PRODUCTIVE KNOWLEDGE IN ANCIENT PHILOSOPHY

This work investigates how ancient philosophers understood productive knowledge, or *technê*, and used it to explain ethics, rhetoric, politics and cosmology. In eleven chapters, leading scholars set out the ancient debates about *technê* from the Presocratic and Hippocratic writers through Plato and Aristotle and the Hellenistic age (Stoics, Epicureans and Sceptics), ending in the Neoplatonism of Plotinus and Proclus. Amongst the many themes that come into focus are: the model status of ancient medicine in defining the political art, the similarities between the Platonic and Aristotelian conceptions of *technê*, the use of *technê* as a paradigm for virtue and practical rationality, *technê*'s determining role in Platonic conceptions of cosmology, *technê*'s relationship to experience and theoretical knowledge, virtue as an 'art of living', the adaptability of the criteria of *technê* to suit different skills, including philosophy itself, the use in productive knowledge of models, deliberation, conjecture and imagination.

THOMAS KJELLER JOHANSEN is Professor of Philosophy at the University of Oslo. He was previously Professor of Ancient Philosophy at the University of Oxford and Tutorial Fellow at Brasenose College. He is the author of *Aristotle on the Sense-Organs* (Cambridge, 1997), *Plato's Natural Philosophy* (Cambridge, 2004) and *The Powers of Aristotle's Soul* (Oxford, 2012).

PRODUCTIVE KNOWLEDGE IN ANCIENT PHILOSOPHY

The Concept of Technê

EDITED BY

THOMAS KJELLER JOHANSEN

University of Oslo

CAMBRIDGE
UNIVERSITY PRESS

University Printing House, Cambridge CB2 8BS, United Kingdom

One Liberty Plaza, 20th Floor, New York, NY 10006, USA

477 Williamstown Road, Port Melbourne, VIC 3207, Australia

314–321, 3rd Floor, Plot 3, Splendor Forum, Jasola District Centre, New Delhi – 110025, India

79 Anson Road, #06–04/06, Singapore 079906

Cambridge University Press is part of the University of Cambridge.

It furthers the University's mission by disseminating knowledge in the pursuit of education, learning, and research at the highest international levels of excellence.

www.cambridge.org
Information on this title: www.cambridge.org/9781108485845
DOI: 10.1017/9781108641579

© Cambridge University Press 2021

This publication is in copyright. Subject to statutory exception and to the provisions of relevant collective licensing agreements, no reproduction of any part may take place without the written permission of Cambridge University Press.

First published 2021

A catalogue record for this publication is available from the British Library.

ISBN 978-1-108-48584-5 Hardback

Cambridge University Press has no responsibility for the persistence or accuracy of URLs for external or third-party internet websites referred to in this publication and does not guarantee that any content on such websites is, or will remain, accurate or appropriate.

Contents

List of Contributors		*page* vii
Acknowledgements		viii
List of Abbreviations		ix
Introduction *Thomas Kjeller Johansen*		1
1	Protagoras on Political *Technê* *Edward Hussey*	15
2	Dynamic Modalities and Teleological Agency: Plato and Aristotle on Skill and Ability *Tamer Nawar*	39
3	*Technê* As a Model for Virtue in Plato *Rachel Barney*	62
4	Crafting the Cosmos: Plato on the Limitations of Divine Craftsmanship *Thomas Kjeller Johansen*	86
5	Aristotle on Productive Understanding and Completeness *Ursula Coope*	109
6	*Technê* and *Empeiria*: Aristotle on Practical Knowledge *Robert Bolton*	131
7	The Stoics on *Technê* and the *Technai* *Voula Tsouna*	166
8	The Epicureans on *Technê* and the *Technai* *Voula Tsouna*	191

9	The Sceptic's Art: Varieties of Expertise in Sextus Empiricus *Stefan Sienkiewicz*	226
10	Plotinus on the Arts *Eyjólfur Kjalar Emilsson*	245
11	Productive Knowledge in Proclus *Jan Opsomer*	263

Bibliography   283
General Index   297
Index Locorum   300

Contributors

RACHEL BARNEY, Professor of Philosophy and Classics, University of Toronto

ROBERT BOLTON, Professor of Philosophy, Rutgers University

URSULA COOPE, Professor of Ancient Philosophy, University of Oxford

EYJÓLFUR KJALAR EMILSSON, Professor of Philosophy, University of Oslo

EDWARD HUSSEY, Emeritus Fellow, All Souls College, Oxford

THOMAS KJELLER JOHANSEN, Professor of Philosophy, University of Oslo

TAMER NAWAR, Assistant Professor of Philosophy, University of Groningen

JAN OPSOMER, Professor of Philosophy, University of Leuven

STEFAN SIENKIEWICZ, Lecturer in Ancient Philosophy, The Queen's College, Oxford

VOULA TSOUNA, Professor of Philosophy, UC Santa Barbara

Acknowledgements

The chapters in this volume, with the exceptions of those by Voula Tsouna and Thomas Kjeller Johansen, derive from papers delivered at a conference on '*Technê* in Ancient Philosophy' held in Oxford in August 2015. The conference was kindly sponsored by the Mind Association, the John Fell Fund and the University of Oxford. Thanks also to Panagiotis Pavlos for compiling the Index Locorum.

List of Abbreviations

Collections of Ancient Texts

SVF: Arnim, H. von (ed.) 1903–1905. *Stoicorum veterum fragmenta*, 4 vols. Leipzig: Teubner.
DK: Diels, H., and Kranz, W. 1952. *Die Fragmente der Vorsokratiker*, 8th ed. Berlin: Weidmannsche Verlagsbuchhandlung.
LM: Laks, A., and Most, G. W. 2016. *Early Greek Philosophy*, 9 vols, Loeb Series. Cambridge, MA: Harvard University Press.
PHerc.: *Papyri Herculanenses*, for which, see Gigante, M. 1979. *Catalogo dei papyri ercolanesi*. Naples: Bibliopolis; Capasso, M. 1991. *Manuale di papirologia ercolanese*. Lecce: Università degli studi di Lecce.

Ancient Texts

Alexander of Aphrodisias

Quaest.　Quaestiones　Questions

Anonymous

in Theaet.　*Commentarius in Platonis Theaetetum*　Commentary on Plato's Theaetetus

Aristotle

DA	*De Anima*	On the Soul
DC	*De Caelo*	On the Heavens
EE	*Ethica Eudemia*	Eudemian Ethics
EN	*Ethica Nicomachea*	Nicomachean Ethics
GA	*De Generatione Animalium*	Generation of Animals

List of Abbreviations

GC	De Generatione et Corruptione	On Generation and Corruption
HA	Historia Animalium	History of Animals
Int.	De Interpretatione	On Interpretation
Juv.	De Iuventute et Senectute	On Youth and Old Age
MA	De Motu Animalium	Movement of Animals
Mem.	De Memoria	On Memory
Metaph.	Metaphysica	Metaphysics
PA	De Partibus Animalium	Parts of Animals
Ph.	Physica	Physics
Pol.	Politica	Politics
Post An	Analytica Posteriora	Posterior Analytics
Pr An	Analytica Priora	Prior Analytics
Rhet.	Rhetorica	Rhetoric
SE	Sophistici Elenchi	Sophistical Refutations
Sens.	De Sensu et Sensibilibus	On Sense and Sense Objects
Top.	Topica	Topics

Asclepius

in Met.	In Aristotelis Metaphysicorum libros A–Z Commentaria	On Aristotle's Metaphysics, Books A–Z

Augustine

De civ. Dei	De civitate Dei	The City of God

Cicero

Acad.	Academica	Academics
De Div.	De Divinatione	On Divination
De Fin.	De Finibus	On Ends
De Inv.	De Inventione	On Invention
De Off.	De Officiis	On Duties
De Or.	De Oratore	On the Orator
ND	De Natura Deorum	On the Nature of the Gods
Acad.post.	Academica Posteriora	Posterior Academics

Damascius (Dam.)

In Phil.	in Platonis Philebum commentarius	On Plato's Philebus

Diogenes Laertius (D.L.)

VF	Vitae Philosophorum	Lives of the Eminent Philosophers

List of Abbreviations

Epictetus

Disc.	Dissertationes	Discourses

Epicurus

KD	Kuriai Doxai	Principal Doctrines
ad. Men.	Epistula ad Menoeceum	Letter to Menoeceus
ad. Herod.	Epistula ad Herodotum	Letter to Herodotus
ad Pyth.	Epistula ad Pythoclem	Letter to Pythocles
De Nat.	De Natura	On Nature

Erotian

Gloss. Hippocr.	Vocum Hippocraticarum collectio	Glossary of Hippocratic Words

Eusebius

praep. Evang.	Praeparatio Evangelica	Preparation for the Gospel

Galen

Contr. Lyc.	Adversus Lycum	Against Lycus
defin. Medicae	Definitiones medicae	Medical Definitions
method med.	De methodo medendi	Method of Healing
sect. ingred.	De sectis ingredientibus	On Sects for Beginners

Hippocrates

Art.	De Arte	On the Art
Loc. Hom.	De Locis in Homine	Places in Man
Nat. Hom.	De Natura Hominis	Nature of Man
VM	De Vetere Medicina	On Ancient Medicine
Vict.	De Victu	Regimen

Homer

Il.	Ilias	Iliad

Iamblichus

Myst.	De Mysteriis Aegyptiorum	On the Egyptian Mysteries

Marcus Aurelius

Med.	Meditationes	Meditations

Philo

Fort.	De fortitudine	On Courage
Leg. Alleg.	Legum allegoriae	Allegorical Interpretation

Philodemus

De elect.	De electionibus et fugis	On Choices and Avoidances
De poem.	De poematis	On Poems
De Sign.	De Signis	On Signs
Oec.	De oeconomia	On Property Management
Rhet.	De Rhetorica	On Rhetoric

Philoponus

in An. post.	In Aristotelis Analytica Posteriora	Commentary on Aristotle's Posterior Analytics commentaria
in Phys.	In Aristotelis physicorum octo	Commentary on Aristotle's Physics libros commentaria

Philostratus

Vit. Ap.	De vita Apollonii	Life of Apollonius

Plato

Ap.	Apologia	Apology
Chrm.	Charmides	
Crat.	Cratylus	
Crit.	Crito	
Euthyd.	Euthydemus	
Euthphr.	Euthyphro	
Grg.	Gorgias	
Hp. Mi.	Hippias Minor	
Lach.	Laches	
Leg.	Leges	Laws
Men.	Meno	
Phd.	Phaedo	
Phdr.	Phaedrus	
Phlb.	Philebus	
Plt.	Politicus	Statesman
Prt.	Protagoras	
Rep.	Respublica	Republic
Soph.	Sophista	Sophist
Symp.	Symposium	
Tht.	Theaetetus	
Tim.	Timaeus	

Plotinus

Enn.	Enneads	

Plutarch

de comm. not.	De communibus notitiis adversus Stoicos	Against the Stoics on Common Conceptions
de Stoic. repugn.	De Stoicorum repugnantiis	On Stoic Self-Contradictions
de virt. mor.	De virtute morali	On Moral Virtue

Proclus

ET	Institutio Theologica	Elements of Theology
in Alc.	in Platonis Alcibiadem Priorem	On Plato's Alcibiades I
in Crat.	in Platonis Cratylum commentaria	On Plato's Cratylus
in Eucl.	in primum Euclidis librum commentarius	On Euclid Book I
in Parm.	in Platonis Parmenidem commentarii	On Plato's Parmenides
in Remp.	in Platonis Rempublicam commentarii	On Plato's Republic
in Tim.	in Platonis Timaeum commentarii	On Plato's Timaeus
Theol. Plat.	Theologia Platonica	Platonic Theology

Ps.-Galen

De hist. phil.	De Historia Philosophiae	History of Philosophy
Def. med.	Definitiones medicae	Medical Definitions

Ps.-Longinus

De subl.	De sublimitate	On the Sublime

Quintillian

Instit. orat.	Institutio Oratoria	Institutes of Oratory

Seneca

Ep.	Epistulae	Letters

Sextus Empiricus

M.	Adversus Mathematicos	Against the Mathematicians
PH	Pyrrhoniae Hypotyposes	Outlines of Pyrrhonism

Simplicius

Ench.	Commentarius in Epicteti Encheridion	On Epictetus' Handbook
in Cael.	in Aristotelis de Caelo commentaria	On Aristotle's On the Heavens

in Cat.	in Aristotelis Categorias commentarium	On Aristotle's Categories
in Phys.	in Aristotelis Physica commentaria	On Aristotle's Physics

Stobaeus

Ecl.	Eclogae	Eclogues

Syrianus

in Met.	in Metaphysica Aristotelis commentaria	On Aristotle's Metaphysics

Themistius

in de An.	in libros Aristotelis de Anima paraphrasis	Paraphrase of Aristotle's On the Soul
in An. post.	Aristotelis Analyticorum Posteriorum paraphrasis	Paraphrase of Aristotle's Posterior Analytics
Or.	Orationes	Orations

Introduction
Thomas Kjeller Johansen

I   The Meaning of *Technê*

What did the Greeks mean by *technê*? The word is hard to translate or paraphrase, and the problems reflect the difficulty of defining the concept. We lack words in modern English with quite the same semantic range. Many of the authors in this volume have chosen to transliterate *technê* or use a range of glosses, 'craft', 'technical understanding', 'productive knowledge', 'productive understanding' or 'art'. The variety mirrors the polysemy of the term, and it would be unwise to legislate in favour of just one translation in all contexts. While tradition prefers 'art', under the influence of the Latin translation *ars*, 'art' today tends to be associated with objects of primarily aesthetic value, as in the 'fine arts', whereas *technê* in many cases has to do with the production and use of tools. 'Craft' does better on this score, but fits less well with the *technai* that are more theoretical – statesmanship, for example – or whose products are less tangible or utilitarian, for example, in medicine.

A Greek term that is sometimes used as an alternative to *technê* is *dêmiourgia*. A practitioner of a *technê*, a *technitês*, may also be *dêmiourgos*, 'a skilled craftsman' as we would say. In ancient philosophy, the term *dêmiourgos* is particularly associated with the divine craftsman of Plato's *Timaeus*, a god who is recognisable as a craftsman, a welder, a weaver, a farmer, notwithstanding all the theoretical knowledge and mathematics that he also brings to the creation. Here the association with making things is clearer, and the term can work with *technê* to specify a *productive* expertise.[1] 'Productive knowledge', as used in the title of this book, has the added advantage of matching Aristotle's account of *technê* as a '*productive* state accompanied by a true account'.[2] Yet here we face the problem that ancient philosophers, Aristotle included, sometimes refer to

---
[1] See *Tht.*146d1: *hai tôn allôn dêmiourgôn technai*.   [2] *EN* VI.4 1140a1–23.

mathematics as a *technê* although it is not obvious how it produces anything.³ Like the Greek *dêmiourgia*, we may think, then, that 'productive knowledge' is too focused on production to be serviceable as a general rendition of *technê*. 'Technical knowledge', finally, is strictly a pleonasm but may seem to offer a conveniently neutral alternative for *technê*. Still here the match is only partial: 'technical' may be used for skills and language in a variety of contexts, from plumbing to mathematics, but it would be misleading today to describe mathematics, medicine or politics as 'technical' professions.

In general, the extension of '*technê*' is blurry around the edges, ranging from highly theoretical forms of expertise, like mathematics, to border-line menial competencies. Sensitive to a wide range of uses, Greek philosophers will sometimes clarify by using the compound 'handicraft' (*cheirotekhnia*) to offset manual skills from more theoretically based crafts.⁴ When Socrates in the *Theaetetus* (146d–e) asks for a definition of knowledge, he is first given examples of *technai*: geometry, astronomy, harmony, cobbling, carpentry. One may reasonably think that the list in part serves to underline the difficulty of finding a unitary account of knowledge.

It may perhaps seem easier to approach *technê* in terms of the people recognised by society as the practitioners of a *technê*. *Technitai*, 'craftsmen', would be those, who because of their knowledge, can be relied on to deliver results within a recognised field and teach others how to do so,⁵ and we might say *technê* is whatever knowledge it is we think so enables them. Yet the status of individuals as *technitai* was no less subject to dispute than the technical status of individual crafts, like medicine or rhetoric. And even if we managed to fix the extension of the term by its members, we still face the conceptual problem of what the knowledge is whose possession qualifies its practitioners as members. We look to the philosophers discussed in this volume for guidance.

---

³ See *Grg.* 450d, Aristotle, *Metaph.* I.1 981b22, cf. Balansard 2001: 56–59. One solution may be that it produces words or statements, for example, proofs. So, at *Grg.* 450d Socrates refers to mathematics as one of the *technai* that operate through words. Clearly, mathematics fails to be productive in the sense that it brings mathematical *truths* into being. Mathematics, as Aristotle would say, deals with the eternal and necessary, not the contingent.
⁴ Cf. Plato, *Plt.* 259c, 304b; Aristotle, *Metaph.* I.1 981a32.
⁵ Compare V. Tsouna's roughly equivalent description in this volume: 'Typically, [*technitai*, 'craftsmen'] are viewed as professionals that achieve valuable results for their communities and, therefore, enjoy wide recognition and respect. Moreover, they are considered entitled to act as instructors in their arts, explaining their methods and procedures and transmitting their expert knowledge to their pupils. So far as the nature of the *technai* is concerned, it is broadly assumed that they involve theory as well as practice, have a sort of generality and universality, and accomplish their functions with varying degrees of regularity and precision.' (166)

II *Technê* before the Philosophers: The Background

It is clear from our earliest sources that the possession of a *technê* bestowed a certain social and professional status. Homer's admiring descriptions of artefacts such as swords, shields, doors, wagons, etc. reflect the high status enjoyed by the corresponding crafts in bronze-age Greece. Such craftworks are worthy of a god, Hephaestus,[6] or the legendary Dedalus, whose many wondrous works had, as Pausanias put it, 'something of the divine in them'.[7] In Aeschylus's *Prometheus Bound* (463–522) it is Prometheus' gift of *technai* that offsets man from the animals. The famous 'Ode on Man' in Sophocles' *Antigone* presents man as capable of great feats of good or evil through his *technai* (365). The power of *technê* may transform human life for the better, enabling us to overcome our natural weaknesses and manipulate natural processes to our advantage.[8] To be sure, craftsmen did not entirely escape the aristocratic disdain reserved for the practical professions. (Even Hephaestus, with his clubfoot, tended towards the uncouth and the ridiculous.) However, the scorn was primarily reserved for crafts of the more manual variety, the so-called *banausic* skills.[9] The attitude is well illustrated by Socrates' remark to Callicles in Plato's *Gorgias* that

> There are times when [the engineer] preserves entire cities .... But you nonetheless despise him and his craft, and you'd call him 'engineer' as a term of abuse. You would be unwilling either to give your daughter to his son or take his daughter yourself. (*Grg.* 512c, trans. D.Zeyl)

Where the *technê* was more liberal, intellectual or integral to the occupations of an Athenian citizen than, for example, engineering, the expertise was held in higher esteem.

In a competitive 'market of ideas', it is not surprising then that disciplines fought hard to establish their credentials as *technê*, or that critics of a discipline would decry competing practices as untechnical. The Hippocratic texts bear witness to these debates and represent an important precursor to the philosophers' accounts of *technê*. It is here we find the first criteria for *technê* of the sort that the philosophers will develop. Prominent amongst these is the requirement that a *technê* should have proper domain. This point is important in the context of defending medicine against the charge that many patients die despite their treatment: extreme cases of

---

[6] E.g., Homer, *Iliad* 1.571, 18.143.   [7] Pausanias, *Description of Greece* ii, 4.5.
[8] See Heiniman 1961: 117–18.   [9] See further Cuomo 2007: 10–11.

illness are simply not within the doctor's remit.[10] Another requirement is that the *technê* should have a characteristic aim, as it is the aim of medicine to bring about health. This is clearly related to the first requirement in the sense that the aim is formulated in relation to the domain, for example, bringing about health in an individual within a group of patients who are not terminally sick. Another distinctive feature of *technê* is that its practitioner understands the causes of the aimed-at result, and on that basis reliably brings it about.[11] This feature emerges in reply to the objection that health is a matter of luck, *tuchê*, not *technê*, since sometimes we see health re-established without medical treatment. The answer is that when this happens the patient has proceeded as the doctor would have recommended but accidentally so and without the doctor's knowledge of the causes involved. The doctor's success is therefore exactly not accidental: *technê* excludes *tuchê* (*Art* 4). Also worth highlighting is the Hippocratic writer's emphasis on the individual circumstances of medical therapy: depending on their individual constitutions cheese may be bad for some patients and beneficial to others.[12] The point re-emerges in Aristotle's claim that *technê* – and again medicine is his example – deals with the particular.[13] Finally, the author of *On the Art* (11) points to the importance of choosing the appropriate time (*ho kairos*) for when the treatment of a disease is attempted, an aspect of the political *technê* that Plato in turn underlines (*Plt.* 305d). The Hippocratic focus is of course medicine but these observations clearly display reflection on what generally constitutes a *technê*.[14] Although it is difficult to be sure about their dates and authorship, the Hippocratic writings seem to have provided a template for Plato's and Aristotle's thinking about *technê*, as will become clear also from several of the chapters in this volume.

Connected to at least some Hippocratic writers,[15] we find the loosely associated group of intellectuals known as the 'Sophists'. They profiled themselves as purveyors of wisdom of all sorts, from literary and linguistic theory, to theology, mathematics, music and athletics.[16] However, a central interest was rhetoric, which Gorgias claimed to be not just a *technê* but the most important one, since practitioners of all other arts could be seen as subject to its persuasive power.[17] In the *Gorgias*, Plato famously attacks the technical status of rhetoric, as conceived of by

---

[10] *Art* 8. [11] See, e.g., *VM* 20. [12] *VM* 20. [13] *Metaph.* I.1 981a1–20.
[14] See, e.g., *Art* 9. [15] See Heinimann 1961.
[16] See the presentation of Hippias in Plato, *Prt.* 318e and Gorgias at *Grg.* 447d–48a.
[17] See Gorgias, *Encomium of Helen*, Plato, *Grg.* 452e.

Gorgias, though a revised notion of rhetoric gets a more favourable hearing in the *Phaedrus*. Another famous sophist, Protagoras, drew on the Hippocratic concept of *technê* to bolster his political expertise as a *technê*, as E. Hussey argues in this volume (Chapter 1).[18] Plato's dialogue *Protagoras* shows the challenges Protagoras faces when defending such a *technê* in a democracy: democrats grant special powers to experts in many domains – they take the advice of a shipwright on how to build their fleet – but when it comes to political decisions they believe that every citizen should have an equal say, as if there was no special political *technê*. In the *Republic*, Plato shows his debt to Protagoras in thinking of ethical and political expertise as a *technê* (as Barney shows in Chapter 3), but this time without the democratic harness.

III *Technê* As a Form of Knowledge

When Greek philosophers of the fifth and fourth centuries BC turn their attention to epistemology, the status of the *technai* as knowledge seems firm; indeed, in some contexts *technê* is what it is to be knowledge. Even Socrates in Plato's *Apology* cannot find fault with the craftsmen's basic claims to knowledge: he examined the politicians and poets and found them ignorant but grants the craftsmen knowledge of many fine things by virtue of their *technê* (23d), even if they do not have the knowledge of the highest things they sometimes think they have.

It is in large part the undisputed status of *technê* as such as knowledge that makes *technê* so important to ancient epistemology. One can dispute whether there is a genuine or objective knowledge of god, or the underlying nature of things, or of mathematical abstractions, or of what makes somebody a good person, and ancient thinkers of a sceptical or relativistic bent, such as Xenophanes or Protagoras, did just that, but it is much harder to dispute that somebody whom you can count on to build a bridge or predict a drought has knowledge. The proof of the knowledge is in its results. So in *On the Art* (14) the Hippocratic author contrasts the practical merits of medicine with more theoretical approaches:

> That medicine can be of value is further demonstrated by the skill of those proficient practitioners whose actions are better proof than their words. It is

---

[18] Hussey argues in Chapter 1 of this volume that this holds for the character of Plato's eponymous dialogue as well as the historical figure.

not that such physicians look down on writers, but they believe that most men are more prepared to believe what they see than what they hear.[19]

While the status of *technê* as knowledge thus was clear, its exact place within the taxonomy of kinds of knowledge was less certain, and could differ according to which *technê* was in focus. We find a generic use of *technê*, for example, in the Hippocratic writings and Xenophon to cover all kinds of expertise.[20] But from at least Plato on, philosophers are wont to distinguish *technê* as a whole from other kinds of knowledge and again to distinguish different kinds of *technê*, some of which may indeed end up under the threshold of knowledge in a stricter sense. So in *Republic* X (601e–602b) there is a distinction between three kinds of *technê*, the user's, the producer's and the imitator's, only the first of which counts as knowledge (*epistêmê*), because only it grasps what the product is for, while the other two are no more than respectively true belief or play.[21] In the *Statesman* (258c–60c), the Eleatic Stranger distinguishes practical from theoretical knowledge and places different kinds of *technê* in relation to the two according to whether they involve using one's hands or giving directions based on understanding. The *Statesman* lies behind Aristotle's distinction between manual crafts and a master or architectonic craft, where only the latter, properly speaking, counts as knowledge since only it possesses an account (*logos*) of what is produces.[22] Most famously, Aristotle in *Nicomachean Ethics* VI divides knowledge into theoretical, practical and productive wisdom, that is, *technê*, all possessing an account of their different objects. A consequence of building up the intellectual element in a *technê* in this way is that a range of more manually or experientially based crafts, which do not provide a causal account, may lose their status of proper knowledge.

The taxonomical manoeuvrings reflect continued efforts to define *technê*. Plato's *Ion* reads like an example of the sort of testing of a putative knower that Socrates refers to in the *Apology*. Here the target is not just the rhapsode but also the poets whom he recites. Socrates argues that neither has a proper craft, since a craft has a proper distinct subject area and requires knowing the entire subject area. In the *Gorgias*, Plato lays down further criteria of *technê*. As in the *Apology* and the *Ion*, the context is critical: the sophist and rhetorician fail to live up to the standards of *technê* in a way that is incompatible with their having any knowledge. Again, a

---

[19] Translation from Chadwick and Mann 1978.   [20] Xenophon, *Economicus* 1.
[21] See also Plato, *Euthyd.* 289b for the distinction between a producing and a using *technê*.
[22] *Metaph.* I.1 981a29–b1.

technê has a proper domain, but it should also be able to produce some good, which is distinctive from the good of other *technai*, and it should also be able to give an account of what it does. Rhetoric fails on all three scores, and counts rather as a knack of bringing about a result. The ability stems from experience (*empeiria*), which bestows no knowledge of how and why the knack works and implies no regard for the real goodness or otherwise of the outcome.

Against the background of such experientially based abilities, it is the ability to give an account (*logos*) that primarily singles out *technê* as a form of *knowledge* for both Plato and Aristotle. As Aristotle explains in *Metaphysics* 1.1 (991a21–30), drawing on the *Gorgias*, the merely experienced can often be as successful as the craftsman, but it is the latter's grasp of why the procedure is successful that shows his possession of a *technê*. For both Plato and Aristotle the ability to give an account is a *general* characteristic of knowledge.[23] When Socrates tested whether politicians, poets and craftsmen had knowledge he asked them to give an account of what they were doing (*logon didonai*), and their success or failure to do so showed if they had knowledge. In several Platonic dialogues, it becomes clear that the account he expects is a definition of the universal attribute that causes the thing to be what it is. At *Meno* 72c he gives the example of the account of a bee, which should give the attribute in virtue of which all bees are bees. Later in the same work (98a) we learn that in order to contribute to knowledge an account has to be causal (*aitias logismos*). This specific notion of an account (*logos*) seems to survive the refutation in the *Theaetetus* of the various notions of an account that by its addition to true judgment might constitute knowledge.

While Plato at least in these works expects, in line with the Hippocratic template, an account to figure in all kinds of knowledge, including therefore *technê*, it is not clear that he expects of the craftsman to have an account at the *highest* level of knowledge. The idea, as expressed for example in *Republic* X (596b), that the craftsman looks to the form of the artefact may give the impression that he must be able to provide an account approximating a philosopher's definition. Yet as we know from the Image of the Line in *Republic* VI (510c), even mathematicians don't and can't be expected to define the forms that they posit in their investigations, for example, what a triangle itself is; this is a matter for dialectic. Still, with these lower expectations one might say that the craftsman must have the ability to account for his practices given a correct conception of

---

[23] See Moss 2014.

the form itself. Aristotle's position likewise is that different kinds of knowledge rely on different kinds of account.[24] This is not surprising: if different kinds of knowledge are differentiated by their proper objects, as Aristotle thinks, then the accounts of those things will also differ accordingly. So, in *Nicomachean Ethics* Book VI, he distinguishes the various kinds of knowledge according to their objects, with each kind giving a true account of its object. Scientific knowledge gives accounts of what is necessary and eternal, practical knowledge of how to act, productive knowledge of how to make things. Productive knowledge is then understood as 'a productive state of the soul accompanied by a true account'. But, as in the case of Plato's productive *technê*, this is not knowledge at the highest level because its object is not the most knowable, that privilege is reserved for theoretical knowledge, knowledge of eternal, necessary truths.

Aristotle agrees with Plato that it is the presence of an account that marks off *technê* as the first step in the hierarchy of *knowledge*. We all desire to know, Aristotle declares at the beginning of the *Metaphysics*. As we proceed from perception to memory, experience and craft we come closer to the goal of wisdom. Craft marks the first point in the ascent where we can properly be said to have knowledge because at that point we come to grasp an account of the cause of what we perceive and experience. But above craft stand scientific knowledge (*epistêmê*) and wisdom, the knowledge of the highest and best causes. Given *technê*'s proximity to the other kinds of knowledge in providing an account of the cause, the question arises also what the differences are and why craft counts as lower: how exactly to understand the relationship between the *logos* of the *technê* and that of scientific understanding? Ursula Coope's contribution to the volume (Chapter 5) illuminates this issue.

Looking in the other direction, from *technê* down at experience, one may wonder just how the craftsman differs from the merely experienced person. We saw that the Hippocratic writers tend to contrast *technê* with *tuchê*, but with Plato and Aristotle it seems to be particularly experience that excludes chance. So, Aristotle says in *Metaphysics* I.1 that the merely experienced person enjoys greater practical success than somebody who just possesses the account of the cause. For a doctor heals not man but the individual person, and experience grasps the individual. Knowing what causes dysentery won't help you cure anybody if you can't recognise it in individual cases. Here it may seem as if the account can be detached from experience and plays no role in ensuring *technê*'s much vaunted practical

---

[24] See Johansen 2017.

success. Is the craftsman's account then merely, so to speak, the theoretical icing on the cake? How one answers this question clearly depends not just on how one understands the power of experience but also on what sort of account we ascribe to the craftsman. If distinctly theoretical, the account may seem too detached from the productive context to be useful. Bolton's contribution to this volume (Chapter 6) is highly relevant to this issue, in arguing for a less theoretical and more practically orientated conception of the craftsman's understanding in other Aristotelian works than *Metaphysics* I.1.

The conception of *technê* as grounded in the possession of a certain account may ring bells with readers familiar with recent debates about the relationship between knowledge-*how* and propositional knowledge. Gilbert Ryle famously argued in *The Concept of Mind* (Ryle 1949) that practical knowledge, know-how, could not be reduced to propositional knowledge, knowledge-*that*. Powerful arguments have been presented to show that he was wrong about this. It has been argued, for example, that knowledge-*how* may be understood propositionally along the lines of knowing that something is a way to do something.[25] This is the position that is known today as 'intellectualism'. Following both Plato and Aristotle, what one would stress in this debate as far as craft is concerned is that grasping a certain kind of proposition is crucial, namely, grasping an account of the cause. However, this point can be made without prejudice to the question whether lower non-technical skills, riding a bike and such, are to be analysed propositionally. But in that case, the propositions entertained will not be of the causal type that distinguishes *technê*. Moreover, Aristotle says that having a causal account is a necessary condition for possessing the *technê*, not that it is a sufficient condition. For he holds that perceptual experience is presupposed by the *technê* and there is no claim that this experience can be exhaustively expressed in propositions.[26] This ancient analysis of *technê* is then in a sense tangential to the modern debate, even if it may at first be suggestive of the 'intellectualist' position.

The role of *technê* in the taxonomy of knowledge is a key theme in several chapters, and the subject relates again to how we understand the sort of account we expect a *technê* to be able to provide. Coope (Chapter 5)

---

[25] See Stanley 2011; Stanley and Williamson 2017.
[26] Aristotle certainly ascribes propositions to the merely experienced: that this medicine helped Socrates on this occasion, and Callias on that occasion (*Metaph.* I.1) but whether grasping these propositions only is what constitutes his practical ability is not clear. On the relationship between experience and *technê*, see further Chapter 5 in this volume.

considers *technê*'s relationship to theoretical knowledge, showing both how it qualifies as knowledge in offering general explanations, but also differs in the openendedness of the explanations that the craftsman works out to deal with individual cases. Bolton (Chapter 6) points to how *technê* in *Metaphysics* Book I seems to fit the picture of the natural sciences of the *Posterior Analytics* in providing an account of the universal cause, but he also argues that this notion of *technê* is not representative of Aristotle's other works, which entertain a much more experientially based and less theoretical conception of *technê*. A similar distinction emerges from Tsouna's discussion (Chapters 7 and 8) of the contrast between the Stoics' more rationalistic understanding of *technê* – *technê* being for them both practical and theoretical – and the Epicurean empiricist conception.

Plato's distinction between productive and directive arts touches on a larger question: is there one account, and one set of criteria, that fits or should be expected to fit all the different *technai*? Sienkiewicz (Chapter 9) brings the question sharply into focus: the account of *technê* that applies to other arts does not apply to the sceptic's. Emilsson (Chapter 10) points out how performative arts such as dancing don't require deliberation and for that reason provide a more fitting model for the Intellect's production of the cosmos. Johansen's argument (Chapter 4) turns on the distinction between the Demiurge's *technê* and the so-called lesser gods' craft, which is imitative of the Demiurge's and has a categorically different object. Another distinction first mooted by Plato in the *Philebus* (55e–57d) is that between stochastic and non-stochastic arts, the former estimating or guessing their outcomes, where the others render a precise and accurate result. This distinction, as Opsomer argues (Chapter 11), corresponds to the different kinds of *technê* that gods and humans employ in production: the divine *technê* dealing merely with eternal intelligible objects while the human concerns itself with changing circumstances involving conjecture and imagination. In Proclus, we thus find a move towards acknowledging a greater role for the imagination in *technê*, which may seem crucial in terms of freeing the arts from the intellectualist paradigm we have seen dominate in previous philosophers. These examples illustrate not just philosophers' awareness of the differences between the *technai* but also how they exploit these differences to make distinctive points within their own epistemology or metaphysics.

IV *Technê*, Ethics and Politics

While we have seen a degree of consensus developing from Hippocrates to Plato and Aristotle about the criteria of *technê*, by no means all ancient philosophers agreed about all of these criteria or how to understand or apply them. We find often that the view of *technê* alters according to the uses to which the philosophers put the concept. As many of the chapters in this volume show, while *technê* work as a central model for a range of disciplines – for example, ethics, politics, cosmology – the concept of *technê* itself is also adapted to accommodate favoured theories within those disciplines. The concept of *technê* develops then not only through discussions about the concept itself but also through its uses as a model for other kinds of knowledge. An important task of this volume is to trace the historical developments of the concept of *technê* through these applications.

Already prior to Plato, *technê* was used as model for ethical and political knowledge. This could mean either seeing ethical knowledge as more or less similar to a *technê* or as being an instance of it. Hussey's contribution (Chapter 1) highlights the question of how the political *technê* in Protagoras can be seen as contributing to the human good, and how the political art on this point is analogous to the medical art as conceived of by the Hippocratic writers. Aristotle, as we saw, distinguishes between productive and practical knowledge as different kinds of knowledge but continues to draw close parallels between the two in his ethical writings.[27] The debate about whether Plato in the earlier works saw, and if so, later ceased to see, ethical knowledge as a kind of *technê* continues. The root of the issue lies in the ability of *technê* to produce opposite results: a doctor can in virtue of his knowledge both cure and kill. *Technê* is, as Nawar calls it here, a 'two-way capacity'. This point goes back to Plato's *Hippias Minor* (375b–c) and has at least since Aristotle (*EN* VI.5) often been taken to limit the similarity of ethics to technical skill: ethical knowledge cannot be properly exercised in doing harm but only in doing good, but technical knowledge can be demonstrated in both ways, therefore ethical knowledge cannot be a *technê*. Some have argued that Plato, by the time he wrote the *Republic*, had reached this conclusion. Barney argues in this volume (Chapter 3) that Plato never abandoned the view of ethical and political knowledge as technical. The key to saving the technical status is, she holds, the conception of virtue as a kind of 'super-*technê*', in Barney's phrase, directing all the other *technai* to their proper end. While a first-order craft may be exercised also for a bad end, the super-*technê* must be realised for the good, because its proper object includes the correct exercise of an art. Barney also makes the original point that adopting craftsman as one's

---

[27] The subject is well explored by Angier 2010.

'practical identity' also commits one to being a good craftsman. When becoming a doctor one undertakes to be a *good* doctor.

Post-Aristotelian philosophers were certainly not deterred by Plato or Aristotle from presenting ethical knowledge as a kind of *technê*, though again not without complications and disagreements. So Sienkiewicz argues (Chapter 9) that the sceptic's art is happiness-producing, but a *technê* only with qualification. For Sextus Empiricus, a *technê* is generally expected to satisfy two of the Platonic criteria, having a proper subject or domain and being useful or 'happiness-producing'. However, the sceptic's art fails on the first count and so amounts only to a kind of 'non-technical' eudaimonistic art. Tsouna (Chapters 7 and 8) analyses the Stoic and Epicurean notions of ethics as an art of living, the Stoics taking the art to be a second-order *technê* that involved the sage's possessing the first-order kinds of knowledge (in so far as they represent perfections of reason), including, for example, natural philosophy, while the Epicureans rejected this demanding requirement.

V *Technê* and Cosmology

Craft plays a central role in the history of ancient cosmology. The ancient philosophers predominantly looked at the world as a *kosmos*, a well-ordered whole as one might translate the Greek. Many of them also saw this *kosmos* as a product of a creating intelligence, with the Epicureans and the other atomists as the important exception, as discussed by Tsouna in Chapter 8. But given the two premises of cosmic order and a creating intelligence, it is natural to turn also to craft as an explanatory model. While the pre-Socratics used notions related to craft to explain the cosmos,[28] they did not articulate what a cosmic craftsman would look like. Plato's *Timaeus*, discussed here by Johansen (Chapter 4), presents the first such account and, as Emilsson (Chapter 10) and Opsomer (Chapter 11) show, the *Timaeus* occupied the centre-stage in Platonist cosmology till the end of antiquity.

Plato's divine craftsman, the Demiurge, is a craftsman of the sort familiar from Plato's earlier dialogues. He has a specific object (here the cosmic animal), works for the good, deliberates, looks to the forms, etc. In antiquity, it became common (though not without exceptions) to read the Demiurge not as personal creator, but metaphorically. As shown by Tsouna (Chapter 7), the Stoics took the Demiurge to be a rational

---

[28] See Sedley 2007 for an excellent survey.

principle internal to the cosmos (cf. their notion of a crafting fire, *technikon pur*). Emilsson (Chapter 10) explains how this sort of reading could lead to changes in the craft model. Unlike a human craftsman, the universal intellect and the World-Soul, which for Plotinus replace the Demiurge, do not deliberate about how to make the world. Instead of rejecting the craftsman model altogether, however, Plotinus points to certain arts –performance arts such as dance – in explaining how natural processes flow from higher principles.

Plotinus' response to the *Timaeus* raises a question going back to Aristotle about the degree to which deliberation is an essential feature of craft. Developing the analogy between craft and nature, Aristotle says in his *Physics* that craft does not deliberate.[29] What exactly Aristotle means by this need not detain us here,[30] but as in the case of Plotinus, the claim shows that deliberation may be seen as an optional feature of craft. Aristotle himself uses the craft model in presenting natural teleology to show the end-directedness of natural substances and processes. Scholars have different views of the limitations and importance of the analogy,[31] but it seems clear that what particularly impresses Aristotle is that natural beings and their parts, like artefacts, have functions that define what they are and that by realising these functions, again like artefacts, they fulfil their end (*telos*).[32] While Plato too in the *Timaeus* would see living beings and their parts as having characteristic functions, for Aristotle such teleology does not depend on the activity of a creative mind:[33] the same natural species have always existed and have, as natural, a principle of change and rest within themselves.

As we see in Plotinus, the variety of arts provides a degree of flexibility in the craft model. It is an important point also in the *Timaeus*, Johansen (Chapter 4) argues, that there are different kinds of arts for different stages of the creation. The Demiurge creates the cosmos but he is limited by his art to producing immortal creatures. The lesser gods possess a *technê* that is similar to the Demiurge's, their creator, but which enables them unlike the Demiurge to create mortal beings. Both of these in turn are different from the arts that humans possess.

Proclus emphasises, as Opsomer (Chapter 11) shows, the differences and similarities between various kinds of production. At the divine level,

---

[29] *Ph.* II.8 199b26–27.   [30] For different answers see Broadie 1987 and Sedley 2010.
[31] For a strongly critical view see Cooper 1982.
[32] For defenses of the centrality of the craft analogy see Witt 2015 and Johansen 2020.
[33] Again, whether this restricts the craft analogy depends also on our view of craft: Broadie 1987 argues that behind Aristotle's analogy between craft and nature is a tendency to de-psychologise craft.

production is the by-product of the unchanging act of thinking by which gods are constituted. Demiurgic production is a subclass of divine production, the products of which are things that become in so far as they change. Demiurgic production is interesting as it resembles human production more closely than higher forms of divine production. Gods only have the higher forms of *technê*, not human *technai* that are based on conjecture and knowledge of circumstances and possible scenarios. Human craftsmanship is analogous to natural and divine production but uses paradigmatic causes as blueprints for artifacts. These are the fruit of genuine invention and not the eternal intelligible objects, which Plato's true craftsman directs his attention to according to *Republic* X. Here Proclus' view of human craft introduces clearly, and for the first time in the history of philosophy, the notion of *creative* imagination.

These are just some of the many themes covered in this volume, which demonstrates the richness and complexity of ancient thought about *technê*. The papers contained are published here for the first time. While each seeks to present an original and focused argument, they also collectively serve as an introduction to the key aspects of ancient philosophical thinking about *technê*.

CHAPTER I

Protagoras on Political Technê

Edward Hussey

Introduction

This chapter aims to reconstruct, so far as possible, the political thinking of the historical Protagoras of Abdera.[1] Since Plato is our only substantial witness, nothing much can be achieved unless Plato's Protagoras is essentially the historical Protagoras, as Plato saw him. That is the simplest assumption, and will be supposed throughout. It carries with it the consequences that the Protagoras of the *Protagoras* is the same as the Protagoras of the *Theaetetus*, and that Plato takes the ideas of Protagoras seriously in both dialogues, though it is only in the *Theaetetus* that he engages with them head on.[2] Any such reconstruction, therefore, must be able to show that the whole depiction of Protagoras in Plato's *Protagoras* and *Theaetetus* can be seen as consistent in itself. If it can, we find in these dialogues a representation, intended to be faithful, of a pre-Platonic structure of ideas, in which the notion of *technê* is central; and the simple and natural assumption is that this is indeed due to the historical Protagoras.

Plato's *Protagoras* is necessarily the first centre of attention. Here Protagoras is made to give an account of the 'political *technê*' that he professes to teach. It is manifestly an incomplete account, and for this there are good dramatic reasons. Protagoras cannot be expected to unveil a

---

[1] An earlier version of part of this reconstruction appeared in Hussey 1996. For critical comment on that essay and on the present chapter, I am much indebted to David Wiggins (in Wiggins 1996, and in personal discussion). The present chapter has also benefited from the contributions and suggestions of participants in the 2015 conference, particularly Rachel Barney and Thomas Johansen, as editor, and of the readers consulted by the Cambridge University Press – grateful acknowledgements to them all.
[2] There are parodistic elements in the depiction of other sophists in the *Protagoras*, but we should at least begin by assuming that Plato is here taking Protagoras' ideas seriously and as deserving of detailed examination. That is not contradicted but confirmed by the fact that he must have held them to be both false and dangerous. Even if Plato's Socrates is ironical when repeatedly praising the 'wisdom' of Protagoras, in both *Protagoras* and *Theaetetus* he is shown as genuinely eager to explore the ideas Protagoras puts forward, and does not consider it a trivial task.

complete outline of his whole thinking, free of charge, in front of his rivals and some of his possible pupils.

The account has also often been found internally incoherent by commentators. The first thing is to consider this charge of incoherence. I shall argue (in Section I) that the apparent incoherence is due in large part to the deliberate incompleteness of what Protagoras is saying; and partly also to the omission of certain assumptions about the nature of a *technê* in general, and the activity of the sophists in general, that Protagoras takes for granted, and takes for granted that his hearers will be able to supply.[3]

That is only a first step. There remains the serious problem of incompleteness. To have any hope of recovering what has been left out of Protagoras' exposition in the *Protagoras*, we must consider his account of truth and opinion as unfolded in the *Theaetetus*. I shall claim (in Section II) that there is a plausible interpretation of this that sits naturally with his claims about the political *technê*, and is the *only* kind of interpretation that gives them any sort of inner unity. It supplies an explanation of what Protagoras is doing, how he himself understands what he is doing and how he represents his own activity to others.

In both sections of this chapter, the conception of 'the medical *technê*' developed in the Hippocratic essay *On Ancient Medicine* proves to offer illuminating parallels and gives welcome support to the claim that we are dealing with a genuinely pre-Platonic line of thinking.[4]

I Protagoras Defended: The Coherence of Protagoras' Account of Political *Technê* in the *Protagoras*

I.A First Problem: The Scope and Content of Protagoras' Political Technê

Protagoras states what he claims to teach, at 318e5–19a2; it is:

> How to make good plans, both about one's private affairs, so as best to administer one's own household, and about civic affairs, so as to be most able to act and speak politically.

---

[3] For pungent statements of the view that Protagoras is shown as incoherent, or at best confused and ambiguous, in the *Protagoras*, see Frede 1992 and Taylor 1991. Many substantial and possibly germane questions about the *Protagoras* must unfortunately be left aside here; in particular, Protagoras' account of punishment (324a3–c5), the interpretation of the Myth (320c8–22d5), the discussion of hedonism and the 'art of measurement' (351b–57e) and, in general, why Plato presents Protagoras' theorising in the way he does and why Socrates doesn't attack it head on.

[4] In this chapter, 'Hippocrates' refers to the character in the dialogue, the young Athenian friend of Socrates. The unidentified author of the Hippocratic essay *On Ancient Medicine* (*VM*) is designated by 'AM'.

Immediately after this, Protagoras assents completely to Socrates' more concise characterisation (319a3–7):

> you seem to me to be talking about the political *technê*, and to be undertaking to make men good citizens.

The word *technê* is thus introduced by Socrates, but accepted immediately and without demur by Protagoras. Protagoras and his audience are prepared to set high value on some *technai* and less on others. Thus, Protagoras has just expressed contempt for certain unspecified *technai* (318d7–e5) as subjects of study; yet has previously (316d3–17b5) admitted that he himself exercises 'the sophistic *technê*' and now agrees that he himself teaches political *technê* (319a). He evidently means, by the unnamed *technai*, crafts with specialised and humble subject matter. But both Protagoras and Socrates are prepared to talk about 'the political *technê*'. So, there must be at least some analogy intended between specialised *technai* and political *technê* – one that both Protagoras and Socrates are happy to accept and be guided by.

In the pre-Platonic period, the word *technê* can cover *all* arts, crafts and sciences, both practical and theoretical. It covers, again, *all* aspects of what we can include under any particular 'art' or specialised skill: the purely theoretical aspect (the 'science') and all the different aspects of the application of theoretical knowledge to actual practical situations, that is, the partly verbalisable know-how and the various kinds of skill, based on experience and natural ability, which are essentially non-verbal. We must expect this breadth and flexibility in its use in this dialogue.[5]

There is a certain doubleness about Protagoras' self-descriptions: he *teaches* political *technê*, and he is himself a practitioner of sophistic *technê*. The latter seems to consist in the teaching of *any* substantive *technê*: he refers (316c5–17c5) to various types of 'wise person', not all of whom could be taken to be teaching specifically *political technê*. The doubleness is even clearer at *Tht.* 167b4–d3, where Protagoras, giving examples, divides 'the *sophoi*', according to their special subject matter or field, mentioning, in particular: (a) medical men, (b) cultivators of the soil (*geôrgoi*), (c) 'wise

---

[5] On the notion of *technê* generally in the later fifth century, see Schiefsky 2005: 5–18. The usage of the term by the Platonic Protagoras, in the *Prt.* or *Tht.*, must not be simply assumed to be identical to its usage in other Platonic dialogues, or by the Platonic Socrates (on which, see Irwin 1977: 71–77). In the *Prt.* there is no sign of any disagreement between Protagoras and Socrates about what, in general terms, a *technê* is.

and excellent' statesmen-orators and (d) *sophistai* as educators. He claims himself to *be* an educator (d); but he claims to *teach* the art of statesmanship (c). In neither dialogue does Socrates press hard on the awkward questions raised by this doubleness, except in the *Protagoras*, and there only briefly in his initial discussion with Hippocrates at 331a9–32b6, not during the confrontation with Protagoras himself. This is one of the many loose ends left hanging in the *Protagoras*.[6]

The statesman's art, in Protagoras' view, like many humbler *technai*, combines a theoretical and a practical aspect: both science (organised knowledge) and the ability to apply it. The medical analogy is apt: the statesman is like a doctor when engaged in actually treating a patient or supervising him in health. He has to have general scientific knowledge; he has to know how to apply that knowledge; and he has to have the practical abilities actually to apply it successfully.

But Protagoras also includes in this *technê* the more fundamental business of being a good citizen. This may be found surprising: what we normally think of as 'good citizenship' is surely something different from the art of statesmanship (if there is such a thing). It consists in keeping the laws and being generally 'public-spirited'. Is there confusion here, as some have thought?

To invoke the medical analogy again: being a good citizen is analogous to co-operating with the doctor when that's needed, but more importantly, keeping the rules of hygiene and of a generally healthy lifestyle. Not only that, but advising others close to us, particularly children, to do likewise, and perhaps also knowing how to give elementary first aid. It's all directed towards the same overall goal of health, as the doctor's professional activity is; but it's related to that goal in a different way. It requires, not science, but common knowledge, and the good sense to listen to what medical science says, to see that it is desirable to follow its advice, and then actually to do that. This low-level but informed and rational behaviour can be seen as part of medical *technê* in a wider sense. In fact, it was so seen by the author of the essay *On Ancient*

---

[6] The solution, suggested at 312a7–b4, that education may just be for 'adornment', and not necessarily for the exercise of a *technê*, clearly wouldn't be acceptable to Protagoras if applied to the training he offers. On Protagoras' educative techniques, there is a scattering of evidence from outside Plato, now conveniently assembled as LM Protagoras D 11–32. References to fragments and testimonia of pre-Socratics and sophists are to Diels and Kranz 1952 (= 'DK') and/or to Laks and Most 2016 (= 'LM').

Medicine: a first indication that that work offers parallels to the thinking of Protagoras.[7]

In *On Ancient Medicine*, the overall unity of the wider *technê* is given by its definition, which specifies its general purpose. This is 'for the health, capacity to survive, and nourishment of mankind' (3.5). The writer asks:

> What difference then can be seen between the intention of the medical man – one recognised as such and acknowledged as a craftsman [*cheirotechnês*] – who discovered the [correct] way of life and nourishment for the sick, and that of the other man who originally discovered and made available the [correct] way of nourishment for all mankind, which we all now use? (7.1)

And, to forestall an obvious objection:

> If [the nourishment of the healthy] is not considered to be an art, that is not unreasonable; for it is not appropriate to call anyone a 'master of the art' [*technitên*] when there are no laypeople, but all are knowledgeable by habit and necessity. And yet, it was a great discovery, demanding much inquiry and much art. (4.1)

It is clear that this conception is parallel to that of Protagoras.

The unity of the overall *technê* that includes both of these parts is given by its definition. We must suppose that the political art, like the medical art, is definitionally bound up with a certain *aim*: namely, the achieving of the success or the flourishing or the good of the city as a whole. Thus, it's defined and made into a unity by that aim. (On how that overall aim is related to the actual aims of actual particular possessors of the art, see Section I.B.)

To this account of the general aim, it may be objected that in Protagoras' 'Myth' speech, the aim of the *technê* is originally stated in purely negative terms: to prevent injustice in human societies (322b1–c3). But it's clear that in his instruction Protagoras aims at teaching how to produce success of a more positive as well as much grander kind. And, on the logical side, the essential unity of the *technê* can only be understood, on the analogy of medicine, as being given by the positive aim of producing and maintaining health/flourishing in the body/city. So: being a good citizen and being an able statesman can perfectly well both be different parts of one and the same complex *technê*. Protagoras must envisage a

---

[7] Translations from *VM* are mine; the text presupposed is that of Jouanna, and references are to the chapter and section numbers of his edition (Jouanna 1990). For a valuable recent introduction to the work, and references to other scholarship, see Schiefsky 2005: 1–71; also Maucolin 2009, for analysis of the language and argumentation of *VM* as polemic.

'*technê* of being a citizen' that covers *three* areas: (i) the dealings of private citizens among themselves (they must be polite, fair, honest, just, non-violent, non-fraudulent in these); (ii) the dealings of private citizens with the city (they must be public-spirited in performing their civic duties, e.g., those of military service, participating in the administration, paying taxes as and when due, loyal to the city, accepting and observing its laws, abstaining from treachery or *stasis,* etc.) and (iii) the official actions of public persons, that is, holders of civic office (they must be wise in deliberating, persuasive in proposing their plans and effective in carrying them out). Private citizens must have at least that part of the *technê* needed for (i) and (ii); those who aspire to public office, like Protagoras' pupils, need (iii) as well. The teaching one gets for (iii) also illuminates (i) and (ii), though, because it is gives a general account that explains not just *what* is in the *technê*, but also *why* the *technê* contains the things it does.

Protagoras doesn't claim to teach basic good citizenship (parts [i] and [ii]); that, as he says, is what gets taught, from the nursery upwards, by parents and schoolteachers, and then by civic institutions and officers. As Protagoras describes it, this basic education in political *technê* is (a) 'elementary', not 'advanced', that is, at a low level of complexity; (b) exclusively concerned with the passive, rule-keeping aspect of the *technê*, corresponding to keeping the basic rules of healthy living, that is, at a low level of attainment and (c) entirely without general insight, that is, at a low level of grasp.

What Protagoras is offering is clearly a higher education in part (iii) of the *technê*; the 'university-level' part, which not every one learns or needs to learn. He can still assent to Socrates' description, though, because of course he sees himself as making people good citizens in the *fullest* sense, in making them able statesmen. In a complex *technê* such as this, with a very general overall aim, just as in medicine, there are necessarily different aspects, different levels of importance and complexity and different levels of attainment and of grasp of the art. AM stresses ([7.3] and [9.3]) that the treatment of the sick, the highest level of medical art, 'is much more complex and demands greater precision' and 'greater effort': there is simply much more to it. Laypeople, he implies, are on a minimal level of attainment, of complexity and of general grasp. They're not required to know or understand anything of a theoretical nature, nor anything at all complicated; they don't have to deliberate; they just have to follow, in a passive way, some simple general rules without understanding why. But, *at that minimal level*, almost everyone can be, and is, fairly good.

There's no need to see confusion, then, in what Protagoras says. In a complex *technê* such as this, as in medicine, there are different aspects, different levels of importance and complexity and different levels of attainment and of grasp of the art. But Protagoras' statements are surely incomplete: he has not specified, other than schematically, what the content of his teaching is. Nor can he realistically do that within the dramatic situation of the dialogue; the detailed content of his teaching is reserved for those who pay for it.

I.B   Second Problem: The Relation of Possession of the Technê to Its Use, and of Political Technê to (Traditional) Aretê

Not only the notion of *technê*, but the association of (some part of) *aretê* with possession of a *technê* is central to the dialogue. It is something that Protagoras insists on: in fact, it's his principal selling-point. He claims that he makes young men 'better', that he (without qualification) 'educates' them or that he teaches them to be 'good citizens' (316c5–d3; 317b4–5; 318a6–9). Any *technê* of course carries with it its own internal notion of 'excellence' – in mastery and application of that very *technê*. But Protagoras' claim is clearly meant more widely: that a political *technê* somehow confers *aretê* in some of its more traditional applications, with their traditional connection with a proper education.

This strong claim is the centre around which the whole dialogue turns. It raises questions that cast doubt on the coherence of Protagoras' position. There is first (a) the question already noticed about the relation between the mastery of the supposed art and the due pursuance of its supposed aim. Then there is (b) another closely intertwined question about the relation between the successful pursuit of the aim, and 'excellence' according to traditional notions. Questions (a) and (b) together are the 'second problem' to be discussed in the present section. If Protagoras can make good his position on both of these, then he has the beginnings of an answer to the question of Socrates: 'how can excellence be teachable?' But for a full answer to Socrates, he needs also to deal with (c) the further question, the one that Socrates raises directly in the dialogue: even if we concede Protagoras' general position on (a) and (b), can he show that any such supposed art is actually possible? This is the problem with which Section I.C is concerned.

As for (d) the obvious fourth question, how Protagoras can show that he himself is in possession of the art, and able to teach it effectively to others, this is not raised by Socrates; it would have been socially inept to do so in the circumstances. That Socrates had doubts about it, may be inferred from his previous warning to Hippocrates (312b7–14b4).

How can possession or mastery of a *technê* guarantee that it is used at all, or, if used, that it is used correctly and in accordance with its defined aim? When Protagoras first claims to teach a *technê*, Socrates' first reply ignores the question. He assumes that Protagoras' pupils will not merely *possess* the *technê* but will make good and proper use of it, that they will not just know *how* to be good citizens but will actually *be* good citizens, and will publicly *display* 'political excellence'; and Protagoras assents. (He is not claiming that his pupils will be pre-eminent, but simply that they will be good.) Socrates is presumably willing to concede all this, hypothetically, for the sake of putting the question that interests him at the moment.

The unspoken assumption of both parties here seems to be this: that any reasonably bright young male upper-class Athenian, after receiving such teaching, will naturally apply it, and apply it effectively and as intended, to the pursuit of political power and influence in order primarily to deserve well of his city, and secondarily, to bring fame and glory to himself and his family. And yet this assumption is problematic, to put it mildly, not only for Plato, but for simple common sense, and especially with the hindsight that is available (as Plato knew) to all readers of the dialogue. The presence of Alcibiades and Critias reminds them that if young men of that generation made anything of the sophists' teaching, it was not necessarily what one might expect from a good citizen.

But apart from that, even on Protagoras' own terms, and even within the dialogue (assuming no knowledge of the later history), one may object that it destroys the analogy with any other known *technê*. For after all, in the case of an ordinary *technê*, those who have mastered it do not of necessity use it, or use it for the purposes for which it was designed. They can choose (a) whether or not to use it at all or (b) whether to use it for its supposed official purpose or for other ones. (Think of the medical case once more.) It seems that the notion of a *technê* is being so stretched as to make any analogy with other *technai* problematic.

Is Protagoras relying on the case of childhood training? This, after all, is supposed not merely to tell children what constitutes elementary good behaviour, but to make them disposed to behave accordingly. But (a) in the first place, all this seems to have nothing to do with its being a *technê*, so the analogy is still defective; (b) it is not clear that that analogy will work for the higher part of the *technê*, since Protagoras' pupils, the future statesmen, are not going to be trained in the way that children are.

Hence, there seems to be no guarantee that they will use their higher education to act always for the good of the city.

A better defence for Protagoras can be found in the 'Myth' (322b3–d5). When presented by Zeus with political *technê*, people made use of it, it is implied, because they could see (by simple common sense, *not* by using the *technê* itself) that it was necessary to their survival and their flourishing. They already had basic everyday practical rationality, as is made clear. Thus, the special status of political *technê* is derived from the fact that it is a *technê* of survival and flourishing for societies and hence also for the individuals composing them. Therefore, it is more or less automatic that people, once they see that it is so, will by and large use this *technê* rightly.[8] Similarly, one obeys medical rules simply because one wants to live longer, and to live healthily, and one reasonably assumes that the medical art knows best how one should do so.

This analogy with medical *technê* fits with what AM says about the discovery and adoption of better diets in prehistoric times:

> Because of this necessity, I think, these [primitive] people searched for nourishment that was in accordance with nature, and discovered that which we now use .... What name can be given more justly or aptly to this discovery and investigation than that of 'medicine', considering that it was discovered with the aim of giving mankind health, capacity to survive, and nourishment? (*VM* 3.4)

This answer meets the objection, without destroying the analogy with other *technai*, but it raises a further question. If it is correct, Protagoras needs to show that his 'higher' part of political *technê* is necessary to civic survival, or, at least, that it is necessary to the construction or preservation of a better kind of life for the society and for the individual citizen. (Also, that anyone instructed by him will be able to see, using only basic rationality, that that is so.) In the *Protagoras*, he does not attempt to do this. But in Athens at least he could have argued from results, along the lines of Pericles' Funeral Speech in Thucydides: 'look at the power and splendour and the internal amenities of this Periclean Athens of yours'. This then does not show that Protagoras is inconsistent or confused in his own mind.

---

[8] The distinction in the myth between the initial gifts of Prometheus and Epimetheus and the subsequent gifts of Zeus seems intended to mark the distinction between natural endowments, transmitted biologically, and cultural achievements, transmitted by education, and embodied in *technai*. The striking claim that in a society 'absolutely everyone' is just (322d4–5; 323c2–d5; 327c4–e1), can be understood and defended in a way coherent with the rest of the speech, though that cannot be argued here.

In the actual discussion, then, it seems Protagoras' grand claims for his *technê* come out unscathed. And yet the dialogue as a whole leaves us with the impression that there is something fraudulent about them. What does Protagoras really think about 'excellence' (*aretê*) in general, and about the particular kinds of 'excellence'? He professes to accept in general the traditional notions, but then he later gets entangled by Socrates when questioned about difficulties in those traditional notions. As Michael Frede has pointed out, this indicates that Protagoras, while invoking the traditional conception of *aretê*, has never properly engaged with the ambiguities, indeterminacies and possible incoherences in that conception.[9] Hence, his vulnerability to Socrates' later questioning on the nature of courage (*andreia*) and on the unity of *aretê*. The weakness is even politely but clearly hinted at by Socrates (316c7–d2); yet here too Protagoras is allowed by Plato to escape, on the surface, almost unscathed. Why this is so is a matter of conjecture; but there is a similar partial reprieve for Protagoras in the *Theaetetus*, possibly for the same reason:[10] Plato wanted to be absolutely fair to his adversary and did not find in his writings any sufficiently definitive statements on which to base a final verdict.

I.C Third Problem: Does Such a Political Technê Really Exist, and If So, What Is Its Content?

Protagoras, then, claims that there is a *technê* that covers good deliberation and effective speech and action, on both domestic and public matters. But can he show that there really can be such a *technê* as he describes? That is what Socrates openly doubts, and he supports his doubts with arguments. The arguments both refer to the high-level art, to statesmanship, 'concerning the administration of the city' (319c8–d1). They are appeals to simple public facts of the present day (not to past history, about which there could be endless argument). (a) Apparently the Athenians don't think that there is any teachable expertise about the governing and administration of their city, since they're willing to listen to anyone on the subject (319b3–d7). (b) Even the acknowledged masters of statesmanship, like Pericles, can't transmit their expertise – not even to their own sons and kinsmen (319d7–20b3).

Protagoras, in his long reply (320c8–28d2), offers parries to both objections. Socrates thereupon professes himself convinced on the point

---

[9] Frede 1992: xvii–xxiv.   [10] See Section II.

at issue (328e1–3), and abandons that line of questioning. But are Protagoras' replies satisfactory?

As to (a), Protagoras claims that the Athenians, by being willing to listen to anyone on the subject of the city's highest concerns, show that they (rightly) recognise that everyone (or, at least, every male citizen) is an expert on these matters. Taylor complains that in this answer the 'concept [of excellence] is so diluted as virtually to vanish. Protagoras claims to make his pupils politically expert in the ordinary sense of pre-eminent'; and Socrates' scepticism about this claim 'is not met by the argument that, in common belief, every normal adult is an expert in some much reduced sense'.[11] This is not quite fair about the content of the claim: Protagoras would say that he claims to make his pupils 'excellent', not in the sense of pre-eminent among their peers (that could hardly be, if he has the training of many of them; in any case, he nowhere makes such a claim), but in that of coming up to some comparatively high standard, which they would not otherwise reach. But Taylor nevertheless points up a serious weakness here. The fact is that Protagoras has done nothing whatever to show that political excellence of the kind he professes to teach, the supposed highest level of the art, can indeed be taught. He answers Socrates' objection in the form in which it was put, but has done nothing to remove any doubts about that part of the art that most interests Socrates and the rest of the audience. On Protagoras' reply to objection (b), the same remarks apply: again he addresses only the question of the teachability of the lower level of the art.

So Protagoras is guilty here of sheer bluff. His evasion of the real question is obscured by a profusion of elegant discourse, which elaborates uncontroversial matters at unnecessary length, in order to conceal the poverty of the content. The most he does towards a real answer, at the end of his long speech (328a8–c2), is the following: He tells us that he satisfies his pupils, who are willing at the end of the course to pay him large sums. So they, at least, who know the content of his thinking in detail, and have experienced its effect on their own minds, are convinced. That 'at least' suggests he has *some* appreciable educative effect. (Here too AM runs parallel: in defence of his claim that there exists a true art of medicine, he insists at *VM* 9.4 (compare 1.2) on the test of results: people recognise that there are good doctors and less good ones, which shows that the good ones make a real difference and do really help people.) But Protagoras still hasn't

[11] Taylor 1991: 83.

done anything towards proving anything substantive about the resulting abilities of his pupils.

In itself, this failure to answer Socrates need not be taken as a sign of confusion. In charity, we may suppose that it's dictated by Protagoras' enforced public reticence about the content and method of his own teaching. As a financially interested provider of that teaching, he cannot afford to reveal anything substantive about it, apart from such generalities as are presumably public knowledge anyway (notably, that it involves intensive discussion of poetry [338e6–39a3]). So he cannot offer any a priori proof that it can meet Socrates' test.

II Protagoras Expanded: An Attempt to Reconstruct His 'Political Art'

So far, using only the dialogue *Protagoras* itself, with the auxiliary evidence of AM, it has been argued that Protagoras' conception of political *technê* need not be seen as internally incoherent. But the indications within the dialogue give us (for good reason) only a radically incomplete picture of that conception. One may still doubt whether it must or even can be completed in such a way as to make Protagoras a political theorist.[12]

In the face of these doubts we must turn to the *Theaetetus*, and especially the long apologia given to Protagoras at 166a2–68c2. The *Theaetetus* is a difficult dialogue, and its treatment of Protagoras is one of the difficult episodes in it. But since it is reasonable to assume that Plato's Protagoras is intended to be the same figure in both dialogues, the *Theaetetus* is the one further source to which we can and therefore must turn.

In this section, therefore, I explore the possibility of filling out from the *Theaetetus* the conception of *politikê technê* expounded in the *Protagoras*. I shall again appeal, for indirect support, to closely parallel passages in *On Ancient Medicine*, without assuming that AM's views must have been entirely the same as those of Protagoras. The case for all this cannot here be argued out: what follows is only a sketch of its main lines.

In the *Theaetetus*, Protagoras is introduced as the proponent of an unusual account of truth, opinion and knowledge. It was not entirely

---

[12] Recent general surveys of ancient political thought, such as Rowe and Schofield (2000), give little space to Protagoras. Among recent studies, Farrar (1988) stands out as a well-argued attempt to see him as a central and original thinker on political matters, though it is forced to suppose that he has been substantially misrepresented by Plato in both *Protagoras* and *Theaetetus*.

novel at the dramatic date of the dialogue, being composed on the basis of thoughts that had been in circulation even in the pre-sophistic period,[13] the original inspiration being the radical epistemology of Xenophanes. The interpretation of Protagoras now to be given cannot be argued for and defended against other views, within the space available. It will be given in summary. The claim that is made for it is that it enables a coherent account to be given and one that fits in a satisfactory way with all of the Platonic evidence.[14]

The first known proponent of radical empiricism is Xenophanes.[15] The fundamental Xenophanean principle, that only that which is experienced at first hand is known, was taken seriously by a good number of others in the following two centuries. A question that faces anyone who takes it seriously is: what should be said about cases where different human observers have apparently different first-hand experiences of one and the same state of affairs? Here Protagoras takes steps that Xenophanes may not have taken, but that did seem to appeal to certain other pre-Socratic theorists (though the details are uncertain).[16] Protagoras' position is found in the *Theaetetus*. After the original elementary exposition by Socrates of the principle that all perceptions are true (151e4–52c7), the development follows in three passages: the first critique of Socrates (163a6–65e4), the 'apologia of Protagoras' offered by Socrates (166a2–66c2) and the second critique of Socrates (169d2–72b7). Any account of Protagoras' position in the *Theaetetus* must be guided by the principles that it should be, as far as possible, not merely compatible with, but closely tied to, the position of Protagoras in the *Protagoras*, and that, if possible, it should make sense of the renewed appeal here to the analogy of the medical art, and to some apparently analogous formulations of AM.

First, the knowledge given by direct perception is infallible. The motivation for this further step is clear: if perceptions were sometimes not wholly infallible, there would need to be, for knowledge to be possible, a

---

[13] This is an example of the general truth that the stock-in-trade of the sophists drew heavily on many predecessors, whether sages, poets or pre-Socratic theorists about the general nature of things. Even the *phusis-nomos* contrast, with which some made great play, was in essence pre-sophistic.

[14] The many divergent opinions on Protagoras' position in the *Theaetetus* cannot be reviewed here. For one recent influential treatment, see Burnyeat 1990: esp. 10–31, 39–42. A lucid statement of the constraints on any possible interpretation of Protagoras' position in the *Theaetetus* is Brown 1993: esp. 205–9, 213–15.

[15] The principal texts for Xenophanes' empiricism are three fragments: DK [Xenophanes] B 18, 34, 35 = LM D 53, 49, 50.

[16] The principal testimony is Aristotle, *Metaph*. IV.5–7 (possibly valuable but difficult); also Sextus Empiricus (denying that Protagoras was a Pyrrhonian sceptic: PH 1.216–19 = DK 80 [Protagoras] A 14 = LM R 21). None of this can be evaluated here.

further, non-perceptual criterion of truth, which would undermine the original conception of perception as the only sure source of knowledge. Then, since knowledge is a grasp of a truth, all perceptions equally must be true. In order to save the truth of perceptions, given the fact that different perceptions may conflict, Protagoras makes a radical revision of the very notion of truth. He declares that there is no such thing as unqualified truth: perceptions are necessarily true, but only for the particular perceiver,[17] and only for so long as they *are* the perceptions of that perceiver. All truth is simply 'truth-for-X-at-time-t', for some perceiver X and some time t. It is in this sense that 'a human being is a measure of all things': any human being is a measure in a very strong sense, an infallible measure of anything that they can perceive.

Secondly, in place of shared truth, Protagoras introduces the notion of 'better opinion'. This too seems to have roots in Xenophanes, who speaks of how humankind makes progress as it 'finds out something better' (B18 D-K = 32 M-P = D53 L-M). We must here include both individual opinions and generally shared opinions. Individual human beings can be persuaded to revise opinions that are founded only on their individual perceptions, and to adopt 'better' ones. So too can whole groups and whole societies.

It is important to note that here, while Protagoras is implicitly distinguishing between people's perceptions and their opinions (that may or may not be founded on perceptions), he is also (though Plato again does not expressly state this) extending to all opinions the principle that they are always true for whoever holds them, but only for them. This goes beyond anything that can be attributed to Xenophanes.

It should be noted also that this position does not exclude, as definitely false, the existence of some objective reality behind conflicting perceptions, or in matters entirely beyond human perception. Indeed, such exclusion would be a breach of the Xenophanean principle, since by hypothesis we cannot experience at first hand the presence or absence of an objective reality in such cases. But, equally, Protagoras cannot possibly assert that there is any such thing.

The central question now is the nature of 'better' opinion: how it is to be defined and recognised, and how it is produced (or destroyed). Here the medical analogy is made to do significant work. The wise man is closely analogous to the physician. Just as the good physician can change people's perceptions of their own bodily states, for the better, so the wise man can

---

[17] *Tht.* 166d1–67b4; at 167b2 we must understand *alêthê* as 'true without qualification'.

change people's perceptions about other matters, from less good to better. But Protagoras does not further explain either the content of 'better', or whether (and if so how) it can be a matter of *knowledge* that any given opinion is better than any other.

It may help to look back at Xenophanes. Having denied the possibility of knowledge about anything beyond the range of immediate experience, he thought it was possible to provide some kind of substitute for knowledge. His prime example (B34 DK = 39 M-P = D49 L-M) of the unknowable was assertions about the gods; and yet he developed a positive theology. And the surviving reports of his cosmological views indicate that they were derived by a minimalist, ontologically parsimonious extrapolation from what can be taken as certainly known by first-hand experience.[18] This is one way of taking the principle of 'resembling what is true', and thereby justifying the claim of 'finding something better'. It is given by another fragment (B35 DK = 40 M-P = D50 L-M) in which Xenophanes speaks of opinions 'resembling truths' (*eoikota tois etumoisin*), and therefore, he implies, acceptable. It can be argued that AM's substantive medical theory is shaped by a Xenophanean approach.[19]

Protagoras now has to explain more fully the practical effects and the public recognisability (which he clearly assumes) of 'better' opinion. If the wise person produces 'better' perceptions in others, for whom, and in whose judgement, are these 'better'? The parallel with the claims of AM about medicine suggests: *for* the individual, but *in the judgement* of all (or most). That must be right for Protagoras too: for if, as pure subjectivism says, it is only in the judgement of the individual perceivers, the whole structure collapses: everyone is wise. So Protagoras' 'better' perceptions and opinions are ones that are *demonstrably* better, and 'demonstrably' must mean: shown by appeal only to what is publicly knowable. This supplies one indispensable role for the 'wise man', if it is only he who is capable of carrying out the needed demonstrations, just as the physician is the only person capable of carrying out the medical treatments needed to improve the patients' sensations. Improvements or the reverse in a person's state of

---

[18] The principle of ontological parsimony may also be seen at work in Heraclitus and some other authors in the empiricist tradition (see n. 27 below). Protagoras too was apparently willing, like Xenophanes, to allow that there can be more or less likely or 'good' opinions about the gods, and himself to speculate on the subject. An essay of his, apparently entitled 'On the Gods' (DK 80 B1 = LM D 10), consistently begins with a disclaimer of knowledge on the subject (cf. *Tht.* 162d5–e4), but the essay cannot have ended there, if it really was about the gods.

[19] See further in this section.

health are publicly demonstrable: not only do patients subjectively 'feel better' (or worse), but their bodily states can be publicly perceived. The expertise of the relevant experts is open to public test.

Sometimes, of course, the wise man is hardly needed. Most people visually distinguish red and green as different colours. But some do not ('red-green colour blindness'). Protagoras tells us that all have true perceptions. But subjective truth, in that case, cannot be the whole story: those colour-blind people who stay within the bounds of what is true for them, cannot function cognitively, in finding their way around the world, as well as those who recognise that their truth is incomplete or misleading in one important respect. And this is demonstrably so.

This shows that opinions based directly on individual sense-perception are just as open to revision as any others. Indeed, there are well-known cases where *everyone's* visual perception can be demonstrated (on the basis of other perceptions) to be misleading. Protagoras must keep the notion of the infallible truth of sense-perception because he needs it as the foundation for everything else; yet he must also say that truth as so defined is always subject to revision in the light of other such truths.

So Protagoras must found publicly accepted 'better' opinion on individual sense-perceptions, taken as being incorrigibly true, and yet allow that these in turn can be criticised, and the opinions founded on them can sometimes be revised and improved, in the light of publicly accepted 'better' opinion. Did he need, and did he feel the need, to define his conception further, and, in particular, to deal with the apparent circularity in his position? It must be admitted that Plato gives us little or no direct guidance on these questions; and he is the only reliable source. But if one accepts, as this chapter has consistently argued, that Plato is trying to be absolutely fair to Protagoras, as he understands him, the natural conclusion is that Protagoras in fact made no effort to define his views more fully. That would be parallel to Protagoras' failure, as shown in the *Protagoras*, to engage closely with the ambiguities and apparent contradictions within traditional Greek values.

A possibly helpful piece of evidence here is Socrates' final attack on Protagoras, at *Tht.* 169d3–72b7 and 177c6–79c1. Here Socrates puts his finger on two vulnerable points. But one should take note of Plato's carefully underlined disclaimers, which once again show the unique respect with which Plato treats Protagoras among all his sophistic and pre-Socratic targets. Socrates insists that he may not be making the best possible case for the absent Protagoras, thereby leaving it finally open whether or not Protagoras could have devised effective answers to his objections. What

Plato is claiming is that, so far as he (Plato) can tell, he could not have done so.

First, Socrates remarks that the doctrine that 'all opinions are true' cannot be squared with the fact that people often believe that their own opinions on many subjects are or may well be radically incomplete, if not downright mistaken. These second-order opinions must then, on Protagoras' account, be both true and (possibly) false, even for those who hold them, and at the time they hold them; an effective reductio ad absurdum, both in itself, and in the further consequence that Protagoras' own opinion, while true for Protagoras himself, is false for everyone, including Protagoras. Secondly, there is a problem about opinions about the future. For here there are matters that are unavailable to direct experience at present, but which eventually become so. Retrospectively, we can see that our opinions about these were false objectively. Once again, this looks sufficient to make nonsense, or mere verbal trickery, of the claim that all opinions are true. Here Protagoras is neatly tripped up by his Xenophanean heritage,[20] and while his conception of 'better opinion' is not thereby directly attacked, it is undermined indirectly, and with it his claims to teach 'good deliberation' (*euboulia*: *Prt.* 318e5–319a3).

In sum, Protagoras tries to develop (without necessarily being able to distinguish them clearly, or to arbitrate between them) both of the two tendencies evident in Xenophanes: that towards radical empiricism, and that towards a form of pragmatism. If they are compatible, as Protagoras in effect assumes, he can enjoy the best of both worlds. The 'man-measure' slogan has correspondingly both a restrictive, empiricist message: 'there is no measure available except human experience'; and an optimistic, pragmatist one: 'using human experience as a measure gives us all we ever need in practice'.[21]

If this reading is correct, Protagoras is, in practical effect, a partial or total pragmatist. He holds (without excluding realism as a theoretical possibility) that what matters, outside the realm of what is knowable, is not truth, but what is most generally and stably accepted as truth. That (though always revisable) is the closest thing to non-relative truth that we

---

[20] Points closely akin to those of Socrates recur in discussions of some modern versions of pragmatism, on which I am indebted for guidance primarily to Brandom 2011, particularly chapter 2, section IX, 'Three Objections to Instrumental Pragmatism'.

[21] The radical empiricist aspect of Protagoras was recognised by George Grote, himself a radical empiricist, in his pioneering studies of the sophists and his attempted defence of them against Plato (see esp. Grote 1875, vol. II, chs. 21 and 26). The pragmatist aspect was recognised by the pragmatist F. C. S. Schiller (see Schiller 1908).

can get. And even if there are some who don't accept this opinion, they are ex hypothesi in a minority and will be, in practical terms, negligible.

It is possible, then, Protagoras recognised (as Xenophanes seems to have done) a limited area within which some objective or inter-subjective truth was attainable; but the way he and Socrates speak in the *Theaetetus* seems to exclude this. In any case, he neither asserts nor denies realism. This again is consistent with his Xenophanean heritage. At least on contentious matters, objective truth is unreachable, and possibly non-existent; but wherever objective truth is unavailable, 'better opinion' can step in to take over the role of substitute for truth.[22]

Two further points about 'better opinion' should be underlined. First, Protagoras must claim that there are generally accepted marks of 'better' opinion, and that in any particular case the expert can persuade others to adopt the better opinion by exhibiting those marks. This is the underlying rationale for the systematic study and practice of rational and plausible arguments, which formed a part of Protagoras' instruction.[23]

In the second place, since 'better opinion' must always be revisable in the light of new evidence, we can see why, though keeping the primacy of sense-perception, Protagoras extends the accolade of 'truth' to all opinions of all human beings. There is no way for him to avoid doing so, once it is admitted that even the most fundamental opinions are subject to revision.[24]

Does Protagoras have to claim that there is long-term *convergence* of 'better opinion' on any question? In the medical case, as AM's claims require, there does seem to be a natural tendency for individual perceptions to converge over time towards a public consensus. This is one reason why it is important to assert that the art of medicine is *ancient*. An effective *technê*, such as medicine, improves this consensus and proves its existence, at the same time as it demonstrates its own effectiveness. The confident

---

[22] Burnyeat 1990: 24 objects that in that case 'it becomes an objective matter that one of two states of mind is better than another', and similarly that experts exist. That need not be so. All that Protagoras needs is an unchallenged general agreement on these questions. There is a possibly infinite regress here: there needs to be general agreement that there is general agreement, and so on; but all that such a regress shows is something that a pragmatist Protagoras must have said anyway, that the enterprise of constructing 'better opinion' must be seen realistically as 'a going concern', always provisional, always proceeding on the basis of limited knowledge, time and energy, and therefore always liable to drastic revision. In any case, it is arguable that general agreement about something already implies general agreement that there is general agreement.

[23] LM D 26–30.

[24] This may also explain the claim attributed to Protagoras that 'every argument [*logos*] admits a counter-argument' (Diogenes Laertius 9.51 = DK 80 A 1 = LM D 26), if it is not simply a pedagogic prescription to practise arguing on both sides of a question.

and optimistic tone of Protagoras, in both dialogues, would seem to suggest that he shared with AM an expectation that the area of unchallenged agreement would in fact grow with time (at least if he and his pupils are allowed to operate on the minds of others). But he makes no outright claim to that effect.

What in the end is the part played in all this by the notion of *technê*? And what is to be made of the parallels of thought and wording between Protagoras (in *Protagoras* and *Theaetetus*), and *On Ancient Medicine*?

To take the second matter first. We have seen how some of Protagoras' formulations in the *Protagoras*, and some of the background thoughts and explanations it seems necessary to attribute to him, are paralleled by AM. The phenomenon recurs in the *Theaetetus*, which indirectly supports the view that the two dialogues are indeed both meant to give a substantially faithful account of Protagoras' thinking, though they concentrate on different aspects of it. The parallelisms seem to be quite unforced, each half of them arising naturally within its context, stated in the author's own way, yet showing both shared thought and some shared terminology (notably the keyword *metron*). They are reinforced by explicit statements of the medical analogy with Protagoras' activity (*Prt.* 352c2–3 (Socrates speaking); *Tht.* 166d3–67a4). Yet there is nothing to suggest that either is directly borrowing from the other, or that the two of them are in agreement on all points. Nor is there any point, for immediate purposes, in speculating about a possible common source. What we need is to grasp the full extent of the parallel thoughts and formulations, and their strategic importance for both Protagoras and AM.

What both insist on, as the foundation of their respective claims, is the actual, public, incontrovertible existence of an effective art of medicine: and one that requires specialised experts, that is, one that goes beyond ordinary commonsense practice. As already said, AM appeals (*VM* 9.4–5) to the fact that people in general recognise the different quality and success rate of different specialist practitioners. And this recognition is possible only because what constitutes success is the (absolute or comparative) restoration or preservation of health, and this too is something subject to public verification (9.3). The patient verifies it most directly, by 'feeling better'; but the patient and others too can inspect, from the outside, the patient's body. It is 'the perception of the body' (*tou sômatos tên aisthêsin*) that is decisive. The phrase is nicely ambiguous: is the genitive subjective or objective? There seems to be no reason why it should not be intended in both ways. There is a point to this pun: for the patient's 'bodily feeling' is part of his 'perception of the body'. There is a publicly available method, a 'measuring device' (*metron*): human sense-perception. This is how, on Xenophanean principles, it needs to be.

Both AM and Protagoras go further along this line, by appealing to the successes of specialised athletic and gymnastic trainers (another very public matter). This is not surprising in AM (7.2); but Protagoras too (*Prt.* 316d8–e5) happily aligns himself with expert trainers of runners and weightlifters, and confers on them the proud title of 'sophists'. He too is following the logic of his position, and in the *Theaetetus* he extends the list of parallel *technai* yet further, to include agriculture and forestry (167b5–c2). For him too the palpable practical successes of other *technai* involving the training of other living beings are essential supports for his claims.

A further point of parallelism is the reference to a supposed 'original condition', a primitive state in which human life began as a grimly basic struggle for individual survival but was gradually improved by purely human effort. This is the scenario underlying the various extant versions, of which the fullest is found in Diodorus Siculus, of a pre-Platonic account of the early human condition and of the origins of civilised life. Here too we are not concerned with the question of authorship: all that needs to be said is that both AM (ch. 3) and Protagoras, in the myth he tells in the *Protagoras* (320c8–23a4), draw on the general conception as something familiar and well-established.[25] They use it, it seems, not as an independent argument, but rather as an explanatory supplement for the claims being advanced. It is the background for the claims that both medicine (*VM*, chs. 2–3, 5) and 'the sophistic *technê*' (*Prt.* 316d3–9) have a long (and increasingly successful) history.

There is therefore a more than superficial intellectual kinship between Protagoras, as portrayed by Plato, and AM, the unidentified Hippocratic writer. Is it possible to specify more precisely what this kinship consists in, as well as where they essentially differ? This brings back the question of the notion of *technê*, and the part it plays within their thinking.

AM is not a follower, or even a close intellectual ally, of Protagoras. AM is interested in some contemporary intellectual debates, but only in so far

---

[25] Diodorus Siculus 1.7–8 = DK [Democritus] 68 B5 = LM [Atomists] D129 and D202. Here the fundamental ideas possibly go back to Xenophanes at least; compare Xenophanes on human progress (DK B 18 = LM D 53). Note also the title of a lost work of Protagoras: 'On the Original Condition of Things' (*peri tês en arkhêi katastaseôs*: Diogenes Laertius 9.55 = DK 80 A1 and B8b = LM D1). In the myth in the *Protagoras*, the appearance of the gods Zeus and Hermes as possessors and givers of *technai* may be taken as part of the mythical apparatus; see n. 9 above. A keyword for this view of human antiquity is *thêriôdês* ('brutish'), used to characterise early human life: Diodorus Siculus 1.8.1, and AM (ch. 3). For general discussion, see Cole 1990 and Dodds 1973.

as he can use them for his own purposes. He is in fact a realist and an empiricist, but shows no sign of concern about the nature of truth, knowledge or reality in general.[26] What interests him is showing the reality of the practical achievements of medical science and the correctness of his own substantive conception of that science. He presents medicine as a self-moving, cumulatively self-improving 'going concern', one that need not and should not pay attention to general ideas originating outside its sphere. All this is summed up for him in the claim that medicine, as he conceives of it and practises it, is a *technê*; one that exists and has long existed and has its own startingpoint and its own method. This has resulted in a substantive theory of health and disease. It is conceived in a radically empiricist way, being tied as closely as may be to observed phenomena. The 'powers' that play the principal role are identified in terms of their observed sensory effects alone, not in terms of any a priori classification. Causal explanations are to be given in terms of the observable effects of these powers and of the manifest structures (*schêmata*) in the human body.[27]

And yet, as the evidence shows, what AM and Protagoras have in common is something very important to both of them. It is the vision of the *technai*, and their transmission by education, as the sources and instruments of human progress, from the 'brutish' beginnings up to civilised life. It is the central role of *technê*, conceived of in this way, and the long history of particular *technai* in the human advance towards a better life, that is the binding thread, both between AM and Protagoras, and between the two halves of Protagoras artificially separated by Plato.

Furthermore, it is not just the notion of *technê* alone that plays this theoretically central role in these authors. For them the notion of *technê* is the vehicle of a thought even more fundamental and powerful: that of the primacy of practice over theory. This is of course a leading thought in pragmatism; but like other powerful thoughts it is Protean, assuming different forms in different minds.

The primacy of practice is not implied by the word *technê* alone, in its earlier usage. In the sophistic period, theoretical studies such as mathematics (not just the techniques of calculation) and theoretical astronomy could also be simply referred to as *technai*.[28] And it might seem that AM does not exemplify it: after all, he does have a general 'theory of health

---

[26] He says without qualification that a failed diagnosis 'will miss reality' (*tou eontos apoteuxetai* [2.3]).
[27] On 'powers' and 'structures', see esp. *VM* chs. 14–18 and 22–24. On the radical-empiricist principle of ontological parsimony ('no new sensibles') in Xenophanes and Heraclitus, see Hussey 1990: 26. What AM calls a *hupothesis* is something that violates that principle.
[28] As at *Prt.* 318e1–3 (where Protagoras himself is speaking).

and disease'. But this is not conceived of as a means of understanding any particular situation: that can only be done by the application of a practically experienced mind to the particular circumstances. Still less is it a means of dictating the actions to be taken in any given case. It merely supplies the invariant background within which the mind and the hand of the physician operate. It is doubtful whether AM saw these general background ideas as anything more than one part of elementary medical training, on a level with (for example) basic anatomical knowledge. What is certain is that in his essay it is the *practice* of medicine that is in the centre of the stage, that justifies his claims for his *technê*, that validates by its success his general ideas about health and disease and that deservedly commands respect and trust. The theory is seen as derivative from, and secondary to, the practice, as a way of summarising the general background rules of 'best practice'.

For Protagoras, the evidence is seriously incomplete. But if there is anything in the quasi-pragmatist interpretation that has been offered, one would expect a corresponding privileging of practice over theory. In fact, what little we know of his educative techniques does not at all suggest that they involved the mastery of a body of scientifically formulated theory. Like some other sophists, he attacked, in a radically empiricist spirit, the theoretical sciences par excellence, mathematics and astronomy.[29] He trained the minds of his pupils by exercises in the interpretation of poetry, the investigation of linguistic phenomena and the composition and delivery of speeches. He must have had some general background conceptions about political life, as he had his general conceptions of language, and of truth, knowledge and opinion, and as AM had his conception of 'powers' in the human body; but there is nothing to suggest that these were any more than the current commonplaces of educated discussion.[30]

Given this reconstruction, it is possible to supply some of what is missing in the account of political *technê* in the *Protagoras*. Thereby it becomes clearer why Plato takes Protagoras so seriously as to devote substantial parts of two major dialogues to his ideas. On this reading, Protagoras was committed to something like the following.

---

[29] Aristotle *Metaph.* III.2, 998b2–4; cf. DK B7a = LM D34.

[30] See n. 6 above. There is no firm evidence for systematic theorising about language, though Protagoras evidently discussed elementary grammar in an analytical spirit (see LM D 17–25); the requirement of 'correctness of speech' (*orthoepeia*: LM D21, 22) may just indicate that he wished to standardise actual usage, an aim of many educators at all times. As Rachel Barney has pointed out to me, further information might possibly be extracted from the writings of Isocrates, whose educational activities seem to have been inspired by those of Protagoras. The primacy of practice in Protagoras is well expressed by Marrou 1948: 84–87.

His 'political *technê*' has as its overall aim the common social and political welfare of the polis (any polis) and hence of all its citizens. This very wide aim, one that embraces the whole of human civilised life, includes a multitude of subsidiary aims, which demand subordinate special *technai*. Like medicine, political *technê* is an overarching, 'architectonic' *technê* (as Aristotle puts it: *NE* 1.1, 1094a27–28). Obviously, too, there must be not just subordinate *technai* but *branches* of the main *technê*, divided by subject matter: those dealing with, for example, (a) the material circumstances of the *polis*; (b) the relations with other *poleis* and other human societies; and, most important, (c) the *minds* of the citizens themselves. This last branch is where Protagoras' particular speciality within political *technê* is to be located.

Protagoras' *technê*, then, is the art of using words to achieve the changing of people's perceptions and opinions, from less good to better. This will mean particularly their perceptions or opinions of what is just and fair, what is good and excellent (in a moral/civic sense), fine and praiseworthy. This includes basic moral and civic education at the lower end, political theory and rhetoric at the higher end. There are different levels, as suggested by the dietetic-medical analogy. But it's in effect an art of education for civilised life within the polis. Hereby, the doubleness in Protagoras' activity, noted earlier, is explained and justified. The sophists are themselves high-level general educators, and they educate their pupils in the art of educating their fellow citizens. These are two levels or aspects of one and the same art. Protagoras' claim, never justified in the *Protagoras*, about the existence of such a *technê*, depends on this kind of general conception; and one can see in outline how to supply from it both the general specification of what it is Protagoras claims to teach and the reasoning that justifies the claim that the *technê* is a necessity for survival and flourishing.

It is an optimistic vision. AM once again provides a parallel, with his explicit, aggressive, even triumphalist optimism about the future continuance and improvement of the medical art; once again, there are already suggestions of such an attitude in Xenophanes.[31] Protagoras does not speak so confidently in Plato. He admits (*Protagoras* 316c5–d3) that sophists often arouse distrust and, sometimes, active hostility. Yet for his part, he is willing to admit to being a sophist, and expresses confidence about his own future (317b3–c1). Above all, his claim to teach effectively a

---

[31] For *VM*, see esp. 2.1, 4.2.; for Xenophanes, DK B 18 (= LM D 53; see n. 15 above). In general, Dodds 1973.

genuine political *technê* that makes the governing classes truly better at governing implies optimism as to political improvements in the future.

His closeness to Pericles, strongly suggested in the *Protagoras*, and independently attested, is not surprising if he is an advocate of a 'Periclean' conception of democracy: a democracy sustained by the consent of the free citizens, but run and guided by an enlightened elite who are capable of persuading them.[32] The members of this elite will, of course, be pupils or at least followers of Protagoras, guided by his ideas. Such ideas could of course also be applied without strain to the justification of other, not necessarily democratic constitutions: a broadly based oligarchy, or even a monarchy. What is required would seem to be an enlightened regime enjoying the consent of the majority of citizens, and responsive to their needs and to the advice of its (Protagorean) experts.

What Protagoras offers, in short, is a *technê* that has the power to change people, permanently and for the better. The moral education of children, which aims to turn them from self-centred animals into decent family members and citizens, is only the first and simplest stage of the process. It is human nature generally, so far as it can be influenced by thoughts put into words, that is Protagoras' concern. He sees it as essentially rational, plastic and adaptable. His conception of political *technê*, even if unrealistically and even dangerously optimistic, contains also, on this reading, a pioneering vision of the general nature of education, lower and higher, and of its power to transform human nature.[33]

---

[32] Closeness to Pericles: *Prt.* 311a1–2, 314e3–15a3; Plutarch, *Life of Pericles* 36.5 (= DK 80 A 10 = LM D); also possibly Heraclides Ponticus ap. Diogenes Laertius 9.50 (= DK 80 A 1 = LM P12), stating that Protagoras was entrusted with the task of drawing up 'laws' (presumably a constitution) for the Athenian colony-city of Thurii. Though Protagoras incidentally expresses sweeping contempt for the views of 'the many' (*Prt.* 353a7–8), that need not mean he is insincere in his support for Periclean democracy, though it does suggest a worrying lack of concern about a danger inherent (if he is right) in any democracy.

[33] On ancient Greek education in this period, Marrou 1948 is a classic work that is still illuminating.

CHAPTER 2

Dynamic Modalities and Teleological Agency
Plato and Aristotle on Skill and Ability

Tamer Nawar

Three important claims are made in *Republic* I concerning the nature of skill or expertise (*technê*) and certain kinds of ability or power (*dunamis*): (a) that skills or the abilities constitutive of skill have a certain 'two-way' nature;[1] (b) that the possessor of skill cannot fail to bring about what they intend or attempt; and (c) that skills or expertise are directed towards some good. These claims are discussed in some detail by Plato and seem to play an important role in Aristotle's account of *technê*, but it is not clear precisely what these claims amount to, why they might be deemed plausible, or to what degree Plato or Aristotle are in fact committed to them. In this chapter, I aim to clarify these claims and the attitudes adopted towards them by Plato and Aristotle and thereby further our understanding of dynamic modalities and teleological agency in the thought of Plato and Aristotle. To this end, I first (Section I) clarify and explain the precise claims being made in *Republic* I, which arguably offers the most detailed surviving treatment of these claims prior to Aristotle. I then (Section II) examine how Aristotle incorporates and adapts the relevant claims in developing his own account of skill and ability.

I Plato's Republic on *Technê*

What has come down to us as the first book of the *Republic* centres on a discussion of the nature of justice. While the conversation focuses on justice, the interlocutors assume or make several claims about *technê* that

---

[1] It is nowadays often claimed that abilities have a two-way nature such that *x has the ability to φ iff x has the ability to refrain from φ-ing*. E.g., 'So, if "*p*" stands for "read", *Cx-p* means "*x* can omit reading".... A fundamental law of ability-logic seems to be this $Cxp \leftrightarrow Cx\text{-}p$. Ability to and to omit are reciprocal' (von Wright 1976: 391). Such claims are often traced back to Aristotle. While there is something to this (see below), as we shall see in this chapter, Plato and Aristotle understand the two-way nature of abilities in ways that differ significantly from this modern understanding.

merit the attention of those interested in ancient views of ability and skill or expertise.

I.A Two-Way Skills

In examining Polemarchus' views concerning justice, Socrates claims that being skilful or clever (*deinos*) has a certain 'two-way' nature. The person who is cleverest or most skilful at hitting is proficient not only at hitting, but is also the cleverest or most skilful at guarding against being hit (*Rep.* 333e3–4). Equally, the person who is clever or skilful at guarding against illness is also proficient at producing it (333e6–7), and the same applies to the person who is a good guard of a camp (333a1–3) in so far as the skilful guard is also a skilful thief (334a5). It seems that the 'two-way' nature of *being skilful* (*deinos*)[2] should be glossed as follows:

> **(Two-Way Skills)** if x is skilful at φ-ing, then x is proficient at φ-ing and x is proficient at ψ-ing (where φ-ing and ψ-ing are opposites).

It is not entirely clear what (Two-Way Skills) amounts to or why it should be deemed plausible because, although the examples in the *Republic* suggest that 'being proficient at φ-ing' amounts to being able to φ well, precisely how the relevant 'opposite' activities should be understood is less clear. Moreover, it is not entirely clear whether Plato's Socrates is putting forward this claim about the two-way nature of being skilful merely dialectically or not in *Rep.* I, whether this claim is meant to hold of *technai* quite generally or to what degree this claim is taken as true in other dialogues. However, given the importance Aristotle gives to similar claims (see Section II.A), the claim merits explication and there seem to be several ways of understanding what (Two-Way Skills) amounts to depending upon how one construes the nature of the relevant 'opposite' activities.[3]

---

[2] Isocrates closely associates being clever or skillful (*deinos*) with possessing a *technê* (e.g., *Antidosis* 33, 35, 117, 230; cf. *Prt.* 312d5–e2).
[3] Plato speaks of opposites (*enantia*) in various ways. In general, it seems that opposites may be:
    contradictories, which are such that everything must be one or the other but cannot be both (e.g., white and not-white) (cf. *Rep.* 491d4–5);
    polar contraries (e.g., *enantiôtata*, *Prt.* 331d5), which are exclusive and partially exhaustive in so far as although *not* everything must be one or the other, everything that instantiates some more general quality must be one or the other or somehow in between (*Symp.* 201e10–b5; *Prt.* 346d1–3);
    contraries, which are such that nothing can be more than one of them in the same respect at the same time, etc. but are not mutually exhaustive (e.g., white, red, green, blue, black) (*Rep.* 436b6–37c10).
    In the *Protagoras*, it is suggested that opposites in the relevant sense, seemingly (ii), come in pairs such that each only has one contrary. Thus, for instance, the beautiful only has one contrary: the

One way of attempting to elucidate the notion of opposite activities focuses upon the fact that each of the examples adduced in the *Republic* involves *guarding* (*phulattein*). Accordingly, one might think that in (Two-Way Skills), φ-ing and ψ-ing are such that if φ-ing and ψ-ing are opposites, then one activity is (or involves) guarding against the other. On this understanding, if someone is skilful at hitting (or poisoning, infiltrating a camp), then that person is able to, for example, hit well *and* able to effectively guard (i.e., 'guard well') against being hit. Thus understood, the possessor of skill is an effective *doer* and an effective guard against 'being done to'. In so far as there are and always have been bruisers as well as featherweights, the claim is not especially plausible and, at best, it seems to only apply to a fairly circumscribed set of activities (for instance, it is unclear how there could be relevant guarding activities in the case of training horses, doing sums, making shoes and many other cases).

The degree to which (Two-Way Skills) is assumed elsewhere in Plato's dialogues is not clear. However, we do seem to be presented with similar views and other ways of understanding the two-way nature of skill elsewhere in Plato. For instance, the *Hippias Minor* seems to offer *two* other ways of elucidating the notion of 'opposite' activities. On the one hand, in the course of discussing whether those who err intentionally are better than those who err unintentionally in the latter part of the *Hippias Minor* (373c7ff), it is suggested that φ-ing and ψ-ing are opposites when there exists some one activity (e.g., running) such that φ-ing is doing that activity well (e.g., running well) and ψ-ing is doing that activity badly (e.g., running badly) (or vice versa) (*Hp. Mi.* 373d5–7). Thus, for instance, the wrestler who falls intentionally is more skilful than the one who falls unintentionally (*Hp. Mi.* 374a1–3), the soul that misses the target intentionally is better at archery (375a7–b2), and the person who intentionally brings about bad results for the body is better at medicine (375b4–7).

On the other hand, earlier on in the dialogue, it is initially suggested that the person who is most able to tell the truth about certain things is also best placed to speak falsely about those things because both effectively speaking the truth and effectively speaking falsely require knowing the truth (*Hp. Mi.* 366e3–67a5). (The person who wishes to speak falsely but doesn't know the truth is not able to effectively speak falsely because they might unintentionally speak truly.) If one equates speaking truly with

---

ugly. Equally, the good only has one contrary: the bad. The high has only one contrary: the low (*Prt.* 331d1–33c9, 338a8–b1).

speaking *well* and speaking falsely with speaking *badly*, one may perhaps see this as offering the same account of opposite activities as is offered later on in the dialogue. However, it seems more natural to say that what is being assumed here is that φ-ing and ψ-ing are opposites when they are activities that bring about contradictory or polar contrary products. According to this suggestion, the φ-ing and ψ-ing constitutive of two-way skills are activities that bring about contradictory or polar contrary products. Such a suggestion finds support in the fact that sometimes *technai* are spoken of as being *set over* these kinds of 'opposites' or having these kinds of 'opposites' as their objects.[4] Thus, for instance, although the object of medical skill is sometimes said to be simply bodily health (e.g., *Chrm.* 165c8; cf. *Phdr.* 270b4–9), other times it is claimed that medicine is *set over* or *directed at* health and illness (e.g., *Chrm.* 170e5–71a9) (with something similar applying to several other *technai*).[5]

Taking skill to have a two-way nature in this manner seems most plausible if we focus on the close connection drawn between *technai*, *measurement* and attaining the right balance,[6] and if we suppose that the relevant 'contrary' states are *polar contraries* (see above) and determinates of some determinable (cf. *Tht.* 186a9ff; *Tim.* 61c3ff; *Soph.* 243d8–e6). Thus, for instance, suppose – as many of the ancients did – that *health* and *illness* are determinates of some determinable(s)[7] and that health (one determinate) is determined by the body being at the right temperature (or having the right balance of cold and hot) while illness is determined by the body being at the wrong temperature.[8] In order to be skilful or clever at healing, one needs to be proficient at both cooling the body down (when it is too hot) and heating the body up (when it is too cold) (cf. *Phdr.* 268a8–b7). This line of thought is not explicitly developed in much detail, but it may explain the thought that skill has a two-way nature in the relevant sense. Simply put, *skill* would require both the ability to manipulate the

---

[4] Plato often has Socrates claim that *technai* are *about* (*peri*) objects or set over (*epi*) objects (e.g., *Grg.* 449d2ff; *Chrm.* 168b2–3; cf. *Grg.* 464b4; cf. *Rep.* 477d1ff), but the nature of this *aboutness* is somewhat fluid. Sometimes it seems like the object of an expertise is an activity that comes about through its exercise (e.g., *Grg.* 449d2–4), other times it is something more like the subject matter or set of facts in the world that the *technē* is directed towards (e.g. *Grg.* 451c1–5).
[5] Cf. *Chrm.* 166b1–3, 174c2–3; *Rep.* 438c6–e9, 523e1–24a3; *Soph.* 253a8–b3.
[6] E.g., *Rep.* 349b1–50c11; *Plt.* 285a3–4; *Prt.* 356e8–57c1; *Phlb.* 55e1ff; *Plt.* 260a9–b1, 283c3–84a3.
[7] Plato, *Symp.* 186d5–e3; *Rep.* 444d3–5; *Tim.* 81e6–82b7; *Phdr.* 268a8–b7; Aristotle, *Ph.* 204a34–b3, 210a20, 246b3–6; *GC* 324a15–19; *PA* 648b2–10; cf. *DA* 408a1–3; *Metaph.* 1032b26–29; 1173a23–28; Hippoc. *Loc. Hom.* 9, 46; *Vict.* 3; *Nat. Hom.* 2.
[8] Much the same story could be told if instead of the contraries *cold* and *hot*, there is simply *heat*, as Philolaus apparently supposed (*Anon. Lond.* 18.8–29). A similar story can presumably be told concerning the humours (cf. Hippocrates, *Nat. Hom.* 4; Aristotle, *Ph.* 246b3–6).

determinable so as to produce one determinate (e.g., health) *and* also the ability to manipulate the determinable so as to produce the contrary determinate (e.g., illness). An agent who could only cool bodies down or only heat them up would not be proficient or skilful.

I.B The Modal Profile of Skill

The second relevant claim in the *Republic* concerns the modal profile of skills and abilities. After Thrasymachus enters into the conversation, he puts forward his account of justice, according to which 'justice is nothing other than the advantage of the stronger' (*Rep.* 338c2–3),[9] and voices commitment to the following claims: (a) an action is just *iff* it is advantageous to the ruler(s) of the *polis* in which the action was performed (*Rep.* 338e1–39a4); (b) if an action is or involves obeying a ruler, then that action is just (*Rep.* 339b9–11, c10–12, d5–10, e4); (c) that rulers are capable of making errors and thus may enact laws which do not benefit themselves (*Rep.* 339c7–8, d5–9). On the basis of Thrasymachus' agreement to these claims, Socrates points out that obedience to laws that were erroneously established (i.e., erroneous because they do not benefit the rulers) will result in actions that are – per (a) – not just (because they are not beneficial to the rulers) and simultaneously – per (b) – just (because they are or involve obeying the rulers). To escape the contradiction, Thrasymachus amends (c) and claims that, speaking precisely, no ruler ever errs and 'no craftsman ever errs' (*Rep.* 340e2–3).

Thrasymachus' views concerning the infallibility of practitioners of a *technê* have attracted significant opprobrium (e.g., Annas 1981),[10] but relatively little in the way of detailed discussion or explanation. However, it is worth taking a closer look at what Thrasymachus actually says:

> [1] When someone makes an error in the treatment of patients, do you call him a doctor in regard to that very error? Or when someone makes an error in calculation, do you call him a calculator in regard to that very error in calculation? I think that we express ourselves in words that, taken literally, do say that a doctor or a calculator, or a grammarian errs. However, I think that each of these, insofar as he is what we call him, never errs. Accordingly, according to the precise account – and you are a stickler for precise accounts – no craftsman ever errs. [2] For it is when his knowledge abandons him that he who goes wrong goes wrong – when he is not a

---

[9] For discussion of what this claim amounts to, see Nawar 2018: 361n3.
[10] For a detailed discussion of the relevant scholarly literature, see Nawar 2018.

craftsman. So that no craftsman, wise man, or ruler makes a mistake then when he is a ruler. (*Rep.* 340d2–e5, trans. Reeve)

In [1], Thrasymachus suggests that when a practitioner of a *technê*, for example, a doctor, makes a mistake, the practitioner is not a practitioner with respect to that mistake. This concerns what an ability (*dunamis*) (which is constitutive of the relevant *technê*) is responsible for and what is constitutive of the actions produced by a practitioner's ability or capacity. The thought here seems to be that a *technê* of φ-ing, or the ability (*dunamis*) constitutive of the *technê*, manifests itself only in φ-ing. If one's action does not amount to φ-ing, then that action does not count as a manifestation of one's *technê* or ability (cf. *Rep.* 341c10–d4; Aristotle *Metaph.* 1046b6). However, in [2], Thrasymachus makes clear that not only are errors *not* to be considered the manifestations of the relevant *technê* (as was claimed in [1]), but that a practitioner's *possession* of the *technê* is incompatible with error and that errors indicate that the relevant *technê* has *abandoned* the practitioner at the time of their error.[11] That is to say, if a person errs (i.e., makes an attempt to φ that does not result in successfully φ-ing), then they did not possess the relevant *technê* or the relevant ability (constitutive of a *technê*) at the time of (cf. *Rep.* 340c7) their error. Thus, Thrasymachus holds or assumes:

(Technical Ability) if S has the ability (constitutive of a *technê*) to φ at t, then if S were to attempt to φ at t, then S would φ at t.

To see how infallibility of the relevant kind is a consequence of (Technical Ability) consider some relevant case, such as that of a gymnast and their relevant ability (e.g., to somersault). If one has the gymnastic ability to somersault, then – according to (Technical Ability) – one would somersault if one were to attempt to. If a person were to attempt to somersault and fail, then that person would *not* have the gymnastic ability to somersault at that moment in time.

Three points about Thrasymachus' views deserve particular attention. First, although Thrasymachus' claims about the infallibility of *technê* have usually been rapidly dismissed by modern readers, claims like (Technical Ability) are not without *some* intuitive appeal (similar views were assumed and put forward in several twentieth-century discussions of ability, cf. Nawar 2018: 367n18).

---

[11] This reading of the passage is expanded and defended in greater detail in Nawar 2018.

Secondly, (Technical Ability) is not idiosyncratically Thrasymachean. (Technical Ability) or views like (Technical Ability) found currency among other ancient theories of *technê*, such as those defended by the Hippocratic authors of *On the Art* and *On Places in Man*. Such authors assumed that *technai*, or at least certain *technai* such as medicine, were complete and perfected areas of rational expertise that guarantee success if they are appropriately practised (cf. Nawar 2018). Thus, for instance, in defending the efficacy of medicine against those who think its successes are due to luck, the author of *On Places in Man* claims that medical skill has been 'completely discovered' and does not rely upon luck and that whereas 'luck rules itself and is ungovernable ... knowledge is governable and successful when the one with knowledge wishes to use it' (*Loc. Hom.* 46, trans. Craik). That is to say, medical *technê* is a complete and perfect *technê* (in much the same way that one might speak of an *ideal physics*). The doctor's knowledge is always successful (*eutuchês*),[12] and whenever the possessor of the relevant kind of knowledge wishes or decides to act or put his knowledge to effect, it will indeed successfully come into effect. Such a view seems to assume (Technical Ability) or some view very much like it.

Equally, in arguing that no medical successes should be credited to luck (*Art* 6), the author of *On the Art* argues that medicine is such that its cure of diseases is *infallible* or *free from error* (*anamartêtos, Art* 9, 13; cf. *Rep.* 339c1, 340d8–e1). In elucidating what such a claim amounts to and attempting to explain away apparent medical failures, the author stresses that when attending to the success guaranteed to genuine doctors one must give attention to the doctor's proper task (*ergasia*) and its perfection or *end* (*Art* 8).[13] He claims that it is foolish to equate the patient not recovering with an error on behalf of the doctor because, even in the case of curable diseases, the doctor's activity is not constituted by the patient recovering but by correctly diagnosing the illness and 'by giving proper orders', that is, prescribing the correct regimen for the patient to follow (*Art* 7; cf. *Plt.* 260a4–7).[14] Notably, the author of *On the Art* supposes that success requires *only* ability and not also luck or favourable circumstance (and shapes his construal of 'success' accordingly).

---

[12] Here *eutuchês* has the same meaning as 'successful' and *tuchê* has the same meaning as 'luck' (i.e., it means a situation or outcome due to factors outside the agent's control). In what follows (*Loc. Hom.* 46), the author moves between this sense of 'luck', and another sense wherein it means positive outcome or successful actions *even if* due to the agent. The same ambiguity occurs with '*eutuchia*' in the *Euthydemus* (cf. Nawar 2017).

[13] The true doctor will only care about the opinion of those who have rationally considered what the task of a craftsman is directed towards and relative to what it may have assessed as perfect *(Art* 8).

[14] We here find important precedent for later thought about stochastic *technai* (cf. Alexander of Aphrodisias, *Quaestio* 2.16). For discussion of stochastic arts, see Tsouna (Chapters 7 and 8) and Opsomer (Chapter 11) in this volume.

Thirdly, Plato's Socrates does *not* dismiss views like (Technical Ability) out of hand and in fact appeals to such views elsewhere. Thus, for instance, while moderation (*sôphrosunê*) and *technê* are assumed to have an unerring (*anamartêtos*) nature in the *Charmides* (171d1–72a5), the *Euthydemus* offers perhaps the clearest example of Plato's Socrates appealing to such views (e.g., *Euthyd.* 280a6–b3; cf. Nawar 2017). In his exhortation to wisdom (*sophia*), Socrates claims that so long as wisdom is present, it guarantees successful action in a manner that is completely free from mistakes (such claims had earlier been made with regard to various *technai*, *Euthyd.* 279d8–e6). Moreover, it is suggested that the agent who possesses wisdom requires *only* wisdom in order to be successful. Even if luck or good fortune is not present, the agent is nonetheless guaranteed to succeed. Socrates repeats this thought, adverting to various *technai* (such as carpentry, musicianship and so on) in order to claim 'knowledge (*epistêmê*) seems to provide men not only with good fortune (*eutuchia*) but also with success (*eupragia*), in every case of possession or action' (*Euthydemus* 281a6–b4).[15]

Plato's Socrates is thus willing to appeal, at least dialectically, to claims like (Technical Ability). However, arguably the most explicit discussion of the modal profile of abilities occurs in the *Hippias Minor*. There Plato's Socrates articulates a view that seems similar to (Technical Ability) but is significantly more modest. Thus, in pressing Hippias on the distinction between being truthful and deceitful (and whether these are two distinct capacities or abilities or not), Socrates discusses what it is to be capable (*dunatos*) of doing something and claims:

> But each person who can do what he wishes when he wishes is able. I mean someone who is not prevented by disease or other such things, just as I might say you are able to write my name whenever you wish. Or don't you say that the person in such a condition is able? (*Hp. Mi.* 366b7–c4)

---

[15] Some readers have suggested that to explain Socrates' views in the *Euthydemus* one should take him to have in mind so-called internal-successes: actions that meet certain success criteria purely in virtue of their internal features (rather than their results). Thus, for instance, while the expert striker will not always score when he shoots (this would be an example of external-success), he does – the thought goes – always hit the ball well (e.g., with good aim). The proponents of such views have not put forward any textual support for this suggestion, but it is attractive and – as we have seen above – something very much like this was suggested by the author of the *On the Art* in attempting to defend medicine from apparent failures (*Art* 7–8). However, even if we suppose that the agent's actions are internal-successes, a problematic gap remains. Putting to one side whether, for example, the archer will hit her target or not, why suppose that she will always make a good shot? What fills this gap is (Technical Ability) or a view very much like it. For detailed discussion, see Nawar 2017; 2018.

Here, Socrates suggests that the capable person is one who can do what they attempt to do *unless they are prevented*. That is to say:

(Ability*) if S has the ability to φ at t, then if S were to attempt to φ at t, and S were not prevented from φ-ing, then S would φ.

(Ability*) allows that preventative factors may *mask* one's ability without eliminating one's ability. (The precise scope of the claim is not clear; it may hold of abilities in general instead of merely the abilities constitutive of *technai*.) In explicitly making allowances for preventative factors and not clearly excluding luck, (Ability*) is more modest (and more plausible) than (Technical Ability). The person with gymnastic ability who fails in their attempt to somersault *need* not lack ability at the time of their failure so long as their failure was due to their *being prevented*. Precisely how *being prevented* should be characterised is not entirely clear, but it seems *not* to be limited to factors extrinsic to the agent since *illness* is cited as a preventative factor.

I.C Directed at the Good

The third relevant claim about *technê* in the *Republic* is that a *technê* is not 'value-neutral' but is instead directed at what is advantageous or good and, more precisely, what is advantageous or good for its object(s). Socrates puts forward this claim in rebutting Thrasymachus' views concerning justice and ruling (*Rep.* 341b3–43a4; cf. Xenophon, *Memorabilia* 1.2.32). The claim is sometimes thought to be held by Plato's Socrates or perhaps even Socrates himself in *propria persona* (and is sometimes even thought to be central to some of Plato's thought about *technê*). However, although there is reason to think the arguments Socrates offers on behalf of the altruistic nature of *technê* are stronger than often supposed (cf. Barney 2006; Nawar 2018), one should remember that the relevant claims in the *Republic* are put forward in a *highly dialectical context*. Socrates aims to show that, due to Thrasymachus' own claims about the perfect nature of *technê*, Thrasymachus himself should be committed to the view that *technê* aims at the good of its object (cf. Nawar 2018).

It is unclear what one may surmise about the attitudes of Plato's Socrates or Plato himself towards the claim. On the one hand, we do find that Plato's Socrates does sometimes assume that a *technê* is directed towards the good of its object.[16] On the other hand, it is sometimes

---

[16] That a *technê* is directed towards the good of its object is seemingly assumed in the *Gorgias* (e.g., 502e2–7, 504d5–e4, 511c7–12b2, 513e2–3, 514d3–16d3) and sometimes suggested elsewhere (e.g., *Euthphr.* 13a4–c2; *Lach.* 195c7–d2; *Plt.* 293a6–e5, 296c4–297b3; cf. *Soph.* 219a10–b2).

assumed that a *technê* will produce something that is good or beneficial partly or principally for the practitioner of the *technê* (e.g., *Chrm.* 164a9–b9) and, as was obvious to Plato's Socrates, many items that seem to be the objects of *technê* – especially inanimate things – are such that it is not clear that they may be benefited by the practice of the *technê*.[17]

One might think that Plato's Socrates is not committed to the view that each *technê* is directed towards the good of its object, but simply that it is directed towards some good or other or that it is somehow beneficial.[18] This would seem to be supported by the fact that in the *Gorgias* rhetoric and cookery seem *not* to be considered genuine *technai* because they are *not* appropriately directed towards some good (500a7–b5, 501a3–4, e1–3; cf. *Rep.* 493a6–c8),[19] and that on several occasions it is assumed that the *ergon* ('task' or 'product') of a *technê* is something of value (e.g., *Chrm.* 165c10–e2; cf. *Ap.* 22c9–d2; *Euthyd.* 288b3–93a6).

Some commentators treat the claim that a *technê* must be directed towards some good (or even the good) as central to Plato's thinking about *technê* (e.g., Woodruff 1990). However, there are several reasons why it is not even clear whether Plato's Socrates should be taken to be strongly or consistently committed to the view that a *technê* is directed towards the good (or even merely directed towards some good or other).[20] First, one might worry that there is a puzzle in reconciling the good-directed nature of *technê* (regardless of precisely how we understand the good towards which the *technê* is directed) with the *two-way* nature of *technê*. Secondly, even if we allow that, for example, weaving produces items of value, there do seem to be occasions on which various disciplines that do not obviously seem to be good-directed or beneficial seem to be viewed as being *technai*. Thus, for instance, in the *Sophist* it might seem that hunting by force (which includes piracy, enslavement and tyranny, *Soph.* 222c5–7) is recognised as being part of some relevant *technê*.

There are various ways in which these difficulties might be addressed by those who think that a *technê* is indeed good-directed. For instance, one might respond to the first difficulty by suggesting that the two-way nature of a *technê* is consistent with its being *directed* towards one of the two

---

[17] Cf. *Euthphr.* 13a1ff; *Plt.* 261b7–8; Aristotle, *EN* 1155b27–31.
[18] E.g., *Lach.* 195c7–d2; *Chrm.* 165c10–e2, 171d1–2; *Grg.* 512b1–2; *Euthyd.* 288b3–93a6; *Plt.* 293a6–e5, 296c4–97b3; *cf. Ap.* 22c9–d2; Aristotle, *EN* 1094a1–2.
[19] Cookery, rhetoric and the like only aim at what is pleasant and it is not clear, in the relevant works, that pleasure is a good (*Grg.* 464e2–65a2, 500b3–5). Cookery also suffers epistemic deficiencies (*Grg.* 465a2–7, 500e4–501b1; *Phlb.* 55e1–56c6).
[20] Cf. Hulme Kozey 2019b.

relevant things (cf. *Rep.* 346a1–47a5), or that the two-way nature of a *technê* is consistent with it being *directed* towards the good and emphasising that, for example, good might be attained through harming as well as healing, or that it is not in any case clear that Plato consistently takes *technê* to have a two-way nature in the relevant way. Equally, one might address the second difficulty by allowing that, for example, hunting by force can be good-directed or, more promisingly, by adverting to the dialectical context of the relevant passages in the *Sophist* (with attention to *who* is making the relevant claims).[21]

The issue of how *technê* is oriented towards the good is important for understanding not only Plato's general views about *technê*, but also Plato's views about virtue (notably with regard to the so-called *technê* analogy), the guise of the good and moral psychology, sophistry and eristic and various other matters. Such issues merit their own detailed discussion (see, for instance, Roochnik 1996 and Rachel Barney's essay in this volume, Chapter 3).[22] Here it suffices to note that it seems that the textual evidence in favour of Plato being committed to each *technê* being good-directed is not entirely clear and, for the reasons already noted (such as the dialectical nature of some of the relevant claims that are sometimes taken out of context), more complex than might be immediately apparent.

I have focused on clarifying three claims made in the first book of the *Republic* about the nature of skill or expertise. First, Plato's Socrates suggests that if *x* is skilful at φ-ing, then *x* is proficient at φ-ing and *x* is proficient at ψ-ing (where φ-ing and ψ-ing are opposites). The claim is treated as obvious, but precisely how that claim should be understood is not entirely clear. In the *Republic*, it seems the contrary activities are such that one is or involves *guarding against* the other. Elsewhere, notably in the *Hippias Minor*, we find it suggested that the contrary activities are such that one is doing a certain activity well and the other is doing *that same activity* badly, and we also find it suggested that the contrary activities are

---

[21] I should add (cf. Nawar 2018) that determining the degree to which Plato's Socrates (or a speaker such as the Eleatic visitor in the *Sophist* and the *Statesman*) is sympathetic to the view that each *technê* is good-directed often requires clarifying the nature of *politikê*, its relation to knowing the good (which, in the *Euthydemus* is said to lead into a labyrinth, 291b7) or knowing things just and unjust (cf. *Grg.* 459c6ff), the nature of rearing (*trophê*) or providing care (*therapeuein*) (e.g., *Plt.* 275d8–e1; cf. *Grg.* 500a1, 513d1–5, 521a2ff) and their relation to *technai*, the relation of subsidiary *technai* to overseeing *technai* (cf. *Grg.* 517d6–18e1), the relation of the various *technai* to architectonic *politikê*, and the relation of *technai* to knowledge of good and evil (as at *Chrm.* 174a10ff).

[22] Roochnik 1996: 27–33 thinks that a notion of value-neutral *technê* may be found in Solon's Prayer to the Muses, and attributes such a conception of *technê* to Plato as well.

such that they are or involve the production or promotion of states that are *polar contraries* (and determinates of some more fundamental determinable).

Secondly, in *Republic* I we also find that Thrasymachus claims that a *technê* is infallible. This modal claim has usually been rapidly dismissed by modern readers, but the view had wider currency among ancient thinkers and its attractiveness may be better understood when we appreciate that the relevant thinkers took *technai* to be complete and perfected areas of rational expertise and that views like (Technical Ability) are not without some intuitive appeal. Plato's Socrates appeals to such views elsewhere and in the *Hippias Minor* he puts forward a similar but more modest and more plausible characterisation of the modal nature of abilities, that is, (Ability*). Thirdly, and finally, it is sometimes thought Plato's Socrates takes a *technê* to be directed towards the good in some substantive sense; however, I have suggested that the evidence on this matter is not entirely clear.

II Aristotle's Account of *Technê* and Rational Capacities

I now turn to Aristotle's account of *technê* and rational capacities or abilities. It seems that Aristotle regards claims (a)–(c) (see Sections I.A–I.C), of which *Republic* I offers the most detailed and focused extant discussion, as being part of the received wisdom of ancient thought about *technê* and several aspects of Aristotle's thought about dynamic modalities and teleological agency are, I suggest, better understood when we examine how Aristotle attempts to incorporate, adapt, or explain claims (a)–(c) while developing his own account of *technê*.

II.A Two-Way Capacities

For Aristotle, a *technê* is a capacity (*dunamis*) of a particular kind (*Metaph.* 1019a15–18).[23] Like other (active) capacities, it is 'a principle of movement or change in another thing or in a thing insofar as it is other' (*Metaph.* 1019a15–16; cf. 1046a10–11, b3–4). However, a *technê* is distinctive in being located in the part of the soul possessing *logos* (*Metaph.* 1046b1),[24] and in being a two-way capacity:

---

[23] In the *Nicomachean Ethics*, it is characterised as a *hexis* (*EN* 1140a20–21), that is, an acquired *dunamis* (cf. *Metaph.* 1047b31–35).
[24] More concretely, it is in the *calculating* part of the rational soul (*EN* 1139a6–15).

> As regards those capacities which involve reason, the very same capacity is a capacity for contraries, but as regards the non-rational capacities a single capacity is for one thing: for example, heat only for heating, while the medical craft for both illness and health. The explanation of this is that the knowledge is an account, and the same account clarifies both the thing and the privation, though not in the same way. (*Metaph.* IX.2 1046b4–9, trans. Makin)

Aristotle here develops and elucidates the view put forward only briefly and somewhat obscurely by Plato's Socrates (who seems to offer the clearest extant parallel to Aristotle's views on this score). He takes a *technê* to be a two-way capacity for *contraries* and explicitly states it to be such (and Aristotle explicitly recognises various senses of *contraries*, e.g., *Metaph.* 1018a25–35; 1055a3–b29). In contrast, non-rational capacities are seemingly one-way or single-track capacities that manifest themselves only in one sort of activity; for instance, *heat* manifests itself only in *heating*.[25] Aristotle does not here discuss why non-rational capacities have a single-track nature so as to manifest themselves only in one sort of activity, but his broader views concerning how agents and patients interact seem to explain it roughly as follows.

Generally, if an agent (*x*) brings about a change in a patient (*y*), such that *y* becomes (actually) *F*, then *x* is actually *F*. The agent's form is the origin of change (cf. *Ph.* 195a11) and, in change, the form of *F*-ness is somehow conveyed from the agent to the patient (*Ph.* 3.2, 202a9–12) so that, once the agent has acted upon the patient, the agent and patient have become alike with respect to *F*-ness (*DA* II.5, 417a18–20; *GC* I.7, 323b18–24a10).[26] Crucially, Aristotle generally *seems* to think that if *x* is actually *F* and *y* has the capacity to become (actually) *F*, then contact between *x* and *y* is both necessary and sufficient for the relevant change to occur (*Ph.* III.2, 202a5–9; 7.2, 244a14–b2; 8.4, 255a34–b1; *GC* 324b7–9).[27] As he puts it in the *Metaphysics*, 'it is necessary, whenever agent and patient approach each other so as to be capable, the one act and the other be affected' (*Metaph.* IX.5 1048a5–7).

Thus, for instance, suppose that something that is actually hot enters into contact with something that is actually cold (and potentially hot). In

---

[25] However, see *Metaph.* 1050b33–34; 1051a4–17.
[26] Cf. *Metaph.* 1034a21–32; 1034b14–19; *GC* 320b17–21.
[27] I hedge somewhat and say 'seems' as it is not entirely clear that contact is necessary (perhaps proximity might do the trick; cf. *Ph.* 260b1–5), or that contact between *x* and *y* is sufficient for *x* to affect *y*, as this is sometimes qualified by a 'nothing intervening or preventing' clause (*Ph.* VIII.4 255b4; cf. *Metaph.* 1047b35–48a8).

such cases, the relevant individuals, or their relevant capacities, are contraries (*enantia*) (cf. *GC* I.7, 324a10–24). The form of heat in the agent is the principle or origin of change and, necessarily, when the agent and patient are suitably receptive to each other and brought into contact, then the agent heats and the patient is heated (*GC* 324b7–9).[28] Thus, 'heat is only for heating' (*Metaph.* 1046b6; cf. *Rep.* 340d2–e5, 341c10–d4). When conditions are right, and two individuals with the relevant capacities stand in a suitable relation (e.g., contact), then the relevant process (in this case heating) occurs. (To be clear, just because the patient is heated does not mean that it comes to be hot.)

Rational capacities, such as *technai*, differ in several respects from non-rational capacities. First, in the case of non-rational capacities, it seems that the form *is* the capacity and the relevant origin of change, and that it is straightforwardly present in the individual. With regard to *rational* capacities, Aristotle does take the form to be the origin of change (*Metaph.* 1032b21–28; 1046a10–11) and supposes that this is somehow conveyed or transmitted to the patient (*GA* 739b12–23), and he identifies the capacity *in a way* with the form (e.g., 'medicine is *in a way* health; house-building is the form of a house', *Metaph.* 1070b33; cf. *GA* 734b37–35a4).[29] However, the form seems to be present in the agent in a somewhat different manner (much like *red* might be present in a soul thinking of red). Thus the medical practitioner has the form of health in their soul but presumably need not themselves be healthy.

Secondly, rational capacities are under the control of the agent in some suitable sense. Non-rational capacities manifest themselves when external circumstances are right. In contrast, rational capacities manifest themselves when external circumstances *and* the agent chooses.

Thirdly, rational capacities are two-way capacities. Unlike heat, which can only bring about heating (and necessarily does so when the agent and a suitable recipient are in contact), medical skill can directly bring about not

---

[28] There are some caveats. First, I focus here on the relevant salient change brought about by the active capacity, but the interactions are more complicated. Secondly, as noted, there is sometimes a 'no prevention' clause (e.g., nothing prevents them from interacting, *Ph.* 255b4). Thirdly, this is sometimes spoken of as a 'transmission model of agency' (e.g., Makin 2006: 48–49) or as 'transference of form' (e.g. Beere 2009), but Aristotle rarely uses this vocabulary and it is not clear that the labels (which seems more fitting to some later thinkers) are entirely apt.

[29] It seems that a number of identity claims are at issue: skills or crafts are identical with forms (*Metaph.* 1070b33); crafts are identical with accounts (1070a29–30); and skills or forms are identical with accounts and knowledge (cf. *Metaph.* 1032b5–6). Aristotle also claims that 'understanding *is* an account' (1046b7–8; cf. 1046b16–17). In so far as skills both are and *have* or *involve* accounts, and we suppose that things may not have themselves, then such remarks present a difficulty when taken literally.

just healing, but *two* things: healing and harming or health and illness (cf. *EN* 1129a13–14). Thus, we might say that if x has a rational capacity of φ-ing, then x can use the rational capacity to φ and to ψ (where φ-ing and ψ-ing are contraries).[30] Crucially, Aristotle thinks such two-way capacities 'involve *logos*' (*meta logou*, 1046b2, 5, 1048a3; *EN* 1140a3–5; cf. *kata logon*, 1046b22–23, 1048a2–3, 13),[31] and it seems to be in virtue of its *logos*-involving nature that, for Aristotle, a *technê* is a two-way capacity.[32]

This requires some explanation. In *Metaphysics* IX.2, Aristotle claims that the *logos* involved in *technê* is about contraries (1046b12–15). More concretely, he claims that a *logos* is about a thing – presumably the relevant form or universal (e.g., health in the case of medicine) – and its privation (1046b8–9). Furthermore, Aristotle goes on to claim: 'the account concerns one contrary *per se*, but concerns the other contrary in a way incidentally: for it is through denial and negation that it clarifies the contrary' (*Metaph*. 1046b12–14). Thus, the practitioner of medicine will have an account of health that positively characterises or defines what health is, and thus concerns health per se. However, since illness is the negation, denial or privation (cf. *sterêsis*, 1046b8–9) of health, the account of health will also thereby state what illness is *per accidens*. Thus, suppose that health is a certain balanced mixture of certain elements (cf. *PA* 648b2–10), illness will then be an *un*balanced mixture of those elements. Furthermore, Aristotle claims not just that the relevant *logos* is of contraries, but that the *logos* 'is in the soul which has an origin of change, so that it will change them [the contraries] both from the same origin, having connected them with the same thing' (1046b20–22). This suggests that the *logos* will specify not just what health is, but how health and illness come about or are related to the same thing (cf. *Metaph*. 1032b3–5).

Aristotle takes the relevant *logos* to impart explanatory knowledge or understanding. The precise nature of the *logos* involved in *technê* and how the cognitive aspects of *technê* compare to the cognitive aspects of scientific

---

[30] Makin offers: 'A capacity to φ is a two-way capacity if there can be exercises of the capacity in normal circumstances which are not (even *inter alia*) instances of φ-ing' (Makin 2006: 43). However, at best that seems to characterise multi-track capacities, rather than specifically *two-way* capacities.

[31] Cf. *kata ton logon*, 1046b22–23, 1048a2–3. Aristotle also claims that knowledge or understanding (*epistêmê*) is an account (1046b7–8; cf. 1046b16–17). For recent discussion of *logos*, see Moss 2014.

[32] For Plato, a genuine *technê* is also characterised by possessing a *logos* (e.g. *Grg*. 465a2–5, 501a1–3). However, Aristotle explicitly grounds the two-way nature of a *technê* in its possession of a *logos*.

understanding (*epistêmê*) are not entirely clear,[33] but the explanatory aspects of *technê* seem divisible into at least two components.

First, Aristotle says a *technê* is or is constituted by cognition 'of universals' (*Metaph.* 981a16). This contrasts with the seemingly less general and more particularised cognition characteristic of *empeiria* (981a15–16; cf. 981a7–12).[34] At least part of what Aristotle seems to mean by such remarks is that *technê* seems to grant more scientifically precise cognition that tracks *natural properties*, that is, what captures facts of resemblance and the relevant causal power or difference-makers (cf. Nawar ms). Thus one with *technê* will cognise, for example, not merely that Socrates is red in the face, but that Socrates has the symptoms of high blood pressure (981a7–12).

Secondly, the person with *technê*, seemingly in virtue of having the relevant *logos*, has insight into the relevant causes and natures: 'For experienced people know the that but do not know the why, whereas craftsmen know the why, that is, the cause' (*Metaph.* 981a28–30). The *logos* will thereby illuminate the nature of the relevant contrary states and their grounds and causes, thereby shedding light on what produces these states. It thus seems that in virtue of having an account of what health is and how it comes about, the practitioner of medicine will also, *per accidens*, have an account of the nature of illness – which is the contrary (a negation or privation) of health – and how it comes about. The account illuminates the nature of health and the activities that promote it, and the nature of the contrary states and the contrary activities (i.e., activities that bring about or promote the contrary states). The practitioner is thereby able to impart health to a person (cause health to come about in them), and they are also able to remove health from (i.e., cause illness in) a person. Something similar holds for the other *technai*.

Finally, what determines which of the relevant contrary actions (e.g., healing or harming) an agent with a rational capacity performs (or whether they will perform any action at all) is something within the agent that controls the relevant capacity. More concretely:

> Then there must be something else which is decisive. I mean by this desire or choice. For whichever it desires decisively, in this way it will act when it is in the condition to be capable, and approaches the patient. And so it is necessary

---

[33] The issue merits detailed discussion. Here it suffices to note that the *logos* and productive reasoning associated with *technê* can, in several important respects, be rather 'scientific'. For discussion, see Makin 2006: 37–39; Moss 2014; Johansen 2017; Nawar ms; and Robert Bolton (Chapter 6) and Ursula Coope (Chapter 5) in this volume.

[34] The relevant content associated with *empeiria* must, it has been argued, have some level of generality. See, for example, Bolton (Chapter 6).

that everything which is capable in accordance with reason, whenever it desires that for which it has the capacity, and in the manner wherein it has the capacity, should act in this way. (*Metaph.* IX.5 1048a10–15)

Non-rational capacities automatically manifest themselves when they stand in a suitable extrinsic relation. In contrast, rational two-way capacities are such that a meeting of suitably receptive (prospective) agents and patients is *not* sufficient for the relevant capacities to manifest or be actualised. Instead, what determines whether an active rational capacity in the agent manifests itself, *and which way (i.e., which of the two contrary activities) it manifests*, is something within the agent: the agent's overarching or dominant desire (*orexis*) or (rational) choice (*prohairesis*). This controls whether a rational capacity will manifest, and which way (i.e., which of two relevant contrary activities) it will manifest. Thus, Aristotle holds that necessarily, if the agent's rational active capacity and the patient's passive capacity are suitably receptive to each and the right conditions obtain and the agent desires to manifest their capacity, then the agent's capacity is manifested.

There are two worries worth raising concerning Aristotle's conception of two-way capacities. The first worry concerns whether *only* crafts and rational capacities have a two-way nature in the manner supposed. We have seen that the two-way nature of a *technê* was grounded in its possession of a *logos*. However, if that is right, then it seems that Aristotle is committed to the view that *empeiria*, which lacks a *logos*, should *not* have a two-way capacity (or at least, if it did have such a two-way capacity, then it should be grounded in something else). The problem is that, as far as I am aware, it is not clear whether Aristotle takes *empeiria* to lack a two-way nature. In fact, he says that *empeiria* and *technê* are 'no different with regard to action' (*Metaph.* 981a12–17) which might be taken to imply that they do not differ in this regard. The second worry, which is perhaps more pressing, concerns whether all rational capacities have a two-way nature in the manner supposed. Thus, for instance, we might suppose that the builder is adept at demolishing houses, and perhaps something similar can be said of some other cases (e.g., perhaps the flute-player or the painter may put disharmony in the souls of listeners), but what about, for instance, the cobbler? Neither worry is decisive, but they are worth signalling.

II.B The Modal Profile of Abilities

I turn now to attempting to clarify Aristotle's analysis of capacities and his claim that, when conditions are right, the rational capacity controlled by desire, necessarily results in efficacious action. In *Metaphysics* IX, Aristotle seems to think that that an appropriate specification of capacities needs to be more fine-grained than one might expect and that what is needed is either:

(a) a more fine-grained specification of the circumstances in which a thing possesses a capacity (e.g., *x* does not simply have the capacity to heal, but has the capacity under certain conditions; for instance, when *x* is not under pressure, *x* has the capacity to heal, etc.); or
(b) a more fine-grained specification of what a capacity does (e.g. *x* does not have the capacity to simply heal, but a capacity-to-heal-when-not-under-pressure or a capacity-to-heal-when-the-equipment-is-handy, etc.).

Aristotle initially remarks: 'since what is capable is capable of something at some time and in some way and with however many other factors it is necessary to add to the specification' (1047b35–48a2). However, while this calls for a more detailed specification of something, it does not make clear whether Aristotle prefers (a) or (b) or some other option (e.g., a specification of the conditions under which an ability can be *exercised*) as a way of proceeding. His later, slightly more expansive remarks are as follows:

> [1] And it has [the capacity] when the patient is present and has [its capacity] in this way; and if not, it will not be capable of acting. [2] For it is not necessary to specify in addition that nothing prevent it; for it has the capacity in so far as it is a capacity for acting, and that is not in any and every condition, but just in some circumstances, in which external things preventing will be ruled out as well; for these are set aside by some of the things present in the specification of the capacity. (*Metaph.* IX.5 1048a15–21)

On a surface reading, [1] seems to claim that an individual only has the relevant capacity when conditions are right for its exercise.[35] That is to say, the doctor has a capacity to heal only when the patient is present and other conditions are right. In [2], Aristotle seems to be saying that an accurate specification of what a capacity does makes a 'no-interference condition' in the antecedent superfluous. As regards this latter, it is important to appreciate that Aristotle is almost certainly here engaging with Plato, particularly with the view articulated in the *Hippias Minor*, that is, with

---

[35] Beere 2009: 147–50 seems to take the view expressed in [1] to be that of the Megarics, but that doesn't seem right. The Megaric view is that a thing has a capacity to act *only* when it is acting.

(Ability*).³⁶ It seems then that he wishes to reject that view, but his reasons for wanting to do so are not entirely clear.

In the most detailed treatment of this issue, Makin (2006) remarks that in *Metaphysics* IX there is no decisive textual evidence in favour of (a) or (b),³⁷ but that (b) is a superior reading that better respects Aristotle's broader commitments (e.g. R: Makin 2006: 103–7, 112–24). In particular, he suggests that (a) should be rejected because it is implausible to suppose, for example, that a person has a capacity to build only when there are bricks present, and that Aristotle seems to think that capacity loss and gain is fixed solely by intrinsic features of the agent (such as their coming to have or to lose some knowledge) (Makin 2006: 113, 120–21). Instead, Makin proposes that Aristotle is *not* here discussing the conditions under which an agent possesses a capacity, but rather the conditions under which an agent is able to *exercise* their capacity (Makin 2006: 113–14). Thus, for instance, a builder might retain their capacity to build when there are no bricks present, but they would not be able to exercise their capacity.³⁸

Makin takes Aristotle to hold the following view: 'As regards two-way capacities: necessarily (if agent and patient are in the right condition and related in the right way, and the agent chooses to act, then action results)' (Makin 2006: 113). The suggestion is charitable and attractive, but it faces various difficulties.

First, Makin's 'are in the right condition and related in the right way' remark seems to be functionally equivalent to 'unless preventative conditions are present'. However, in [2] (1048a16–21), it seems that Aristotle wishes to reject any specification of an ability that makes reference to the absence of preventative conditions and thus seems to wish to reject (Ability*) or views akin to it. Secondly, if Makin is correct, Aristotle's aversion to talk of preventative conditions is not entirely consistent with his practice (Makin recognises this, 2006: 119).³⁹ Thirdly, if Makin is right, Aristotle's aversion to talk of preventative conditions is somewhat mysterious (and it is not clear to me that Makin's remarks render

---

[36] Aristotle explicitly engages with that work elsewhere in the *Metaphysics* (e.g., *Metaph.* 1025a1–13).
[37] Makin's two options are put slightly differently: 'What is capable is capable of something [it is capable] at some time and in some way, etc.' (which he calls 'POSS' and is seemingly similar to my [a]) and 'What is capable is capable of something-at-some-time-and-in-some-way-etc.' (which he calls 'CONT' and is seemingly similar to my [b]).
[38] Makin adduces *Ph.* 251b1–8 and 260b1–5, but neither is decisive.
[39] E.g., 'Each of these are not capable [of knowing] in the same way. One [is capable] because his genus and matter are of a certain kind; the other [is capable] because he has the capacity to contemplate whenever he wishes, so long as nothing external hinders him' (*DA* II.5, 417a26–28; cf. *Ph.* 199b15–18).

Aristotle's aversion less so).⁴⁰ Finally, it seems that on Makin's own view, Aristotle resists an analysis that appeals to preventative conditions (e.g., *S* has the ability to play the piano at *t iff*, at *t*, *S* were to attempt to play the piano and *S* were not prevented from playing the piano, then *S* would play), and instead ends up proposing an analysis according to which: *S* has the ability-to-play-the-piano-unless-people-are-watching.⁴¹ However, this makes what capacities *do* seemingly too fine-grained (they are multiplied beyond predictive or explanatory necessity) and if Aristotle does indeed wish to avoid talk of preventative conditions, then this doesn't seem like a very satisfactory way of doing so.⁴²

However, despite the objections just raised to Makin's interpretation, the other salient alternative, which makes capacities context and relationally dependent, seems damaging to Aristotle's broader aims and inconsistent with his remarks about the acquisition and retention of capacities, which suggests that they are stable features (not easily lost) and contextually robust (such that it is not the case that an agent has a capacity relative to one situation or circumstance, but not according to another situation or circumstances).⁴³ It does not seem that it will do to have someone who is a doctor at one moment but not the next, or to have someone who is a doctor when-the-case-is-an-easy-one but not a doctor when-there-are-complications.⁴⁴

What is needed then is an analysis of rational capacities that avoids the problems so far raised. Ideally, it should also allow for: (a) *occasional* failure (e.g., *Ph.* II.8, 199a33–35; *Metaph.* 981a20–24); (b) manifestation of the capacity where the typical result aimed at is not possible (*Rhet.* 1355b12–14); and (c) some (but not total) adaptability to circumstance or the manifestation-form of the capacity (e.g., *Top.* 101b8–10).

---

⁴⁰ Makin 2006: 119–20 suggests that Aristotle resists any specification of preventative conditions 'because it is important for him to privilege the role of active and passive capacities (agent and patient); and it is important to do that because it is the active and passive capacities which stand to the change as something potential to something actual' (120). However, that doesn't seem to be suggested by the text and neither is it especially compelling. Specifying the conditions under which a match acts (e.g., by saying 'if the match were struck and nothing interfered, then it would catch light') does not, as far as I can see, rob the match of causal power.

⁴¹ Cf. Makin 2006: 121.

⁴² To be clear, Makin allows that one may have a capacity at a time or in a situation where it is not possible that it be exercised, yet he maintains that some finessing of what capacities do is nonetheless necessary (Makin 2006: 123–24).

⁴³ Cf. *Metaph.* 1046b36–47a2.

⁴⁴ Cf. also Johansen 2012: 75–78 for the point that the explanatory role Aristotle wishes to assign to capacities, for example, in his psychology, would be undermined if they were generally made too context specific.

While matters are difficult, it seems that if one is to provide a unified account, then what is required is something (very roughly) along the following lines:

> (**Ability****) if S has a rational capacity of φ-ing, then *if S were to attempt to φ or ψ* (where φ-ing and ψ-ing are contraries) at t, then – *most of the time* – S would perform the activity they had attempted.

(Ability**) might seem to run counter to some of Aristotle's remarks in *Metaphysics* IX (e.g., *Metaph*. 1048a13–15 suggests *infallibility* and would seem to require success *all of the time*). However, Aristotle's remarks about how generalisations that hold only *for the most part* (i.e., claims of the form, *for the most part*, α holds of β) are characteristic of the *logos* constitutive of *technai* suggest that what Aristotle is committed to (or perhaps what he *should say*) is (Ability**) or something like it.[45] (The thought being that the skilled practitioner will be limited in his effectiveness by the limitations of the generalisations upon which he or she relies.) A full discussion of this issue merits its own detailed treatment (cf. Nawar ms), but here it suffices to note that (Ability**) seems to better reflect Aristotle's thought in some works and also seems to be a rather good characterisation of abilities (or rational capacities) of the relevant kind.[46] Moreover, in line with (β), such an account *could* be supplemented by the specification that the activity in question would be strictly the *doing* of action, rather than the achievement of a specific result (or perhaps the achievement of a *modest* result, cf. *Rhet*. 1355b12–14).

II.C Directed at the Good

Finally, I turn to consider Aristotle's conception of how *technai* are directed towards the good. The *Nicomachean Ethics* famously opens with a proclamation to that effect, stating that every *technê* seems to seek some good (1094a1–2) in a manner that suggests that the claim has wider currency and that it is important. However, Aristotle is clear that a practitioner of *technê* does not need to know the good (*EN* 1097a5–13) and it seems that, contra some readers (e.g., Beere 2009: 88–90), Aristotle's understanding of the claim that *technai* are directed towards the good should ultimately be understood in a rather deflationary manner.

---

[45] E.g. *Metaph*. 1026b27–27a28; *EN* 1180b8–10; see also the essays by Bolton (Chapter 6) and Coope (Chapter 5) in this volume.
[46] For recent discussion of generic and modal accounts of ability (and the virtues of hybrid accounts), see Maier 2018.

In so far as every *technê* has a *logos* of some universal and, *per accidens*, of its privation (*Metaph*. 1046b6–14), we may suppose that, for Aristotle, the universals that are the objects of *technai* are goods (cf. *EN* 1140a25–28; *EE* 1216b16–19). Thus, for instance, just as medicine takes as its object, health (which is a good), so too we might expect that something similar applies to other *technai*, and – as Aristotle notes – it is indeed a fine thing to have cognisance of fine things or goods (*EE* 1216b19–20). However, the problem with this line of thought is that even if *all* the non-privational objects of *technai* were in fact goods, and even if Aristotle might say that *technai* are naturally directed towards the good (cf. *EE* 1246a26–35), it is not easy to see in what manner a *technê* can meaningfully be said to be aimed at the good rather than its privation. As we have seen, it is ultimately the agent's desire that is in control, and it seems that the agent's desire might be directed towards the good or not (e.g., the doctor's desires may be directed towards healing *or* harming).

Aristotle does not, as far as I am aware, explicitly speak of any *dark arts* in any detail and does not explicitly countenance a *technê* or a pseudo-*technê* that is directed towards evils or non-goods, but with regards to those *technai* that have been put to nefarious ends he claims:

> What makes a man a sophist is not his abilities but his choices. In rhetoric, however, the term 'rhetorician' may describe either the speaker's knowledge of the art, or his choices. In dialectic a man is a sophist because he makes a certain kind of choice, a dialectician in respect not of his choices but of his abilities. (*Rhet*. I.1 1355b17–21)

On Aristotle's view, the sophist and the dialectician differ only in their respective desires and the ends towards which they direct the *technê* (cf. *Top*. 126a30–b3). If that is right, then although Aristotle might say that each *technê* is directed towards the good, it is not clear what this being *directed towards* amounts to. Like Plato, Aristotle would probably rule out a *technê* that manifests itself in reliably bringing about bad works (*erga*), that is, *erga* that are not brought about *adroitly* or *skilfully* (e.g., badly executed paintings, lousy playing of music and the like). However, more explicitly than Plato (and, indeed, perhaps against Plato's Socrates, depending upon how and whether Plato's Socrates takes a *technê* to be good-directed) Aristotle seems to allow that there are *technai* whose *erga* are or may be morally bad. Accordingly, it seems that the principal way in which a *technê* can be said to be directed towards the good is that it is useful (cf. *chrêsimos*, *Rhet*. 1355a21) and that, on the whole (or, for the most part), the practitioners of a *technê* (and their desires) tend to be directed towards the good. However, if that is right, then it doesn't seem that a *technê* can be said to be good-directed in any particularly strong sense and the claim is less important than is sometimes thought.

III Conclusion

In this chapter I have attempted to clarify three important but poorly understood claims in the thought of Plato and Aristotle: (a) that skills or the abilities constitutive of skill have a certain 'two-way' nature; (b) that the possessor of skill cannot fail to bring about what they intend or attempt; and (c) that skills are good-directed. We have seen the precise form these claims take in *Republic* I, why they might be thought plausible, and how Plato's Socrates and Aristotle engage with them. Each of the claims deserves further attention, but in the course of this chapter I hope to have advanced our understanding of these claims and of Plato's and Aristotle's views on the modal and teleological aspects of *technê*.[47]

---

[47] Thanks to two anonymous readers for the press and audiences at Oxford and, especially, Kyoto for comments on earlier versions of this piece.

CHAPTER 3

Technê *As a Model for Virtue in Plato*

Rachel Barney

I Introduction

One of the most striking features of ancient Greek ethics is the pervasiveness of analogies between virtue or excellence (*aretê*) and *technê*: craft, art, skill or expertise. In Plato's early, Socratic dialogues, it seems that virtue *is* a craft; at any rate, his Socrates is obsessed with the idea that it might be. The Stoics speak of the 'art of living' (*technê biou*) as a craft equivalent to all of moral virtue, and Epictetus makes pervasive use of analogies between this 'greatest craft' (*megistê technê*, *Discourses* I.20.13) and the specialised ones.[1] Aristotle vehemently rejects the idea that either the ethical virtues or practical wisdom (*phronêsis*) could be identified with craft (*EN* II.4, 1105a26–b2; *EN* VI.5, 1140b1–7, 21–25); and yet of all ancient ethics his works are the most saturated with craft analogies. (In *EN* III.3 alone, his account of deliberation is worked out by reference to medicine, money-making, navigation, gymnastics, medicine again, oratory, statesmanship and baking.) If Aristotelian virtue is not a craft, it still comes close enough for virtually every feature of the one to have an illuminating counterpart in the other.[2]

In this chapter, I will discuss this craft model (or *technê* model), using the phrase to cover both the view that virtue *is* a craft and whatever weaker presumption underlies Aristotle's practice. The model is a rich one, with a long and complex history; a wide range of authors use it in diverse ways, and I won't be trying to give a full inventory of them. Rather, my agenda will be to bring out a side of it that has, so far as I know, been somewhat

---

[1] On the Stoic moral *technê*, see SVF s.v. *technê*, and the contribution of Voula Tsouna to this volume (Chapter 7).
[2] For this ambivalence, see Broadie 1991 and Angier 2010. I will set Aristotle largely aside here, apart from certain moments in which he seems to illuminate Platonic ideas.

Technê *As a Model for Virtue in Plato* 63

ignored:[3] what I will call the *deontological* dimension of the model, which invites us to think of the life of virtue as involving a norm-imposing function or work (*ergon*). This conception is, I think, of great ethical significance; and it has little or nothing to do with the 'intellectualism' about virtue with which the craft model is usually associated.

The basic concept of craft (*technê*) on which the model depends is reasonably clear and easily grasped: a craft is a specialised kind of knowledge that leads to reliable practical success and provides some benefit.[4] We can add that for Plato and his successors, a craft is a social practice marked by discursive rationality: one that can be reliably taught, learned, systematised and explained.[5] This is already the import of craft in what is probably the earliest (philosophical) text in which we can detect the model at work, Plato's *Apology*. Here Socrates likens the knowledge claimed by anyone who undertakes to teach virtue, as the sophist Evenus does, to the kind involved in training horses; but he also disavows it himself, as requiring superhuman wisdom (19d–21c). Later on, he allows that, alone of the claimants to wisdom he has interrogated, the practitioners of the crafts really did know something (22d). Given the contrast he is drawing with the politicians and the poets, this must mean that they were able to explain and defend their practices in question and answer – able to give a *logos*, an account, of what they do and why. And this turns out to be a definitive feature of craft in Plato's *Gorgias* as well (465a, 501a–b).

This Socratic association of craft with a kind of explanatory knowledge, together with the ubiquitous craft analogies in the early dialogues, leads naturally to what I will call the *intellectualist story* about the craft model.[6]

---

[3] So my treatment will be very selective, and will not aim to deal in a general way with the huge scholarly literature on *technê* and its ancient ethical uses: in addition to the works on Socrates and Plato noted in n. 11 below, I have especially benefited from Annas 1993: 67–73, 396–405, 442–43; Menn 1995; and the papers on Stoic ethics in Striker 1996a.

[4] For background on the early Greek understanding of *technê* and related concepts, see Schaerer 1930; Heinimann 1961; Kube 1969 and Löbl 1997 as well as ch. 1 of Roochnik 1996.

[5] It is worth contrasting the most famous use of the craft model in the ancient Chinese tradition, in the *Zhuangzi* (discourse 3). As in the Greek tradition, the craftsperson, here an expert chef butchering an ox, is a model for the expert ruler. But this version of the model seems to be *anti-intellectualist*: the emphasis is on the chef's ability – acquired from long meditation and self-training, apparently, rather than instruction – to act without conscious deliberation or even awareness. This suggests that we should see the intellectualism of the Greek version of the model as a contingent feature, and driven from the start by an interest in craft as something *taught*.

[6] This story is an oversimplified composite; no scholar says anything quite as crude as what follows. Still, I take it to stand as a kind of baseline to the various richer, differentiated accounts many modern scholars do offer. (The most important and philosophically sophisticated account of the craft model in early Plato remains Irwin 1977; but Irwin's account is distinctive and controversial in many ways, particularly in its handling of the relation of a craft to its end.) Thus, it is also part of what the

On this story, the craft model is distinctively Socratic and part of his legacy to the later tradition. (In that light it should come as no surprise that Aristotle is ambivalent about it, while the Stoics are unconditionally Socratic.) It serves as a vehicle for his extreme ethical intellectualism or rationalism (terms I will use interchangeably), embodied in the infamous Socratic paradoxes: all desire is for the good, *akrasia* is impossible, wrongdoing is involuntary and virtue is sufficient for happiness. These are organised around the central thesis that virtue consists in a kind of knowledge; the point of the craft model is to elucidate how this moral knowledge works. Moreover, this intellectualist thesis gains some of its plausibility from reflection on the existing *technai* as sources of reliable practical success: so craft is part of the grounding for Socrates' position as well as a tool for developing it. In short, Socrates starts from a rationalistic conception of craft, which emphasises its susceptibility to expression in *logos*, and leverages this to support an equally rationalistic understanding of virtue. But in this strong version at least (the story continues) the model is short-lived, and for good philosophical reasons: for Socratic intellectualism is highly problematic, most obviously in its sidelining of affective and non-rational motivations as irrelevant to virtue. Plato acknowledges its deficiencies and repudiates it in *Republic* IV (at the latest); once the theory of the tripartite soul is in place, nothing like craft knowledge could be thought sufficient for virtue. Aristotle recognises even more fully that virtue depends on non-rational factors, and motivates in ways that craft does not: this recognition is what ultimately underlies his rejection of the model. And it's because the Stoics revert to a kind of Socratic intellectualism, holding as they do that every desire and impulse involves rational assent to an evaluative proposition, that they revert to it.

Once made explicit in this rather simple-minded way, the intellectualist story should immediately raise doubts. For the craft model is not really an apt tool for ethical rationalism. After all, many of the recognised *technai* depend heavily upon non-rational factors like physical dexterity and self-discipline. Relatedly, to learn almost any craft takes training and rote practice – not just rational instruction.[7] Moreover, craft is *obviously* an odd analogue for virtuous motivation: as Socrates is perfectly well aware, doctors sometimes act as poisoners and guards as thieves, but the just

avowedly revisionist accounts of Roochnik 1996 and Balansard 2001 are arguing against, cf. especially Roochnik 1996: 1–11 (with references) and Balansard 2001: 160–65.

[7] Thus Aristotle is being tendentious and unfair at *EE* I.5 1216b4–10. The closest thing to a supporting text in Plato is *Grg.* 460a–c, but this is an ad hominem elenctic context, not necessarily indicative of Socrates' own assumptions.

person never chooses to act against the demands of justice (see Section IV below). So if the point were to support an intellectualist conception of virtue as wholly rational, acquired purely through instruction, and yet consisting in a knowledge that is motivationally compelling, the model would be strikingly ill-chosen.

The intellectualist story also sits oddly with our texts. It predicts uses of it that we find rarely or never, and fails to predict those we do. We never see Socrates argue that virtue is wholly a matter of rational rather than affective factors, or that learning a craft requires only instruction. We do not see ancient philosophers citing various kinds of craft education to argue for different theories of moral education, or arguing about just *which* craft provides the closest analogue to moral knowledge.[8] It is far from clear that the model really disappears from Plato's post-tripartition work;[9] and Aristotle continues to draw promiscuously on craft analogies despite his firm rejection of intellectualism. And if the Stoics revive the model for the purposes of ethical rationalism, why do their preferred examples of *technai* include dancing, acting, wrestling and volleyball?[10]

I think that the intellectualist story gets at only a small part of what makes the craft model interesting, and gets that part mostly wrong. The rest of this paper is an attempt to supplement and correct it. In Section II, I offer a different picture of the origins of the model; Section III discusses *Republic* Book I, which I take to be the key text for Plato's mature and distinctive version of it. In Section IV, I turn to two related ideas that are needed to defend the model against the most obvious objection ('the motivational objection'), and which together complete it; Section V briefly points out that the model also has a canonical rhetorical function, one that the reading offered here helps to explain. My focus throughout will be on Plato; I will refer only occasionally to Aristotle and to the Stoics (particularly Epictetus and Marcus) for points where their version of the model remains Platonic and can help to illuminate it.

---

[8] Possible exceptions would be (1) Isocrates' critique of 'technocratic' ethics in the *Against the Sophists* and *Antidosis*, especially if this is aimed at Plato; and (2) the Stoics' emphasis on dancing and acting as paradigms for the art of living, especially if this is aimed at Aristotle.
[9] For the art of living as a theme of the *Philebus*, see Harte forthcoming; and for the art of the *politikos*, obviously, the *Statesman*. If the *technê* model is *less* prominent in Plato's post-*Republic* works, it may be because he has come to doubt that these two can be a *single* art, with the dual scope I discuss in Section II.
[10] Dancing, Cicero *De Fin.* III.24; claimed by Marcus Aurelius to be less apt than wrestling, *Med.* VII.61; acting, Epictetus *Disc.* IV.1.165; volleyball (or at any rate a partially cooperative ball-tossing game), *Disc.* II.5 (and cf. the wrestler of I.2.25–27 and other athlete analogies passim).

II The Origins of the Craft Model

Let's begin with a look at the indisputable ground zero for the model, at least given the state of our evidence: Plato's early 'Socratic' dialogues.[11] The intellectualist story takes these as depicting a Socrates committed to the thesis that virtue is knowledge, and using the craft model to develop it. But, in fact, the dialogues present a more confusing picture. Socrates does on several occasions argue that some kind of knowledge or wisdom is necessary and sufficient for happiness (*Prt.* 356c–57e; *Men.* 86d–89d; *Euthyd.* 278e–82d; *Chrm.* 173a–74e), sometimes supported with an induction over the crafts (*Euthyd.* 279e–81b); and this does seem to be intended to show that this knowledge is *virtue* (*Euthyd.* 278d, 282e, 292c). However, when Socrates considers intellectualist definitions of particular virtues in the *Euthyphro, Laches* and *Charmides*, and of virtue as such in the *Meno*, the discussion invariably leads to *aporia*. Since acquisition from teaching is taken to be a standard marker of craft (*Grg.* 513e–14b, *Lach.* 186a–87a), Socrates also problematises the model by arguing repeatedly that virtue cannot be taught, or at any rate *is* not taught by those who claim that it can be (*Men.* 89d–96d; *Prt.* 319b–20b; implicitly at *Ap.* 19d–20c). In the *Gorgias*, Socrates claims to be the *only* person of his time to undertake the true *politikê technê* – and he rather pointedly does not claim to succeed (521d).

At the same time, Socrates clearly supposes that his *interlocutors* accept at least some weak form of the craft model; rather than argue for it, he tends to presume it in order to examine their claims. In doing so, he deploys a canonical set of crafts such as shoemaking, horse training and medicine, and applies a checklist of markers he takes them to share. The expert in a craft aims successfully at some good or benefit; he uses a proprietary set of methods and techniques; he can give a *logos*, a rational defense, of his practices; and he can make another like himself by teaching (*Grg.* 464b–66a, 500e–501a). (Thus each craft really has two kinds of 'product', its distinctive work and further experts of the same kind.) The most far-reaching of these markers is the *determinacy criterion*: a real craft must have some determinate and distinctive object – something it is 'set over' and acts upon – which differentiates it from all the other *technai*.

---

[11] For *technê* in Plato, see Schaerer 1930; Kube 1969; Kato 1986; Cambiano 1991; Isnardi Parente 1996; Roochnik 1996; Irwin 1997 and Balansard 2001. I make the now-customary assumption that we can usefully distinguish a set of 'early' or 'Socratic' dialogues without commitment to any strong claims either about the historical Socrates or about the chronology of Plato's writings; I take the Socrates of these dialogues to be above all the instrument of Platonic philosophical inquiry.

This point is used by Socrates both to investigate problematic candidates for craft status, such as rhetoric (*Grg.* 453b–54a) and poetic recitation (*Ion* 537e–41b), and to raise puzzles about the putative knowledge which is virtue in the *Laches, Charmides* and *Euthydemus*.

Socrates' complex, ambivalent treatment of the craft model has the look of a provisional, critical engagement with a popular intellectual trend: it invites us to ask, who *did* firmly and unequivocally believe that virtue can be taught? And the answer is obvious: the sophists, including Evenus in the *Apology* (19e–20c), Gorgias in the *Gorgias* (459c–60e) and above all Protagoras in the *Protagoras*.[12] This first and greatest of the sophists is introduced, with some fanfare, as a self-proclaimed teacher of virtue, and this seems to be constitutive of sophistic practice as he understands it.[13] Protagoras promises to make his students better people every day, by teaching them excellence in deliberation (*euboulia*) (318a–19a). This term 'deliberation' has political connotations, and Protagoras is happy to accept Socrates' identification of it with the *politikê technê* (319a4), though he emphasises that it covers both the management of one's private life and the matters of the city.

> What is to be learned is good judgement in private matters, how best to manage one's own household, and in matters of politics – how to be most able [or powerful, *dunatôtatos*] in things to do with the city, both in action and in speech. (*Prt.* 318e5–19a2)[14]

It's unlikely to be a coincidence that the phrasing here is identical to that used by Thucydides to describe the statesman Pericles (I.139): Protagoras (whom we know to have been an associate of Pericles) is offering to make his students effective statesmen along familiar and respectable lines. And that all this is intended to count as a *technê*, in *most* ways just like the others, is then confirmed in Protagoras' 'Great Speech' (*Prt.* 320d–28d). Here, in response to Socrates' arguments that virtue *cannot* be taught, Protagoras represents political or social virtue, justice and shame as collectively a craft, taught by all to all just like the Greek

---

[12] For a fuller account of the Protagorean *politikê technê*, including some illuminating parallels with the art of medicine, cf. Hussey's chapter in this volume (Chapter 1).

[13] Protagoras' disparagement that Hippias' polymathy suggests that he takes the proper business of a sophist to be teaching virtue and nothing but (317d–e); but his genealogy of crypto-sophistic predecessors (316d–17a) implies this to be recognisable under many guises. I here take Plato's presentation of Protagoras in the *Protagoras* to be broadly historical, setting aside the *Theaetetus* as very much less so (cf. Gomperz 1900–1912: vol. 1: 457–58). Compare, however, Hussey's chapter in this volume (Chapter 1).

[14] All Plato translations are from the various hands in Cooper 1997, sometimes with revisions.

language. It differs from flute-playing or medicine only in having to be acquired by all members of the community. And this presumption that virtue is a craft is sustained throughout the dialogue. With his presentation of the *metrêtikê technê*, the 'measuring art', Socrates proposes that it must be less closely analogous to flute-playing or language than to kinds of scientific expertise, able to cut through deceptive appearances by establishing the comparative quantities of pleasures and pains (356c–57e).

So, as Plato himself presents it, the impetus for the *technê* model originates not with Socrates, but with the sophistic movement, and, in particular, with the promise of Protagoras that political virtue can be taught.[15] This sophistic project needs to be seen in context for the excitement around it to be understood. As a number of memorable fifth century BCE texts make clear, including Aeschylus' *Prometheus Bound* and Sophocles' *Antigone*, thinkers of the day are already bedazzled (and a little troubled) by the uncanny powers of the recognised crafts, seen as distinctively human, rational, systematic achievements – powerful triumphs over nature and chance, providing the goods on which civilised life and our collective happiness depend.[16] That fascination naturally gives rise to a troubling question: why do we have no such reliable, publicly agreed upon art for the political realm, where we need it the most? (A question all the more urgent given that without it, all the other *technai* may come to naught.) And with that puzzle comes the tantalising speculation that perhaps such a thing *is* within our reach. Perhaps a general art of political decision-making *could* be systematised and passed on from one generation to the next. This is the aspiration Protagoras represents. In fact, we should distinguish two aspirations here, marked by the two halves of Protagoras' boast: one for a *politikê technê* able to produce expert statesmen on a reliable basis, and one for an art of living enabling any agent to pursue his own interests with success. Both take the form of a general art of deliberation, an unspecialised counterpart to the specialised practical wisdom of the craftsperson: indeed, they constitute a *single* 'dual-scope' (as I will term it) deliberative art. That makes Protagoras' *technê* perfectly tailored to the ambitious young men clustered around him, since for them political power is in any case the main constituent of private success.

So if a certain rationalism is built into the Greek version of the craft model (unlike, say, the Chinese one), it's because its allure is from the start that of an educational programme; and teaching, at least at the advanced

---

[15] Cf. Kamtekar 2006 on the sophistic origins of the idea of politics as a 'profession'.
[16] See Nussbaum 1986, ch. 4.

level here relevant, is assumed to take the form of explicit instruction and explanation. What exactly the teaching of virtue requires was clearly contested among the sophists. But we have a pair of precious fragments of the real Protagoras on education: 'Teaching requires natural ability and practice', and 'in learning, one must start from early youth'.[17] These sound like bland truisms, but applied to the case of virtue, they imply a substantive position on just this controversial question. At the start of Plato's *Meno*, Meno asks, 'Can you tell me, Socrates, can virtue be taught? Or is it not teachable but the result of practice, or is it neither of these, but men possess it by nature or in some other way?'[18] As both the fragments and the *Protagoras* suggest,[19] Protagoras' own answer was a three-factor account: virtue comes from teaching, but to benefit from that teaching one needs both natural ability and practice or training. And this rather plausible three-factor view seems to have been incorporated into the philosophical tradition, as common ground among otherwise diverse theories. When in the *Republic* we finally get a positive Platonic account of moral education, it turns out that the Guardians require both the right natural ability and education, which in turn subdivides into early non-rational affective training and a higher education involving formal, highly rational instruction. A similar three-factor, two-stage model is accepted by Aristotle: for him, virtue requires the right natural endowment, non-rational habituation (i.e., practice) and completion by practical reason. This somewhat boring pluralistic consensus is just what we would expect given a widespread acceptance of the craft model; for it seems obvious that all three factors have their role to play in mastering most of the canonical crafts.[20]

In sum, Socrates' invocations of the craft model in the early dialogues are exploratory and critical in spirit: they're Plato's way of taking the Protagorean promise seriously, *au pied de la lettre*, and using the recognised crafts to elaborate and assess it. His purpose is to bring out what virtue *would have to be like* if it really were a craft: and this turns out to be far beyond anything Protagoras could have imagined. The prospective and

---

[17] *Anecdota Parisiensia* I.171, 31; translation from Dillon and Gergel 2003.
[18] *Men.* 70a; for the popularity of the *topos* cf. *Dissoi Logoi* 6 as well as the opening arguments of the *Protagoras* itself.
[19] Plato's Protagoras is strikingly vague about what he himself provides as a higher education, given that his students will already have mastered the civic virtue taught by all to all (328c–d). But the language of *technê* quietly evaporates from the latter part of the Great Speech, perhaps hinting that what ordinary people acquire from their moral education falls short of being a *technê* in the full sense. That makes good sense of his role: by teaching deliberative wisdom, he converts rudimentary civic virtue (in the appropriately gifted and trained person) into the full political craft.
[20] Cf. Hutchinson 1998: 29–32.

aspirational character of the model, and the critical character of his engagement with it, is resounding in passages like *Protagoras* 356c–57e, *Euthydemus* 291b–93a, *Meno* 99e–100a and *Charmides* 173a–77e: to me it suggests that we would do well to think of the craft model as a kind of gigantic multi-author *thought-experiment*.[21] Let us postulate a dual-scope craft of deliberation, one that is constitutive of political virtue and also guarantees private success – but which is otherwise just like the other crafts. What follows? What do the features of the recognised crafts look like when transferred to the case of the *politikos* and the virtuous man? And what further difference do its stipulated distinctive features turn out to make? The craft that is virtue will be special, to be sure; but does it turn out to be special in ways that exclude it from being a craft at all?[22] What, if anything, does our thought-experiment reveal to us about the nature of craft as such? We will look at Platonic answers to these questions in Sections III and IV.

If all this is on the right track, the intellectualist story is wrong on at least three counts. The craft model is essentially a sophistic aspiration – not a Socratic dogma. It is first and foremost political, and only by extension ethical. And it is not a vehicle for rationalism or intellectualism, at least not in any form stronger than is required for virtue to be teachable along Protagorean three-factor lines. In its original and most basic form, the idea of virtue as a craft is just the optimistic vision of a generalised deliberative skill, sufficient for private happiness as well as the skillful exercise of power, which could somehow be taught.

III The Platonic Model

I turn now to the shape the model assumes once Plato takes it over: for the critical explorations of the early dialogues are preliminary to a full appropriation. This is most visible in Book I of the *Republic*, where, more than

---

[21] Less anachronistically, we might say that it is a hypothesis, in very much the manner envisaged by the 'method of hypothesis' of *Phd.* 100a and 101c–2a, and that the early dialogues are in large part devoting to working out and testing its consequences. It is striking that Julia Annas' influential contemporary revival of the craft model (Annas 2011) also proceeds in a 'holistic' way (2–3, 7), as she puts it, working out the implications of the model rather than arguing directly for it either point by point or on the basis of one central similarity.

[22] This is Aristotle's answer, I take it: the postulated craft turns out to be a combination of things – *phronêsis*, the ethical virtues, *politikê* – each of them rather different from a craft strictly speaking. (Notably, the adjective *politikê* standardly goes nounless in Aristotle; but while it would be problematic to supply *technê*, given his official rejection of the model, the same is true for any alternative feminine noun. So perhaps the ambiguity is deliberate.)

anywhere else, Plato most fully expounds his own constructive vision of the craft model and uses it to do load-bearing work.[23] Here the model is common ground between Socrates and Thrasymachus, who uses it to explicate his conception of the 'ruler in the strict sense'. He claims that the true ruler is the practitioner of a *technê*: for he unerringly practises injustice in his own interest, and this inerrancy is characteristic of any craft practitioner correctly conceived:

> No craftsman, expert, or ruler makes an error at the moment when he is ruling, even though everyone will say that a physician or a ruler makes errors. It's in this loose way that you must also take the answer I gave earlier. But the most precise answer is this. A ruler, *insofar as he is a ruler,* never makes errors and unerringly decrees what is best for himself. (340d–41a, trans. Grube-Reeve)

The craft model is here being flagged as sophistic in origin and political in orientation, as we should expect given its Protagorean lineage.[24] Socrates takes it up and responds with a suite of four arguments. First, the *argument from ends* (341c–47d) shows that each craft has the characteristic work or function of benefiting the object it is set over, rather than itself. So, contra Thrasymachus, the expert ruler exercises justice – 'the good of another', as he himself says – not injustice. Second, the *argument from action* (349b–50c) shows that just action resembles expert action in aiming at a uniform right amount,[25] rather than at any kind of maximisation or self-interested outdoing. Socrates infers from this formal similarity a kind of identity: justice must be a craft and therefore (since craft makes its possessor 'wise and good' in its domain) a kind of virtue. So Thrasymachus was wrong to class injustice with virtue and justice with vice. Third, the *dunamis argument* (351b–52b) spells out the characteristic causal power, the *dunamis*, of injustice: it is to cause disunity and dysfunction wherever it is found, be it in a city, a gang of thieves or an individual soul. So Thrasymachus was wrong to celebrate injustice as 'more powerful' than justice. The closing *ergon argument* (352b–54a)

---

[23] I here assume that *Republic* I is not a false start but a foundation for the *Republic* as a whole; the rest of Sections III–IV should provide some support for that presumption (cf. also Barney 2006). On *Rep.* I, cf. also Nawar's chapter in this volume (Chapter 2), which gives a more detailed account of the argumentation than I can do here.

[24] As Kato 1986 notes – though the evidence for presenting Thrasymachus' view as *the* 'sophistische Konzept der *Technê*' is thin (28). Thrasymachus also thereby contributes the more abstract point that agents act under descriptions, *qua* this or that. This insight too probably has its origins in sophistic thought, as a tool for disambiguation in eristic arguments, and is likewise crucial to Plato's development of his own position.

[25] A thought developed more fully at *Plt.* 283b–5c.

exploits this relocation to the level of the individual soul: it argues that justice must be what enables the soul to perform its function, *ergon*, of deliberating and managing things, thereby enabling a person to live well. So, against Thrasymachus' most important and alarming claim, it is not the unjust person but the just one who lives happily.

I cannot here work through these extraordinarily rich arguments in the detail they deserve. But it is worth noting that they are more tightly unified than they might appear, both with each other and with the subsequent argument of the *Republic* – and that the craft model is in play throughout. Craft is explicitly discussed only in the first two; but crafts are individuated by their powers,[26] so that the *dunamis* argument pursues the contrast between justice and injustice as candidate crafts. The *ergon* argument proceeds without explicit allusion to the *erga* of crafts, instead using an induction over animals, instruments and parts of the body. But the fact that its central concept is shared with the initial argument from ends is enough by way of ring-composition to suggest that the two, and thereby the whole chain of arguments, are to be read as a unity. And the connections are not hard to see. The argument from ends establishes that crafts have *erga*; the argument from actions tells us that justice is a craft. The *dunamis* argument offers an indirect suggestion as to what its *ergon* might be – for if the power of injustice is to generate disunity and dysfunction, justice must do the opposite, and do it likewise *within* the soul of the just person. This suggestion is left as a placeholder or promissory note for the account to be developed in Book IV. In the meantime, the *ergon* argument establishes a more basic and abstract point: the function of justice is to bring about good deliberation (just like the original Protagorean version of the craft), and with it happiness itself. And in Book II, though it is in some ways marked as a new beginning, Glaucon's challenge will be presented as a demand to substantiate just this point: *by doing what* in the soul itself does justice accomplish this (366e, 367a–b, e)? What he wants to be shown, in effect, is the connection between the *dunamis* argument and the *ergon* one: how exactly is it that justice's distinctive power within the soul enables us to live well?

For our purposes, the key features of the craft model are those brought out right at the start, in the argument from ends. Here Socrates emphasises that, as he puts it in a striking personification, no craft seeks out what is to its own advantage, but provides for the good of the object it is 'set over'

---

[26] *Grg.* 447c2, 509e1–10a4; *Hp. Mi.* 376a; and cf. *Rep.* 332d10, e4.

(341c–42e).[27] Here and elsewhere Socrates speaks interchangeably of the craft and its practitioner: the latter – the 'doctor qua doctor' – is simply the art operationalised. What the art of medicine seeks is the health of the patient. In response, Thrasymachus offers a rather effective counterexample: shepherds, surely, do not do their work in order to benefit the sheep (340c–41a, 343b–44c). Socrates' defense is to object that Thrasymachus has not identified the shepherd as such, but only a further activity all craft-practitioners have in common – the additional craft, as Socrates presents it, of wage-earning.[28] After all, the doctor can perform his craft, and confer the benefits distinctive of medicine, whether he earns anything from it or not; and likewise the shepherd, if his work really deserves the name of craft.[29]

In the course of this rebuttal, Socrates clarifies that the other-benefiting results of craft have to do with their each having a distinctive power (*dunamis*) (346a2, b1) – thus setting the stage for the third, *dunamis* argument. He eventually identifies this with its constitutive function or work: 'each craft accomplishes its own work [*ergon ergazetai*] and benefits what it is set over' (346d5). (This language of 'accomplishing a work' is a flag for the craft model even when the term *technê* isn't present: it is also pervasive in the *ergon* argument [353a11, c1, c7, c10].) So the idea that craft is ordered to an end or function emerges here as a result of conceptual clarification, starting from the familiar and uncontroversial understanding of it as involving a distinctive, beneficial, other-oriented specialisation. And Socrates' principal concern is to insist that, on this teleological understanding, craft can be seen to be *disinterested*. That is, the end for which the craftsperson acts is unrelated to his own advantage. Even if the doctor heals herself, or the navigator saves his own life along with the ship, it is strictly speaking qua patient or passenger; and it's a matter of accident that the situation makes this exercise of their craft appropriate.

This picture of craft as essentially teleological and disinterested is at the heart of the Platonic craft model, or at any rate of the dimension of it that I hope to articulate here. It is reaffirmed in a text whose importance as

---

[27] For puzzles about this good-directedness, see also Nawar (Chapter 2) in this volume.
[28] A problematic solution since wage-earning itself seems *not* to fit the other-oriented conception of *technê* that it is introduced to support; and it is not obvious why it should count as a craft at all. But Plato does sometimes use 'technê' very loosely – for instance, in the *Sophist* for the activity of the sophist (cf. *Soph.* 265a–68d, and for discussion Brown 2010).
[29] Socrates need not assume that the shepherd's aim must be to make his sheep happy: craft always aims at making something *better*, but that betterness needn't be construed in terms of the *welfare* of its object. Given the hierarchy of crafts (see Section IV), what makes a sheep better is likely its suitability for use by the crafts of cooking, weaving, tanning, etc.

evidence for the model (and for its continuation in late Plato) is often underappreciated: Plato's account of God as the craftsperson par excellence – literally, the Demiurge or Artisan – in the *Timaeus*.[30] What interests Plato most in introducing the Demiurge is his motivation: he creates the *kosmos* because he is good, and what is good is never 'jealous', but wants other things also to be good insofar as possible (*Tim.* 29d–30b, cf. 28a–29a). Now in the case of ordinary craft-agency, we can ask two very distinct questions: why did *the doctor* act as he did, choosing such and such a treatment in this particular case? And why did *that person* choose to act *as* a (qua) doctor? The first question is properly medical, asking for the rationale of the doctor's procedures in a particular case. Socrates emphasises in the *Gorgias* that the doctor himself will be able to answer it – to give a *logos* of what he does, an answer ultimately relating his action to the end of medicine, health (*Grg.* 465a, 501a–b). The second is a question about the contingent motivations of the person who adopts that medical role, and Socrates' talk of wage-earning in the *Republic* is an acknowledgement that it is a question calling for an answer of a different kind. The *perfect* craftsperson, though – aka divine Nous, the agent who is *nothing but* pure practical reason (*Tim.* 47e–48a) –needs no wages: his reasons for action, both in adopting his craft and in practising it, form a single continuum of ungrudging beneficence. This motivation is not exactly our familiar benevolence or altruism; for those standardly aim at the welfare of other sentient beings, and there are none of those around when the Demiurge takes up his work. What he seeks from the start is simply to *make things better*. This then is the nature or orientation proper to craft itself, here visible in a uniquely pure form: disinterested beneficent teleological rationality.

Returning to the arguments of *Republic* I, Plato here means to show that our conception of craft – for Plato thinks that Socrates can win this argument, that our practices and preconceptions side with him and not Thrasymachus – is essentially *functionalist*. Each craft has a distinctive function or work proper to it, and to be a doctor is simply to act as the art requires. Such functionalist categories are inherently normative, in a slippery-slope sort of way: the *good* doctor is one who instantiates the art correctly and well, while one who does so badly enough may fall out of the category altogether.[31] In the case of craft, this functional normativity has a

---

[30] On the complexities of this passage cf. Johansen 2014, as well as his contribution to this volume (Chapter 4).
[31] I take this to be the corrected Platonic version of Thrasymachus' claim that the craftsperson as such is infallible, discussed by Nawar in this volume (Chapter 2). Note also that (as I hope to show in 'Platonic Predication', ms) Platonic claims about agency-qua are primarily causal; and

social dimension: a craft is something an agent undertakes, and this undertaking is both a social performance and a psychological stance. In undertaking the role of doctor, I present myself to the world under that description and, unless something fraudulent is going on, resolve to adopt the medical standpoint in my deliberations.

So while the doctor qua doctor is in the first instance a norm and a metaphysical abstraction, it is also a role that an agent can choose to instantiate. And to genuinely undertake the art of medicine means not only acquiring the relevant base of knowledge, but adopting the deliberative standpoint of medicine in the relevant contexts ('locally', as I will put it): internalising its end, treating the reasons it provides as sufficient and aspiring to meet its norms. This entails that the doctor, properly speaking, is an agent who not only knows certain things but is motivated in a certain way: and these motivations are *insulated* from considerations external to medicine, including whatever external motivations may have initially led her to undertake it. Imagine, for instance, the doctor propelled to take up medicine by greed – or a naïve teenager who undertakes to become a firefighter just because it sounds so exciting. For her *really* to act as a firefighter will involve internalising the ends and norms of the art of firefighting, and being guided exclusively by them when deliberating in the relevant contexts. And 'because it would be exciting' is not an acceptable reason for action in firefighting. This kind of motivational transformation through the internalisation of a new deliberative standpoint is routine, familiar and itself part of the norms belonging to every craft: it's something we expect a correctly educated firefighter or doctor to do. Our evaluative practices would be unintelligible otherwise: even Thrasymachus does not try to claim that 'good doctor' means 'doctor who *could* promote the health of the patient, if he ever felt like it', or 'doctor who is super-efficient at making money out of medicine'.

The disinterestedness of craft has some implications worth exploring. It has been much debated whether we *ever* find genuinely disinterested or non-egoistic motivations in ancient philosophy, equivalent to the motives of duty and altruism we find in modern ethical theories.[32] The question arises because in ancient ethics the *eudaimonia* of the agent – his happiness or well-being, taken to be the human good – seems to be assumed as the

---

Thrasymachus is right that it is not *because of* his medical expertise that the doctor-loosely-speaking makes a mistake.

[32] For a starter-kit of relevant arguments, see e.g., Irwin 1977; Kraut 1989; Annas 1993: chs. 10–12 with references and White 2002.

natural and necessary starting point of ethical reflection. The worry is that this eudaimonist orientation renders all his motives ultimately egoistic: if the *ultimate* reason for an agent's actions is always his own good, then surely his virtuous motivations are always merely instrumental in relation to ultimately egoistic ones, and his practice of virtue as a whole is reducible to the pursuit of self-interest. I can't properly address this controversy here, but I would suggest that the craft model is the place to look for a solution to the problem – or, more accurately, for an explanation of why it never looks like a problem to Plato himself (or to Aristotle, or the Stoics). For in the humble and familiar context of craft, the alleged prison of egoistic motivation starts to look illusory: even the humble shoemaker steps out of it daily, every time he deliberates about how to make a good shoe, without consideration of his profit margins or career goals. More deeply, the everyday insulation found in the practice of the crafts shows, contra Thrasymachus et al., that there is nothing inherently or by default self-interested about successful practical rationality – quite the opposite, in fact, in the cases of it which we understand the best.

On the conception of virtue informed by the craft model, then, to become virtuous is to take on the motivations provided by the virtues in the same way as the well-trained doctor or firefighter. Firefighting really *is* exciting; and committing to the life of virtue is indeed the key to obtaining your own happiness. But part of what it means for firefighting or virtue to be a craft is that undertaking it involves committing to a genuinely new motivational standpoint, one internal to the craft itself and providing reasons for action that are insulated from any external ones. So read, the principal import of the craft model is deontological rather than epistemological; its point is to provide a way of construing the demands of morality as categorical.[33] For what is demanded of a craft-practitioner in any given situation is quite independent of the agent's inclinations and self-interest, including the motivations that led him to adopt that identity; the adoption of the identity consists precisely in grasping those demands and committing to them as authoritative. The obvious problem with this as a model for moral motivation is, of course, that the adoption of any craft-identity in the first place is only ever optional. I turn in Section IV to ask whether the craft model can accommodate this disanalogy.

It might be objected that this emphasis on craft as disinterested is at war with the eudaimonistic stance, and most vividly with the picture of virtue

---

[33] This is not to say that the reasons provided by craft are never *defeasible*: see Section IV (also Barney 2008b) on normative insufficiency and the hierarchy of crafts.

we get from the early Socratic dialogues. For there the end of the craft of virtue is straightforwardly the agent's own good[34] – just as we should expect, given the origins of the model in Protagorean careerist self-help. Moreover, there is no reason to think that Plato's mature version of the model is any different in that regard: in *Republic* I too, the conclusion of the *ergon* argument is that the just person himself will live well, and so be blessed and happy (354a). However, this does not necessarily conflict with the claim that craft is disinterested in its structure. It implies only that the virtuous person's pursuit of his happiness involves commitment to a strategy of indirection – like that of the adventure-seeker who genuinely commits to the norms of firefighting, or the shoemaker who, persuaded by the myths of capitalism, never doubts that his best strategy for personal profit is to make the best shoes he can.

The starkest evidence for this strategy of motivational indirection is the infamous 'Return to the Cave' in *Republic* VII. This is where the rulers in the strict sense as Plato conceives them, the masters of the craft of political virtue, formally undertake to adopt that role. Not by coincidence, it's a moment heavily foreshadowed in the deployment of the craft model in Book I (345d–47e). Just as Socrates argues there, the Guardians, as we discover in Book VII, will rule 'unwillingly'; for as true rulers, they benefit not themselves but those they rule. In fact, they rule at massive cost to their own happiness, which would be maximised by a life of philosophical study.[35] Yet they will reliably undertake this political role, we are told, simply because they are just people, and the demand that they do so is just (520e). Recent scholarship has found this maddeningly unsatisfactory, and sought for more complicated reasons;[36] but Plato's whole point is that nothing more needs to be said. To be a just person is to be committed to a deliberative standpoint from which the demands of justice are unconditionally authoritative, insulated from any considerations about one's own interest. Agents come to adopt that standpoint, of course, on the basis of

---

[34] E.g., *Euthyd.* 278e–82d; cf. Irwin 1977 for a reading taking this as central.
[35] To be clear, the world in which a true Guardian decides to act as a free-rider is internally contradictory and thus impossible. So there is in a sense no answer to the question whether a free-riding Guardian would *really* be happier; and a pseudo- or proto-Guardian who unjustly free-rides cannot be happier overall than his just counterparts. What remains true, though, is that each Guardian would be much happier in a society that (though otherwise like the *kallipolis* in the relevant respects) exempted him from political responsibilities, so that he could avoid them with his justice unimpaired. (This is the magical possibility represented by the divinely governed Isles of the Blessed [519c].) He thus rules 'unwillingly' inasmuch as doing so is not for him a good; his life would be better without it, if only all else were equal.
[36] See, e.g., Kraut 1991 and Brown 2000.

some motivation external and antecedent to it, standardly their ongoing desire for their own happiness. In fact, Plato thinks, a rational agent will recognise it as the only strategy for the pursuit of happiness that has any chance of working. But that does not change the structure of virtue as a craft, or the force of its demands.

What is most striking about the craft model in *Republic* I, then, is that craft is here conceived as a vehicle for the demands and norms of a disinterested practical reason. Seen in this deontological light, the recognised crafts are important to Plato not as special kinds of knowledge (and so not as grounding any particularly intellectualist conception of virtue) but as instances of a broader category of reason-giving, norm-imposing identities. These are what Christine Korsgaard calls *practical identities*; and her argument that they ground normativity seems to me a kind of recovery of this side of the ancient craft model. According to Korsgaard, a practical identity is

> a description under which you value yourself and find your life worth living and your actions to be worth undertaking. Conceptions of practical identity include such things as roles and relationships, citizenship, membership in ethnic or religious groups, causes, vocations, professions, and offices .... Our conceptions of our practical identity govern our choice of actions, for to value yourself in a certain role or under a certain description is at the same time to find it worthwhile to do certain acts for the sake of certain ends, and impossible, even unthinkable to do others.[37]

We might compare here Epictetus' claim that to discover my *kathêkonta*, the duties or actions appropriate to me, I need only look at the 'names' I am called, such as human being, citizen, son, brother, city councillor and youth. For each of these, he says, has its own proper function or work (*Disc.* II.10.1–12; cf. Cicero, *De Off.* I.107–17). That is, just like craft-identities, roles like 'brother' and 'city councillor' are norm-imposing, and (as I will argue in Section IV) vehicles for the more general norms binding on us as human beings. Indeed, to think of other identities in this way amounts to thinking of them as craft-like: as jobs to be done, with all the expertise we can muster. This suggests that the ethical significance of craft, for Plato and his successors, is as the species of practical identity whose normative and motivational structure is most

---

[37] Korsgaard 1996: 100–2 and Korsgaard 2009: 20–24, 42–44. Korsgaard's emphasis on the voluntary adoption and construction of such identities is perhaps distinctively modern (not to mention Kantian, and American). But she too grounds the authority of virtue in an identity that is *not* optional: 'our identity as rational or human beings' (2009: 22).

transparent to us, because its connection to a work or function is most obvious.[38] I will have more to say about the relation of *technê* to *ergon* in Section IV.

IV The Motivational Objection and the Completion of the Model

I now want to consider the most powerful objection to the craft model, and what I take to be Plato's rejoinder to it: doing so will help to bring out some other key features of the model. The objection is one raised by Plato himself in the *Hippias Minor*.[39] A *technê* can be abused: that is, the person who has acquired it can choose to use its methods for purposes opposed to the good that it standardly provides. In fact, the doctor will be the *best*, most expert poisoner or torturer. If virtue is like *technê*, then, it must be a body of knowledge that the agent can choose to deploy for good *or* for harm. Socrates concludes:

> Therefore, it belongs to the good man to do injustice voluntarily, and the bad man to do it involuntarily; that is, if the good man has a good soul . . . . So the one who voluntarily misses the mark and does what is shameful and unjust, Hippias – that is, if there is such a person – would be no other than the good man. (Hip. Mi. 376b)

This is a paradox, and clearly unacceptable to Socrates himself[40] – hence, as many scholars have noted, the crucial stipulation 'if there is such a person', which we are presumably meant to see is counterfactual. For the just person is one who will never choose to do injustice *at all*. Again, that was the simple solution to the problem of 'the return to the Cave': 'we'll be giving just orders to just people' (520e1). Because the Guardians are just, all non-moral considerations will be silenced for them in cases of prima facie conflict, including considerations about their own happiness. But the

---

[38] Craft names do not appear in Epictetus' list here; but they come in immediately after, when he reproaches the person who fails to live up to his roles as being like a smith who forgets he is a smith and uses his hammer incorrectly, or like someone who loses the use of language or of music (*Disc.* II.10.13–16).

[39] T. Nawar's essay in this volume (Chapter 2) discusses this under the heading, 'two-way skills'.

[40] This is not to say that it is an impossible view. The springboard for the discussion, occupying the first part of the *Hippias Minor*, is the question of whether truth-telling and lying should be seen as a single bivalent power; and the traditional Greek answer, immortalised in the boast of the Muses at the start of Hesiod's *Theogony*, is yes. Still, in the case of the virtues, and justice in particular, the parallel answer seems wrong. It is not an unintelligible conception of justice so much as a clearly corrupt one – the view of someone like Odysseus in Sophocles' *Philoctetes*, who boasts that nobody is better at justice than him, whenever circumstances make it to his advantage (83–85, 1049–52).

existence of doctor-poisoners and the like shows that no *technê* is motivationally compelling in this way; therefore virtue (or at any rate the key virtue of justice) must not be a *technê*.

Now the motivational objection is recalled in *Republic* I itself during the discussion between Polemarchus and Socrates: as part of a whole barrage of eristic paradoxes, Socrates here uses craft analogies to show that the just person, as a skilled guardian, 'turns out to be a kind of thief' (333e–34a). That the teleological, deontological conception of craft discussed in Section IV is wheeled out by Socrates against Thrasymachus immediately *after* this passage, and used to ground the craft model, strongly suggests that Plato thinks that this conception enables the model to exclude or withstand the objection. And it is easy to see how it provides at least a first line of response. According to the argument from ends, a craft properly understood is *not*, as the objection implies, an instrumental collection of techniques used for whatever purpose the person trained in it might choose; rather, it is inherently structured around a beneficial end. So the doctor may be best *able* to produce disease; but the doctor strictly speaking can never choose to do so. And so the craft analogy does not imply, disastrously, that the just person ever *is* a thief. (This is not just a matter of terminological fiat: Plato can plausibly argue that the person who thinks of his craft as merely a grab-bag of techniques, without seeing how they are organised around an end, does not possess the art in full; and whatever he does grasp of it will not by itself guide him to act in *any* particular way [*Phdr.* 268a–9c].)

Still, the objection survives this first line of response. For it does not address the central charge that, be the nature of the craft itself what it may, the knowledge it gives is evidently not motivationally compelling, as any knowledge constitutive of virtue must be. Even if the medically knowledgeable poisoner is not strictly speaking a doctor, the fact that such a person is possible suffices to show that there is a deep motivational disanalogy here. Moreover, Socrates' invocation of wage-earning in the argument from ends seems to admit the point: the just person surely practises justice without requiring any such 'wage'.

I think we can see why Plato might nonetheless presume the craft model to be immune to the objection, precisely on the basis of his teleological or deontological conception of crafts as practical identities. To begin with, we need to see that on this conception, the crafts *do* motivate, not as magically powerful kinds of knowledge but in the way that all our practical identities do: by providing a deliberative standpoint that imposes authoritative norms and demands on those who commit to it. This is less visible than it should be because the motivational force of craft-identities is inherently *weaker* than that of virtue: the objection is right that there is a real difference here. But this difference is not as deep as the objection claims; and far from invalidating the craft model, it is explained by it. To see how, we need to turn to two ideas that I take to represent a kind of necessary extension or completion of the model.

The first is Plato's conception of the political craft as *architectonic*: that is, as having the function of managing and integrating the work of the specialised crafts. The single text in which this vision is worked out in the fullest detail is the opening of the *Nicomachean Ethics*; but Aristotle is here clearly picking up on themes that we also see developed in the *Charmides*, *Euthydemus* and *Republic* (both in the conception of the role of the Guardians and in more abstract terms in *Rep.* X 601b–e). The point of departure for these discussions is the pervasive pattern of organisation by which one craft is related to another: one craft provides the tools or materials that are used by another craft, and so is practised under its supervision as subordinate. If we ask where these chains of hierarchy end, and how they are integrated into a social and economic unity, the obvious answer is that they rest in the hands of the *politikos*. For the wholly general art of deliberation that he possesses is the perfect qualification for this supervisory task – for adjudicating and harmonising the diverse claims and contributions of farmer and sailor, general and trader, doctor and cook. If we ask what the distinctive end of such an art consists in (the determinacy criterion again), the answer must be: the good of the community as such, that is, the human good writ large.

Moreover, we can now see that the regular crafts *require* the existence of a craft that has this distinctive end and special status. For only if there is such a thing can they hope to be reliably beneficial in the way they are standardly assumed to be – an assumption built into the very conception of craft, and so into the model from the outset. As I argued earlier, the demands of medicine must be insulated from the extra-medical motivations of the doctor; but it's a familiar modern observation that this insulation can be a bad thing. We are perturbed by the doctor who cares only about the body part he specialises in and not about the patient's health overall, and the rocket scientist indifferent to where his bombs come down. In short, due to their local or specialised character, the crafts are incomplete or *normatively insufficient* in a number of ways.[41] That is, the reasons they give are defeasible, and there are situations in which the

---

[41] Cf. Barney 2008b: 297–300.

pursuit of their end ought to be curtailed as no longer beneficial all things considered. And the craft itself can tell you nothing about these. Plato is acutely aware of this shortcoming: the case that worries him is the art of medicine, which cannot tell you about cases in which a patient would be better off dead (*Lach.* 195c–d; *Grg.* 511e–12b). His solution is that medicine and the other ordinary crafts need to be supervised by a higher art possessed of a more encompassing vision of the good and able to give rationally non-defeasible commands; by, ultimately, the art of the *politikos*. Without it playing this authoritative role, the normative standing of the other crafts would be deeply compromised (cf. *Chrm.* 171d–75d). On this account, the *politikê technê* is a special kind of craft in the same way that a general is a special kind of soldier: while squarely belonging to the broader genus, it plays a distinctive role that the rest of the genus (arguably, at least) requires.

To see how this becomes an answer to the motivational objection, we need to turn to the private counterpart of *politikê*, which has its own version of this architectonic function and special authority. For instance, Epictetus' *Discourses* begin by asking what human ability (*dunamis*, here clearly including the crafts) studies itself and so knows how to employ itself (I.1.1–6, cf. I.20.1–6). Grammar and music will tell you *how* to write your friend or play the lyre; but not *whether* it is appropriate to do so, and when. That calls for a higher deliberative capacity, one able to address questions about 'what is to be done' in a perfectly general and regress-ending way. This conception of the craft that is virtue as involving use of the other crafts can be found already in the *Euthydemus* and *Charmides*.[42] So the virtuous person, just as we would expect from the original Protagorean 'dual-scope' conception of the craft, is a small-scale version of the *politikos*. And so he must know the small-scale, private version of the human good: that is, his own *ergon* and flourishing as a human being.

This private version of the art also adds something new. The art of politics is especially authoritative; but from the perspective of the practitioner, it is still like all the other crafts in providing a merely optional practical identity. The craft that fulfils the human *ergon* is not like that. Its end is unique in being universally non-optional; for it corresponds to our inalienable identity as human beings, which is prior to and independent of

---

[42] It is striking that both dialogues temporarily shift the focus to the political level, with the *basilikê technê* in the former (289c–92e) and the dystopian city of all the sciences in the latter (171d–74d). The dual scope of the craft in question makes this unproblematic; and as in the *Republic*, the 'large letters' of the *polis* can reveal principles that are also present, but less visible, in the case of individual human beings.

the more specialised identities we may choose to adopt. Virtue is special as a craft, then, not only because there is no higher craft on the basis of which its reasons might prove defeasible, but because I cannot refuse to adopt the practical identity that makes its end an end *for me*.

This individualised version of the *politikê technê* also allows us to see why, though defeasible, practical identities such as crafts can be genuinely normative. For as was already apparent from Epictetus' emphasis on 'names' or roles as the key to our duties (*kathêkonta*), the craft that realises the human *ergon* operates to a great extent *through* our more specialised practical identities.[43] Our duties are incumbent on us as human beings; but an action often *becomes* a duty for us on the basis of a more specific role. You cannot be a good human being if you are an abusive son or a negligent citizen. And elsewhere Epictetus argues along the same lines with craft identities explicitly in the picture:

> There is, besides, a particular end and a general end. First of all, I must act as a human being. What does that involve? That one shouldn't act like a sheep, even if one is gentle in one's behaviour, and one shouldn't act injuriously like a wild beast. The particular end relates to each person's specific occupation and moral choice. The lyre-player must act as a lyre-player, the carpenter as a carpenter, the philosopher as a philosopher, the orator as an orator. (*Disc.* III.23.4, trans. R. Hard)

If the duties of that abstract figure, the lyre-player qua lyre-player, ever become real duties for the person who *is* a lyre-player, it must be because being a lyre-player becomes part of her job as a human being, so that the normativity of her role is grounded in that of the human *ergon* as such.[44]

In short, the motivational objection misrepresents as a deep difference in kind what is just a necessary complementarity built into the craft model itself. On the Platonic conception, craft *does* motivate, in the way of any practical identity: for to practice a craft is just to understand its demands and embrace them as sufficient reasons for action. Where ordinary crafts fall short is that such craft-identities are only ever local, defeasible and optional. The craft that is virtue is the necessary complement to them: authoritative in the reasons it provides, it grounds in turn their weaker

---

[43] I discuss this thought as the 'realisation reading' of the Aristotelian function argument in Barney 2008a: 309–18.
[44] Thus in the *Republic*, the justice of the *kallipolis* depends on its fulfilling the diverse natures [*phuseis*] of its citizens: Plato seems to have an almost Leibnizian optimism that the professions that will enable practitioners to do work appropriate to their natures are *also* just the ones that will contribute to the good of the city. For a just and happy city to be possible, the twin perspectives of the architectonic art and of the *ergon* argument must deliver the same roster of *technai*.

form of normativity. This picture also explains why virtue, so understood, is necessarily motivationally compelling. For the possessor of this craft must grasp that the reasons for action it gives are non-optional and non-defeasible; and – and this is where it at last becomes important that virtue is not just a practical identity, but a kind of wisdom or rational perfection – in such a person what is irrational is also impossible.

So the idea of a human *ergon*, on the one hand, and the architectonic hierarchy of the crafts, on the other, are pathways to the same conclusion: that there is – there *must* be – a craft of deliberation that has for its end the human good as such, both at the individual level and the political one, and which therefore has an authoritative relation to all the others. To pursue the craft model further would mean exploring the grounding of our *ergon* in human nature (*phusis*): for we would need an account of human nature in all its complexity and diversity in order to see not only what the human *ergon* is in general, and how virtue enables us to attain it, but how it relates to its large-scale counterpart, the good of a political community and to the particular *erga* of the crafts within it. In short, we would need something very much like *Republic* II–IX. And this suggests that if the craft model seems to evanesce from the *Republic* after Book I, it is because for the rest of the argument we are deeply *inside* it. It is only from the perspective of the craft model that the vindication of justice would naturally take the form of an account of the happy city as one in which the right jobs are assigned to the right natures – including, above all, the assignment of political power to rulers with a craft-like grasp of and commitment to the common good.

V Conclusions

I've argued that the craft model enters ancient ethics when Protagoras promises to teach excellence in deliberation – the virtue of the *politikos* – as a craft that is also sufficient for private happiness. Plato thinks that Protagoras himself has no hope of making good on this; but he too is mesmerised by the very idea of an all-encompassing deliberative craft, and thinks that by taking a serious look at the existing crafts we can discover a lot about how it would have to work. In doing so, though, what he comes to find striking about the crafts is less their epistemic content than their normative structure. So the craft model comes to be used by Plato (and at least some of his successors, some of the time) to spell out a conception of virtuous action as structured by practical identities oriented to disinterested ends. And this deontological dimension of the model points in two further directions. First, it calls for an account of the political craft that will suit it for an essentially architectonic role, supervising the web of crafts and other practical identities that make up a community. Second, it calls for a theory of human nature that will show how the human *ergon* grounds the norms imposed by our specialised practical identities.

In all this, the *technê* model is an exercise in what Aristotle calls reasoning from what is more familiar, or better known to us, to what is less so. We are familiar with the idea that the carpenter has a job to do – much less so with the idea that a human being does (cf. *Rep.* 406c–7a). And this form of reasoning is not just a theoretical exercise: it also has a psychagogic and rhetorical function. As used by Socrates, Plato and the Stoics, the craft model often performs a shaming of the presumed audience, leisured gentlemen with a halfhearted aspiration to virtue or philosophy.[45] The message to them is simple and abrupt: do your job! Put real care and effort into that virtue you claim to be committed to, the way the lowly carpenter over there does with his lesser task. And this rhetorical dimension of the craft model is useful confirmation for the deontological reading I've been presenting, for it has nothing to do with rationalism or intellectualism in ethics. When Socrates, Epictetus and Marcus Aurelius hold up the shoemaker, carpenter or athlete as a role model, it is not for their systematic knowledge but their dedication and commitment. Indeed, the lower and less intellectual the *métier*, the stronger the reproach.

So the craft model in ancient ethics is not just an analytical tool but a mode of exhortation – a strikingly egalitarian one, for the ancient world – and a prompt to our moral imagination. Imagine understanding human happiness as fully as a carpenter understands buildings. Imagine making political decisions as reliably as an expert shoemaker makes shoes. Imagine taking the demands of justice as seriously as an obsessive athlete takes his sport. *That's* what it would be like to be a virtuous person: now *get on with it*, say Plato and the Stoics, the way the athlete and the shoemaker do.[46]

---

[45] Cf., e.g., *Rep.* 406c–7a; Marcus Aurelius, *Med.* V.1.3; Epictetus, *Disc.* II.13.15, III.23, IV.5.22, IV.8, IV.12.14, etc.; I discuss *Rep.* 406c–7a briefly in Barney 2008a: 315–16.

[46] Over different incarnations, this chapter has benefited from comments from so many people that I fear I cannot remember them all: still, I would like to acknowledge the help of James Allen, John Cooper, Mark Gatten, Chris Gill, Tom Hurka, Brad Inwood, Terry Irwin, Rachana Kamtekar, Richard Kraut, Gisela Striker, Voula Tsouna, Roslyn Weiss and Thomas Johansen, to whom I am also indebted for patient and thoughtful help as an editor. It began life as a contribution to a Symposium at the Eastern APA in December 2008, attempting to address the question: where in ancient philosophy, if anywhere, do we see something like the Kantian conception of a distinctively moral motivation? So my thanks to Iakovos Vasiliou for that invitation, and to my co-panelists Barbara Herman and Allen Wood for discussion.

CHAPTER 4

Crafting the Cosmos
Plato on the Limitations of Divine Craftsmanship

Thomas Kjeller Johansen

I Introduction

The Demiurge made the whole cosmos as a living being, with a body and a soul. But he didn't create man or the other mortal creatures. This task he left to the 'lesser' gods. Why? The question is a classic in the scholarship on the *Timaeus*. However, the way I shall approach it in this chapter, from the viewpoint of craft, is, I believe, novel.

It is clear from several works that Plato thinks that craftsmen generally work to make the best possible product.[1] So, in the *Gorgias*, Socrates says that a craft considers not just the good but what is best for its subject (501b). Again, in *Republic* I (345d, 347a), Socrates says of crafts that they aim at the best (*to beltiston*) for that which they are concerned with.[2] In the *Timaeus*, the divine craftsman, 'the Demiurge' henceforth, makes the cosmos to be as beautiful and fine as possible (29a, 30a–b). Yet he only creates parts of it himself, leaving the creation of mortal beings to his first creation, the heavenly bodies, who are themselves gods, the so-called lesser gods. But if the Demiurge was the best of all causes, seeking to make the finest cosmos possible, why did he not make the mortal beings too? Here is the passage where Timaeus raises and answers the question:

> T1 When all the gods were born, both those whose circuits we see in the sky and those who only appear to us when they wish, the father of this

---

[1] See Nawar (Chapter 2) and Barney (Chapter 3) in this volume for more detailed consideration of this claim.
[2] Though Plato shows no awareness of the distinction in these passages, one might in general distinguish between making the best possible product and doing the best possible for the subject. Perhaps forcing your child to be the best possible pianist is not the same as doing what is best for your child. However, where Y is also what X essentially is, it is reasonable to say that making X the best possible Y will also be doing what is best for X. So it seems intuitively right to say that making somebody the best possible human being is also doing what is best for her. These (making the best possible cosmos, making the best possible human being, etc.) are the sorts of cases the *Timaeus* is concerned with.

universe addressed them as follows: 'God among gods, works whose maker and father I am, what was created by me cannot be dissolved without my consent. Anything bonded together can of course be dissolved, though only an evil will would consent to dissolve anything whose composition and state were good. Therefore, since you have been created, you are not entirely immortal and indissoluble; but you will never be dissolved or taste death, as you will find my will a stronger and more sovereign bond than those with which you were bound at your birth. Hear therefore what I now make known to you. There are three kinds of mortal creature yet uncreated, and unless they are created the world will be incomplete, as it will not have in it every kind of living creature which it must have if it is to be sufficiently complete. But if these were created and given life by me, they would be equal to gods. In order therefore that there may be mortal creatures and that the whole may be truly a whole, turn your hands, as is natural to you, to the crafting [*dêmiourgia*] of living things, imitating my power when I created you. And in so far as there ought to be something in them that shares the name with the immortals, something called 'divine' and guiding those of them who are always ready to follow you and justice, I will begin by sowing the seed of it and then hand it on to you; it remains for you to weave mortal and immortal together and create living creatures. Bring them to birth, give them food and growth, and when they perish receive them again. (*Tim.* 41a-d)[3]

The argument seems to be the following:

(1) The cosmos has to contain mortal creatures (otherwise it won't be complete).
(2) Anything created is created by either (a) the Demiurge or (b) the lesser gods.
(3) Anything created by the Demiurge will be immortal.
(4) Anything created by a created creature (even if it is de facto immortal) will be mortal.
(5) The lesser gods are created.
(6) Therefore, the mortal creatures are created by the lesser gods.

The argument bears a superficial similarity to the famous Theodicy problem. We are familiar with this problem in the following form:

(a) God is all powerful.
(b) God is all good.
(c) God is all knowing.
(d) Therefore, the world is as good as possible.

---

[3] Translations of the *Timaeus* with some adaptations from Lee (revised Johansen) 2008.

(e) The world contains evil.
(f) So not (d).

Therefore, not (a) or not (b) or not (c).

Like the Theodicy, Plato seems to argue from an aspect of the world that is less than ideal to showing that God's abilities in some way must be limited.

However, the similarity with the Theodicy is superficial. The Theodicy is not a problem for Plato in the *Timaeus*. Plato's God may be entirely good, (b). But he nowhere suggests (a), that God is all-powerful. Indeed, Timaeus recognises that the divine intellect made the cosmos good only in so far as Necessity allowed it (48a). Nor does Timaeus claim that (c) God knows everything, if this claim is taken with its most general scope: for particular sensibles as such are not knowable according to Timaeus (51c–e).

However, there is a problem to be constructed about God as a craftsman. We might call it the 'Technodicy': how does a good craftsman as such make a product that is worse than what he is capable of? Consider the following argument:

(i) God is a craftsman.
(ii) A product created by a craftsman (as such) will be the best possible.
(iii) An eternal product is better than a mortal one.
(iv) Therefore, a craftsman will create an eternal product if possible.
(v) At any time, it was possible for God to create an eternal product instead of a mortal one.
(vi) Therefore, God will never create a mortal creature.

One question here is about the scope of (vi). Does it mean
(vi)* God will never *himself* create a mortal creature.
 or
(vi)** God will never *himself or with the help of others* create a mortal creature?

Construed as (vi)*, the argument is consistent with the Demiurge's reasoning: the Demiurge realises that he himself can't directly make mortal creatures, but that doesn't prevent him from letting the lesser gods to do so, even though the lesser gods were his own creation and will do as they're told by him.

However, construed as (vi)**, the claim seems inconsistent with the Demiurge's reasoning: for if it was in the Demiurge's power to create further creatures in such a way that they were immortal, then he should as a craftsman, that is, according to (i)–(iii), have done so. Handing the job over to the lesser gods, who are able to create mortal creatures, hardly alters the situation. Imagine a craftsman who oversees the work of his assistants, allowing them to make a poorer product than he himself would have made. One would surely be right to blame him as a craftsman for allowing his assistants to proceed in this way. So the Technodicy seems to reemerge on reading (vi)**: the Demiurge, as the perfect craftsman, should in no way allow mortal beings to be created.

II Craft and Holistic Goodness

So why does the Demiurge allow for the creation of mortal creatures? The answer lies in Timaeus' holistic conception of goodness. The thought is that the cosmos *as a whole* is better because of the existence of mortal creatures. This consideration overrides the concern one might have for individual beings. So even if it would be better for any individual creature to be immortal, it is better for the cosmos as a whole to contain mortal beings. Since the Demiurge's primary concern was always with the cosmos as an ordered whole – indeed *kosmos* comes close to meaning 'ordered whole' in Greek – his practice seems justified.

Plato shows his awareness of the distinction between what is good for the individual and what is good for the whole in other dialogues. In *Phaedo* 98b Socrates says that he expected that Anaxagoras, when he said that Reason (*nous*) was the cause of the cosmos, would explain 'what is best for each and what is good for all in common'. Here Socrates does not say that such a cause would be a craftsman. However, in *Laws* X Plato presents a craftsman's primary concern as the good of the whole: 'every skilled craftsman always works for the sake of some end-product as a whole' (903c, trans. T. Saunders).[4] Of course, such holism allows also for the individual itself to be seen a whole, though we would still expect priority to go to the greater whole, which is not itself a part, or at least a whole of more wholes.

Factoring in the craftsman's concern with the whole, Timaeus' argument would go:

(a) God is a craftsman.
(b) A product created by a craftsman qua craftsman will be the best possible.

---

[4] See also *Tim.* 30b, *Grg.* 504a.

(c) The goodness of the whole is greater than the goodness of the part.
(d) Therefore, when making a product a craftsman is always primarily concerned with the goodness of the whole.
(e) There is a whole (the cosmos) which is the best possible and contains both immortal and mortal creatures.
(f) God can create such a whole.
(g) Therefore, God will create a whole containing both immortal and mortal creatures.

This argument gets the Demiurge off the hook of the Technodicy. However, it doesn't reflect Timaeus' thinking in T1. For (f)–(g) claim that God can create such a product and that he will do so. But T1 tells us that the Demiurge did not and cannot create mortal creatures.

Why he can't do so is not immediately obvious, since holism now allows him as the best craftsman also to create mortal creatures. Compare the case of the lesser gods' creation of the human skull (75c–d): they decided to make the human skull thinner than it could be in order to increase man's intelligence, although it has the negative consequence of making human life briefer than it could have been. This is a way of maximising the good of the whole arrangement that is perfectly in line with the expectations of a craftsman. Similarly, the Demiurge might have created mortal creatures to improve the quality of the whole cosmos, even if mortal creatures considered in isolation are less good than immortal ones.[5]

Why, then, is the Demiurge not himself able to create mortal beings as part of a better whole? Given holism, the problem is no longer why God didn't make everything in the world as good as it could have been, but why God did not himself make all the world given that it as a whole is as good as it could have been.

I want now to consider three kinds of answer to this problem. The first tries to give an answer in terms of the Demiurge's role as a father, the second focuses on his goodness, while the third returns to his function as a craftsman.

---

[5] See in this vein Plotinus, *Enneads* III.2.3 'It is, therefore, impossible to condemn the whole on the merits of the parts which, besides, must be judged only as they enter harmoniously or not into the whole, the main consideration, quite overpassing the members which thus cease to have importance. To linger about the parts is to condemn not the Kosmos but some isolated appendage of it.' (trans S. Mackenna and B. S. Page).

III God As a Father

Now there is a significant detail in T1 that may help explain why the Demiurge couldn't create the mortal creatures: he is not just a craftsman but also a father.[6] He is the father of the lesser gods (41b7). This helps explain why the lesser gods are themselves gods (41c2–3): they are the children of a god. Admittedly, the lesser gods are qua generated in principle subject to dissolution, but as children of the Demiurge they are so well put together that it would take an evil will to dissolve them. As far as the mortal creatures are concerned, the Demiurge will create what is immortal about them, namely, their rational soul. Because the lesser gods are generated, and so in principle mortal, they in turn will create the mortal creatures' mortal soul and body. Again, the Demiurge puts the point in T1 in a way that highlights that whatever is the offspring of an immortal god is itself divine:

> And in so far as there ought to be something in them that shares the name with the immortals, something called 'divine' and guiding those of them who are always ready to follow you and justice, I will begin by sowing the seed of it and then hand it on to you.

There is something divine about human beings too, our immortal reason, which appropriately the Demiurge created, not the lesser gods. So we might say that the answer to why the Demiurge can't make the mortal creatures is that while he could produce them as a craftsman, he can't do so as a father.[7] For a father only creates something like himself, in this case, something divine and immortal.[8]

But why then does Timaeus choose to make the Demiurge a father as well as a maker? One answer lies in the basic principle of Timaeus' cosmology.[9] At 29e2–3 Timaeus said that the Demiurge 'being without envy wishing *all things to be as like himself as possible*. This indeed is the most proper principle of becoming and the cosmos' (my emphasis).

---

[6] The double role of the Demiurge as craftsman and father was mentioned early on in Timaeus' account: 'to discover the maker *and father* of this universe is indeed a hard task' (28c3–4, my emphasis).

[7] Cf. Plutarch, *Platonic Questions* 2, 'Also in the case of a maker, such as a builder ... his work when done is separated from him, whereas the principle or force emanating from the parent is blended in the progeny and constrains its nature, which is a fragment or part of the procreator.' (trans H. Cherniss).

[8] Later Platonists assign a higher status to the father than the maker, cf. Opsomer 2005: 52.

[9] Druart 1999: 169 claims that the Demiurge's 'fatherhood cannot be construed as a begetting' since he doesn't create but orders the chaos he finds. If this were true, Aristotle's father, who orders the matter provided by the mother, would not count as a begetter either.

'Making another like oneself' is a favored description of procreation in Plato (as in Aristotle),[10] so it should not surprise us that Timaeus uses the notion of fatherhood to express the distinctive manner in which the Demiurge creates the cosmic god, the whole cosmos or the gods within it, in his own likeness.[11]

We might think that here the artistic and biological models of causation are on a collision course with one another. As a rule, craftsmen aren't like their products, while parents are like their children. Even if we allow for the special case of an artefact that is like its maker, we would think of this as an accident from the point of view of craft itself.[12] However, the Demiurge says that when he produces an ensouled being, it necessarily becomes divine, like himself. There is no indication that the Demiurge is engaged in reproductive processes – no mention of copulation or such as in earlier cosmogonies – which would ensure or explain this necessity. Rather, the mixing, molding and bonding by which he creates both the world soul and the immortal human soul are all processes of traditional crafts (41d).

To be sure, Timaeus talks about the Demiurge's planting the seed of the soul but the image here is agricultural, and so technical, rather than reproductive. This is made clear also when the Demiurge hands over the seed (*sporos*) of the immortal souls to the lesser gods for them to plant them in mortal bodies (41d1, 42d6).[13] There is no suggestion that the seed he plants is his own sperm, and so no suggestion that he is reproducing himself in the creation of the souls.[14] And, as I said, craft as such gives no reason why the offspring should necessarily be just like its parent.

Consider this point also from the perspective of the distinction between being and becoming, the fundamental ontological distinction Timaeus draws at the beginning of his account (27d–28a). Alongside the Forms, the Demiurge belongs to the kind 'eternal and changeless being', while the cosmos including the created gods belongs to the kind 'becoming' (cf. 37a1–2). When the Demiurge creates the cosmos he shapes becoming in the likeness of being (29b–c). Time, for example, is a moving image of eternal being (37d). This sort of creation is in line with the craftsman model: in general, craft causes something to come into being by modelling

---

[10] Cf. *Symp.* 207d–208b, Aristotle, *DA* II.4 416b15–17.   [11] Cf. also *Tim.* 37c7.
[12] Rather in the way that for Aristotle it is an accident when the doctor cures himself (cf. *Ph.* II.8 199b31–32): there is nothing in the notion of a doctor to suggest that he will also be the patient.
[13] Plato may here be appropriating the role of Anaxagoras' *nous* as a 'farmer god', cf. Sedley 2007: 23–24.
[14] Timaeus' vocabulary (*sporos, sperma, speirō*) is itself ambiguous between the planting and reproducing.

it on a formal paradigm. Yet when we think of the father as the cause of something that comes into being, we expect the cause necessarily to make an offspring of the same sort as himself, and so the offspring would share certain essential characteristics of the father, including, say, his immortality, divinity, goodness. But these are characteristics that the offspring cannot possess since it belongs to the category of becoming.

Timaeus' solution to this problem, such as it is, is to stress the likeness relation across the ontological divide between being and becoming. Sphericity is an image of the completeness of the Forms (33a–b), time of eternity (37d), so by bestowing on becoming features analogous to those of being, Timaeus can maintain that the crafted product is like its cause, and so within the remit of paternity. Compare the Image of the Sun in *Republic* VI: the Sun belongs to the world of becoming but is an image of the Good, and therefore not inappropriately also called the 'offspring' (*ton ekgonon*) of the Good (508b13), and a 'god' (508a9).

A key reference in the *Timaeus* for thinking about the notion of fatherhood across the ontological divide is the 'receptacle passage' (50b), where Timaeus compares the so-called receptacle to the mother, the model to the father and the likenesses of the model in the receptacle to the offspring. No reference to the Demiurge here, but the point of immediate interest is that something belonging to the category of eternal being can be seen as the father of offspring belonging to the category of coming into being, exactly in so far as the one causes the other to be like it.[15] This likeness can be limited to a specific feature and need not include the basic ontological characteristics of the father, such as his eternity or divinity.

The apparent exception is the case we are interested in where the Demiurge creates another living being. Here the father must make something that is immortal and divine like himself. However, the exception is only apparent: it is not hard to see why this case is still compatible with the others. Here again are the exact words of the Demiurge:

> Anything bonded together can of course be dissolved, though only an evil will would consent to dissolve anything whose composition and state were good. Therefore, since you have been created, you are not entirely immortal and indissoluble; but you will never be dissolved or taste death, as you will find my will a stronger and more sovereign bond than those with which you were bound at your birth. (*Tim.* 41a8–b5)

---

[15] So Timaeus here refers to the forms as 'that from which, by being made in its likeness, what comes to be is born' (50d1–2).

The Demiurge does not confer the same immortality onto the lesser gods that he himself possesses. He makes them immortal like himself but contingently so in that they could be dissolved if he himself wanted so. The likeness between the Demiurge and his offspring is then comparable to the examples above, the likeness between the completeness of the forms and the sphericity of the cosmos or the likeness between the eternal being and time. The lesser gods' immortality is modelled on the Demurge's own, but not the same as it. And the reason why the lesser gods' immortality can be no more than contingent is again their ontological status as created and so as necessarily dissolvable.

Rather than saying that the craft model and the biological model are in conflict with each other here, one might maintain that the biological model *requires* the complement of the craft model to explain how this kind of reproduction happens. The biological model explains why the offspring resembles the parent. But it doesn't capture how an offspring resembles the parent in the manner of an image or likeness. For here the image belongs to another ontological category, so it cannot possess the same features in the same manner as God himself, but only ones that are merely *like* or analogous to his across the ontological divide. But this is what craft can explain. For craft, as we know from *Republic* 10, is a cause that looks to eternal being and makes an image of it in the realm of becoming.

In making the cosmos like himself, the formal paradigm serves as a kind of proxy for God himself. We see this in God's first creative act. The Demiurge sets out to make the world as good as possible in the sense of as good as *something visible* can be. This requires the world to have reason (*nous*), and therefore soul and a body (30b). In this way, the world ends up also being an animal or a living being (*zôion*).[16] There is no indication that the Demiurge himself is an animal or that he has soul, but he certainly has or is reason (*nous*). So, we can say that the Demiurge makes the cosmos like himself by endowing it with reason but works this out for the cosmos in the manner that is appropriate and best for a visible being, that is, by its being a rational animal with a soul and a body. The question next arises for Timaeus *which* animal the cosmic animal was modelled on, and we are told that it was a complete one, containing all the intelligible animals (30c). For this is the model that would make the cosmos complete and so best and most beautiful. The model helps the Demiurge find the sort of

---

[16] Though I shall use 'animal' for simplicity, I take no position in this chapter on whether *zôion* should be understood as 'living being' or as 'animal', see further Sedley 2007: 108n36.

goodness that is appropriate to the cosmos, and so indirectly for the cosmos to become like himself. We might say that the model directs the Demiurge in his attempt to assimilate the cosmos to his own goodness. If world-making was simply a matter of standard reproduction, there would be no need for a model: the likeness of the offspring to its father would be established simply by the transfer of the father's own form.

Consider in this light 37c6–d1, where Timaeus begins his account of the creation of time:

> T2 When the father who had begotten it perceived that the universe was alive and in motion, an image [*agalma*] of the eternal gods,[17] he was glad, and in his delight planned to make it still more like its pattern; and as this pattern is an eternal living being, he set out to make the universe resemble it in this way, as far as was possible.

Timaeus could not have confronted us with a more striking juxtaposition of the biological with the technical: a father generating an offspring that is an *agalma*, an image or statue. Yet the forms on which the image is modelled is referred to as 'eternal gods', like the father himself. So while the product is an image of the model, in accordance with the craft model, the image is also a reproduction of a living being, the forms. It is as if the forms work here as a proxy for the Demiurge. But this is not so surprising if, as I argued, the forms of intelligible animals (at 30c) are the model by which the Demiurge makes an image of his own goodness. The craft model helps explain, then, how the father creates an offspring that is like himself but still only as an image.

I have argued that the craft model and the biological model are mutually implicated for Timaeus.[18] The biological model is appropriate to the Demiurge's wish to make the world like himself, but it does not constrain him in a way that precludes the craft model.[19] For the craft model helps explain how the likeness relation can hold across the ontological divide, through the notion of a craftsman looking to an eternal model to make a particular image.

By the same token, the solution to the question why the Demiurge didn't make the mortal creatures does not lie, as one might have thought, in saying that while God as a craftsman could make something lesser, like the mortal beings, he couldn't do so *as a father*. For being a father is not

---

[17] D. Lee followed Cornford who had 'shrine for the eternal gods' in his first edition of the Penguin translation. My reasons for the reading adopted here are given in the revised edition, Lee 2008, comment on 37d.
[18] Plato is no doubt developing a tradition going back to Hesiod and Empedocles 'of locating our biological origins in divine management decisions', as Sedley 2007: 57 puts it.
[19] For the coupling of father and craftsman, see also *Plt.* 273b.

supposed, for Timaeus, to exclude producing likenesses of a lower ontological standing.

IV God As Good

I have considered one answer to the question why the Demiurge couldn't create mortal beings directly, his status as a father, and that answer seemed on its own insufficient. I turn now to another possible answer: God as the best can only produce the best things, and therefore only divine and not mortal souls. I think a version of this answer is right but it is important to be clear about which.

In relation to the creation, God's goodness has in some respects explanatory priority over his role as a craftsman. This is made clear when Timaeus asks why we should say that the cosmos was made by a craftsman looking to an eternal paradigm (28c6–29a2). A craftsman could, in principle, look to a generated paradigm, but if so, his product would not be beautiful (28b1–2). We can be confident that the maker of this cosmos looked to an eternal paradigm because he was good (29a3). It is God's goodness that in turn justifies the denial of envy (*phthonos*) as well as the assertion of his wish to make everything as like himself as possible (29e1–3), what Timaeus called the principle of becoming and the cosmos. One could read the priority of God's goodness as determining also his role as a craftsman. So, the thought might be that God wants to make a good world, being good, and chooses to do so as a craftsman because that is the best way to make the world good. When he is confined to making only immortal beings it may follow directly from his goodness: as good he makes only the best, but that means only immortal offspring.

However, it would be wrong to say that God's goodness is fundamentally prior to his status as a craftsman. There is no suggestion that God chooses to be a craftsman because he is good. The assumption that he is a craftsman is brought in primarily as the only imaginable cause of the generation of a beautiful cosmos. God's goodness is mentioned at 29a3 to explain why he chose to exercise his craftsmanship the way he did rather than in the bad way that is, in principle, possible for any craftsman. But given the general aim of craft, which I noted at the outset, of doing the best possible thing for its product,[20] God's choice may be seen to be just his choice to exercise his craft properly.

---

[20] Cf. *Rep.* I 342e. As Nawar (Chapter 2) and Barney (Chapter 3) in this volume highlight, as a general claim about the crafts this assumption is not unproblematic. However, in the case of the Demiurge we may also resort to the notion of an *architectonic* craft, the highest *technē* that includes an

This point may in turn help explain why Timaeus conspicuously formulates God's motivation for creating the world negatively: it would be *phthonos* or envy not to make a world. The thought may be that since it follows naturally from God's status as a craftsman that he would want to use his craft for the good, it would take a defeating circumstance such as envy to prevent him from so exercising his craft. Or as one might say: only an actively preventing factor like envy could stop a craftsman, and particularly one so well qualified as God, from exercising his skill for the good. God's goodness is then more a guarantee that he will act properly as a craftsman than it is an extra factor explaining his motivation to do so.[21]

Timaeus may have a similar point in mind when the Demiurge explains in T1 why his creation won't be dissolved:

> what was created by me cannot be dissolved without my consent. Anything bonded together can of course be dissolved, though only an evil will would consent to dissolve anything whose composition and state were good. Therefore, since you have been created, you are not entirely immortal and indissoluble; but you will never be dissolved or taste death, as you will find my will a stronger and more sovereign bond than those with which you were bound at your birth.

The question addressed in these lines is, to be clear, not the same as the question why God made the world. Rather the question here is why God wouldn't allow his creation to be dissolved. This question, as we saw, is premised on the fact that the lesser gods qua created are not strictly or necessarily immortal. However, as artefacts of the Demiurge they are well put together and so have the potential to persist unless interfered with.[22] Again the point is made negatively: it would be an exercise of an evil will to dissolve the beautiful product, just as earlier it would have been an act of

---

understanding of the ends of other *technai*. Given both his divine status and the range of crafts employed by the Demiurge it is in any case reasonable to ascribe the highest craft to him. On this suggestion more below.

[21] Cf. here Barney (Chapter 3) on the motivational commitments that being a craftsman entails.

[22] Admittedly, it is not clear from these lines whether God's good will just ensures that he doesn't actively dissolve his own work, or whether it also means that he will, more positively, step in to maintain his own work given its fundamental goodness. On the second reading the words 'you will find my will a stronger and more sovereign bond than those with which you were bound at your birth' may seem appropriate in the following way: It is relevant that God's will is stronger than the bonds exactly because those bonds may not themselves be sufficient to ensure continued life. On the first reading, the greater strength of God's will might look like a threat: exactly because of its strength he could dissolve the bonds if he wanted to (but he won't because he is good). But, less menacingly, one might also take him, on the first reading, simply to emphasise the strength of his good will by saying that it is still (*eti*) greater than the bonds by which the lesser gods were bound, great as we have seen *those bonds* to be.

envy not to have made it in the first place. Indeed, it is tempting to identify the evil will imagined here with the envy mentioned earlier. However this may be, God's good will serves as a guarantee of the continued existence of the cosmos rather than as a positive factor in actively maintaining it. No craftsman other than one who also happened to be a bad person would wreck an artefact that had been beautifully made and was still in fine condition. A craftsman normally respects and cares about craftworks. In letting the lesser gods live perpetually, the Demiurge behaves as any proper craftsman would.

What these considerations show is that there is a sort of goodness that characterises God, his good will, or his absence of envy, which is not so much an added explanatory factor but an assurance that God's craftsmanship was properly realised. But then we need to turn to God's craftsmanship again to explain why it could be realised in the manner only of creating immortal beings, and not also mortal ones.

V   God As a Craftsman, Again

Though we have added to the craftsman model, we have not moved away from it by describing the Demiurge either as a father or in attributing to him good will. So when we turn to the following lines in T1 there is reason to think that we still need to think of what God would or could do as a craftsman: 'if these [sc. the mortal creatures] were created and given life by me, they would be equal to gods'. The point would still be that a craftsman of his sort could not make living beings that were less than gods, though the lesser gods could. But why that should be remains to be seen.

When Timaeus said at the beginning of his account that the maker of the world was the best of causes (29a6) or that it was just (*themis*) for the best only to do the finest (30a6–7), we may take him to refer to what the best cause in the sense of the best *craftsman* would do. The best craftsman possesses the best craft, which is the craft to produce the best. If the best is the divine, then it is right for this craftsman only to produce the divine. This reading depends on taking craftsmen to be the only causes under consideration, but this appears already to have been assumed from the outset of Timaeus' account (28a6–b2) where the only possible causes of the world are two kinds of craftsman. The restriction on what God can create comes then from the craft he possesses as the best craftsman.

This argument seems abstract and rather a priori, and leaves us wondering what this craft is that the Demiurge possesses. Thankfully, there is a more specific notion of God's craft that connects specifically with our text

T1. Notice how Timaeus in T1 describes the creation of the lesser gods in terms of being 'bound together' (*deomai*) and their being dissolved in terms of being 'dissolved' or 'untied' (*luomai*). The exercise of a special skill in combining and dissolving can reasonably be seen as the most general description of God's creative activity in the *Timaeus*.[23] Throughout the creation, God divides and mixes. We see this in the creation of the world soul whose different elements were fitted and bound together,[24] and before that, in formation of the world body. Here the Demiurge bound the four elements together by proportion, the strongest of all bonds:

> T3 So for these reasons and from these four constituents the body of the world was created to be at unity through proportion; and from these the body acquired friendship, so that having once come together in unity with itself, it is indissoluble by any but him who bound it together. (32c)

T1 clearly refers back to the thought in T3 that something bound together in the manner of the world body is dissoluble only by God himself. But T3 gives us the reason: this sort of geometrical proportion is a bond of the sort that will otherwise last. As F. Cornford argued, it is the same kind of geometrical proportion that is involved in the formation of the world soul.[25] So both in body and soul, the gods are formed by a bond that is indissoluble because of its peculiar geometrical character.

When we ask why God is not able to create something mortal, the answer would seem to lie in the sort of craft or skill he has: it is the ability to bind elements together proportionally so that they form an unbreakable unity. It must be this power that the Demiurge refers to when in T1 he bids the lesser gods to 'turn your hands, as is natural to you, to the crafting [*dēmiourgia*] of living things, imitating my power when I created you' (41c4–5).

The Demiurge's power does not imply having the power to create something mortal. Describing him as the 'best of all causes' and the producer *only* of the finest would suggest rather that his power is limited to immortal beings. But, independently, it is also reasonable to say that the craft that is the power to produce the finest products isn't also exercised in the production of lower quality products. One case where the same craft *is* involved in producing lower quality products would be where, since, as

---

[23] For the thought that God has as special knowledge about combining and dissolving, cf. also *Tim.* 68d. For a discussion of the range of arts that the Demiurge employs, see Zedda 2000.
[24] 35a8: *sunarmottôn*; 37a4: *sundetheisa*.   [25] Cornford 1937: 68–69.

Aristotle says, a craft allows you to produce two opposites,[26] the craftsman produces the worse of the two, a doctor killing rather than curing, a cook spoiling the broth. But these are cases where the worse opposite is to be understood as the privation of the first. But mortal life is not simply the privation of immortal life: it is an imitation and likeness of immortal being.

There are clearly also cases where we think that there is a distinct craft related to producing another product, which happens to be of a lower quality. This would be the case where we see the product not just as an inferior version of the higher product but as a kind of product in its own right. So a hot dog may be inferior to *cailles en sarcophage*, but it doesn't follow that the art of making *cailles en sarcophage* allows you to make a good hot dog. The case of the Demiurge's craft would seem to be like that: his craft is related to the product of immortal living beings, while the lesser gods are assigned the crafting of mortal living beings, and these, as we were told are *distinct* kinds, both contained in the complete kind of living being (T1, cf. 30c–d).

Recall the notion of distinctness of powers from *Republic* V: powers are distinct if and only if they are set over against distinct objects and produce different things.[27] On this criterion, the Demiurge's and the lesser gods' crafts are clearly distinct powers. An immortal creature is a different kind from the various kinds of mortal creature. We do not arrive at an understanding of the mortal creatures simply by negation of the immortal. Nor is the similarity between the immortal and the mortal creatures such that we can simply derive the features of the mortal from our knowledge of the immortal, as we shall see. It makes sense therefore to see distinct crafts as involved in the production of the two kinds. The Technodicy arises, we might say, from the restriction of the Demiurge's craft to the production of immortal creatures. His limitation is primarily a practical-cognitive one. Mortal creatures are beyond the field of his expertise.

It is common in Plato and Aristotle to think of the arts as forming a hierarchy.[28] At the top presides an architectonic craftsman, giving instructions to the lower crafts about how and when to execute their crafts. The architectonic craftsman clearly has a general understanding of the ends and uses of the lower crafts. But his craft doesn't include theirs: he couldn't do *their* job.[29] One may similarly compare the Demiurge to an architect who

---

[26] On the notion of *technē* as a two-way capacity, see further Nawar (Chapter 2) in this volume.
[27] Cf. *Tim.* 51c–e, which seems to rely on this criterion. See also Barney (Chapter 3) in this volume on the proper object of *technē*.
[28] See Plato, *Plt.* 260a; Aristotle, *Metaph.* I.1, *EN* I.1; and Barney (Chapter 3) in this volume.
[29] Cf. *Plt.* 305c–d.

knows what is required to build a house, who may also himself be able to build the structure and the foundation, but lacks certain technical skills in, say, plumbing, plastering or carpentry to complete the house, and therefore needs the assistance of lesser craftsmen. It is of a piece with such a hierarchical view of the arts to think that the Demiurge is not able to execute all the tasks of the creation.

To sum up the argument of this section. The problem faced by the Demiurge was a Technodicy after all, rather than a Theodicy. It was the problem of how a good craftsman could make a world containing less than perfect things rather than how a craftsman who is also good could do so. God's goodness was primarily referred to as a way of ensuring that the craftsman acted properly as a craftsman, rather than as a distinct motivating factor, and it was the limitations of God's craft that prevented him from creating mortal creatures, even though their presence made the cosmos as a whole better. But as the problem arises from the limitations of the Demiurge's craft, so the answer to the problem seemed to lie in positing another limited craft, that of the lesser gods, which is such as to create mortal creatures. What exactly this craft looks like is our next subject.

VI   The Craft of the Lesser Gods

When the Demiurge in T1 bade the lesser gods imitate his own power, the point was not that they should exercise the same power in a similar but lesser way, but that they should exercise a different power that resembles his. So what are the points of community and difference between the powers of these two crafts?

One shared feature must be looking to an eternal, formal model. The Demiurge reminds us (41b7–8) that 'there are three kinds of mortal creature yet uncreated, and unless they are created the world will be incomplete'. This is clearly a reference back to 30c where Timaeus said that the Demiurge sought to make the universe complete by looking to a model that contained intelligible animals of all kinds. The state of play now is that, looking to the model, the Demiurge has created one of these kinds, that is, the lesser gods themselves, and they, the lesser gods, are now to make the remaining kinds. If they didn't do so by also looking to the eternal model, then, given what Timaeus said earlier about craftsmen in general (28a–b), their product would not be beautiful, the cosmos would not be beautiful and they would not be working as proper craftsmen.

> shape the part of the marrow (the ploughland, as it were) that was to contain the divine seed and called it 'the brain', indicating that when each creature was completed the vessel containing the brain should be the head. The rest of the marrow that was to contain the mortal parts of the soul he divided into long, cylindrical sections, called by the general name 'marrow', to which the whole soul was bound, as if to anchors. And around brain and marrow, for which he first constructed a bony protective covering, he went on to frame our whole body. (73c–d)

Recall that the mortal part of the soul contains the various irrational affections that Timaeus figures as linear motions. They contrast geometrically with the circular revolutions of the immortal rational soul (cf. 43a–e). But the marrow is constructed to accommodate both: a spherical part in the head, which is continuous with the elongated cylindrical sections that extend down along the spine.[31] The result is an integrated psycho-somatic system with reason set apart in the head, on the 'acropolis', but connected and integrated with the rest of the soul through a single marrow.[32] One might say then that the life principle of a mortal being is contained in the marrow as a whole: immortal and mortal together.

Setting aside the details, what is of interest here is the way the lesser gods[33] have not copied the Demiurge, but *extrapolated* on the basis of his example: just as he made the world spherical to accommodate its rational soul, so the lesser gods made the head spherical to house its motions, but also the rest of the body elongated to accommodate the characteristically linear motions of the irrational soul. The principle here is that of geometrical suitability: it is this thought that the lesser gods adopt and extend from the Demiurge's paradigm. Imitating the Demiurge's creation is then not a matter of copying his work but of understanding the rationale underlying it and extending it in a manner suitable to the mortal product.

The same reasoning applies to another of the lesser gods' tasks: that of creating the remaining animals, the air, land and water creatures required to make the cosmos complete. In T1 the Demiurge told the lesser gods:

> it remains for you to weave mortal and immortal together and create living creatures. Bring them to birth, give them food and growth, and when they perish receive them again.

---

[31] For this interpretation, see Johansen 2004: 150–52.
[32] The integration through the marrow is illustrated again in the account of the emission of the seed (91a–b).
[33] The singular 'god' (*theos*) should not detain us: it is the job of the lesser gods, not the Demiurge, to create the human body, one god or other happens to do the job. The singular may also be used for the collective, 'all gods', or the generic, 'deity', cf. van Riel 2013: 37–38.

The brief is to create animals (*zôia*), not just human beings. It might come as a surprise, then, that the entire account of the mortal body up until the final pages apparently concerns the human body only. The creation of the non-human animals is only sketched at the very end of the work in the context of a reincarnation story (91d–92c). And here the account does not take the form of an account of the different parts of the various animal bodies, but simply a brief reference to the features by which the soul in question is punished. The main thought is that the soul is reincarnated in a body suited to the soul's particular deformation. The sort of body a soul acquires is then entirely dependent on the sort of intellectual shape it is in, with 'shape' taken quite literally. The rational soul originally moved in perfect circles but was upon embodiment twisted out of shape by the linear impulses affecting it from without (43c–e). Our mission in life is to re-establish those circular motions in our heads to the extent possible; failure to do so will lead to reincarnation in a body that reflects the manner and degree to which we have allowed our souls to lose shape. So Timaeus says that the skull of the animal accommodates the particular way the soul's rational circles have been deformed:

> T7 Wild land animals have come from men who made no use of philosophy and never in any way considered the nature of the heavens because they had ceased to use the circles in the head and followed the leadership of the parts of the soul in the breast. Because of these practices their fore-limbs and heads were drawn by natural affinity to the earth, and their fore-limbs supported on it, <u>while their skulls were elongated into various shapes according to the particular way in which each man's circles had been crushed through lack of use</u>. (91e–92a, my underlining)

We have then a further application of the principle of embodiment through geometrical appropriateness,[34] the principle which, as we saw, the lesser gods learnt from the Demiurge and applied in the first instance to the human head. When Timaeus concludes in the lines following T7 that 'these are the principles on which living creatures change and have always changed into each other', it is this principle he is primarily referring to. For it is this principle that explains how and why a soul is removed to the body of a particular kind of animal.

---

[34] For a discussion of the notion of geometrical appropriateness in the *Timaeus* and how it differs from Aristotle's hylomorphism, see Johansen 2016.

VII The Technodicy of the Lesser Gods

We have seen how the Demiurge, given his craft, could not create mortal beings. He left this task to the created gods, who could do so, as created and so in principle mortal. We have also seen how the lesser gods created man in imitation of the Demiurge's creation, and how the other animals arose from man.

How far down, as it were, does the lesser gods' craft reach? The lesser gods are never called 'the fathers' of human beings, though the language of creating, nurturing and receiving the mortal beings (41d) calls to mind parenthood (including motherhood?).[35] One might suspect that the focus on the creation of man again reflects the lower limit of what gods can do. Just as the Demiurge can only create immortal creatures, that is, gods, so the lesser gods too are limited to creating the best mortal beings in so far as they are good, that is, human beings. As craftsmen, they are constrained to produce the best possible product within their range.

The Demiurge said in T1 that the lesser gods

> were to fashion mortal bodies and, for the rest, to devise the necessary additions to the human soul and their consequences, and so far as they could control and guide the mortal creature for the best, except, that is, insofar as it because a cause of evil to itself. (42d–e, my underlining)

The lesser gods will guide mortal creatures for the best and will not be responsible for the evils that befall them. When a soul becomes reincarnated as a lower animal, it is clearly then the result of the mortal creature's own efforts or lack thereof. It is man who is himself responsible for the creation of the other animals.

We might still say that the lesser gods create the other living beings by creating man. Also, the lesser gods create the animal bodies, as we have seen, that match the souls that have emerged from human lives, and they anticipate that some humans will be embodied as lower animals. The lesser gods facilitate the incarnation of souls in suitable animal bodies, bodies that, as the case of the fangs show (76d–e), will help these animals lead their characteristic, less rational lives, but they do not directly cause any individual human being to become reincarnated as a lower animal. This could only mean making some souls worse,[36] since the only factor that

---

[35] Cf. 'receive'(*dexesthe*) with 50d3: 'Indeed we should liken the recipient (*to men dekhomenon*) to the mother.'

[36] There is no suggestion that being reborn as a lower animal provides *correctional* punishment and so in the longer run makes the soul better.

determines whether a soul is reincarnated as an animal is the state of their soul. So, for the lower gods to cause a human soul to be reborn as a lower animal would require that they made a human soul worse. Nor, on the other hand, is there any indication that the lesser gods give the lower animals a leg up to help them return to a more rational state. All of these demotions and promotions are the direct result of the soul's own efforts.

The lesser gods' position is a delicate one. It is one familiar also from *Laws* X, mutatis mutandis,[37] a text we looked at earlier in connection with holism. The Athenian Stranger continues his argument by explaining how god's world order ensures that the virtuous are rewarded and the vicious punished:

> T8 since a soul is allied with different bodies at different times, and perpetually undergoes all sorts of changes, either self-posed or produced by some other soul, the divine checkers-player has nothing else to do except promote a soul with a promising character to a better situation, and relegate one that is deteriorating to an inferior, as is appropriate in each case, so that they all meet the fate they deserve .... With this grand purpose in view he has worked out what sort of position, in what regions, should be assigned to a soul to match its changes of character but he left it to the individual's acts of will to determine the direction of these changes. (903d–4c, trans. T. Saunders)

Here in the *Laws* the talk is of souls' moving location in the cosmos according to their just deserts, rather than, as in the *Timaeus*, their assuming various animal bodies. However, the fundamental thought seems the same in the two works. Humans are themselves responsible for the consequences of their actions. The role of God is limited: applying the rules of the game, he responds to the individual's acts by moving him to the appropriate place, but it is the individual who determines where he ends up. The moves on the checkerboard are in a sense made by the pieces themselves, the gods ensure that the rules are enforced.[38]

---

[37] The Athenian stranger operates with one cosmic god, not the Demiurge, nor the plurality of lesser gods, yet as immanent in the cosmos his world soul is comparable to the lesser gods. The world soul of the *Laws* was commonly identified with the Demiurge of the *Timaeus* by Plato's successors, see Dillon 2003.

[38] Plotinus expresses a similar thought using the image of actors whose characters determine the roles they play in a drama: 'Thus, every man has his place, a place that fits the good man, a place that fits the bad: each within the two orders of them makes his way, naturally, reasonably, to the place, good or bad, that suits him, and takes the position he has made his own. There he talks and acts, in blasphemy and crime or in all goodness: for the actors bring to this play what they were before it was ever staged.' (*Enn.* III.2.17, trans. S. Mackenna and B. S. Page).

We can see this view as a response to the same sort of worry that made the Demiurge step back from creating man. The lesser gods cannot take direct creative responsibility for outcomes that, taken individually, are less than ideal, even if these outcomes work collectively for the greater good of the whole. They are responsible instead for the mechanism that ensures that individual bad outcomes lead to the greater good of the whole: that by which individual souls are reallocated to other animals. It is this mechanism that ensures that the cosmos contains all the different living species. Again, this is a proper exercise of craft: ensuring given the materials available the greater good of the whole product.[39]

Given the hierarchy of crafts involved in the generation of the cosmos, one might wonder if there is a craft by which the humans themselves produce the lower animals. There are indications in the *Timaeus*, though no explicit reference, that there is a craft of living *well*. A Stoic reader, for example, might well find inspiration in passages such as 47b–d and 88b–89d, where Timaeus describes the various motions, psychic and somatic, that one should cultivate to become a well-formed human being. Knowing how to order oneself clearly involves imitating the cosmic soul and body. However, if this is a human craft of living, it is also a craft meant to ensure no less than a human life, and by preference, a better astral life; it is most definitely not a craft meant to ensure one's own passage to a lower animal. There is then no craft of producing lower animals, other than the one possessed by the lesser gods. Here we seem to have arrived at bedrock as far as craft is concerned: both the Demiurge and the lesser gods make something better out of the materials they find. That is what craft does. But to make oneself worse, to order the materials and potentials one is given into something worse, less ordered or less rational, can be the proper work of no craft, only ignorance.

---

[39] Another way to put the point is in terms of necessity: the disorderly motions of irrational souls are the product of necessity, not design. When using souls deformed by these motions to form non-human animals, the lesser gods are making the best possible use of this fait accompli. Thereby the irrational souls might be seen as a contributory cause (*sunaition*) of the greater cause (*aitia*) of an ordered cosmos (46d–e).

CHAPTER 5

Aristotle on Productive Understanding and Completeness

Ursula Coope

In *Metaphysics* IX.2, Aristotle describes craft (*technê*) as a special kind of understanding (*epistêmê*): productive understanding.[1] Elsewhere, he classes certain particular crafts as forms of understanding (medicine and gymnastics at *Metaph.* XI.7, 1063b36–64a1, the craft of building at *Metaph.* VI.2, 1026b4–10). My topic in this chapter is this notion of productive understanding. Aristotle himself sometimes simply identifies understanding (*epistêmê*) with theoretical understanding.[2] In what follows, I shall ask in what sense productive understanding is a genuine kind of understanding, and how exactly it differs from the kind of understanding that is theoretical.[3]

I shall argue that both kinds of understanding essentially involve grasping explanations, but that they differ in the following way. Someone who fully possesses a certain theoretical science (and hence, has full theoretical understanding within a certain domain) has explanations for everything

---

[1] I take the '*kai*' at IX.2.1046b3 to be epexegetic: 'all crafts, that is all productive forms of understanding, are powers' (following Ross 1924, ad loc). One reason for taking the '*kai*' in this way is that the subsequent argument seems to depend on identifying *technê* with productive understanding. Aristotle justifies the claim that *technê* is of opposites by arguing that productive understanding is of opposites. However, as we shall see below (Section III), there are some grounds for doubting whether a *technê* can be strictly identical with productive understanding. Arguably, the ability of the craftsman, qua craftsman, also includes a specific kind of perceptual ability: an ability he needs if he is to apply his productive understanding to particular circumstances and hence to act successfully on the basis that understanding.

[2] For example, at *EN* VI.3.

[3] There are several passages in which Aristotle divides *epistêmê* into three kinds: theoretical, practical and productive (*Metaph.* VI.2.1026b2ff, VI.1, 1026a21, *Metaph.*1064a10ff – where the *epistêmê* of nature is contrasted with productive and practical kinds of *epistêmê*, *Top.* 145a16 and 157a10–11.) At *Metaph.* I.1, Aristotle says that theoretical *epistêmê* is closer to being a kind of wisdom than is productive *epistêmê*. In this chapter, I focus on the differences between theoretical and productive understanding. I leave aside the more difficult, though obviously interesting, question of the relation between theoretical and practical understanding, though I hope that my discussion here will serve as a useful preliminary to tackling that further question.

within the scope of that science.[4] There is, by contrast, nothing analogous that would count as fully possessing a certain productive science: the content of productive understanding is indefinitely extendable. I shall use the label 'completeness' to characterise this difference: a science is potentially *complete* (as I am using the term) if and only if *having explanations for everything that is explicable within its scope* is in principle possible. Thus, I shall be arguing that theoretical science is in this sense potentially complete, whereas productive science is not. A consequence of this is that productive understanding requires a special kind of creativity. The ability to work out new explanations is essential to productive understanding in a way that it is not essential to theoretical understanding. In what follows, I first look at the ways in which Aristotle's account of productive understanding is similar to his account of theoretical understanding, and then look at the crucial respect in which the two kinds of understanding differ from each other.

I Explanations in Theoretical and Productive Science

Understanding, whether theoretical or productive, involves grasping explanations. Aristotle says that craft is like theoretical understanding in that it involves knowing 'the why and the cause' (*to dioti kai tên aitian*, Metaph. I.1 918a30). This concern with explanations is a feature of any kind of understanding:

> Every science [*epistêmê*] seeks certain principles and causes for each of its objects – e.g. medicine and gymnastics and each of the other sciences, whether productive or mathematical. For each of these marks off a certain class of things for itself and concerns itself with this. (*Metaph.* XI.7 1064a1ff)

As Aristotle says in this passage, a science will concern itself with explanations *within a certain specified domain*.

Theoretical understanding is exercised in actively thinking explanations. Its goal is contemplation. For instance, each of astronomy, physics and geometry aims at 'knowing and contemplating the nature of the things' within its domain. Productive understanding is exercised in acts of

---

[4] Aristotle uses the same word, '*epistêmê*', both for the content understood (a branch of theoretical or productive science, e.g., the organised body of knowledge that makes up the science of geometry or of medicine) and also for the cognitive state of the person who has that understanding. In what follows, I shall use the English word 'science', where what is meant is clearly the content understood and 'understanding' where what is meant is the cognitive state of the person who grasps that content in the right way.

production that are guided by the grasp of explanations. Its goal is a certain product. For instance, health is the goal of medical understanding, good governance of political understanding.[5]

Theoretical explanations take the form of demonstrations. A demonstration is a kind of syllogism in which the premises are explanatory of the conclusion. All the theorems that fall within the scope of a given science can be derived by demonstration from the first principles of that science, these first principles being themselves indemonstrable.[6] Aristotle claims that the principles of a theoretical science must be finite in number, since otherwise the science as a whole would be unknowable. This is the reason he gives in *Physics* I.4 for rejecting Anaxagoras' view that there are infinitely many first principles. The infinite is unknowable, so if there were infinitely many first principles, it would be 'impossible to know the things that are from them'.[7] Aristotle's syllogistic implies that if the first principles are finite, then only finitely many theorems can be deduced from them.[8] Thus, within any science there will be finitely many first principles and also finitely many demonstrations and demonstrated theorems. In other words, the fact that there are only finitely many principles implies that the theoretical science as a whole is finite: it is in principle possible to have demonstrative understanding of *all* the theorems of a given theoretical science.

The explanations that guide exercises of productive understanding are different in structure.[9] Aristotle says that in a productive science, the starting point is the goal to be achieved. This goal plays a role that is analogous to the role of a hypothesis in a theoretical science:

---

[5] *EE* I.5 1216b11–19.
[6] Aristotle allows that there is also an extended sense of 'science' in which one science can be subordinate to another. For instance, the science of optics falls under that of geometry. In such cases, the explanations are given by the higher science (*Post An* I.13 78b35ff).
[7] *Ph.* I.4, 187b10–11. See also *DC* 302b10ff on figures.
[8] As Smith 2009: 54 emphasises, this is a way in which the syllogistic differs from modern propositional logic: in modern logic 'if we start with just a single proposition p, its logical consequences include not only all the infinitely many tautologies, but also all the infinitely many propositions equivalent to it: p & p, p & (q v -q), p v p etc'.
[9] For a contrasting view of the relation between the explanations of theoretical science and the explanations that constitute the content of productive understanding, see Bolton's discussion of *Metaphysics* I.1 (Chapter 6). Of course, even on my interpretation, it will often in fact turn out that having the relevant productive explanations will only be possible for someone who also has a certain amount of theoretical understanding. For instance, it may turn out that a certain level of understanding of the science of trees is needed in order to be a good gardener. My claim is only that the explanations that directly guide what the craftsman does are explanations that are differently structured from the explanations that are grasped as part of a theoretical science. That is compatible with the view that, in certain cases, a level of theoretical understanding is required in order to possess the relevant productive explanations.

as in the theoretical sciences the hypotheses are the starting points, so in the productive the end is the starting point and hypothesis. Since this body is to be made healthy, it is necessary for this thing to be if that is to come about, just as there [in geometry], if the angles of the triangle are equal to two right angles, necessarily this is the case. (*EE* III.1227b28ff)[10]

In this passage, Aristotle is comparing the kind of demonstrative syllogism that is grasped by a geometrician to the productive syllogism that might be grasped by a doctor attempting to cure someone. This suggests that there is an analogy between demonstrations in theoretical science and productive explanations in productive science. The geometrician grasps certain first principles (e.g., that the angles of the triangle are equal to two right angles) and demonstrates certain theorems from these first principles. In grasping these demonstrations, he grasps why the theorems hold. The first principle grasped by the doctor is the goal to be achieved (e.g., that health is to be brought about in this body). The doctor reasons about what should be done in the light of this first principle. In so doing, she arrives at a productive explanation of why such and such should be done.

How exactly is the productive explanation the doctor arrives at *explanatory*? In theoretical demonstrations, the explanatory work is done by the middle term.[11] For example, 'sap-solidifiers' is the middle term in the demonstrative syllogism: 'all broad-leaved trees are sap-solidifiers, all sap-solidifiers lose their leaves, so all broad-leaved trees lose their leaves'. This shows that the explanation of why broad-leaved trees shed their leaves is that they are sap-solidifiers.[12] Is there anything analogous to this in the case of productive explanation?

---

[10] My discussion here and in what follows is especially indebted to Moss 2014. The parallel between theoretical and practical/productive explanation is also helpfully discussed in Allen 2015. Moss 2014: 214 n. 41 suggests that Aristotle's point would have been clearer had he used as his example of a theoretical first principle a claim about the essence of triangles (since elsewhere, he is quite clear that 'the angles of a triangle add up to two right angles' is itself demonstrable, rather than an ultimate first principle, *Metaph*. V. 30 1025a30–34; *Pr An*, I.35 48a36–37). However, there is perhaps a reason for Aristotle not to use an ultimate first principle as his example here. The first principles of a *technē* are not, strictly, analogous to *indemonstrable* first principles within a theoretical science. Rather, they are first principles that are explicable, but not explicable *within the technē*. There is an explanation of why this patient should be made healthy, but knowing that explanation is no part of the doctor's craft. Thus, for Aristotle's purpose here (of comparing theoretical and productive understanding), a better example of a theoretical hypothesis would have been something that is assumed, and hence not demonstrated, within a subordinate theoretical science, but that might be demonstrated within a higher science. (For Aristotle's account of subordinate theoretical sciences, see *Post An* I.13.)

[11] See *Post An* II.2 (90a6–7) and II.11.   [12] For the example, see *Post An* II.16–17.

Consider the following chain of productive reasoning:

> Starting point or goal: To make a chilled patient healthy.
> The way to make a chilled patient healthy is to heat her.
> The way to heat the patient is to rub her.
> CONCLUSION: The way to make a chilled patient healthy is to rub her.

We can think of this as analogous to a demonstrative explanation. The middle term is 'heating', and this connects in an explanatory way the two terms mentioned in the conclusion ('producing health in a chilled patient' and 'rubbing'). The doctor who knows this productive explanation knows why rubbing is the way to make a chilled patient healthy. The explanation is that rubbing her is a good way of heating her and heating her is a good way of making her healthy. Thus, the doctor who knows the whole productive explanation knows the explanation that connects *rubbing* to *producing health*, just as the natural scientist who knows the demonstrative syllogism about trees knows the explanation that connects *being a broad-leaved* tree and *losing leaves*.[13]

Thus, productive explanations are in certain respects analogous to the demonstrative explanations of theoretical science. Nevertheless, we can already see that there are two important differences between theoretical and productive explanations. First, the conclusion of a productive explanation is, in a certain sense, essentially comparative. If I know that rubbing is generally a good way to produce health in a chilled patient, then I know that rubbing is good *in comparison to other possible ways of producing health in chilled patients*. I either know that rubbing is the best possible method of producing health in such patients, or at least that it is among the better methods. This already suggests that productive understanding is *in a certain sense* unlimited in its range: grasping a single productive explanation requires knowing indefinitely many facts about other things not mentioned in the explanation (e.g., about alternative possible methods of producing health). By contrast, the conclusion of a theoretical demonstration is not, in the same way, essentially comparative.

Second, the conclusion of a demonstration, unlike the conclusion of a productive explanation, is entailed by its premises. Of course, Aristotle

---

[13] This suggestion is confirmed by the way in which Aristotle applies his theory to final cause explanations in *Post An* II.11 94b12–21: the way to make yourself healthy is to walk after dinner, because walking after dinner makes the food not remain at the mouth of the stomach, and this produces health. (The explanatory middle term is *the food not remaining at the mouth of the stomach*.) An experienced person might know that the way to keep yourself healthy is to walk after dinner without knowing the reason why this is so (that is, without knowing the relevant middle term), and hence without having the relevant craft knowledge.

thinks that it is because the craftsperson grasps the goal that she is able to come up with productive explanations, just as it is because the theoretical scientist grasps the principles of the science that she is able to come up with demonstrations.[14] But Aristotle never suggests that the steps in a productive explanation are *logically entailed by* the first principles of the craft, as the steps in a chain of demonstrations are entailed by the first principles of the relevant theoretical science. This difference bears on our question about completeness. As we saw earlier, Aristotelian syllogistic ensures the finitude of theoretical science: if there are finitely many first principles, then only finitely many theorems can be deduced from them. Since productive explanations are not constrained in the same way by Aristotelian logic, there is no analogous reason to insist that productive understanding must be finite (that is, that there must be finitely many explanations within the scope of any given productive science).

However, although Aristotle does not have this formal reason for insisting on the finitude of productive understanding, in spelling out his account of productive understanding, he is clearly concerned to limit its scope. As we shall see, he claims that productive understanding is limited in three key ways, each corresponding to a limitation on the scope of theoretical understanding. If we can get clearer about these ways in which productive and theoretical understanding are analogous, this will help to bring into focus the important respects in which they differ.

II Limitations on Scope: Productive and Theoretical Understanding

I shall argue that there are three limitations on the scope of theoretical understanding, each of which has a parallel in a limitation on the scope of productive understanding. The first is that understanding is of general truths. The second is that there is no understanding of the accidental. And the third is that chains of explanation are finite.

II.A   Understanding Is of General Truths

Aristotle says that 'every science [*epistêmê*] is of what holds either always or for the most part' (*Metaph.* VI. 1027a20–21). His account of theoretical understanding places constraints on what can count as a theorem of a

---

[14] It is because the doctor has a full grasp of what health is that she is able to explain how to cure; it is because the housebuilder has a grasp of what a house is that she is able to explain how to build.

science (and hence, what can be explained within a science). A theorem must be the kind of thing that can be the conclusion of a demonstration. Aristotle sometimes says that only necessary truths can be demonstrated and hence only such truths can be the theorems of a science: 'if something is understood demonstratively, it must hold from necessity'.[15] However, this constraint on demonstration would rule out the possibility of natural science. A complete natural science could not consist simply of explanations of necessary truths about the things in its domain: the behaviour of natural things is too irregular to be explained in this way. To accommodate the possibility of natural science, Aristotle in some texts allows that there can be demonstrations, and hence scientific knowledge, of what holds for the most part (i.e., as a rule, *hôs epi to polu*).[16]

Our understanding of general truths gives us a *kind* of derivative understanding of the infinitely many particulars to which they apply (though this derivative, applied kind of understanding does not fall within the scope of theoretical understanding itself). For instance, if I understand on the basis of demonstration why vines as a rule lose their leaves in autumn, then provided that this particular vine lost its leaves in virtue of a natural causal regularity, I thereby understand why *it* lost its leaves in autumn. Similarly, if I understand why all triangles have angles adding up to two right angles, then I thereby also understand why any particular perceptible triangle has angles adding up to two right angles.[17]

Elsewhere, Aristotle says that productive understanding too is of general truths. In the *Posterior Analytics*, he gives an example from medicine: 'the doctor does not say what is healthy in the case of some individual eye, but either in the case of every eye, or determining some species of eye' (*Post An* 97b25–28). In the *Rhetoric* he appeals to his view that the particular is 'not knowable' in support of his claim that craft is, strictly speaking, of the universal:

---

[15] *Post An* I.6 75a12–13. See also *EN* VI.3.1139b19–21 for the claim that *epistêmê* can only be of necessary truths.
[16] For instance, at *Post An* I.30 87b21–23, he says that demonstrations are of either what happens of necessity or what happens as a rule, since 'every syllogism is either through necessary premises or those that hold as a rule'. If the relevant syllogisms are to be valid, then holding 'as a rule' (*hôs epi to polu*) here must mean holding in virtue of some natural causal regularity, not merely something that holds as a matter of statistical frequency (although Aristotle is elsewhere prepared to use the expression '*hôs epi to polu*' for mere statistical regularity). For some discussion of this point, see Henry 2015: 179–85.
[17] This point is nicely made in a paper by Callard (unpublished). At *Pr An* II.21 67a12–16, Aristotle implies that someone who knows that every triangle contains angles equal to two right angles, in a sense already knows (universally) of any particular triangle, that it contains angles equal to two right angles.

> No craft [*technê*] looks to the particular [*to kath' hekaston*]. For instance, medicine does not look to what is healthy for Socrates or for Callias, but rather what is healthy for someone of this type, or people of these types: for this is a matter of skill [*entechnon*], but the particular is unlimited and not knowable [*apeiron kai ouk epistêton*]. Similarly, neither will rhetoric study what seems plausible [*endoxon*] to this or that particular person e.g. to Socrates or to Hippias, but rather what seems plausible to people of a certain type. (*Rhet.* I.2 1356b30–35)

Technical explanations might tell us why a certain type of treatment heals a certain kind of patient, or why a certain type of rhetorical technique is effective in persuading a certain type of listener; they do not refer to particular patients or particular listeners.

As with theoretical understanding, this leaves open the possibility of understanding *certain* facts about particulars, provided these facts are instances of explicable general truths. Just as my understanding of why vines as a rule lose their leaves gives me a kind of derivative understanding of why this vine lost its leaves, so also the doctor's understanding of why honey water should be given to patients with bilious fever enables her to have a kind of derivative understanding of why honey water should be given to *this* patient with bilious fever. Thus, Aristotle can still allow that a productive syllogism ends in a particular action (an action of treating *this* patient in *these* circumstances). His point is that the explanation of why this particular action is the right one for producing health must be general. What gets explained is, in the first instance, why an action *of this sort* will produce health; that this particular action is health-producing is just an instance of this more general explanandum.

II.B There Is No Understanding of the Accidental

Aristotle tells us that the accidental 'is not the concern of any science, whether practical, productive or theoretical' (*Metaph.* VI.2, 1026b2ff). It is relatively easy to see why the accidental is excluded from theoretical science. Something counts as accidental from the point of view of a natural science if it is not explained by the natures of the things that fall under that natural science. Since natural things do not always behave in accordance with their nature, there will be truths about particular natural things that are not instances of either universal or as-a-rule (*hôs epi to polu*) generalisations, and hence that cannot be explained by appeal to a demonstrative syllogism. Aristotle says that such truths fall outside the scope of natural science and are, in that sense, accidental. For example, the science of trees will not explain why this particular broad-leaved tree lost its leaves unnaturally in the spring rather than in the autumn. Of course, we might be able to tell a story about why the tree lost its leaves then: it was diseased, it was hit by lightning, some children came and picked all the leaves. But this kind of explanation is not a part of any natural science. Any particular tree will presumably have many such accidental features that are not explained by the science of trees.[18]

It is less clear what counts as being accidental to productive understanding. After all, productive understanding is not confined to explaining *how things are by nature* as natural scientific understanding is. In *Metaphysics* VI.2, Aristotle goes some way towards clarifying the relation of craft to the accidental. He says that there will be features of any particular craft-product that are accidental to its being a product of that craft. For example, the house that the builder produces may be pleasing to some people and unpleasing to others, but these features of the house are accidental to its being a product of the building craft. The building craft aims at making a house stable and weatherproof, and the builder should be able to explain how his actions further these aims, but the builder is not, as such, expected to know how to make the house pleasing to any particular group of people. For instance, it is not part of the craft of building to know what type of house will please stockbrokers.

Although Aristotle does not himself spell this out, it is plausible to suppose that there are also other ways of being accidental in relation to a craft. Many things can prevent even the right medical prescription from producing health: the patient may be struck by lightning before the treatment takes effect or the medicine may be stolen before the patient has a chance to take it. Presumably, it is not the job of the medical craft to guard against failures of this kind. Moreover, because of interference,[19] it can sometimes happen that though the patient recovers after treatment,

---

[18] Aristotle's point is not merely that such accidental facts about the tree are inexplicable *given our current state of knowledge*. Of course, *sometimes* what might appear to be an exception to an explanatory generalisation is in fact evidence that one has picked the wrong generalisation. For example, the fact that fir-trees keep their leaves shows that the relevant general *explanandum* should be *broad leaved trees lose their leaves in autumn*, rather than simply *trees lose their leaves in autumn*. Aristotle's view, however, is that there will be exceptions even to the maximally refined generalisations of a fully developed natural science. Particular natural things do not always behave in accordance with their natures, and hence there will be exceptions to any generalisations that describe the behaviour of natural things as the behaviour they engage in when acting in accord with their natures. Such exceptions will be accidental to the science: even a complete science will not include explanations of them.

[19] On whether the absence of interfering factors enters into the specification of the *technē*'s capacity, see also Nawar in this volume (Chapter 2).

the treatment is not the *cause* of the recovery. Perhaps the doctor gave the wrong medication, but something else intervened with the result that the patient recovered anyway. In this case, the medical craft does not explain the recovery: there is no general medical-craft-explanation of why giving the wrong medication results in recovery. Perhaps the doctor gave the right medication, but the patient accidentally took an antidote and then went on to recover without medical help. In this case too, the medical craft does not explain the recovery: though there *is* a general explanation that connects giving the right medication to recovery, what happens in this case (where the patient accidentally takes an antidote) is not an instance of that general explanation.

These are some respects in which Aristotelian productive understanding, like theoretical understanding, is not concerned with the accidental. Nevertheless, as we shall see, what counts as accidental to a craft is importantly different from what counts as accidental to natural science. In Section IV, I shall argue that, because of the way in which productive understanding is oriented towards particulars, productive understanding differs from natural science in being essentially concerned with certain types of exceptional circumstance. Something can be an exception to one of the generalisations explained by a branch of productive understanding without thereby being accidental to that branch of productive understanding.

II.C Finite Explanatory Chains

In his account of theoretical understanding, Aristotle emphasises that chains of demonstration are finite. They start from indemonstrable first principles[20] and they arrive, after finitely many steps, at a conclusion from which nothing further can be demonstrated (*Post An* I.19–22).[21] I shall

---

[20] Or, in the case of a subordinate science, principles that are indemonstrable *within that science*.
[21] This claim might seem to be threatened by the unlimited possibilities for classifying things into more and more specific types. One problem arises from the natural variations that Aristotle describes as differences of more and less. (For some discussion of how these phenomena relate to demonstrations, see Henry 2015: 184–85.) Suppose, for instance, we have a demonstration that explains why male dogs lift their leg to urinate when they develop appropriate strength. Aristotle says that this happens at around the age of six months, but that there is a range of natural variation (*HA* VI.20). If we need a separate demonstration for each *precise* time of developing strength, then there will be infinitely many demonstrations and infinitely many relevant subspecies (dogs that develop the appropriate strength in their fifth month, those that develop it in the first week of their fifth month, those that develop it on the first day of the first week of their fifth month and so on). To counter this, Aristotle needs to be able to allow that there are some levels of natural variation that fall below the level of detail that is explained by the relevant science. The science of dogs need

argue that some remarks Aristotle makes about the finitude of deliberation imply that productive explanations are also finite in length.

When we deliberate, we inquire into how to bring about some end; in doing so, we work out both how to act and also why acting in that way is a successful means to bringing about the end. Thus, deliberation is a way of coming up with productive explanations.[22] Aristotle makes two points about the finitude of deliberation. First, it is no part of a craft to deliberate about whether to produce the craft's end. For instance, the doctor (qua doctor) does not deliberate about whether to produce health (*EN* III.3 1112b13). Aristotle's point here is about the scope of the medical craft, not about the practice of actual doctors. As we have seen, he compares the end aimed at by a craft to the first principles of a theoretical science. Just as a science does not demonstrate its first principles, so also 'no craft asks questions about the end' (*EE* III.11 1227b27). A medical productive syllogism will explain how to produce health, but it will not go further and explain how health is itself a means to producing some further good.

Aristotle's second point about the finitude of deliberation concerns its limit in the other direction. In *Nicomachean Ethics* III.3, he says:

> So there will not be deliberation about particulars either, as e.g. about whether this is a loaf, or whether it has been cooked as it should; for these belong to the sphere of perception. And if a person deliberates at every point, he will go on *ad infinitum* [*ei de aei bouleusetai, eis apeiron hêxei*]. (1112b34–13a2, trans. based on Broadie and Rowe 2002)

Again, I think, this point must be about the scope of the craft, rather than just about the practice of actual deliberators. Aristotle is not merely saying that actual processes of deliberation eventually come to an end (when the

---

not explain why one dog develops the relevant strength an hour before another. That seems rather plausible. However, it is harder to see how Aristotle can justify ruling out infinite demonstrative chains in mathematics. Suppose that even numbers are a species of number and that the proper attributes of even numbers are demonstrated within arithmetic; it might seem that *numbers that are divisible by four* will be a further species of even number, with certain proper attributes of their own; and if so, then presumably *numbers that are divisible by eight* will be a further sub-species, and so on ad infinitum. (For this example, see Barnes 2003: 126–27.) This threatens to produce a potentially infinite chain of demonstrations. No finite chain would explain the proper attributes of all the sub-species: wherever the chain stopped, there would always be a further sub-species whose attributes would remain undemonstrated and hence unexplained. Aristotle needs to deny that all the kinds in the series *numbers divisible by four, numbers divisible by eight and so on* are genuine sub-species of the kind *even numbers*. But it is hard to see how a complete mathematical science could avoid postulating infinitely many kinds (of numbers in the case of arithmetic, or of figures in the case of geometry). Aristotle himself never attempts to explain in detail how this might work.

[22] Allen 2015: 53 emphasises that deliberation culminates in, and is aimed at, the grasp of a whole syllogism (not merely the grasp of the conclusion of a syllogism).

deliberator stops deliberating and starts acting). His claim is that deliberation must eventually come to an end because beyond a certain point there are no further explanatory accounts to be grasped. For example, suppose the final explanation in a chain is 'the way to finish the bread-making process is to take the loaf out of the oven when it has been cooked just enough'. The baker is guided by his knowledge of this explanatory chain, but his ability to act on this knowledge by taking out the loaf at the right time is not based on his grasp of some *method* for telling just when the loaf has been cooked enough, a method that might be captured by a further step in the explanatory chain: 'the way to take the loaf out when it has been cooked just enough is to ...'. Rather, Aristotle says that at this point the baker simply acts on the basis of perception. Because the baker is experienced, he can simply see when the loaf has been cooked enough. Aristotle's more general claim here is that any such chains of explanation will eventually reach a point at which there is no further explanation to be had. At that point, the craftsman must draw upon his experience in perceiving how to act.[23]

III Craft and the Fine-Tuning Needed for Acting on One's Productive Understanding: A Difference between Craft and Theoretical Understanding

In Section II, I described three limitations on the scope of craft-explanations, each corresponding to a limitation on the scope of theoretical explanations. These parallels between craft and theoretical understanding help to justify thinking of a craft as itself a kind of understanding. In Sections III and IV, I focus instead on two important differences between craft and theoretical understanding, both of them resulting from the way in which craft and theoretical understanding differ in their goals. The goal of a craft is successful production, whereas the goal of theoretical understanding is contemplation.[24] I shall argue that because of this difference, exercising a craft requires engaging with particulars in a way that exercising theoretical understanding does not.

One reason for this is that exercising a craft requires more than simply grasping that, and why, such and such a course of action will best achieve a certain end; it requires, in addition, *acting* on this understanding. The

---

[23] It must be admitted that if I am right about what Aristotle is claiming here, the examples he uses are not very helpful: neither 'this is a loaf' nor 'this has been cooked enough' are claims about how to do something, so neither of them are the kinds of things that could be steps in such an explanatory chain.

[24] As Aristotle says in *EE* I.5.

craftsman must be able to apply his understanding to the particular circumstances in which he finds himself. Aristotle says that this adjustment to particular circumstances does not itself 'fall under any craft [*hupo technēn*] or set of rules [*hupo paraggelian oudemian*]'; rather, 'the agents themselves have to consider the circumstances relating to the occasion [*ta pros ton kairon skopein*], as is the case in medicine too and in navigation' (*EN* II.2 1104a7–10). When Aristotle says that this adjustment to particular circumstances does not fall under any craft, I take it that he means that the craftsman's explanations (of what he should do and why) cannot capture precisely every detail of how he should adjust what he does to the circumstances. As Aristotle says in *EN* III.3, the craftsman needs to make use of perceptual powers in order to act on his explanatory knowledge. For instance, at a certain point, a craftsman must just be able to *see* whether this loaf has been cooked enough, or whether this is the right amount of medicine to give to this patient. Though not a part of the craftsman's explanatory understanding, much of this ability to see is itself acquired as part of learning the craft. Though one does not need any special craft to see *that this is a loaf*, the ability to see *when a loaf has been baked enough* is an ability that is acquired through the repeated practice of baking loaves; similarly, the ability to see that this is the precise amount of medicine to give to this patient is an ability acquired through repeated experiences of treating particular patients. That is, one acquires this perceptual ability in just the way that one acquires productive understanding: by practice.

In claiming that the craftsman must use this experience-informed perceptual ability, Aristotle is introducing a *kind* of unlimitedness into the nature of the craft. In acting on his explanatory understanding, the craftsman must respond perceptually to unlimitedly many potential features of his environment.[25] He must fine-tune his action to suit the circumstances. Achieving the goal of a craft requires not only having the ability to come up with relevant productive explanations, but also having the perceptual ability that enables one to act in just the right way on the basis of those explanations.[26] The doctor will not only understand why

---

[25] Of course, it is also true that in order to apply your *theoretical* understanding to the world around you, you will need to be responsive to such features of your environment. The difference is that the goal of theoretical understanding is contemplation and this does not essentially involve applying such understanding to the world around you. By contrast, the goal of productive understanding is production and producing something necessarily involves interacting with your environment.

[26] As I mentioned above (n. 1), this puts some pressure on the identification of craft with productive understanding, at least if 'productive understanding' is simply an ability to come up with appropriate productive explanations.

such and such medicine is appropriate and why giving too much or too little would be harmful; he will also be able to discern *what counts as just the right amount* for *this* patient. To discern this is to be responsive to details of the circumstances, beyond those that can be mentioned explicitly in a finite productive explanatory account.

The claim that successful craft-production depends on this kind of unlimited ability is quite compatible with the claim that the *explanations* that form the content of productive understanding are finitely specifiable; that is, it is quite compatible with the claim that craft-understanding is potentially complete: its explanatory content could in principle be fully grasped. However, in what follows I shall argue that there is a further respect in which a craftsman's ability is unlimited, and that this does imply the essential incompleteness of craft-understanding. Productive understanding is unlike theoretical understanding because its explanatory content cannot be finitely specified.

The source of this further kind of unlimitedness lies in the way in which productive understanding treats of exceptional circumstances. As we have seen, Aristotle holds that neither craft nor theoretical science provides explanations of accidents. However, this similarity hides an important difference. What it is to be an accident relative to a theoretical science cannot be quite the same as what it is to be an accident relative to a craft. The difference lies in the relation between accidents and exceptions to rules. In natural science, anything that is an exception to one of the generalisations explained by the science is an accident from the point of view of that science and hence is not explicable within the science. A natural science thus explains the behaviour of the things within its scope, *in so far as those things are behaving naturally*. By contrast, I shall argue, the generalisations that are explained within a craft have exceptions that are themselves also explicable within the craft. Such exceptions do not, then, count as accidents relative to the craft. I shall argue that because there is no limit to such potential exceptions, the explanatory scope of a craft is similarly unlimited.

IV Craft and Exceptional Circumstances: A Second Difference between Craft and Theoretical Understanding

The generalisations that are explained by both craft and the science of nature are generalisations that hold only for the most part, or as a rule (*hôs epi to polu*). For example, the science of tree frogs explains why male tree frogs as a rule produce sperm in summer. Of course, there will be exceptions to this generalisation: there will be individual male tree frogs that fail to produce sperm in summer, perhaps because their organs are defective, or perhaps because they are not in their natural habitat. Similarly, the medical craft explains why, as a rule, honey water should be given to patients suffering from bilious fever (perhaps, in order to thin the blood and hence produce health). But there will be exceptions to this generalisation. For instance, honey water should *not* be given to patients who are suffering from bilious fever but are allergic to honey. The building craft explains why, as a rule, foundations in gravel should be dug to a depth of 70 cm. But there will be multiple exceptions to this generalisation. For instance, the foundations will need to be dug to a different depth if the ground is waterlogged.

My claim is that a craftsman, unlike an expert in the science of nature, needs to engage successfully with such exceptional cases. An expert in the science of tree frogs can explain how tree frogs are *in so far as they are developing and behaving in accord with their nature*; she does not concern herself with defective tree frogs or with tree frogs that are outside their natural habitat.[27] By contrast, an expert doctor will need to know what to do when the patient is allergic to the normal treatment (and why) and an expert builder will need to know what to do when the ground is waterlogged (and why). As Aristotle says, a craftsman will be able to act successfully in nonideal circumstances: 'a good general uses the available army in the most militarily effective way and a good shoemaker makes the finest shoe out of the leather provided to him, and the same also for all the other kinds of craftsmen' (*EN* I.10 1101a3–6). The craftsman will even need to be able to act well in circumstances in which fully achieving the goal of the craft is impossible: 'it is not the function of medicine simply to make man quite healthy, but to put him as far as may be on the road to health; it is possible to give excellent treatment even to those who can never enjoy full health' (*Rhet.* I.1.1355b12–14).[28] These are claims about

---

[27] Of course, someone who knows the science of tree frogs may in fact also be able to say something about how a tree frog will react in such exceptional circumstances, but the ability to do so is not part of understanding the science of tree frogs.

[28] Aristotle does make certain superficially similar remarks about nature. For example, at *PA* II.14 658a23–24, he says that nature makes the best arrangement *out of those that are possible*. And at *GA* II.6 744b15–16 he explains the way in which bodily residues are used for making bones, nails, etc. with the remark: 'nature, like a good householder, is not in the habit of throwing away anything from which it is possible to make anything useful'. Neither of these, however, concerns something that is an exception to one of the generalisations explained by the science of nature. Neither is a case in which the matter is defective or unsuitable for its purpose. Aristotle's point is that when things operate as they should by nature, there will be certain residues that are used for making bones, and things will be organised in the best way given the materials that nature makes available. The natural

what is involved in having a certain craft, not merely claims about what the practitioners of a craft will in fact be able to do.

The reason for this difference is that a natural thing's nature specifies both its matter and its habitat, whereas a craft does not determine in the same way the environment in which it is exercised and the matter it is exercised upon. Of course, a craft will limit the materials and environment to some extent. As Aristotle says, 'the carpenter would not make a box except out of wood' (*GA* II.6, 743a25). Moreover, it is the job of the carpenter to know what would be the best kind of wood to use. But the craft will often need to be exercised in circumstances in which the best kind of material is not available. The reason for this is that the craft itself does not determine the circumstances of its exercise. *Whether or not to exercise the craft in this case* is determined externally, by the employer (or by the craftsman himself but not qua craftsman). If the employer wants shoes made out of unsuitable leather, the shoemaker will be able to make the best possible shoes out of that leather. If the employer wants a house on earthquake-prone ground, the housebuilder will be able to produce the best house possible for that situation. Because of this, the craft-expert will need to operate successfully in unlimitedly many cases that are, in a certain sense, 'exceptional': cases in which the generalisations that explain what one should do in normal circumstances do not apply.[29]

This introduces a further respect in which a craft is unlimited, and hence a further way in which craft differs from theoretical understanding. In Section V, I shall argue that this further kind of unlimitedness suggests

---

scientist needs to be able to explain these facts. But the natural scientist does not need to explain the functioning of a defective animal, or how an animal might function if it were made of some material other than the material of which it is naturally made. (I am grateful to Thomas Johansen for pressing me on this point.) Of course, an understanding of natural science (that is, an understanding of why things develop as they do when acting in accord with their natures) could incidentally also shed light on what happens in defective cases. Thus, in *GA* IV.4, Aristotle himself attempts to explain the causes of certain monstrosities (where monstrosities, properly speaking, are things that occur contrary to nature and contrary to what happens as a rule, 770b9–11). My point is just that the content of natural science does not include such explanations: a natural science does not need to provide such explanations in order to be complete.

[29] This is consistent with Aristotle's remark, discussed in Section II above, that there is no productive understanding of the accidental. As we saw above, there are certain types of accidental feature that the craft is not concerned with. The housebuilder does not need to be able to explain how to produce a house that will increase in value. Even with this limitation on the scope of craft, there will still be unlimitedly many cases in which the craftsman will need to explain how to act in unusual circumstances. In theoretical science, anything that is an exception to one of the generalisations explained by the science counts as an accident (and hence as something that falls outside the scope of the science). My claim is that this is not true of a craft: something can be an exception to one of the as-a-rule generalisations explained by the craft without thereby being an accident (and thus something that falls outside the scope of the craft).

Aristotle on Productive Understanding and Completeness

that productive understanding is never complete. The expert craftsman, unlike the expert in theoretical science, has a capacity for working out potentially infinitely many explanations.

V Exceptional Cases and Productive Explanations

The fact that an expert craftsman must be able to act successfully in a potentially infinite range of circumstances does not, *by itself,* show that he must be able to work out potentially infinitely many explanations. Someone might argue that the craftsman's ability to respond to exceptional cases does not depend on an ability to work out new explanations. As we saw earlier, the craftsman makes use of a kind of perception-based ability in applying an explanatory account to his particular circumstances. For instance, a kind of trained perception might enable the doctor to tell that *this* is the right amount of honey water to give to *this* patient, and thus enable him to act successfully on his explanatory account of why honey water needs to be given to this patient (and of why the patient should not be given too little or too much). In doing this, the doctor does not need a new explanation; instead, he uses his perceptual power in applying the explanation he already has to new circumstances. It might be argued, then, that the craftsman's ability to respond to exceptional cases is based in a similar way on trained perception rather than on a capacity for working out new explanatory accounts.

However, the ability to respond to exceptional cases is importantly different from the ability to fine-tune one's action to the circumstances in acting on a given explanatory account. The doctor who uses trained perception to see just how much honey water to give this patient (basing this on his sense of the patient's general health, the progress of the disease, etc.) is still acting on his understanding of why honey water should be given to patients with this kind of fever. The doctor who grasps that this patient should not be treated with honey water (because he is allergic) needs to find some alternative method of treatment. Presumably, if he is acting as a craftsman, he will need, in acting, to understand why that alternative method is successful. This requires him to grasp a new explanation.

Of course, the doctor's grasp of the original productive explanation will often help him to come up with a new one. This is, in part, because (as we saw earlier) grasping a productive explanation is grasping something comparative. If the doctor understands why administering honey water is generally a good way to cure bilious fever, then he understands why this method of treatment would generally be better than others (or at least as good as certain others). This understanding will inform his choice of alternatives in cases in which honey water would not be suitable.

Moreover, the new productive explanation might (and often will) be closely related to the original one. For instance, if honey water cures by thinning the blood, then the doctor might look for some alternative blood-thinning substance. In judging that some alternative blood-thinning substance should be given to the patient, he is acting on a new explanatory account: 'such and such a substance should be given to patients with this kind of fever who are allergic to honey, because such and such a substance produces health by thinning the blood, and does so without causing an allergic reaction'.

In grasping, and acting on, a new explanatory account, the doctor is exercising a rational power, not simply employing trained perception. The doctor might arrive at this new account by deliberation or he might just grasp it immediately without having to spend time working it out. In either case, though, the cognitive power he is using is the same: it is a rational power for grasping explanatory accounts.[30]

VI Why Theoretical Understanding Must Be Complete but Productive Understanding Need Not Be

The arguments I have given above strongly suggest that productive understanding necessarily involves the capacity to come up with new explanations: the explanatory content of a craft cannot be encapsulated in a finite list of explanatory accounts. The craftsman's ability to use trained perception is not itself a substitute for his ability to come up with new explanatory accounts to fit exceptional circumstances.

What I have said does not, I think, provide a *conclusive* argument for the incompleteness of productive understanding. I have not demonstrated that there are, in fact, *infinitely* many different types of exceptional cases that fall within the scope of the craft. What I have shown is that there is no obvious way in which the finitude of productive understanding could be ensured by limiting the range of exceptional cases. Moreover, it might still be possible to defend the view that craft understanding was complete, by allowing a single (though relatively vacuous) explanation to account for a

---

[30] I take this to show that this rational power cannot simply be what Aristotle calls 'experience' (*empeiria*). For a very different view on the role of experience in Aristotle's account, see Bolton's discussion of *Metaphysics* I.1 (Chapter 6).

wide range of cases. For instance, it might be argued that the doctor acts on an account of the form 'to cure the bilious patient, thin the blood; to thin the blood, administer treatment that thins the blood', and uses trained perception to see what treatment, in the circumstances, will be best for thinning the blood. The explanation he acted on would just be 'administering treatment that thins the blood cures the bilious patient by thinning the blood'. This would allow for a very wide range of treatments to be explained by one and the same account, but it would do so at the expense of making such explanations rather vacuous.

In this last section, I want to step back from this question and ask instead why one should expect understanding (whether theoretical or productive) to be potentially complete. I shall argue that Aristotle has a good reason for wanting to maintain that theoretical understanding is potentially complete, but that this reason does not apply to productive understanding. As we have seen, Aristotle does introduce certain limitations on productive understanding, corresponding to limitations on theoretical understanding: in both, what are explained are generalities; in both the length of explanatory chains is finite; in both, there is no explanatory grasp of the accidental. These correspondences bring out certain important similarities between theoretical and productive understanding. However, there is no reason to suppose that productive understanding must be like theoretical understanding in being finite in its explanatory scope.

Why, then, does Aristotle insist that theoretical understanding must be potentially complete, while allowing that productive understanding need not be? I want to suggest that his position on this is a consequence of his view that divine beings exercise theoretical, but not productive, understanding. Aristotle claims that the gods must be active, and that the kind of activity they engage in is contemplation, rather than either production or practical action (*EN* X.8 1178b18–22). In other words, the gods exercise theoretical, but not productive or practical, understanding.[31] Now Aristotle's views about divine perfection imply that a god could not have a kind of infinitely extendable ability to work out new explanations. On his view, gods are pure activities: they do not have abilities that might or might not be exercised.[32] In *Metaphysics* XII.8, he says that divine contemplative activity cannot be the exercise of some potential (*dunamis*),

---

[31] In this, of course, Aristotle departs from Plato's view in the *Timaeus*. For a discussion of Plato's account of divine craftsmanship, see Chapter 4 in this volume.
[32] At *Int.* 13 23a23–24 he says that primary substances are 'activities [*energeiai*] without potentiality'. In *Metaph.* IX.8 1050b6–22 he argues that eternal things do not have potentialities (nothing eternal is *dunamei*). For discussion of this argument, see Makin 2006: 209–15 and Beere 2009: 317–24.

since if it were, it would be the kind of activity that could become wearisome.[33] Rather, a god simply *is* contemplative activity. It follows that divine understanding must, being perfect, consist in a grasp of *all* the explanations within its scope. This does not imply that gods are *omniscient* – Aristotle says that the objects of divine understanding can only be the most divine and honourable things[34] – but it does imply that the activity of divine understanding is a grasp of *everything* that is explicable about the objects within its domain.

Aristotle's view that there is no actual infinite implies that grasping infinitely many distinct explanations is impossible.[35] This is not merely something that is impossible for finite human intellects. Thus, if divine understanding is complete, in the sense that it is a grasp of *all* the explanations within its domain, it must also be finite. Within the scope of such understanding, there must be only finitely many explanations *to be grasped*.[36]

Of course, someone could agree with Aristotle's account of the divine and still hold that human theoretical understanding is infinitely extendable. But if Aristotle were to agree with this, he would have to give up on the idea that divine activity is a model for human theoretical understanding. For Aristotle, it is important that humans, in exercising theoretical understanding are engaging, albeit imperfectly, in a divine kind of activity. A human should, by exercising such understanding, 'become like the immortals' (*athanatizein*) in so far as this is possible.[37] Aristotle needs, then, a single account of theoretical understanding that applies both to the kind of understanding exercised by the gods and to human understanding. What humans aim at in their theoretical inquiries must then, like divine understanding, be complete and finite.

There are no such constraints on Aristotle's account of craft (*technē*), since he denies that the gods exercise productive understanding. Aristotle allows that there is a sense in which one can be in complete possession of a craft: 'a doctor is complete (*teleios*) and a flute-player is complete, when in respect of the form of their proper excellence nothing is lacking' (*Metaph.* V.16 1021b16–17). But there is no reason to suppose that 'lacking nothing' with respect to a craft implies already knowing *all* the explanations needed to act on the craft. Instead, I have suggested that productive understanding essentially involves the capacity to work out new explanations, as the circumstances demand. If this is right, then a craft essentially

---

[33] *Metaph.* XII.9 1074b28–29. [34] *Metaph.* XII.9 1074b25–26. [35] *Ph.* III.4–8.
[36] The importance both of the fact that divine beings engage in theoretical understanding and of the view that grasping the infinite is in principle impossible are recognised by Crager 2013.
[37] See *EN* X.7 1177b26–34.

involves a kind of capacity for innovation. To 'lack nothing' with respect to a craft is to have a fully honed capacity for working out and acting on new explanations, as they are needed.

VII Conclusion

I have argued that the content of a particular theoretical science must be finite: such a science consists of finitely many explanatory demonstrations. Of course, to have understanding, one must grasp these explanations *in a particular way*. It is not enough simply to be able to recite the demonstrations; one must, in addition, grasp how the conclusion of each demonstration follows from, and is explained by, its premises. The content of any particular branch of craft-understanding is, by contrast, potentially infinite. Fully possessing a craft does not, then, involve grasping *all* of that craft's productive explanations. Instead, someone who fully possesses the craft will grasp a certain limited number of productive explanations and will have the capacity to come up with further explanations. Having a craft, like having theoretical understanding, involves grasping explanations in a particular way. Like the person of theoretical understanding, the craftsman must be able not merely to recite the relevant explanations but also to appreciate their explanatoriness. However, grasping the relevant explanations *in the way that constitutes having a craft* also involves more than this. Having productive understanding involves having the capacity to reason about what to do, and why, when faced with new circumstances. You grasp the relevant explanations *in the way that constitutes having a craft* only if your grasp of these explanations is such as to allow you to extrapolate from them so as to work out new explanations to suit new circumstances. Thus, you only count as having productive understanding if you have developed, through training and instruction, this reason-based capacity for innovation.

Aristotle's view about the difference between productive and theoretical understanding is of interest in itself. If I am right that this view is underpinned by his assumptions about the divine and the infinite, this suggests interesting avenues for further inquiry. Later philosophers differed from Aristotle on many of these assumptions. For instance, certain Christians held both that God exercises a kind of craft and also that God's knowledge (unlike human knowledge) can be infinite.[38] Are these departures from

---

[38] For the view that there is a divine craft, see Aquinas, *On Physics* II, Lecture 14, 268, where nature is described as 'the divine craft, impressed upon things'. For the view that God, unlike human beings, could grasp an actual infinite, see Aquinas, *Summa Contra Gentiles* I.69.

Aristotle reflected also in differing views about the completeness of productive understanding? More generally, to what extent can we explain the views these ancient and medieval philosophers adopted on the nature of craft understanding by looking at their views on the divine and the infinite?

CHAPTER 6

Technê *and* Empeiria
Aristotle on Practical Knowledge
Robert Bolton

There is a certain kind of *technê* (*technê tis*) which is not of the same sort as are those [*technai*] which are able to prove things (*deiknousai*).[1]
(*SE* 11 172a39–b1, cf. *Pol* III.11 1282a3–6)

Absolutely, it is better to try to make things that are posterior known through things that are prior; for such a procedure is more scientific. Nevertheless, for those who are unable to come to know things by such [scientific] means it is presumably necessary to provide an account through things that are known to them.
(*Top.* VI.4 141b15–19; cf. *EN* I.4 1095b2–3)

I Aristotle's Study of *Technê*

Towards the conclusion of his life of Aristotle, the ancient biographer Diogenes Laertius tells us this:

He [Aristotle] wrote an enormous number of books (*biblia*) which I have thought it appropriate to catalogue because of the man's excellence in every type of discussion. (Diogenes Laertius, 'D.L.', V.21)

Among Aristotle's works of 'excellence', Diogenes lists the following:

Compilation (*sunagogê*) of *Technai*, 2 books
Technê, 1 book
Another Compilation of *Technai*, 2 books. (D.L. V.24)

The other ancient lists of Aristotle's works contain equivalent titles.[2] So in so far as we may judge from this, it would seem that not only did Aristotle produce a treatise on the general nature of *technê*, or skilled

---

[1] In this chapter, round brackets are used in quotations for words explicit or implicit in the Greek, while square brackets are used for the author's explanatory glosses.
[2] See Düring 1957: 46, 85, 224. I follow ms F, with Hicks 1925 and Moraux 1951, for Diogenes' third listing.

practical knowledge, he also assembled collections of what may well have been *manuals* for the practice of various existing *technai*, or branches of skilled know-how, acquired by him for his use as a basis for a general treatise on the nature of the subject. If so, this would parallel Aristotle's dual interest in not only producing his *Politics* but also, as Diogenes confirms (V.27), in collecting the working constitutions of 158 States, grouped into different types, as his initial basis, so Aristotle himself indicates in *EN* X.9, for his subsequent general treatise on that subject (1181b15–23).[3]

Such a dual procedure would also parallel Aristotle's well-known project in the *HA* to assemble first a full collection, from a variety of sources, of often rough, preliminary empirical and other data concerning the differences among animals, as his basis, so he says in *HA* I.6, for his subsequent systematic zoological theory (491a6–19). It would conform also to Aristotle's general insistence that such a two-stage procedure – first to collect the relevant experientially based data then to produce the systematic study starting from and based on that – is the proper way to proceed in the treatment of any disciplined area of inquiry whatsoever (*Pr An* I.30 46a17–27; *DA* I.1 402b16–403a2; cf. *Ph*. I.1 184a16–b14). So the approach that Diogenes' report opens up for us concerning Aristotle's treatment of *technê* is in close conformity with Aristotle's clear views on the proper procedures for systematic inquiry overall.

Most regrettably, we know but little of compilations by Aristotle of data on the practices of various standing *technai*, and even less of a systematic treatise by him on *technê* itself. In *EN* X.9 Aristotle does refer to various medical writings collected it seems by him that 'try, at least, to state not only the treatments [for various ailments] but also, in distinguishing different ailments, to state how each sort of individual should be cured and treated' (1181b2–5). These medical writings, or manuals, could well be among the works on the *technai* that Aristotle collected. His reference to them likely indicates further that his collections did not only concern rhetoric as many have supposed. That restriction would not fit his standard recommended procedure for dealing with all disciplined subjects.[4] But, in any event, with Diogenes' report as an opening, it may be more possible to

---

[3] Aristotle uses similar language in *EN* X.9 to describe his compilations of constitutions (*sunêgmenôn politeiôn*, 1181b17) as Diogenes uses (*sunagogê*) to offer what are presented by Diogenes himself as Aristotle's own titles of his compilations of *technai*.

[4] For manuals of Aristotle's acquaintance on the *technê* of rhetoric, see *SE* 34. 184a25–b8, and cf. Cicero *De Inv.* II.6.

fill the gap in our understanding of Aristotle's treatment of these matters than has so far been attempted. That will be a main aim of this discussion.

II *Technê* and *Empeiria* in Aristotle's Extant Works

In the absence of the lost works or collections of Aristotle concerning *technê* and the *technai*, scholars have devoted the bulk of their attention to his most detailed discussion in his extant works, of *technê* and its basis in extensive, accumulated experience or *empeiria* in *Metaph*. I.1 (sometimes in the following referred to simply as 'I.1'), taken with more brief remarks elsewhere, especially in the *EN* and in *Metaph*. IX. Aristotle's remarks in I.1 are worth quoting at some length. There he says:

> By nature (*phusei*) [all] animals are born with [the power of] perception (*aisthêsis*), and *from* [active] perceiving (*aisthêsis*) (alone) memory is generated (by nature) in some (animals) . . . . The other animals (than humans) *live* [by nature] by use of appearances and memories. And (in addition) they share a little (*mikron*) [along with humans] in *empeiria* while the human race *lives also* by use of *technê* and reasoned calculations (*logismoi*). And *from* memory [alone] *empeiria* is generated in humans, since *many* memories of the same [sort of] thing [by themselves, by nature] bring to perfection (*apotelousin*) a power (*dunamis*) [for active living] which is a *single* [unified] item of *empeiria*. It is held (*dokei*) [by some] that *empeiria* is much the same as scientific knowledge (*epistêmê*) and *technê*. However [against this], *epistêmê* and *technê* in humans come about *by means of* [prior] *empeiria* . . . . (That is) *technê* is generated when, *from* the (already present) many cognitive states (*ennoêmata*) [i.e., the many memories of similars] that [collectively] make up an item of *empeiria*, a single [true] universal conviction (*katholou hupolêpsis*) comes about concerning those *similar* things [which, as naturally, psychologically collected together as similar in memory, constitute an item of *empeiria*]. For, to have the [true] conviction that when Callias was ill with this disease this [treatment] benefitted him, and also in the case of Socrates and, in this same manner (*houtô*) [i.e., similarly], in *many* an individual case (*kath' hekaston*), constitutes an item of *empeiria*. But to have the [true] conviction that it benefitted *all* people of a certain sort *marked off in a single kind* (*kat' eidos hen*) [not just collected together in *empeiria* as a large group naturally unified in memory by similarity] . . . is an item of *technê* . . . . *Empeiria* (thus) is knowledge (*gnosis*) of particulars (*ta kath' hekaston*), *technê* of universals (*ta katholou*) . . . . If, then, someone has the account (*logos*) without the [relevant] *empeiria*, i.e. he knows (*gnôrizei*) the universal [in question] but is ignorant of some single particular (*to kath' hekaston*) covered by this, he will often fail to cure [that single individual of whom he is relevantly ignorant] . . . . We think, however, that knowledge (*to eidenai*) in the sense of understanding (*to epaiein*) belongs rather to [those

with] *technê* than to [those with only] *empeiria*, and we hold [thus] that those with *technê* are *wiser* than those with [only] *empeiria* ... because the former [with *technê*] know the cause (*aitia*) the others do not. For, those with *empeiria* know *that* the thing is so (*to hoti*) but do not know *why* (*dioti*), while the others [with *technê*] know the why and the cause [of *to hoti*]. Wherefore, we think that artificers-in-chief (*architektones*) [who have *technê*] ... are wiser than manual artificers (*cheirotechnai*) [who have only *empeiria*] because the former know the causes of the things that are [correctly] done [by the latter]; the latter do things [correctly] rather as certain lifeless things do, which do things [successfully] but do not understand what they do, as for instance fire burns [without knowing why it burns]. However, the lifeless things [such as fire] do each such thing *by virtue of some nature* (*phusis*) [that they possess], while the manual artificers [with *empeiria*] act [correctly] *from habit* (*di' ethos*). Thus the former [artificers-in-chief, with *technê*] are *not* wiser [than the manual artificers, with *empeiria*] in virtue of being able to act [correctly] but rather in virtue of possessing, themselves, the account (*logos*), in the sense of knowing the causes [of the correctness of what is successfully done by those with *empeiria*] .... No one thinks that our perceptual powers (*aisthêseis*) provide wisdom (*sophia*). Although they [these perceptual powers] provide *most authoritative knowledge of particulars* [i.e., *empeiria*], they do not tell us *why* anything is so; they do not tell us, for instance, *why* fire is hot, but only *that* it is hot. (980a27–81b13)[5]

In this multifaceted, crucial text, one matter especially stands out in importance for our purposes. Aristotle stresses that '*empeiria* is knowledge of particulars, *technê* of universals'. It is evident, however, that though *empeiria* is here identified with 'knowledge of particulars' it must have a very strong element of generality to it. To begin with, it involves, in the first case illustrated above (981a7–12), the grasp of a *kind* of treatment for a *kind* of ailment with a *kind* of result, namely, cure of that *kind* of ailment in numerous particular cases. Some understanding of these various general *kinds* must be in play even at the most basic initial level of *perception* itself, which is, as Aristotle describes it, of the instantiation of such kinds in particular individuals in particular situations.[6] However, the most direct indication of the generality in *empeiria* that is especially relevant for us here is Aristotle's claim that both *technê* and *epistêmê*, or scientific knowledge, are finally reached in the same way, by finding the true cause and explanation *of* what is known by those with *empeiria* who, as such, know

---

[5] Here as elsewhere glosses and emphasis are supplied, to be discussed below. Primavesi 2012: 454 attempts a reconstruction of 981a30–b6 that avoids the somewhat unruly grammar of the manuscripts (452). This issue does not however affect the sense of the passage for our discussion.
[6] Cf. *Post An* II.19 100a16–b1.

that something is so but not *why* it is. For Aristotle, causal explanation of the sort that yields *epistêmê*, for instance, must be causal explanation of some *general* regularity. There is for him no causal explanation, yielding *epistêmê*, of facts about ground level particulars, such as Socrates and Callias as such. In *Post An* I.31, for instance, Aristotle maintains that no causal scientific explanation is possible of the ground level particular fact 'that the moon is now eclipsed'. Rather, it is only when, by virtue of frequent perception of similar particular events, 'we have captured the universal (*katholou*)', namely here that *generally* the moon is subject to eclipse, that we first have a fact ready for causal explanation (87b39–88a4; cf. *Post An* I.8).

In *Post An* II.1–2 also, Aristotle uses his standard expression 'knowledge-*that* (*hoti*)' specifically for items ready for scientific explanation (89b23–31; cf. II.8 93a16–21). *Empeiria*, then, *as* knowledge-*that*, which *is* ready for the search for its scientific explanation, *must* be somehow general in character. In *Post An* I.13, as also in II.1–2, Aristotle uses the term *epistêmê* and its cognates, in a broad sense, for this very knowledge-*that* which is ready for scientific explanation (78a22–26, 89b23–31), and thus as covering *empeiria*, which, as *Metaph*. I.1 tells us, *is* such knowledge-*that*. *Empeiria* would also count thereby, in suitable practical cases though not of course in purely theoretical cases, as one of the 'productive forms of *epistêmê* (*poiêtikai epistêmai*))' in the broad sense of the term *epistêmê*. These are states, which, as productive, Aristotle groups directly with *technê* in *Metaph* IX.2 (1046b2–24), states whose possession he connects there with the capacity for the use of *logos*. This fits with the fact that both *empeiria* and *technê*, in humans, are productive capacities to use *logos* or reason in successful reasoned *deliberation* about practical matters though not, in the case of *empeiria* alone, to use *logos* in scientific explanation and demonstration, as is the case for *technê* here in I.1 as also in *Pr An* I.30 46a22 and *Post An* II.19 100a9.[7]

Such a reading of the generality that the type of 'knowledge of particulars' in question in *Metaph*. I.1 involves is further supported by Aristotle's second example there of knowledge-*that*, namely, 'that fire is hot' (981b13). Since Aristotle says directly that it is those with *empeiria* who have such knowledge-*that* (981a28–29), this is clearly meant to be an example of *empeiria*, and this example of *empeiria* evidently has a certain generality to it; in fact, as we have just seen a generality, as Aristotle himself presents it, sufficient to make it a suitable basis for the search for

---

[7] On these different uses of *logos* see *EN* VI.1 1139a3–17.

knowledge why and thus, when it is causally explained in a proper way, for *epistêmê* or *technê*. Since, moreover, this knowledge-*that* is said to be provided, and provided 'most authoritatively', simply by the senses, not at all by the use of reason, we can also see that the *acquisition* of such a general item of causally explicable *empeiria* must be for Aristotle a natural function of our perceptual faculty alone, even though its practical *use* by humans can involve deliberative reason or *logos*. In *Post An* I.13 Aristotle confirms that 'it is the work of *perceivers* (*aisthêtikoi*) to know the *that*', but of theorists to know the why and the cause of this (79a2–4). Aristotle does indicate further in *Post An* I.13 that knowledge-*that* can come also by argument, from previous knowledge-*that* but, still, it comes originally and 'most authoritatively' by the senses, so I.1 directly tells us, and it comes, in this authoritative form, as ready for the search for its causal explanation, which not all knowledge-*that* reached by argument, as understood in I.13, does (78a26–38). Some have recently supposed, rather surprisingly, that the type of knowledge-*that* in question in I.1, as *empeiria*, is not itself subject to or ready for the search for a causal explanation that gives rise to *epistêmê*, unlike the knowledge-*that* which figures in, for instance, *Post An* II.1–2.[8] This, however, is directly contradicted by the text of *Metaph.* I.1.

III Knowledge of Particulars and Universals in Other Texts

Scholars have pointed to other passages where Aristotle again speaks of universals and particulars, where it is also clear that a certain generality is involved in those so-called particulars, so it is worth considering them for the assistance they may offer for an understanding of his distinction between the two in *Metaph.* I.1. In *Top.* I.12, for instance, Aristotle says, concerning the use of inductive argument in dialectic:

> Induction (*epagogê*) is the advance from particulars (*ta kath' hekaston*) to universals (*ta katholou*). For example, if the knowledgeable (*epistamenos*) pilot is the best and also the charioteer, then, generally, the knowledgeable individual is the best in any sphere. (*Top.* 105a13–16)

Aristotle's examples here, first of 'particulars' and then of a 'universal', where the grasp of each is described using a cognate of *epistêmê* in the broad sense, show us that, on one version of the distinction that he can employ between universals and particulars, *both* are *propositional* items that are *general*, even items that may hold for all cases of a certain sort. The

---

[8] Charles 2000; Lennox 2021.

salient difference between them is only that what is universal is broader in scope, or less determinate, than what is particular, not that what is universal is, so to speak, universally quantified, while what is particular is something less. However, the distinction in the *Topics* is introduced to explicate the use of inductive argument in dialectic. Here, in *Top*. VIII.14, Aristotle counsels the use of such inductive argument by questioners to secure the concession of general propositions of broad scope from an answerer, due to the special value that such general propositions of broad scope have for use as premises, for example, for refutation, in dialectical deductions (163b33–64a3). On the other side of the coin, Aristotle counsels answerers in dialectic to try to avoid such general concessions of broad scope, no doubt to forestall or limit the possibilities of refutation (164a7–8). Still, he supposes, since particulars as understood there, as the more determinate generalities, are the sorts of things that are more commonly grasped by people in general, and thus are more likely to be granted by ordinary interlocutors in dialectical discussion, they have a special use for subsequently reaching inductively those generalities of broader scope that are of special further value in dialectic.[9]

Clearly enough then, given these things, the distinction between universals and particulars in *Top*. I.12 is not directly relevant to Aristotle's more theoretical interests in *Metaph* I.1, where the advance from particulars to universals, and the knowledge thereof, marks an advance from *empeiria* to unqualified *epistêmê* or *technê*, not simply an inductive advance from one generality to another generality that is broader in scope and thus may serve as such as an especially useful premise for deduction in dialectical encounters. Thus, as we shall shortly further confirm, this version of the distinction between universals and particulars, in *Top*. I.12, will be of limited value for our final understanding of the more theoretically geared version of the distinction in I.1.

Yet another central passage to which scholars have often appealed to gauge the generality involved in that 'knowledge of particulars' which is in question in *Metaph*. I.1 is found in *EN* VI.7, where Aristotle says:

> Nor is moral wisdom (*phronêsis*) [knowledge] of universals (*ta katholou*) alone, but it is necessary to know (*gnôrizein*) also the particulars (*ta kath' hekasta*). For, *phronêsis* is practical and practical action is concerned with particulars. Wherefore, even some who do *not* know [certain universals], and, in other areas [than ethics], those with *empeiria,* are more successful in action than others who do know [those universals]. For, if someone knew

[9] See VIII.1 155b34–56a10 with VI.4 141b6–14.

[the universal] that light meats are digestible and healthy, but was ignorant [i.e., lacked *empeiria*] of which [particular] meats are light, he would not produce health. Rather, the one who knows [as a matter of *empeiria*, the particular] that bird meats are digestible and healthy will produce health. (1141b14–21, reading *krea* for *koupha* at b20)

Here again, as in the *Topics*, the distinction between universals and particulars is a distinction between two types of general, even, possibly, universally quantified, *propositions*, of greater and lesser scope or breadth of application, not between items that are and are not in themselves universally quantified or otherwise general. It is agreed that there is clear indication here that the 'particular' general conviction of more narrow scope, namely, that bird meats are digestible and healthy, is taken to qualify as an item of *empeiria*, where this is understood, importantly, as a distinctive type of *general* propositional knowledge of relatively narrow scope. Some have also seen here the suggestion that the 'universal' in question, that light meats are digestible and healthy, would serve to causally explain some particular in question, for example, that chicken, as a light meat, is digestible and healthy, and thus give rise to *technê* or *epistêmê* in line with what we find in I.1. But, very significantly, Aristotle does not say that, nor is that his interest. His stated interest in *EN* VI.7 – as also in the parallel passage in II.7 (1107a28–b8) where the particulars (a33–b8) are again lower level propositional generalities – is not in what explains what, or in what is or is not subject to causal explanation, but only in what is, or may normally be, more *actionable* or usable for successful action than what is less so, as 'chicken is healthy', Aristotle supposes, is typically more directly usable for successful action than 'light meats are healthy' (cf. IX.2 at 1165a35). Thus, once again, as with *Top*. I.12, the difference of interest here will limit the value of this passage for our understanding of the distinction between universals and particulars found in I.1. There in I.1, crucially, the notion of universal in question, as something reached *only* in *technê* or *epistêmê*, is essentially connected with that of what is reached *only* by or in causal explanation not simply or at all with what is relatively broad in scope and thus may be less directly actionable than some particular, however it may be acquired.[10]

---

[10] Nothing in the text of *EN* VI.7 rules it out that knowledge of a 'universal' of broad scope, as understood there, could be reached by suitably extensive *empeiria*, as well as, say, by inference or reliable testimony. But even so it would remain less actionable for Aristotle than knowledge of a particular as understood there.

Quite strikingly in fact, even in his official definition, as it were, of *technê* in the *EN*, in VI.4 1140a1–23, there is no mention of the point, so strongly emphasised in *Metaph*. I.1, that *technê* requires the possession of the causal explanation as to why the things that are correctly done by empirically successful agents are correctly done. Nor, more importantly, is there in VI.4, or anywhere else in the *EN*, any mention of the connected need found in I.1 for *technê* to involve knowledge of universals of the special sort described in I.1. As is clear from the text, in I.1 knowledge of universals is *not* general knowledge that is broader in scope than some other general knowledge, as it is in *EN* VI.7 or II.7. Rather, knowledge of universals in I.1 is knowledge that some general subject *of whatever scope* has some general attribute *as a kind* (*kat' eidos*, 981a10). This language and doctrine are absent from the *EN*, as we shall further find below. These omissions in the *EN* may well be connected with Aristotle's notice to us, in *EN* VI.4 again, that:

> Concerning these matters [*technê*, *phronêsis*, and their functions] we regard even our *exoteric* [i.e., popular] discussions as reliable. (1140a2–3; cf. I.13 1102a26–32, I.4 1095b2–13)

This methodological warning or restriction concerning the mode of the treatment of *technê* and other matters in the *EN* contrasts directly with what we find in I.1 where there is no such qualifier. This could well help to explain the relative lack of fit and thus the lack of value of what we find in the *EN* for our understanding of the account of *technê*, and thus of universals and particulars, as found in I.1. This is an important question to which we shall later return.

IV Types of Knowledge of Particulars and Their Uses

Before approaching that issue, however, still more needs to be said about the sense in which, according to *Metaph*. I.1, *empeiria* is 'knowledge of particulars'. While, as we have seen, this does require that *empeiria*, as ready for the search for its scientific explanation, has some type of strong propositional generality to it, still, as accumulated memory knowledge of the sort described in I.1, the power of *empeiria* must *also* incorporate explicitly (and/or implicitly) accessible habituated memory knowledge of many concrete past individual cases of, say, fire being hot, not in isolation one by one but naturally grouped together, again in habituated memory, as appropriately *similar*.[11]

---

[11] Since the unified memory knowledge of such a class of similars is possessed and accessible for use in the form of a habit (981b5), implicit access through memory will doubtless be in play in many cases as we shall see in the rest of this section.

This is quite evident from Aristotle's first example of *empeiria* in I.1, which is directly described as brought to completion or perfection, as a power for successful action, *as* the accumulated memory knowledge of what cured Callias, and also Socrates, and *many* other actual particular individuals, of a certain type of ailment in a *similar* way. Reference to these specific individuals *by name* is explicitly stated to be a part of the very content of a certain conviction (*hupolêpsis*) that constitutes an item of *empeiria* (981a7–9). When Aristotle characterises *empeiria* as constituted by the collected grasp in memory of many *similars*, the similars in question are clearly ground level individual cases or events of, for example, healing involving such particular individuals (981a7–9). For, those many similars, the memories of which collectively constitute a unified item of *empeiria*, are each, on Aristotle's account, naturally retained items of perceptual knowledge, and perceptual knowledge, for him, is always *of*, in content, ground level individuals as well as of cases or facts involving them (*Post An* II.19 99b36–100a2, I.31 87b28–34). As we have further seen, Aristotle conceives of the initial collecting together of the knowledge of these similars in distinct groups in *empeiria* as an authoritative function just of our *perceptual* powers, and thus not of reason, which shows how at least some *empeiria* can also be acquired and used by certain other animals, who have suitable memory but, as animals, lack reason (980b25–26).

Aristotle's stated basis for his requirement of this special mode of knowledge of particulars for *empeiria*, as understood in I.1, is that medical *empeiria*, for instance, is a power to cure and:

> The doctor does not cure a human being, except incidentally, but rather Callias or Socrates, or some other *thus spoken of* [*by name*] *individual*, who happens to be a human being. (981a18–20)

Here the doctrine is quite different from that in *EN* VI.7. There the need for knowledge of particulars for successful cure or other action, as particulars are understood there in VI.7, is a need for 'particular' knowledge consisting of the most directly actionable *generalities*, such as, say, 'chicken is healthy', as opposed to the normally less easily actionable 'universal' generality 'light meats are healthy'. In I.1, by contrast, the need for knowledge of particulars, as understood there, is rather a need for habituated memory knowledge of many distinct large unified collections, each consisting of, for example, concrete *similar past successful healings* of actual named or nameable individuals, as a necessary basis lodged in memory to enable *successful present or future cures*. Aristotle's strong emphasis in I.1 on the necessity, for successful action, of this very content for *empeiria*, as extensive accessible memory knowledge of similarity classes made up of concrete named individuals and past individual successful cases involving them, shows us that for him, there in I.1, it is in virtue of a present case being recognised to be *sufficiently and selectively similar* to a certain particular concrete past *successful* case, or cases, lodged in accessible habituated memory, that *empeiria* is successfully exercised in that present case. It is this that explains, and well explains, the need for *empeiria* to embody this special type of extensive memory knowledge of unified collections consisting of past concrete named or nameable individuals and similar successful particular cases of action involving them. *Empeiria* thus, in I.1, is not simply an ability to recognise how to deal successfully with new cases. It *is* such an ability of course, but one whose actual operations, and effectiveness in exercise, Aristotle, in I.1, undertakes to account for in some psychological depth.

There is a Platonic antecedent that helps us to understand Aristotle's approach here. For Plato, at least in *Republic* VII, skilled practical success in a concrete new case requires properly judging its suitable, if inexact, *similarity* to a non-concrete *ideal* case such as that grasped by one who has knowledge of the Platonic form of justice, or of health or of the good (VII 520a–d; cf. IV 443c–44a). Aristotle replaces this with the doctrine that reliable practical success in a concrete new case requires properly judging its suitable *similarity* to other *concrete* past *successful* cases lodged in memory, not similarity to some Platonic ideal since, so he often argues, there is no such thing (*Metaph.* I.9 991a20–92b9; *EN* I.6 1097a10–15). The more Aristotelian approach, depending for success on access in habituated memory to past concrete cases, is in fact condemned by Plato in *Rep.* VII (516c–e). For Plato there, no knowledge, or even practically adequate opinion, that concrete cases of, say, healing, were or are or will be successful is possible without proper recourse to some ideal theory, in his sense, of the nature of health. Aristotle rejects Plato's epistemology on this point and even holds further that without genuine *prior* perceptual *knowledge* of the success or correctness of past *concrete* particular cases there would be no epistemic basis for coming to know *any* true theory, ideal or otherwise.[12]

Thus, Aristotle's special conception in I.1 of what gives *empeiria* as 'knowledge of particulars' its power for present or future successful action

---

[12] *Pr An* I.30 46a17–27; *Post An* I.31 87b39–88a17, II.19 99b28–100a2. In Irwin 2000, by contrast, a reverse, Platonic mode of epistemic priority, for knowledge of theory over concrete cases, is falsely assigned also to Aristotle.

is entirely absent from what we find in *EN* VI.7 or II.7. It is not that, on the latter account, one might not need to have had some experience of past actual concrete instances of, say, chickens, as surely one must, in order to acquire and to use the determinate 'particular' knowledge that, in general or always, chicken is healthy, for successful action.[13] It is rather that the 'knowledge of particulars' in question in *EN* VI.7 is not simply such experiential knowledge of past or present concrete named or nameable individuals as chickens as would be sufficient to generate the ability to identify chickens in the present or future. Nor, more to the point, is the knowledge of particulars in *EN* VI.7 collected memory knowledge of actual concrete instances not of chickens, but of many propositional items or facts on which actual individual chickens were *known to be healthy to eat*, facts grouped naturally together in habituated memory as a class of similars, as it is in *Metaph*. I.1. There is no mention in VI.7 or II.7, or elsewhere in the *EN*, of such a special type of unified memory knowledge of collected facts about similar *successful* past cases, each involving concrete individuals, nor any role for it. Rather, to repeat, the knowledge of particulars, and thus the *empeiria* expressly in view in *EN* VI.7, is simply knowledge of suitably determinate and thus suitably actionable propositional generalities. It is just this that is said to be crucial for practical success there.[14]

Thus, as we can now clearly see, there are *two quite different models* for the kind of 'knowledge of particulars' it is that is required for practical success in our two main passages. There is, as Aristotle indicates, an avowedly popular or exoterically based model in *EN* VI.7, where regular success depends on the grasp of suitably many generalities of appropriately narrow scope; and there is another, esoteric, much more psychologically sophisticated, model in *Metaph*. I.1, where regular success depends on memory access to suitably many unified collections of similar actual concrete past successful individual cases involving particular individuals.[15]

Aristotle does, of course, offer some further general remarks elsewhere in the *EN*, outside of VI.7 or II.7, on how *technê* or *phronêsis* or *empeiria* are

---

[13] See, e.g., *EN* VII.3 1146b35–47a9, where this is in play. But what is called universal (*katholou*) there could, and should, count as what is called particular in VI.7 if it is, in line with VI.7, a general propositional item suitably narrow in scope properly to facilitate action; as is also the case for the *empeiria* of X.9 1180b30–81a12. We will return to this issue later in this section and in Section X.

[14] We find this same approach as here in the *EN* in *Rhet*. I.2 1356b30–57a7, by contrast again with that in I.1, a matter to which we shall return in Section IV.

[15] The first model might well have been one made especially evident to Aristotle, by contrast with the second, in some of the *technai*, or manuals, for successful medical practice that he collected, which are noted and described in this very mode by him in *EN* X.9 1181b3–12.

successfully activated in new cases and these are also in need of consideration. In II.6, he advises that the doctor or trainer, in dealing with concrete new cases, should aim to hit the mean and avoid both excess and deficiency, in prescribing food and drink for instance (1106b5–28). In VI.11, he famously adds that to successfully deal with concrete new particular cases in this manner 'it is necessary to have perception concerning them, and this perception is [practical] intelligence (*nous*)' (1143b5; cf. II.9 1109b20–23, IV.5 1126b4). He there closely associates the possession and use of this practical intelligence with the possession and use of *empeiria* (1143b6–14). These remarks, as far as they go, are not directly inconsistent with the esoteric account in *Metaph.* I.1 of the detailed mode of the successful, psychological operation of *empeiria*, but they altogether lack specificity on that more scientific, psychological issue, and Aristotle offers no departure in *EN* VI.11 from the direct implication of VI.7 that the *empeiria* in question that is to be used for successful 'perception' is and need only be of *generalities* of suitably narrow scope, acquired of course in a way such as to enable one perceptually to identify instances of the terms or kinds involved in those generalities of narrow scope for purposes of action.[16]

Elsewhere in the *EN* we do perhaps find reason why Aristotle would not in the end be content with his approach there in VI.7 from the more esoteric or scientific point of view. He emphasises again and again in the *EN* that in practical matters all types of generalities *of whatever scope* typically hold only for the most part, so that special information applicable to each particular individual at hand is necessary for regular practical success.[17] But unlike what we find in I.1, Aristotle tells us nothing in the *EN* about how such individualised information is psychologically acquired or used. This is no doubt appropriate in an exoteric treatment addressed just to those youths – in fact, exclusively to young male citizens of the *polis* – who 'have been well brought up in good [i.e., virtuous] habits'. This is Aristotle's audience in the *EN*, which consists thus largely of those who are educated to the point of 'ordinary understanding', rather than being addressed to those 'few ... whose understanding is precise and exceptional', who would be ready or could be made ready for an esoteric approach from natural psychological science not suitable for the *EN*.[18]

---

[16] Cf. *EN* II.7 and IX.2 with III.3.
[17] Cf. *EN* II.2 1104a5–10 with I.3 1094b19–22; I. 9 1109b20–23, III.3 1112b9–16, V.9 1137a13–18, V.10 1137b12–32, X.9 1180b8–10.
[18] Cf. *EN* I.5 1095b4–13, X.9 1179b24–31; II.2 1103b28–1104a11 with *Top* VI.4 141b12–14; *EN* I.3 1094b12–27.

In *EN* VIII.1, in fact, Aristotle explicitly says:

> Questions in natural [e.g., psychological] science we may leave aside, since they are not *proper* (*oikeia*) to our present investigation. (1155b8–9)

Such a non-scientific level of treatment will of course also be appropriate for the discussion in the *Politics*, which continues the discussion in the *EN*, and is thus proper for more mature members of the same group addressed in the *EN* (VI.13 1102a19–25). Aristotle's principled avoidance of any account in the *EN* and *Pol.* of the reliable natural psychological processing that takes place when a correct and warranted practical choice is made by the skilled *technitês* or *phronimos* has opened the way to a reading of this by some on which such a correct choice is in the end for Aristotle a matter of immediate self-warranting (practical) insight or intuition, with no reasoned natural psychological processing or warrant available to account for its reliable correctness. This version of a so-called particularist or intuitionist approach finds in the silence of the *EN* and *Pol.* an answer to a question that Aristotle does not intend to address there.[19] As we have noted, Aristotle indicates that he is not speaking in the *EN* to those who know about, or need to know about, natural science, psychological or otherwise.[20]

V Aristotle's Scientific Treatment of Practical Knowledge

There is somewhat more information than that found in *Metaph.* I.1 provided on practical knowledge and its exercise from the side of scientific psychology in *DA* III.11, where Aristotle says:

> The deliberative use of appearance (*phantasia*) is found in those animals which can calculate, since [to deliberate] whether to do this or that [to reach some given goal] is directly the function (*ergon*) of calculation (*logismos*) [in the consideration of alternatives]. Since one would pursue the better [alternative] it is necessary to evaluate [alternatives] by use of a single metric (*heni metrein*), so that one has the power [as an effective deliberator] to

---

[19] An especially clear instance of this approach remains Woods 1986.
[20] He does often refer in the *EN* to things that hold 'by nature' but he regularly uses this term there, appropriately, in traditional generally intelligible common exoteric ways where this is opposed to what holds by convention or set law, or is opposed to what comes about by habit or instruction (I.3 1094b16, II.1 1106a9, V.7, X.9 1179b20), and not, inappropriately as he himself says, where it would refer to what holds as a matter of natural science (VIII.1 1155b2–15). Where he does, once at least, apparently introduce the latter (VII.3 1147a24–31) it is as an aside by clear contrast with the quite different general procedure that, earlier in that same context, he has recommended as sufficient and proper for the *EN*. Cf. *EN* VII.1 1145b2–7 with VII.2 1146b6–8.

constitute one (*hen*) [single metric for evaluating alternatives] *out of many appearances* (*phantasmata*). (434a7–10)

This scientific account of how a skilled practical agent successfully selects a correct course of action from among alternatives conforms quite easily to Aristotle's account in *Metaph*. I.1 of the use of *empeiria* for successful action in, say, healing. There, as Aristotle says, the doctor who is experienced (*empeiros*) has built up out of many groups of memories of successful similar past cases – memories that are of course for Aristotle naturally stored collectively by means of appearances or *phantasmata* (*Mem*. 1 450a11–25) – a single unified power (*mias empeirias dunamis*, 981a1) usable as a metric for choosing the better alternative in a given case by review of past successful cases.[21] In the also scientific *Mem*. 2, successful reasoned deliberation as to how properly to act is directly associated by Aristotle with a form of recollection where it is, in standard cases, a suitably *unified* collection of things fixed by habituation *via* multiple phantasms in memory that serves as the base or metric by access to, and review and use of which, either explicit or implicit, successful deliberation is accomplished in the present (453a4–14 with 451b10–16).

To explore yet further Aristotle's account, or accounts, of deliberation and successful choice by those with practical knowledge, it will be useful to consider still other texts in his scientific works that are often thought to assist us on this topic, beginning with his outline sketch of the standard deliberations of a doctor who has medical *technê* in *Metaph* VII.7, where he says:

> Since health is *this*, if someone is to be made healthy then *this* [which health is] must be present – say it is a uniform state [of the body] – and, if that is to be present, then ... heating; and this [heating] he [the skilled doctor] accomplishes by rubbing. (1032b6–26)

It is important to see first that Aristotle offers us here in *Metaph*. VII.7 essentially no information as to just how, as a matter of reliable psychological processing and review, a skilled doctor comes to a correct final decision on the proper course of treatment in a particular case. Even accepting his assumed definition of health as bodily uniformity, which

---

[21] Some would suppose rather that the single thing in question in *DA* III.11 (*hen*, 434a9) is not a single metric but simply a single phantasm or internal presentation composed of the presentations of different alternatives and, perhaps also, of a metric for comparing them. But *hen* here clearly refers back to *heni* (a8), and that single thing is something *by which* one measures, which metric it is Aristotle's aim to expose here. On the alternative account he tells us nothing about this. For further discussion of this and related passages, see Bolton forthcoming.

seems to be put forward simply as a familiar enough description that is adequate for his purposes (*Top.* VI.2 139b21; *Post An* I.13 78b18–27), Aristotle offers us no account of how it is psychologically, in deliberation, that the skilled doctor reliably and correctly decides in some case at hand that heating is appropriate rather than say cooling, or some entirely different course of action to restore suitable bodily uniformity if the patient has, for instance, a broken leg. In addition, even if heating is appropriate, Aristotle offers us here no account of just how the doctor correctly decides in deliberation that rubbing, as opposed to the drinking of wine, or wrapping the patient in blankets, etc., is the preferable alternative. Suppose that the patient has a severe rash where the rubbing would need to take place (cf. *EN* IX.2). To assume, as some would, that Aristotle takes it that the fully skilled doctor will have knowledge of numerous exceptionless universal generalisations of narrow enough scope sufficient to cover each such variation is to ascribe to him a position, never stated by him, that is both highly implausible in itself and does not fit Aristotle's oft stated view of the inexactness of practical knowledge where its non-trivial generalities, no matter how broad or narrow in scope, typically hold only for the most part.[22]

This is not to criticise Aristotle's account in *Metaph* VII.7 or 7–9. His aim there is to analyze *coming to be* – by nature, by *technê* and by spontaneity – in order to isolate the roles of *form* and *matter* in such coming to be for strictly metaphysical purposes, in particular, to help him heuristically to determine how, or whether, *form*, in some suitable sense, counts as *substance* or primary reality, in some suitable sense (1032a12–33a22). His aim is not, as it is in I.1, or *DA* III.11 or *Mem.* 2, to describe the full mode of psychological review and processing, explicit or implicit, which results reliably in correct decision-making in particular new cases by the *empeiros* or *technitês*. Still, the limitations of the example in VII.7 on this score – and also of the often discussed related examples in, for example, *MA* 7 701a7–32 – show us how little assistance even a proper universal theoretical conception of the nature of health, by itself, would offer for regular correct decision making and how crucial the role of the unified knowledge in accumulated memory and experience of collections of similar past successful particular healing actions, as understood in *Metaph.* I.1, is for that purpose.[23] In any event, moreover, as in *Metaph.*

[22] *EN* II.2 1104a3–10 with I.3 1094b19–23. Contrast Coope (Chapter 5), and, earlier, Cooper 1975.
[23] To add, moreover, to the example in *Metaph.* VII.7, so-called particular premises of the sort that figure, e.g., in the expanded examples in *MA* 7 and in *EN* VII.3 would not address the problem in

VII.7, Aristotle's aim in *MA* 7 is again not to detail the type of psychological processing that reliably results in correct decision-making but, there in *MA* 7, to identify the efficient cause of action, or other animal movement (700b4–11). His concern in I.1, by contrast, is not to identify what causes one to act in the right way when one knows it but how the right way to act is correctly decided.[24]

This issue comes to the fore again, of course, in the *EN* in III.3, where, in his account of proper ethical deliberation and wise choice of correct action in particular cases, Aristotle may seem to be more concerned than he is elsewhere in the *EN* with the fine details of correct decision-making. There he notoriously offers us the following:

> We deliberate not about ends but about what promotes ends .... Having set down the end we deliberate about how and by what means it is to be achieved. If it appears to come about by several means we consider by which of these it will come about most easily and finely, while if by one means only we consider how it is to be achieved [most easily and finely] by that means, and then how [i.e., by what means] this further means is to be achieved, [and so on] until we come to the first cause [directly within our power to enact for reaching the end] which is the last in the order of discovery. (*EN* 1112b11–20)

Here again Aristotle does not describe in any manifest way the psychological processing and review by which correct choices are made *at each stage* of discovery, at each of which the deliberator will normally be dealing with things that only hold for the most part. This is, in the first instance, because his clear and stated aim here is to show that deliberation is not about ends and to show how a proper, if sketchy, account even of the multiple stages that may be involved in deliberation supports that result, not to describe the internal psychological processing that reliably leads to a correct choice or decision *at each stage*. In addition, as we have seen, his discussion there needs to be easily accessible to and proper for the general audience that he is addressing, and thus exoteric, not esoteric and scientific as is his discussion in *Metaph.* I.1, *DA* III.11, and *Mem.* 2. In *EN* II.1, Aristotle does attribute such practical knowledge as comes with the

---

question here, which is created already by the so-called universal premises in play that must, typically, only hold for the most part. See *Pr An* I.2 for guidance on the notions of universal and particular in play in such contexts.

[24] Compare *EN* VII.3 1147a24–b5 where Aristotle has a similar aim to that in *MA* 7, as he does also in *DA* III.11 434a16–21 and in other passages where the so-called practical syllogism is under discussion. His sketchy examples are adequate for his purposes in those contexts but not for his different purposes in *Metaph* I.1.

acquisition of moral virtue to the same source as does the acquisition of the practical knowledge that comes with having properly learned how to build houses, namely, to habituation (1103a14–25). Such an emphasis may further open the door to a scientific account of the mastery and exercise of practical knowledge of the type developed in *Metaph.*1 and *Mem.* 2, where habituation again plays a crucial role, as we have seen and will see, but, given the audience of the *EN*, there is no more than an open door to that, and no departure is offered there, or in X.9 1180b30–81a12, from the clear doctrine of *EN* VI.7 or II.7.

In sum then, and most importantly as we can now see, *empeiria*, as understood in I.1, must somehow *both* have sufficient generality in its content for it to be ready for the search for its causal explanation *and* the very special type of particularity in its content required by the necessity for it to incorporate extensive accessible memory knowledge of collections of similar concrete named or nameable individuals and individual past successful cases involving them, the grasp of suitable selective similarity to which is the effective psychological and epistemic basis for select present or future successful action. We shall later explore just how this rather puzzling but little addressed *dual* requirement for *empeiria* is satisfied.

VI *Technê* As Knowledge of Universals

Before addressing that puzzle, however, it is necessary first further to investigate Aristotle's claim in *Metaph.* I.1 that *technê* is 'knowledge of universals'. This often is taken to mean that, perhaps unlike *empeiria*, *technê* involves the knowledge of universally quantified truths such as: In every case, fire is hot. This would fit Aristotle's familiar logical use of the terms universal and particular in *Pr An* I.2 (25a1–13). Such a reading might also seem to be confirmed in *EN* X.9, where Aristotle says:

> Care can best be provided in an individual case (*kath' hen*) by a doctor, or trainer or anyone else, who knows *as a universal* (*katholou*) what is good for everyone, or at least for people of certain sorts, since the *epistêmai* [such as medicine or gymnastics] are said to be, and are, concerned with what is common (*koinon*). Not but what *some* single individual (*hen tis*) may perhaps be well cared for by some unlearned person who has accurately observed in experience what happens in that individual case (*eph' hekastô [i]*), just as people hold that some are their own best doctors though unable to cure anyone else. Nevertheless, it would presumably be held that if someone wishes to become *technikos* or *theoretikos* he must advance to what holds *katholou* and come to know that as widely as possible since, as was

said, this is what the *epistêmai* are concerned with. (1180b13–23; cf. *Rhet* I.2 1356b30–33)

This passage might seem to support the view that, for Aristotle in *Metaph*. I.1, the knowledge of *katholou* or universals that is required for *technê* and its successful use is always knowledge of what holds in every case of a certain sort. However, the passage cannot in fact be used to show this since in the lines prior to this passage Aristotle has just said this:

> Though *as a universal* (*katholou*) rest and fasting are good for someone with a fever, in some individual case (*tini*) [of someone with that fever] it may not be so. (*EN* X.9 1180b8–10)

Here what holds *katholou*, as a 'universal', cannot be what holds in every case of a certain sort but only, rather, what holds in general, or on the whole. So when Aristotle goes on right away in the text to speak of what holds *katholou* and as such is a matter of *technê*, he cannot mean by what holds *katholou* what holds strictly in *every* case of a certain sort; he means rather what holds in general or on the whole. What holds *katholou*, as what holds in general but not in every case, is contrasted *in this context* with what holds in some single ground level individual case or cases. This is, then, a yet different contrast between universals and particulars, and the knowledge thereof, from the one in *Top* I.12 and *EN* VI.7, and also different from the contrast in *Metaph* I.1. In each of those texts, the particulars, and the knowledge of particulars, in question must have a greater generality than here where knowledge of particulars is only very limited experiential knowledge concerning single individuals and individual cases, even for instance by a lay person who can only cure himself, not knowledge of relevantly determinate generalities of narrow scope, or knowledge of groupings each made up of many past concrete individual particulars and particular successful cases grasped in habituated memory as suitably similar. 'Particular' knowledge of determinate *generalities* of narrow scope such as 'chicken is healthy', as understood in *EN* VI.7, would thus count as knowledge of universals not of particulars by the lights of X.9.[25]

Thus, *technê* here, in *EN* X.9, as the grasp of the universals in question here, is a grasp of suitably many generalities in the sense of many things that obtain on the whole in various sorts of cases whatever the scope may

---

[25] Aristotle's Greek can use the term (an) *empeiria*, as here in X.9, to refer to single items of perceptual experience, as well as for a certain general understanding or power for action based on extensive such experience, as in I.1.

be of those generalities, not simply of generalities of broad not narrow scope, nor of things that obtain in every case of a certain sort or sorts; nor, as we shall shortly further confirm, of cases where one type of thing belongs to another as a kind (*kat' eidos*) as in I.1 (981a10). Nor is there any mention here in X.9, as there also is not elsewhere in the *EN*, of a need for *technê* to involve knowledge of scientific causes, or any indication that *technê* as understood here, as knowledge of many generalities (*katholou*), is superior, or even equal, for purposes of action to *empeiria* as understood in *Metaph.* I.1. *Technê* as understood here in X.9, as knowledge of suitably many generalities of whatever scope, is judged best by comparison with *empeiria* understood as experiential knowledge of isolated individual cases, but, as we have seen, the latter is not what *empeiria* is in *Metaph.* I.1. Nor does Aristotle indicate in X.9 how knowledge of universals as understood there, as generalities (whether of broad or narrow scope) which typically have *exceptions*, can function to secure success in new cases. In *EN* II.2, as we have noted, Aristotle says that the proper procedure in new cases is to pay special attention to each individual at hand as a way of making effective use of generalities that hold only for the most part (1104a5–10; cf. I.6 1097a10–15). But, again, unlike what we find in *Metaph.* I.1, he tells us nothing there in *EN* II.2 about how, psychologically and warrantedly, this is to be reliably and successfully done. As bears repeating again, to say simply that the generalities should be of narrow scope would hardly provide an adequate answer to the problem arising from the fact that practical generalities *of whatever scope* typically have exceptions, a serious problem to which the account in *Metaph.* I.1, *DA* III.11, and *Mem* 2. does directly offer a compelling solution not found in the *EN*.

VII Knowledge of Universals in *Metaph* I.1

This shows us in some detail now, as we had already earlier begun to see, that there are many contrasts between particulars (*kath' hekasta*) and universals (*katholou*) and the knowledge thereof in Aristotle, contrasts that differ markedly depending on the context of discussion, so that we must be careful when we try to use what we find in one such context to interpret what we find in another. But, in any event, we clearly cannot use what we find in *EN* X.9 to support the result that in *Metaph* I.1 knowledge of universals is knowledge of regularities that hold in every instance of a certain sort since what holds as a *katholou* in X.9 is only what holds in general or on the whole. Nevertheless, there is compelling evidence in I.1 itself that by what is *katholou* or universal, and thus is required for *technê* as

Technê *and* Empeiria 151

understood there, Aristotle does not mean (1) what only holds in general or on the whole but not necessarily in certain individual cases, as in *EN* X.9. Nor does he mean (2) what holds, either generally or in every case, with wider scope than for some other more 'particular' generality of more narrow scope, as he does in *EN* VI.7 or II.7. Nor does he simply mean by what is *katholou* in *Metaph.* I.1 (3) what holds in *every* case of a certain sort, as opposed to what holds only in *some* case or cases of a certain sort, as he does in *Pr An* I.2. He is rather using *katholou* in I.1 in still another, quite different, *fourth* way, one that he in fact defines for us in *Post An* I.4–5. As we have seen, in *Metaph.* 1.1, Aristotle glosses his reference there to what holds *katholou*, knowledge of which is required for *technê*, by indicating that it is what holds of some group of things marked off 'as a single kind (*kat' eidos hen*)'. (981a10). In *Post An* I.4–5, he explains this special use of the term universal or *katholou* as follows:

> I call universal (*katholou*) a case where one [kind of] thing belongs to another *both* in every instance (*kata pantos*), *and* in itself (*kath' hauto*) and as that [kind of] thing (*hê[i] auto*) .... Hence [to illustrate], even if someone proves separately ... of *every* type of triangle – equilateral, scalene and isoceles – that it contains [angles equal to the sum of] two right angles, he still does not know as a *katholou* that the triangle contains [angles equal to] two right angles ... even if [he knows that] there is no other type of triangle than these; for he does not know that having two right angles belongs to the triangle *as a triangle* (*hê[i] trigônon*), nor even that it belongs to every triangle except collectively, but not to every triangle *as a kind* (*kat' eidos*), even if there is no triangle which he does not know to have it. (73b26–74a32)

It is just his last language here, employing the phrase *kat' eidos*, as a kind, that Aristotle uses also in *Metaph* I.1 where he characterises *technê* as the type of 'knowledge of universals' that requires the grasp that some type of subject has some feature *kat' eidos hen*, as a single kind (981a10). Thus, it is this very special sort of *katholou* or universal, and knowledge of this, that he has in mind in I.1 for *technê*. In the *Post An*, moreover, Aristotle tells us just how knowledge of universals in this special sense is reached. In brief, he says that, for instance, knowledge of the universal that the triangle *hê(i) auto* or *kat' eidos*, as that very kind, has interior angles equal to two right angles is reached by, and only by, strict scientific demonstration of this fact from the proper first principles of the relevant science (*Post An* I.4 73b32–74a3, I.5 74a32–b4).[26] In *Post An* I.33, Aristotle again refers to

---

[26] Thus, the universals in question in *Metaph.* I.1 are not, as such, items that do explaining, as some have supposed the universals are that figure both in I.1 and in *EN* VI.7. They are rather, in typical cases, things that get demonstratively explained and are made evident only by demonstrative

the truths grasped by, and only by, proper demonstration as those where the predicate is seen to belong to the subject *kata to eidos*, as the kind of thing the subject is, by derivation from proper principles (89a20). These proper or special principles that do the explaining, moreover, will necessarily, and importantly, include both those principles, called by Aristotle 'hypotheses' (*hupotheseis*), that are necessary to fix and delimit the special subject or *genos* to which the triangle, say, and the study of the triangle pertain, and also the basic definitional principles that state what the causally ultimate essences are of the triangle and other geometrically relevant entities (*Post An* I.2, 10, 28; cf. *DA* I.1). We shall shortly see the special significance of this requirement.

In any event, this confirms for us now that, in *Metaph* I.1, Aristotle does indeed mean to say in speaking of the *technê* of medicine, for instance, as 'knowledge of universals', as universals are understood in I.1, that medical *technê*, when mastered, essentially involves a genuinely *theoretical scientific component*, one whereby the medical *technitês* knows by proper scientific demonstration that certain specific types of ailments, not only in every case but also as the specific natural kinds of ailments that they are (*kat' eidê*), are cured by certain specific treatments. As Aristotle directly says in *Metaph*. I.1, knowledge of such a special fact and universal (*katholou*) is not knowledge that one could have prior to the grasp of a causal demonstration. It is exclusively a matter of *technê* and, as such in I.1, it is *only* acquired by proper causal explanation (981a5–30).[27] It is, then, this demonstrative scientific knowledge,[28] coupled with the relevant extensive empirical memory knowledge of groups of similar ground level particulars and particular successful cases, extensive empirical knowledge that it would in any case have been necessary to accumulate as a prior condition of acquiring this scientific component (as Aristotle says in *Metaph*. I.1; *Post An* I.31 and II.19) that fully constitutes medical *technê*.[29]

---

explanation, from proper principles, as in the case of the 'universal' truth that triangles as a kind have angles equal to two right angles.

[27] Thus, the universal or *katholou* in question in I.1 cannot be the same as that *katholou* introduced in *Post An* II.19 100a6, as many allege, since unlike the case in *Metaph*. I.1, the universal in question there in II.19 *must* be known *prior* to the possession of *technê* or *epistêmê* and, thus, prior to the grasp of the causal explanation and demonstration that there alone yields it (100a6–9).

[28] On the relationship of *technê* to scientific demonstrative knowledge, see also Coope (Chapter 5).

[29] There is still a fifth use of the term *katholou* in Aristotle found, for instance, in *APo* II.19, where he says: 'It is some particular (*to kath' hekaston*) that is perceived, but [active] perceiving is of [i.e., has also for its content] a *katholou*, for example it [perceiving] is of [the *katholou*] human being, not rather [i.e., merely, in content] of [the particular] Callias, who is a human being' (100a17–b1). Here we have the familiar use of *katholou* found in *Int* 7 17a37–b16 where it designates a general *property* predicable of many things by contrast, also there, with a particular such as Callias, which is

Technê *and* Empeiria 153

It is worth emphasising at this point that, as we can now see, the theoretically demonstrable component of medicine, described in *Metaph.* I.1 as universal in the sense in question there, does *not* consist of things that may hold only for the most part. Rather, as in *Post An* I.4–5, it consists of truths where one kind of thing belongs to another in every case, in itself and as that kind of thing. So, for Aristotle, even where, or especially since, the demonstrable scientific component in a *technê* has this character, there is the necessity for *technê* as a whole, which includes its demonstrated empirical base, to involve the type of collected memory knowledge of groups of similar ground level particulars and particular events that is in question in I.1, in order to permit its successful use in the practical domain where things typically hold only for the most part. Elsewhere, of course, Aristotle does note that in a domain considered by natural science, such as health, regularities may well hold only for the most part (e.g., in *Post An* I.30). But that is absent from I.1 and it plays no role in explaining the need for the kind of knowledge of (demonstrated) universals or *katholou* in play there for *technê*.[30]

VIII Non-Scientific Modes of *Technê* in Aristotle

Aristotle's account of *technê* in *Metaph.* I.1, as containing a theoretical, strictly scientific, component, fits well with the close parallel drawn also by

---

not so predicable. Aristotle's point in II.19 is that perception does not have for its full content mere particulars, so to speak, but always is of, in its content, a particular, such as Callias, *as* a such and such, where the such and such introduces a general property, as we have seen perception always does in the examples offered of items of strict perception in *Metaph.* I.1 (cf. *Post An* I.31 87b29–30). Commentators from antiquity on often take *katholou* in this use in II.19 (100a17) to designate a general *concept*. See Sorabji 2010 for the early views. But a general property is not a general concept. Some also connect this use of *katholou* with the use earlier in II.19 (100a6) where, however, as in many of the other passages we have been considering, it designates a *propositional* item that, as subject to explanation, must be general in a suitable way, not a general property *or* a general concept, which are not so subject to explanation. For completeness, there is also an important use of *katholou* by Aristotle in *Ph.* I.1 184a23–b14, on which see Section XI.

[30] In *Metaph.* II.3 995a15–20 and *GA* V.10 778a5–9, one mode of inexactness endemic to things in the natural world is ascribed by Aristotle to the fact that physical particulars contain matter and thus may only imprecisely fit into the kinds with which natural science is concerned. This may well indicate that there is for Aristotle, in the end, no proper scientific logic, so to speak, for propositions that hold for the most part. The logic of science is, as it were, just the logic of exact science, for example, of universal truths in the sense of *Post An* I.4 and *Metaph.* I.1, however inexactly this may fit or apply even to the actual non-accidental, but imprecise, regularities in the material world. (That natural science and scientific explanation may concern things that are only 'usual' does not require that the propositions actually *demonstrated* in such a science themselves have 'usually' as a part of their very content. This is not required by, for example, *Post An* I.30. Nor could such propositions be *explained as* having this very content by the demonstration since the causes of such 'usual' status are indeterminate.) This would mark an accommodation to some degree on Aristotle's part to Plato's idealisation of science, but without the extra metaphysical baggage of Plato's theory of forms.

him in *Post An* II.19 and *Pr An* I.30 between the proper mode of the acquisition of *technê* and that of *epistêmê*, where *both* are finally reached in the same way, by demonstration of items of prior knowledge of just the same sort from indemonstrable principles (100a3–9, 46a17–27). This helps to explain also why Aristotle treats *technê* and *epistêmê* together, as reached through knowledge of explanatory causes, again in I.1 (981a1–3). It also fits well with Aristotle's references in the *PN* to medical *technê* as including the knowledge of health and disease by doctors as a proper part of natural science, a part that he indicates that he himself aims to pursue. Thus, as he asserts there:

> Not only the doctor but also the natural scientist [e.g., Aristotle himself] must, up to a point, state the causes [of health and disease] ... since those doctors who are refined and accomplished do treat in part of natural science and deem it right to find the causes [of health and disease] there. (*Juv.* 480b22–28)

This passage confirms that *iatrikê*, or medical *technê*, for Aristotle himself does indeed include a theoretical scientific component, one that he may himself have pursued in another now lost work in two books, entitled *Medicine* (*Iatrika*), which is also listed by Diogenes.[31] But, while this 'scientific' conception of *technê*, as we may call it, is clearly the one offered in *Metaph* I.1, and in *Post An* II.19 and *Pr An* I.30, and is one that fits closely with the details of Aristotle's apparent allusions in the *PN* to his own now lost scientific study of health and disease, there are other main texts which make it clear that Aristotle did not have only this one monolithic theoretical, scientific conception of a *technê*. There are signs of this elsewhere in the *PN* where Aristotle says, in *Sens* 1:

> Most natural scientists *and most doctors* who pursue the *technê* [of medicine] more philosophically [i.e., more theoretically, than do other doctors] ... begin their study of medicine with a study of natural science. (436a19–22)

This singular passage bears witness to the existence, in Aristotle's acquaintance, both of a standing group of 'doctors' who took the *technê* of medicine to involve a substantial explanatory scientific component and also of another standing group of doctors who viewed the *technê* of medicine very differently.[32] That Aristotle himself was more than

---

[31] D.L. V.25; see Düring 1957: 88, 228, for mention of such a work under related titles in the other ancient lists.
[32] On the significance of this the discussion here draws on Bolton 2018, which see also for further details.

sympathetic to the idea that a genuine *technê* need not, and in certain cases could not, involve or require a theoretical scientific component of the sort mandated for medical and other *technê* in *Metaph.* I.1, *Pr An* I.30, and *Post An* II.19 is made quite evident in the opening lines of *Rhet.* I.1, where he says:

> Rhetoric is a partner of dialectic. For both are concerned with the sorts of things which it is in a certain way common to everyone to know and which [in order to know] do not involve any distinct scientific knowledge (*aphorismenê epistêmê*). This explains why everyone [not simply some few with *epistêmê*] takes part [successfully] in a way in both [dialectic and rhetoric]. For everyone, up to a point, engages in [the dialectical] examination [of others] and in submitting to argument [i.e., to dialectical examination from others]; and also [everyone takes part] in the [rhetorical] defense of himself and accusation of others [e.g., before a jury]. Now most people do these things [successfully] either at random (*eikê[i]*) or due to a capacity reached through habituation (*sunêtheia*). Since both are possible, it is evident that their [successful] procedures can be reduced to a system (*hodôpoiein*), since it is possible to see why some succeed [regularly] due to habituation and some succeed [at random] by chance (*apo tou automatou*), and everyone would agree that this sort of thing [i.e., practical success due not to chance but to the mastery and use of procedures that can be systematised] is the function (*ergon*) of a *technê*. (*Rhet.* 1354a1–11)

Here, to focus first on dialectic, Aristotle tells us that dialectic is a *technê*. It is a *technê* because its successful procedures can be reduced to a system that can be mastered, one then suitable for use for regular practical success. However, Aristotle says, dialectic is a *technê* whose mastery and skilled use does not involve the possession of any *epistêmê*, any scientific knowledge, at all. These points are echoed in *SE* 11 where Aristotle affirms again that dialectic is a genuine *technê* (172a34–36) and says:

> Now dialectic is not concerned with any definite kind (*genos ti horismenon*), nor does it establish anything concerning any [definite *genos*], nor is it such as to be of what is universal (*katholou*) [pertaining to a given *genos*]. For [dialectic deals with all things and] all things are not contained in any single *genos* nor, if [*per impossibile*] they were, could all things fall under the same principles (*archai*). So no *technê* [of the type] that establishes things [from special principles] that concern a particular nature (*tina phusin*) proceeds by asking for concessions .... Dialectic, however, does proceed by asking for concessions, while if it aimed to establish things [universally concerning a particular nature and kind] it would refrain from asking for concessions, especially about the primitive things (*ta prôta*) [that fix the kind or *genos* in question] and [more generally] about the special principles (*tas oikeias archas*) [e.g., also the definitions that concern the *genos* in question]. (172a11–20)

Here it is evident that dialectic, though a genuine *technê*, *cannot* involve a scientific component, since this would require that dialectic, like medicine or gymnastics in Aristotle's view, be concerned with a special *phusis* and *genos*, a natural kind such as health or bodily fitness, and with special principles of explanation that determine and that apply strictly within that *genos* (*Post An* I.2, 10). This is not the case for dialectic because it is concerned with everything that is, not with what has to do with a particular *genos* since, contrary to Plato, *what is* (*to on*) is not a *genos* or natural kind (*EE* I.8 1217b34ff; *Metaph.* VII.1 1028a10–15). Thus, unlike the *technê* of medicine in *Metaph.* I.1 for Aristotle, the proper norms or strategies (*topoi*) for the practice of the *technê* of dialectic cannot, at any level, be reached or confirmed or understood by scientific causal explanation, since, as earlier noted, this can only take place where the subject concerns a particular *phusis* and *genos*.[33]

IX How to Learn a Non-Scientific *Technê*

Nevertheless, as we have seen Aristotle tell us in the *Rhet.*, since it is a genuine *technê*, the proper procedures or rules of dialectic can be 'reduced to a system'. If this system cannot have any of its practical norms reached, or confirmed or understood through scientific explanation, unlike norms of the *technê* of medicine in I.1, how then are these norms to be reached or learned? In the *Rhet.*, Aristotle informs us that highly successful dialecticians have been guided in practice by norms of proper procedure that they internalised by habituation without the grasp of any distinct science or *epistêmê*. We know, in addition, that Aristotle himself undertook, for the first time as he says in *SE* 34, to collect and to offer as the basis for a *methodos* for the successful practice of dialectic a systematisation of a sort of the norms that did govern the reputedly successful practice of dialectic as it actually existed in his day. This is of course just what we are presented with in the *Topics* (including the *SE*). There Aristotle commonly introduces those *topoi*, or strategies for successful argument, which he collects and systematises for use in dialectic, *as* the ones that are themselves generally

---

[33] In *Metaph* IV.2, Aristotle does also say that dialectic and sophistry deal with the same *genos* as does philosophy/science (1004b22). This does not mean however, which would be contrary to what we find in *SE* 11, that dialectic, like a science, concerns a distinct *genos* or natural kind. For one thing, dialectic importantly concerns the accidental that is the concern of no science (*Top.* II-III; *Metaph.* VI.2). Aristotle means rather that any scientific subject or domain (*genos*) can be treated not only scientifically but also, like everything, dialectically, or indeed, again like everything, sophistically, cf. *SE* 11 172a21–b4, and Bolton 2013.

taken to be proper and accredited (*endoxoi*) and thus to have been successful.³⁴ So, not only are the proper *premises* for dialectic generally accredited (*endoxa*, *Top.* I.1), so are the strategies or *topoi*, and they are collected only on that basis, not on the basis of any scientific *genos* under which they all fall.

Thus, the *Top.* provides us with a paradigm example of a systematised manual for the exercise of a genuine *technê*, as Aristotle calls it, where that *technê* is one whose mastery does not and cannot include the grasp of any scientific explanatory component. Rather, Aristotle offers us this in *Top.* I.2 as a prime use for his manual for dialectic:

> That this endeavor (*pragmateia*) [as codified here for the first time in the *Top.*] is useful for training (*gumnasia*) is apparent on its face. For if we have a systematic procedure (*methodos*) [acquired by this training] we shall be able quite easily to tackle the thing [i.e., any problem] proposed. (*Top.* 101a28–30; cf. I.3 101b5–10, *SE* 34 183a37-b14)

Here Aristotle indicates that the *methodos* whose mastery constitutes the *technê* of dialectic is acquired by training or repeated practice, and thus by habituation, in the use of the various standardly well-regarded strategies of argument, or *topoi*, that he catalogues. Elsewhere in the *Top.*, especially in VIII.14, he emphasises the necessity of such repeated practice on particular successful, and unsuccessful, examples – of which the *Topics* is full – for acquiring the 'habituation' (*to ethizesthai*) and the 'trained memory' (*mnêmonikê*) that underwrite the mastery of the *methodos* and *technê* of dialectic (163a29–b16, b24–33; cf. VIII.9 160b14–23). This shows the importance for Aristotle of habituated memory access to groups of similar past examples for the skilled practice of the *technê*. As commentators have noted, the reference to *topoi*, or, literally, *places*, in the title of the work, apparently alludes itself to the elements of typical mnemonic devices used to accomplish recollection that were popular in antiquity.³⁵ This would seem to show further that the organisation of the *Topics* by types of *topoi* or 'places' is itself specifically designed to facilitate its habituated assimilation, through practice on the proper groups of particular similar examples, for subsequent use as a mnemonic system (*Top.* VIII.14 163b23–33; *Mem.* 2 452a13).

This need for reliance on habit and trained memory does not mean, of course, that the skilled dialectician cannot give or use explanations or

---

³⁴ *Top.* I.14 105b30–31, IV.2 121b29–22a2, 3 123b20–32, VI.1 129a28–31, VI.4 142a13–16.
³⁵ See *Mem.* 2 452a14, and Solmsen 1929; Sorabji 2004a (1st ed. 1972), followed by Smith 1997.

reasons, in an ordinary sense, for moves that he may make in employing the *topoi*. He may, for instance, avoid or object to some proposed definition, say of a human being as *a rational animal*, on the ground that it does not put the *genus* of the *definiendum first* in the proposed definition (*Top.* VI.5). But the correctness or truth of the norm in question is not something that can be *scientifically demonstrated*, or learned or understood thereby. It is embedded in and has its standing only as a reasonable part of an accepted practice and, as such, it is mastered *for use* by habituation and training (*gumnasia*), which provides a base for suitable memory as a means to such use.

There is, in addition, clear indication that in the standing practice of dialectic a given *topos* will be more accredited (*endoxoteros*) for use in certain circumstances than in others, or with certain people than with others, so that there is an analogue to the situation in ethics where general norms of practice will hold only for the most part, and one where their holding for the most part, in dialectic, clearly cannot in any way be scientifically demonstrated, even with a rider such as 'if nothing prevents'.[36] One may, for instance, wisely choose in some context to put the differentia first, as grammar permits for a desirable emphasis on it, as in the above definition of a human being. Here too, then, as for deliberation and wise choice of correct action in other practical matters, reliance on trained memory concerning particular successful past cases and situations would be crucial for success. Nor does this reliance on habituation and trained memory mean that the skilled dialectician cannot be creative, or experimental, in dealing with new cases where, for instance, access to past successes does not easily determine a present course. But this will be done by imaginative use and warranted adaptation, through recognition of similarities, of the particular past successes and failures lodged in memory not by use of any scientific theory or by appeal to any exceptionless rules no matter how narrow in scope (cf. *Top.* I.3 with VIII.14).

This type of genuine *technê*, however, one acquired and effectively used only by proper habituation and trained memory, is of course not what Aristotle calls a *technê* in *Metaph* I.1. This type of *technê* is rather what Aristotle calls an *empeiria* in I.1.[37] As we can now infer then, the *Topics* gives us an early example of a systematised codification or manual of practical procedures previously found successful in groups of similar

---

[36] See, e.g., *Top.*VI.4 141a23–b2 at 142a12–16.
[37] This fits well with the fact that in the *Rhet.* and *Top.*, unlike the case in *Metaph.* I.1, Aristotle does not oppose *technê* to *empeiria*. Rather, as we have seen in *Rhet.* I.1, he opposes *technê* and what its use may regularly accomplish to *chance*. Contrast Schiefsky 2005.

particular past cases, procedures to be mastered and exercised by habituation and trained memory, for use in the practice of a *technê* as *technê* came to be understood in the later so-called *medical empiricist* school. That is, the conception of *technê* found in the *Top.* is one variant, at least, of the very conception of *technê* as *empeiria* defended by the later medical empiricists.[38] The further study of the *Top.* then can only help to improve our grasp of the early history of that empiricist conception of *technê* as *empeiria*, by contrast with the later so-called rationalist conception of *technê* that is anticipated, if not articulated, by Aristotle in *Metaph* I.1.

Dialectic is not, however, the only example of a *technê* for Aristotle that must be understood in this empiricist way. We have already seen Aristotle pair rhetoric with dialectic in this regard. In *Rhet.* I.2 he says:

> Neither dialectic nor rhetoric concerns how any distinct *epistêmê* stands; both are [simply] certain powers to invent arguments [on any subject] (*Rhet.* I.2 1356a32–33).

Apart from rhetoric, Aristotle also commonly speaks, for instance, of the *technê* of housebuilding (*oikodomikê*). This in fact is his prime example of a *technê* in *EN* VI.4 (1140a6f). But there can be no theoretical scientific component of this *technê* of housebuilding *as such* for Aristotle since, for him, there is no natural kind or *phusis* of the house – or of the couch or the shuttle for weaving either, contrary it seems to Plato (*Rep.* X, *Crat.*). The house is an artifact whose proper function, for Aristotle, depends on our interests and conventions, whether these simply concern shelter or also narcissistic trophy display or whatever. Houses are the object of study of no explanatory theoretical science – neither of mathematics, nor of physics, nor of theology, which are for Aristotle the only theoretical sciences (*Metaph.* VI.1 1026a18–19). How then is the full *technê* of housebuilding acquired? Aristotle's answer in the *EN*, in II.1, is this:

> We learn (*manthanomen*) a *technê* by [repeatedly] producing the very products which we must produce [by using it] when we have learned it. For example, we become [skilled] housebuilders by building houses. (1103a32–34)

This is Aristotle's conception of a *technê* and of its mode of full acquisition in the *EN*. In line with this, in *EN* VI.4 Aristotle says flatly:

> A *technê* does not concern things that are or come about ... by nature (*kata phusin*). (1140a14–15)

---

[38] See, e.g., Galen in Frede 1985 for the views of this school and for indication of variations within it.

This exoteric account, in the *EN*, of a *technê* clashes sharply with what we have seen in the esoteric account offered in the *PN* where one type, at least, of genuine medical *technê* concerns, in substantial part, the natural kind of health as something that does come about by nature, and requires for its mastery the study of health and its natural causes as a proper part of natural science.

This, further, answers for us now the intriguing question: Why is full *empeiria*, given its acquired power for regular practical success, not a virtue, even, with its acquired power for excellent deliberation, an intellectual virtue, for Aristotle? The answer is that, by the lights of the *EN* itself, as one type of *technê*, *empeiria* is an intellectual virtue, not because it contains a reasoned explanatory scientific component, since it does not, but because, at least in humans, it embodies an acquired power for successful *reasoned* deliberation, and calculation (*logismos*) in that mode, one based on extensive habituation and the subsequent ability reliably to recollect and to review relevant past cases to achieve new success. In *Mem.* 2, in his chapter on recollection, Aristotle counts the use of trained, skilled memory (*mnemonikê*) as an operation of reason in view of its ability to draw, in deliberation, on relevant past cases and to make a proper selection from among them applicable for success in present cases, even where no explanatory demonstration or even strict deductive reason is necessary or possible to reach a successful result in this reasoned process (453a4–14). It is a serious mistake, then, to rely too heavily on *Metaph.* I.1 and its more rationalist conception of a *technê*, especially there of medical *technê*, for Aristotle's conception of a *technê*, or of practical knowledge, overall.

X The Practical Value of Scientific *Technê*

A *technê* of the type to which dialectic or rhetoric belongs does not, therefore, rely at all for success on the grasp or use of any theoretical or scientific component, since there is no such component. But it is still worth asking whether a *technê* of the more rationalist type such as medicine, where there is a scientific component for Aristotle, does, for him, rely on its theoretical component and the knowledge of *causes* that it brings for full *practical* success beyond what is provided by its empirical component. Many interpreters would answer yes. But Aristotle never directly says that it does in the *Metaphysics*, or in other works where this rationalist conception of *technê* is under discussion, as one would expect he would if he believed it; and there is very good reason why he should not. To see this, consider first the famous case that he discusses in *Post An* I.13

78b34–79a16. Here he claims that an empirical doctor will know *that* circular wounds heal more slowly than non-circular wounds of equal length of outer boundary (something that of course in fact holds only for the most part), while a mathematical theoretician will supply *why* this is so, namely, because circular figures have a greater geometrical area than do those others. It is extremely implausible that the *practical* skill of the fully experienced doctor, who knows well how to treat circular and other wounds in all of the individual variability in which they come, would be enhanced by learning this explanation, and Aristotle certainly does not say or suggest in I.13 that it would. Again, the experienced housebuilder will know that oak timbers will bear a greater weight than pine and will know how to make use of this in select ways, which again apply only for the most part, in building. But it would be highly implausible to claim that knowledge of the true scientific *cause* of this – due for Aristotle to the differing *imperceptible* mixtures and ratios of hot, cold, wet and dry in the different materials (*Mete.* IV.4–5) – would improve his practical ability, and Aristotle does not say otherwise. Consider finally another, perhaps even clearer, case from *Post An* I.13, on which the experienced navigator will know and remember well the movements of the stars and planets, and will be able effectively to use this knowledge for the successful steering of his ship. It would be again extremely implausible, indeed absurd, to propose that theoretical knowledge of the causes of the various regular movements of these heavenly bodies – due for Aristotle to the special circular movements of the imperceptible ethereal spheres in which they are imbedded – would improve his practical ability and, again, Aristotle does not suggest otherwise.[39] In *EN* VI.1, Aristotle assigns the use of scientific reason (*to epistêmonikon*), for example, in reaching knowledge of causes, exclusively to the sphere of things that cannot be otherwise, as opposed there to the sphere of things that can be otherwise, such as, he indicates, practical matters involving *technê*, where it is *not* scientific reason but *only* deliberative reason (*to logistikon*) that is of use (1139a6–17).[40] So it is in this sense alone that *technê* is reason involving (*meta logou*) in *EN* VI.4

---

[39] In *EE* I.5 1216b2–25, Aristotle suggests that astronomy is not prevented by its theoretical status from having practical use. But he does not say that such practical use would be due to a grasp of its demonstrative explanatory component rather than to the mastery of its necessarily full empirical component.

[40] For a contrasting account of the role of *logos* in *technê*, which brings Aristotle's account in *Metaph.* I.1 closer to that of *EN* VI, see Johansen 2017.

(1140a3–24, particularly a10–13), by contrast, as we have seen, with what we find in *Metaph* I.1.[41]

XI The Status of *Empeiria* in a Scientific *Technê*

There remains, however, one feature of Aristotle's conception of the more rationalist type of *technê*, the type that *is* opposed to *empeiria* in I.1, which requires attention. On that conception, as we have seen, *empeiria*, as a component of full *technê*, as *technê* is understood in I.1, has both to be general enough in its content somehow to allow the search for its scientific causal explanation, and also to embody enough by way of memory knowledge of distinct groups of ground level similar concrete past successful cases to enable that *empeiria* to serve psychologically for present and future practical success in the day to day world where practical generalities typically hold only for the most part. How then is this *dual* status for *empeiria* possible? We can begin to see Aristotle's answer if we concentrate on a particular case of *empeiria*, or of knowledge-*that* as Aristotle describes *empeiria* in *Metaph*. I.1. In *Post An* II.8, a main example offered of knowledge-*that* is the knowledge concerning the lunar eclipse that the moon is subject to 'a certain loss of light (*sterêsis tis photos*)' (93a23). This instance of knowledge-*that* is presented in II.8, as are the cases of knowledge-*that* in I.1, as a prime candidate for causal explanation and thus for knowledge why and *epistêmê* or, in a practical case, *technê* (93a16–24). In *Post An* I.31, as we have noted, Aristotle indicates further that in this case our initial knowledge-*that* comes from 'observing repeated instances' of the loss of light in question, instances that are, as *Post An* II.19 makes clear, lodged together in a unified collection in memory (88a2–4, 100a3–6). Nevertheless, in *Metaph*. VIII.4, concerning this very case of knowledge-*that*, to the effect that the moon from time to time undergoes a certain 'loss of light', Aristotle says this:

---

[41] In *Metaph*. IX.2 (1046b2–24), Aristotle treats *technê* and other modes of human productive knowledge as capacities of a special sort whose exercise can involve the use of reason or reasoning (*logos*) in the determination *either* of how to bring about some practical result *or* its opposite. But nothing there indicates that it is the scientific use of reason in providing knowledge of causes by demonstration that he has in mind rather than the deliberative use of reason available to the *empeiros* as well as to the scientific *technitês*, which use of *logos* Aristotle distinguishes from the former, scientific use in *EN* VI.1. In any case, moreover, Aristotle's interest in IX.2 is in the, for him, metaphysical question as to what kind of potentiality or power (*dunamis*) a practical skill is – as a power to produce opposites – and not in the psychological question of just how in detail such a power is successfully actualised or exercised by an agent in particular cases.

> A [lunar] eclipse is ... a [certain] loss of light [by the moon] .... But this account [of the eclipse as a certain loss of light] is unclear (*adêlon*) if it is not accompanied by the cause (*aitia*) [of that loss of light] .... But if we add 'by the earth coming in between' [the moon and the sun], this will be the account accompanied by the cause [of that loss of light]. (1044b12–15)

This passage shows us that, for Aristotle, it is quite possible to look for the cause or the *why* of some still 'unclear' or less than precisely grasped or formulated *that*, as one can ask, quite reasonably, why the moon repeatedly undergoes those many similar actual losses of light, without wanting, or being able, to state precisely which losses of light are involved. We could mean initially to leave it open, for instance, in asking why, whether or not the partial eclipses, as we call them, are a different phenomenon with a different cause than the so-called total eclipses. Further, Aristotle says here, one will only reach a clear or precisely formulated *that* by or as a result of the process of proper causal explanation and demonstration. Prior to this, as I.1 tells us, the knowledge-*that* will be captured only in *empeiria* where, as we have seen, one's grip on the kind in question, such as the lunar eclipse, while looking for its cause, is essentially constituted by accumulated memory knowledge of many past individual instances, instances grouped together as similars that are naturally and correctly taken to belong on the whole to some single real natural kind, but a kind that is as yet not clearly specified. In *DA* II.2 also, Aristotle explicitly describes our initial knowledge-*that* (*to hoti*) as unclear (*adêlon, asaphes*), and he says there again, as in *Metaph.* VIII.4, that for a final clear grasp of the *that* it is necessary to 'make evident the cause (*aitia*)' (413a8–20).

This point is duplicated and developed further in *Ph.* I.1 where, as in *DA* II.2, Aristotle again describes our cognitive and epistemic ascent to scientific knowledge as starting from what is unclear in itself though clearer to us (184a19–21). This *first* stage is further described as involving the grasp of one sort of universal or generality (*katholou*), one that captures what is in accord with perception (*kata tên aisthêsin*) prior to knowledge of any causal principles, and as a special type of 'universal' in the grasp of which the kinds involved are not clearly and precisely demarcated (*adioristôs*, 184b2). Rather, as in *Metaph.* VIII.4, it is

> [starting] from the grasp of these things [these universals wherein the kinds involved are not precisely distinguished] that ... the principles (*archai*) become known and *serve to render distinct* (*diairousin*) these [previously not precisely distinguished kinds of] things. (184a21–26)

In *HA* also, Aristotle offers various examples of *empeiria* or knowledge-*that*, which, as generalities, have similar imprecision and unclarity. In VIII.24, for example, he says: 'Those with *empeiria* say that in general (*holôs*) the horse and the sheep have nearly (*schedon*) as many ailments as affect humans' (604b25–26). Elsewhere in *HA*, he cites as matters of *empeiria* what happens in some cases (*eniote*) and, very frequently, what happens often (*pollakis*) (IX.49 631b8, 633a9; IX.8 614a12–30). These imprecise or unclear facts are for Aristotle nevertheless, in *HA* itself, facts of which one may begin to look for an explanation, one that will jointly make 'apparent (*phaneron*) *both* the items to be explained *and* the things [the causes or *aitiai*] on the basis of which it is necessary to demonstrate them' (I.6 491a10–13). So, again here, it is only in or as a result of proper causal explanation that previous items of *empeiria* are made precise. In *Ph.* I.1, Aristotle cites, as parallel to cases of our initial imprecise knowledge-*that*, the case where 'children call all women [not *mother* but] mothers (*mêteras*)' (184b3–4). He again there treats such an imprecise fact, that women are mothers, as a fact of which, though imprecise, it is possible to look for an explanation, as obviously it is, an explanation in virtue of which, as he says, the two previously unclearly distinguished kinds, women and mothers, will, again obviously, become clearly distinguished.[42]

Nevertheless, and crucially now, when such unclear initial knowledge-*that* is refined and clarified in or by the process of reaching a proper causal demonstration, the prior *empeiria* with its special involvement of the extensive habituated memory knowledge of ground level particulars and particular facts will of course still remain, as a suitable basis for practical action, should the *empeiria* in question be of the sort that serves for action and not simply for causal explanation (*Post An* II.19 100a8–9). What the clarification through demonstration brings with it is knowledge why and, with this, more precise knowledge-*that*, it does not add any further power for action. Aristotle makes this clear, as we have seen, in I.1 when he says that those with *technê* are not wiser than those with *empeiria* 'in virtue of being able to act [correctly] but rather in virtue of knowing the causes [of the correctness of what is done by those with *empeiria*]' (981b5–6). In any event, we can also see now how it is that our original genuine *empeiria* or knowledge-*that* has the dual status that Aristotle requires of it in I.1, both to be sufficiently general as to be ready for the search for its causal explanation and the full refinement in its content that that alone can

---

[42] See further Hasper and Yurdin 2014 and Bolton 2009; 2017 with references there.

bring, and also to be sufficiently particular in its content, in the required sense, as to be fit to enable successful present and future action.

XII Conclusion

Finally, then, we are in a position to begin to offer a reasoned conjecture as to what the contents of Aristotle's lost treatise on *Technê*, if indeed there was such a treatise, might have included. On the model of *Metaph.* I or of *DA* I, it might well have begun with an account of the differing opinions of Aristotle's predecessors and contemporaries, both on the nature of *technê* and on its mode or modes of reliance, or not, on knowledge both of universals and of particulars, understood in various ways. On the model of *Metaph.* III, Aristotle's treatise on *technê* might well then have turned to a review of problems generated by conflicts among these different views of *technê* and different views of the required knowledge of universals and particulars.[43] On the model of *Metaph* IV.2 (cf.1003a33-b10), the treatise might well then have proceeded to offer a resolution of these conflicts and problems, beginning with the announcement that:

Hê technê men legetai pollachôs.

Technê is, in fact, so-called in many ways.

---

[43] In *DA* I.2 403b20ff Aristotle depicts these first two required stages, as he sees them, as compactly combined into one.

CHAPTER 7

The Stoics on Technê *and the* Technai

Voula Tsouna

I Introduction

By the time of Aristotle's death, which also conventionally marks the beginning of the Hellenistic era, the notion of *technê* had been debated for a long time by philosophers and non-philosophers alike.[1] However, there is a fair level of consensus[2] to the effect that *technê* commonly refers to expert knowledge of a specific subject matter corresponding to a particular art or craft or discipline,[3] and also that *technitês* as well as other semantically related terms[4] designate the practitioners of different *technai*, arts, as expertly knowledgeable people in their respective fields. Typically, these latter are viewed as professionals who achieve valuable results for their communities and, therefore, enjoy wide recognition and respect. Moreover, they are considered entitled to act as instructors in their arts, explaining their methods and procedures and transmitting their expert knowledge to their pupils. So far as the nature of the *technai* is concerned, it is broadly assumed that they involve theory as well as practice, have a sort of generality and universality and accomplish their functions with varying degrees of regularity and precision. Everyone would agree that good mathematicians are typically successful in their proofs, whereas well-

---

[1] The chapter on the Stoics and the chapter on the Epicureans (Chapter 8) are envisaged as a fairly close-knit pair. Those who will read only the Stoic section will encounter a rather abrupt ending, whereas those who will read only the Epicureans will have missed some early groundwork. To acquire a complete picture, it is best to read both chapters in sequel. The Introduction to the volume highlights the organic unity of these two chapters and provides useful guidance to the readers.
[2] A useful survey of the earlier uses of *technê* is offered by Roochnik 1996: 17–88.
[3] In this latter sort of case, *technê* is used as a synonym for *epistêmê*. As we shall see, Plato as well as the Stoics and the Epicureans often use these terms interchangeably in non-ethical contexts. As has been convincingly argued (Hulme Kozey 2019), in many cases the *technai* are also called *epistêmai* by synecdoche: the arts do not consist *only* of sciences, but nonetheless scientific or expert understanding does constitute the most essential aspect of an art. As will become evident, I favour this sort of approach regarding both the Stoics and the Epicureans.
[4] Such terms include *ergatês* and *dêmiourgos*, which ordinarily designate experts in first-order arts.

166

reputed doctors do not always cure their patients nor do able sea-captains always bring their boats safely to shore.[5] The examples of carpentry and weaving used by early Greek authors highlight a feature crucial for every other *technê* as well: namely, the core idea of craftsmanship, of systematically putting together a certain sort of material to constitute a coherent whole. Past experience and current input, traditional knowledge and newly formed beliefs, theoretical aptitudes and practical skills, reasoning and intuition and talent and other relevant elements, are all methodically woven together with a view to the goal that each *technê* aims to fulfill.[6] Such structures are dynamic and open-ended. However, the domain of each *technê* can be fairly clearly delimited at a given time. The experts can usually reach a consensus as to what constitutes technical knowledge and what does not, who is an expert and who is not, and what are the criteria according to which the expert can be distinguished from the non-expert.

Plato appears especially concerned with this latter issue. Moreover, he addresses a question first raised by Solon, namely, whether the successful practice of the *technai* has value in its own right. In tandem with Solon, Plato's Socrates appears strongly inclined to answer that question in the negative, and discusses from different perspectives a distinction also found in earlier literature between the first-order *technai* or *epistêmai*, arts or sciences, which are morally neutral and can be used for good or evil, and a putative second-order *technê* or *epistêmê*, whose consistent practice can secure happiness. Notably, he explores the limits of the so-called *technê*-analogy, which is usually taken to suggest that the first-order *technai* are importantly analogous to a higher-order *technê* whose object is good and evil and whose peculiar function is the attainment of happiness. While Socrates' commitment to the aforementioned analogy is disputed,[7] it is relatively uncontroversial that Socrates favours a rationalistic account of *technê*. In short, his view seems to be that a genuine art or science differs

---

[5] It is important to keep in mind the idea that in certain arts, the so-called stochastic arts, the experts do not always achieve successful outcomes even though they always are in full possession of their *technai*. For, as we shall see, this idea underlies the Stoic conception of the art of living especially associated with Antipater, according to which the sage acts like the archer, whose expertise consists in aiming right even if he does not necessarily hit the target. I thank James Warren for his comments on this topic.
[6] Strictly speaking, the subject matter of the *technê* is distinct from its goal as well as the activity aiming to fulfill the latter. For example, the subject matter of medicine is commonly considered to be health and disease, while the goal of medicine is to treat or cure the patient and the activity of the medical doctor consists in whatever it takes to attain that goal. For the most part, I shall not draw attention to these distinctions, but the immediate context shall make clear, I hope, which one of these aspects of *technê* we are focusing on.
[7] The interpretation of the *technê* analogy is controversial, as shown, e.g., by Roochnik 1996.

from mere empirical practice because, unlike the latter, the former has a method, is governed by principles and rules, admits of a *logos*, account, in virtue of which it is transmissible to others and aims to achieve a good as opposed to mere pleasure. Also relevant to present purposes is another element found in certain dialogues of Plato,[8] namely, the suggestion that a hierarchical relation could obtain between the first-order *technai* and a second-order *technê* or *epistêmê* whose function comprises the orchestration of the first-order arts with a view to the common good.[9]

These ideas constitute the core of the philosophical background that the Stoics and the Epicureans take into consideration in order to form their own positions about *technê*, first-order or higher-order. Hence, I shall frequently refer to Plato in relation to each of these schools and, especially, the Stoics. In the first chapter of this study, I shall discuss the Stoic definitions of *technê*, argue that they belong to a unified conception of the notion, explore the implications of the latter for the first-order *technai*, compare them with the higher-order art whose only expert is the sage and indicate ways in which the Stoic position on art and the arts can be fruitfully interpreted as a complex reaction to Plato. In Chapter 8, I shall follow a similar course with regard to the Epicureans, shifting, however, the foci of emphasis to reflect the distinctive interests of Epicurus and his followers. In addition to defining *technê*,[10] they account for the origin of the arts and the phases of their development, identify the main criteria of technicity and draw distinctions between different sorts of arts, ask how the *technai* are profitable and to what extent they may be practised by the sage and determine clearly and firmly the axiological relation between the first-order *technai* and the *technê* by which one lives the philosophical life. To conclude, I shall venture a few comparative remarks concerning the views of these two schools on *technê*, their respective stances vis-à-vis Plato's heritage, and their value for us.

However, Aristotle will be nearly absent from these two chapters, and I wish to explain why. Despite contentions to the contrary, I am convinced that Aristotle does have a coherent conception of *technê* and a carefully worked-out view of the complex relations between *technê* and *epistêmê*, as

---

[8] These dialogues include the *Charmides*, the *Euthydemus*, the *Republic* and the *Statesman*.
[9] See Rachel Barney, Chapter 3 in this volume.
[10] Properly speaking, Epicurus and his adherents do not define, but describe or outline the subject of enquiry. Henceforth, references to Epicurean 'definitions' should be understood in a catachrestic, Epicurean sense of the term.

The Stoics on Technê *and the* Technai   169

well as *technê* and *phusis*.[11] Some of his assumptions and positions find parallels in the extant remains of the Hellenistic schools. Nonetheless, his approach to the subject of *technê* is largely motivated, first, by his interest in different kinds of understanding and explanation[12] and, second, by his investigation of metaphysical issues regarding reality, change and the potentialities of matter.[13] For instance, Aristotle discusses the potentialities of a certain material to produce a certain type of artefact, its proper or improper uses[14] and the limitations that the natural properties of a given material can set on the process of artistic or technical transformation. On the other hand, as far as we know, neither the Stoics nor the Epicureans discuss *technê* in connection with such issues. Rather, they concentrate on *technê* primarily for epistemological and ethical purposes. Even when they extend the concept of *technê* to the realms of physics and cosmology, they do so chiefly to defend or, alternatively, reject creationism and its implications for the good life.[15]

II The Stoics: Definitions of *Technê*

We may begin with the definitions of *technê* attributed, respectively, by the sources to the three leaders of the early Stoa. According to Zeno, the school's founder, 'an art[16] is a system made out of cognitions [*sustêma ek*

---

[11] Regarding this topic, I am indebted, most of all, to Vattimo 1961 and Natali 2007. I am grateful to Carlo Natali and Cristina Viano for drawing my attention to this latter study. Natali 2007 argues convincingly against the thesis defended by Isnardi-Parente 1962 and 1966, namely, that Aristotle's views about *technê* cannot be integrated into an organic whole, mainly because of Aristotle's twofold concern, on the one hand, to respect his commitment to Platonism and, on the other, to preserve his empiricism.

[12] See Ursula Coope, Chapter 5 in this volume.

[13] Natali 2007 substantiates this point by providing detailed discussion of several passages mainly drawn from the *Physics* (notably, 193a9–17, 193a23–28, 199a33-b7, 200a7–13, 200b5–7) and the *Metaphysics* (notably, 1032a3–6, 1032b9–22, 1036a31–32, 1044a25–32, 1047a24–26, 1048a32–33, 1049a5–12, 1069b29–34). Among other things, Natali's analysis provides greater perspective and depth to a claim first advanced by Vattimo 1961, that is, that Aristotle conceives of *technê* in terms of work accomplished not *against* nature but rather *beyond* nature.

[14] On this point too, see the account by Natali 2007, who argues that, although, according to Aristotle, the sphere of the accidental is indefinite, a distinction should be drawn between a 'proper' accidental and an 'improper' accidental use of a material, e.g., wood or straw. As he points out, this distinction makes good sense in the broader context of Aristotelian physics and, in particular, Aristotle's analysis of different sorts of change.

[15] Regarding the Stoics, the fact that their extant remains do not contain discussion of the ontology of artefacts is especially surprising in the light of notable similarities between Aristotle and the Stoics themselves. However, perhaps these similarities are due not to a direct influence of Aristotle on the Stoics, but to the fact that both Aristotle and the Stoics have Plato as their starting point. I am grateful to Carlo Natali for this suggestion.

[16] In this and other similar contexts, I usually render *technê* by 'art' or 'expertise'. In some cases, it can be translated, more specifically, as 'craft', and in cases in which the term is a synonym or near synonym of *epistêmê*, I render it by 'science' or 'discipline' (see above, n. 2).

katalêpseôn)[17] that have been practised together [cf. *suggegumasmenôn*)[18] with a view to some goal useful for life'.[19] A different sort of definition of art in terms of tenor (*hexis*), a notion drawn from Stoic physics, is attributed by the sources to Zeno as well as Cleanthes, Zeno's successor and the principal rival of Arcesilaus, head of the Academy.[20] According to this latter, 'an art is a tenor [*hexis*] that brings to completion all things[21] by following a certain road' (Olympiodorus, *in Plat. Gorg.* p. 53). The same source attests that Chrysippus found Cleanthes' definition unsatisfactory for the reason that it is too broad: nature too is a tenor that accomplishes its goals in the same manner as art. 'Therefore, he added the phrase "with impressions" [*meta phantasiôn*] and claimed that art is a tenor that proceeds by following a certain road with the aid of impressions.' In addition, he probably conceived of art also in the way Zeno did, as 'a system or collection of cognitions' (Sextus, *M* VII.227) applied together to achieve some profitable aim. A closer look at these definitions should help us acquire an initial idea about what, according to the Stoic authorities, a *technê* is and what are its prominent characteristics.

In the first place, Zeno's definition stresses the cognitive character of a *technê* as well as its complexity and systematicity. An art does not consist in a single *katalêpsis*, cognition, but in a collection made out of cognitions (cf. *ek katalêpseôn*) conceptually related to each other in some systematic manner. Given their systematic character, it seems reasonable to infer that each such set of cognitions is governed by principles and rules, and also can be modified and enriched over time.[22] Moreover, Zeno's contention that the cognitions constituting a *technê* must be practised together suggests, I think, that no sharp dividing line should be drawn between the theoretical elements and the practical application of a *technê*. Typically, an art consists of both, although this does not necessarily mean that they stand on an equal footing as constitutive elements of it. Like all other cognitions, art-related cognitions result, in Zeno's view, from assenting to cognitive

---

[17] On the variant ἐγκαταλήψεων occurring in the mss. of ps-Galen, *Def. med.* 8, p. 350, 7–8 K, see Gourinat 2011: 245 and n. 11.

[18] A compelling defense of the genitive plural συγγεγυμνασμένων over the accusative singular συγγεγυμνασμένον attested by the mss. is offered by Mansfeld 1983.

[19] Olympiodorus, *in Plat. Gorg.* 53, 54 Jahn. In most cases, I follow the system of references and abbreviations of the sources on Stoicism used by von Arnim 1903–1905.

[20] Scholia ad Dionys. Thracis Gramm. ap. Bekk. Anecd. 663,16.

[21] In this instance, 'all things' probably means any given thing in any domain. I thank Sara Magrin for this clarification.

[22] Sparshott 1978: 284 claims that the phrase *ek katalêpseôn* is intended to convey the idea that a *technê* evolves over time. Compare Gourinat 2011: 255, who takes Zeno to claim, simply, that a *technê* is a system consisting of interrelated cognitions, without reference to its development over time.

impressions, and cognitive impressions are typically empirically derived. Hence Zeno appears to believe that arts typically have an empirical basis and depend on experience for their further development and practical applications.

Chrysippus' claim that *technê* advances by following a certain road on the basis of impressions also highlights the empirical dimensions of art. Moreover, the metaphorical reference to a road draws attention to what we may call the orientedness or directionality as well as the forward-looking nature of every *technê*. The experts do not act at random, but advance step-by-step in accordance with the methods peculiar to their respective *technai*. They observe certain principles and rules but not others, pursue certain lines of enquiry but not others, act in certain ways but not in other ways. And thus they make steady progress, moving from one point to another, towards the final goal of their art. This latter is determined by the object or subject matter of a *technê*, that is, what a *technê* is *of* or *about*: weaving cloth, making things out of wood, building houses, restoring health, dancing or administering one's property and wealth.

While both Chrysippus and Cleanthes compare progress in the *technai* to advancing along a certain path towards a destination, Cleanthes differs, so far as we know, from his successor in that he chooses to explain *technê* in physiological and psychological rather than epistemological terms. As mentioned, Cleanthes defines *technê* as a *hexis*, tenor, of a certain sort – a tenor moving forward systematically from one point to another. Whether this definition originates with Cleanthes or, more probably, can be traced back to the school's founder (Scholia ad Dionys. Thracis Gramm. ap. Bekk. Anecd. p. 663,16),[23] to understand its meaning we need to consider what *hexis* stands for in Stoic physics.[24] The term is related to the verb *echein*, to have or to hold, and refers to that in virtue of which a body is sustained or held together. Probably reflecting the canonical view, Chrysippus describes tenor as a current of air or breath expanding and contracting, pushing and pulling simultaneously and in opposite directions and, in virtue of the tension involved in this dynamic continuum, causing a thing to be what it is.[25] Thus, tenor is responsible for the essential quality

---

[23] See Gourinat 2011: 251 and n. 43. As Mansfeld 1983: 61 points out (cited by Gourinat 2011: 251 n. 44), a parallel can be drawn between the definition here under discussion and Zeno's definition of nature as 'artful fire proceeding towards generation by following a certain road' (D.L. VII.156).
[24] *Hexis* has a different meaning in Aristotle: see Ursula Coope, Chapter 5 in this volume.
[25] Plutarch, *de Stoic. repugn.* 1053F–54B; cf. also Alexander of Aphrodisias, *de mixtione*, p. 223, 225 Bruns.; Plutarch, *de comm. not.* 1085C; Galen, *de musculorum motu* I, 7 and 8. See further the analysis by Long and Sedley 1987: 1: 286–89.

of a thing, whether this latter is something lifeless, such as a stone, or a power of intelligence (Philo, *Leg. Alleg.* II & 22). Moreover, tenor is supposed to account for the defining feature of a given class of things, even though the members of the class may exhibit that feature in different degrees or variations. Technically, *hexis*, tenor, differs in this respect from *diathesis*, character: the former can accommodate variety and imperfection within a class of things, whereas the latter cannot. But also, *hexis*, tenor, differs from *schesis*, relational state. For while a tenor is an essential and defining characteristic, states such as 'well-organised leisure, undisturbed stability, manly concentration' (Stobaeus, *Ecl.* II p. 73,1) are acquired features that a thing may or may not come to have.[26] A *technê*, then, is a tenor that makes its possessor be what he or she is: a weaver, a builder, a doctor, a geometer, a dancer.[27] One can be better or worse at these arts, and one can have greater expertise in certain aspects of an art than in others.

Although Zeno's conception of art as a collection of systematically interrelated cognitions was far more influential in antiquity than the conception of art as a tenor directed to a certain goal (cf. Quintillian, *Instit.orat.* II.17.41), there is no indication they were treated as mutually exclusive. Rather, they complement each other, in so far as they highlight different aspects of *technê*. While Zeno's more widespread formula focuses on the epistemological content of a *technê*, the alternative, psychological formula highlights the fact that expertise in a given art constitutes, as we might say, a dispositional state orienting the people who possess it to apply systematically a particular method in order to attain the goal of their art. As for Chrysippus' aforementioned definition, we may take it to combine these two approaches, since it both underscores that art is a tenor and specifies that it is a sort of tenor relying on impressions to pursue the attainment of a final goal.[28]

I wish to make an additional remark regarding the nature of this latter. While many arts aim at the production of something distinct and independent from the artistic process itself, for example, a house or a cloak, this is not always the case. As Cleanthes makes clear, an art's production should be understood in a broader manner, as a methodical process successfully brought to completion (cf. *anuousa*: SVF I.490).[29] Curing a patient, bringing a ship to port, tending one's flock, dancing, playing music and wrestling are all recognisable goals of their corresponding arts. The same

---

[26] See Long and Sedley 1987: 1: 289.
[27] Striking parallels are found in Plato, e.g., *Prt.* 311b–12b.
[28] See Long and Sedley 1987: 2: 263.
[29] This point is stressed by Gourinat 2011: 252.

holds to some extent for theoretical activities that Aristotle classifies under the heading of *epistêmê*, science, for example, the activity of a geometer going through a proof or of an astronomer calculating the motions of a planet.[30] Barring ethical contexts, in which the Stoics need to distinguish first-order knowledge of the *technai* from the *epistêmê* of the sage,[31] I suggest that the Stoics tend to treat as *technai* all sorts of methodical activities: theoretical as well as practical, prestigious or pedestrian, productive as well as performative[32] and so on. Two related elements of Stoic *technê* also call for further comment: the intuitive assumption, shared by all Stoics, that the final end of each art is something beneficial for life; and the idea, briefly mentioned above, that the cognitions constituting an art must 'have been practised together' to attain the art's final objective.

As mentioned, it is commonplace that a *technê* must be good for something: it must bring some benefit to *bios*, human life; and in so far as a *technê*'s product or function is beneficial, it is also good (*agathon*) or fine (*kalon*). In the context of Stoic philosophy, however, these terms take on a special meaning. Since virtue is the only good and vice the only evil,[33] the arts and their achievements cannot be evaluated in absolute terms as good or profitable.[34] Rather, they are 'things to be preferred' (*proêgmena*) as opposed to 'things to be dispreferred' (*apoproêgmena*), and they derive their relative value from the fact that 'they can contribute further to living in accordance with nature' (Stobaeus, *Ecl.* II.80, 22) – the ultimate moral goal, which, according to the Stoics, is equivalent to living the good life. We shall return to this topic later, but for the moment the implication to retain is that, in the eyes of the Stoics, the arts can have only relative value. While the accomplishments of a given art are perceived as advantageous from a perspective internal to that art, they can be judged to be neutral or harmful when viewed from a different perspective. This observation points to the possibility that there may be a sort of expertise that transcends the limits of the first-order *technai* and supplies objective criteria for assessing the value of their functions and products.

Turning to Zeno's claim that an art entails 'having practised together' (cf. *suggegumnasmenôn*) the set of cognitions constituting that art, the quoted phrase suggests that one's mastery of a *technê* requires knowledge

---

[30] Again, see the study by Ursula Coope in this volume (Chapter 5).   [31] See Section V.
[32] On the importance of the performative arts for Plotinus' conception of divine craftsmanship, see Emilsson, Chapter 10 in this volume.
[33] Also, the Stoics allow for goods, such as the good person himself or herself and good friends. However, these too qualify as goods ultimately because they are assessed in terms of virtue.
[34] Inwood 2015 argues briefly and convincingly to that effect.

as well as a certain sort of training. Not only does a doctor possess the set of cognitions essentially constituting the art of medicine, but he is also able to bring his expert cognitions (or subsets of them) jointly and systematically to bear on particular cases requiring treatment. It is significant that several Stoics active in different periods appear to deliberately avoid drawing a wedge between knowing *that* and knowing *how*, theory and training, the principles governing an art and their application to practice. Rather, the Stoics generally underscore the interaction between these elements and the ways in which they are yoked together in the service of a common goal. Despite contentions to the contrary,[35] there is no solid evidence that the orthodox Stoics privilege the practical application of first-order arts over their theoretical and epistemic elements. The opposite is more likely to be true. In my view, what turns a system (*sustêma*) of cognitions into an art is, first of all, the conceptual relations tying these cognitions together and the methodological path that the practitioner of the *technê* is expected to follow. These are the elements primarily accounting for the 'tenor' in virtue of which one is an expert in a given art.[36]

III The Stoics' Debt to Plato

Before moving on, we should pause to consider the considerable extent to which the Stoics are indebted to Plato's explorations of the notion of *technê*. Leaving aside the fact that the Stoics view *technê* as a corporeal state of the commanding faculty – a position with which Plato is evidently at odds, the first affinity to note is that both sides greatly emphasise the importance of method. The four *technai* mentioned by Socrates in the *Gorgias* qualify as genuine arts mainly because they are systematic and pursue a beneficial goal in a methodical manner. In virtue of their methodical character, they are able to 'always tend to the best advantage, the ones the body, the others the soul' (464c), and also can be properly taught and learned. The expert is the only competent teacher (cf. *Prt.* 319b–c). He is a *technitês*, or *technikos* (*Lach.* 185a), or *dêmiourgos* (*Grg.* 452a, *Chrm.* 171c), or *epistêmôn* (448e, 449a; *Chrm.* 174a). Very similar ideas are found in Stoicism too, and the same goes for the Socratic belief that a genuine *technê* admits of a *logos*, explanation or account (cf. *Grg.* 465a). Zeno's view that a *technê* proceeds by following a certain

---

[35] Notably, see Sellars 2003, who defends a similar approach regarding Plato as well.
[36] See n. 2 above, and also the incisive observations by Sparshott 1978: 281–82.

path implies that every step can be explained by reference to what precedes and what is to follow.

To be sure, while Plato is notoriously diffident towards experience, the empiricist aspects of the Stoic notion of *technê* should not be underrated. In addition to the importance that Chrysippus ascribes to the experts' systematic use of cognitions paradigmatically deriving from the senses, the following distinction is drawn between artful and artless ways of practising divination: true experts foretell the future by conjecturing on the basis of careful empirical observation of signs, whereas people that have no real expertise prophesise merely by stimulating or relaxing the mind, like dreamers or people falling in a trance (Cicero, *de div.* I.34). On the one hand, it seems virtually certain that Plato's Socrates would reject that sort of distinction, together with the cardinal role ascribed to empirical observation and inference (cf. *Tim.* 71d–72b). On the other hand, first, the gap between the two approaches under discussion is narrower than it might seem. For, much of what Plato's Socrates says about first-order arts is consistent with the assumption that these latter progress in part on the basis of experience. For instance, he characterises the person who really knows how to use the products of a *technê*, for example, a horse's reins or a flute, as someone who is *empeirotatos* (*Rep.* 601d), most experienced about such matters. And recent research on scientific practices in the Academy indicates ample if cautious use of empirical data.[37] Second, if the Stoics determine technicity, first of all, by reference to the principles and cognitions constituting a *technê*, they probably find congenial Socrates' suggestion that a person who has no knowledge of the theoretical elements of an art but nonetheless tries to teach it would be a strange teacher (*atopos paideutês*: *Rep.* 493c). And, furthermore, they certainly agree with Socrates that a *technê* differs from a mere knack acquired through familiarity and habit (cf. *Grg.* 465a).[38]

Another Socratic/Platonic feature that finds a new home in Stoicism is the large scope and flexibility of the notion of *technê*, which includes as I have suggested all sorts of first-order arts and disciplines. Arts such as carpentry, architecture and medicine, but also arithmetic and geometry and calculation, religious ritual, draught-playing (*Grg.* 450d), money-making (cf. 450e), fencing, horse-riding, shepherding and many other activities fall under Plato's concept of *technê* as they would under its Stoic counterpart. Also, the criteria of arthood intimated by Plato's

---

[37] See Kalligas 2016.   [38] The Epicureans too draw a similar contrast: see Chapter 8.

dialogues find close parallels in Stoicism. According to Plato's Socrates, if there is to be a genuine *technê*, one should be able to tell what it is (*Grg.* 448e), what it is *of* (*Grg.* 451a–c; *Chrm.* 165c–66b), and what it is good *for* (*Lach.* 185c–e; *Chrm.* 167b, 171d–75a). Not unlike the Stoics, then, he determines a *technê* by reference to its domain and its final end. This idea is defended by Plato's Socrates at some length, together with the contention, implicitly endorsed by Stoicism, that the domain or the goal of *technê* must be distinct and different from the *technê* itself (*Chrm.* 165c–66c).[39]

Further affinities between the two approaches under discussion concern the relative value of artistic products and, importantly, the idea that their value depends on their good or bad use. Socrates argues that 'for every thing', including every first-order expertise, there are three *technai*: the maker's, who has true belief (*pistin orthên*: *Rep.* 601d); the user's, who has genuine knowledge (*epistêmê*: 601e) and the imitator's, who has neither (cf. 601c–2b). The distinction relevant to our purposes is between the maker and the user: according to Plato's Socrates, while all first-order experts can be considered makers in a broad sense of that term, only a higher-order *technê* may be capable of assessing 'the excellence, beauty, and rightness of each instrument, animal, or action according to nothing other than its use for the purpose for which each of them has been made or has been naturally constituted for' (601d). The user's art, then, is higher-order because of the kind of knowledge that it involves: knowledge concerning the teleological purpose of everything, including the products of the first-order arts. Arguably, a similar thought lies at the core of the Stoic *technê biou*, the art of living, in so far as the Stoics conceive of it as a higher-order *technê* whose only expert is the sage. The latter can be considered a user not just in the sense that he uses the products of the other crafts but, importantly, in the sense that he has complete understanding of what everything is for in the light of what is good. However, it is important to stress that for the Stoics more than for Plato the art of living, in addition to being a superordinate art, is also concerned with every aspect of daily life.[40]

---

[39] In my view, the refutation of Critias' position in the second half of the *Charmides* vindicates Socrates' contention that, if temperance is a *technê* or *epistêmê*, then, like other *technai* or *epistêmai*, it must be of something distinct from itself. In any case, the Stoics clearly think that the first-order *technai* as well as the virtues have respective spheres distinct from themselves (e.g., Stobaeus, *ecl.* II.62, 15).

[40] I thank Thomas Bénatouïl and Emily Hulme Kozey for their comments on this point.

IV Technê and Epistêmê

Since the sage is also the only person to have *epistêmê*, a term that in certain contexts has the specific meaning of scientific knowledge, we should broach the subject of the art of living, first, by looking at the relation between *technê* and *epistêmê*. As I indicated, the Stoics tend to blur the semantic boundaries between these two notions to the point of often using them as near synonyms. However, this occurs mostly in non-ethical contexts, whereas in ethical contexts the Stoics tend to distinguish the cognitions of moral progressors (who presumably include first-order experts) from the stable and coherent manner of knowing that constitutes the *epistêmê* of the wise man. The following passage indicates the complexity of the relation between *technê* and *epistêmê* and the different ways in which the Stoics put these notions to use.

> *Epistêmê* is a cognition [*katalêpsis*] which is secure and cannot be shaken by argument. Secondly, it is a system of such *epistêmai*, like the rational cognition of particulars existing in the virtuous person. Thirdly, it is a system of expert *epistêmai* [*epistêmôn technikôn*] which has intrinsic stability, as the virtues do. Fourthly, it is a tenor for the reception of impressions [cf. *hexin phantasiôn*] which is unshakable by reason and consists, as they claim, in tension and power. (Stobaeus, *Ecl.* II p. 74, 16;[41] see also D.L. VII.47; Cicero, *Acad. post.* I.41; Sextus, *M* VII.151)

Further evidence attests that, taken in the sense of tenor, *epistêmê* invariably leads to the acquisition of true beliefs formed by reason on the basis of the relevant impressions (Galen, *defin. medicae* II.7 vol. XIX p. 350).[42]

Thus, on the one hand, technical expertise and scientific knowledge share essential features in common. Both consist of systematically interrelated cognitions deriving from assent to cognitive impressions. And both are dispositional states of distinct but comparable sorts. On the other hand, they also have crucial differences that the Stoics point to in order to defend the epistemic and ethical superiority of the sage vis-à-vis the rest of mankind. While *technê* as a *hexis* must admit of degrees, *epistêmê* is a

---

[41] I follow the translation by Long and Sedley 1987: 1: 256, with modifications.
[42] Even though the substitution of 'belief' (*doxa*) for 'reception' (*prosdexis*) may be historically inaccurate (see Gourinat 2011: 244–45), it is not philosophically untenable. Surely, Zeno would accept that, since *epistêmê* is a perfected disposition regarding the reception of *phantasiai*, it must invariably lead to the acquisition of truths.

permanent character (*diathesis*)[43] not susceptible to variation. And while *technê* can presumably be shaken by argument, *epistêmê* cannot (cf. Anonymous *in Theaetetum* XV.26–30 Bastianini – Sedley).[44] A doctor can be brought to question his own judgement, whereas the sage's *epistêmê* is firm and steadfast: if he gives his assent or decides to withhold it, no argument can make him change his mind. Ultimately, the stability and irrevocability of the sage's *epistêmê* derives from its global and consistent character. While the set of cognitions constituting a *technê* is confined within a narrow domain and draws no support from other such domains, the set equivalent to the sage's *epistêmê* is entirely coherent and grounded in his perfected rational faculty. According to Stobaeus, this observation applies to the virtues as well: their absolute stability is closely comparable to the stability of an entire system of first-order arts (cf. *technikai epistêmai*: Stobaeus, *Ecl.* II p. 74, 16). From the cognitive state of the sage 'Zeno removed error, rashness, ignorance, opinion, conjecture, and, in short, everything alien to firm and consistent assent' (Cicero, *Acad.* I.42).

What are the contents of *epistêmê* understood as scientific knowledge? And how is it related to the *technê biou*? There is some confusion about this question. For some sources treat the two notions as coextensive, while others reserve *epistêmê* only for the sage but allow that the art of living may be practised by moral progressors as well. On balance, the canonical position seems to be that, since only the sage has the perfected disposition to always do the right thing in the right circumstances and in the right manner, only the sage is a true master of the art concerned with life. Sextus is particularly helpful regarding this point.

> In response to this objection they [sc. the Stoics] say that, while all deeds are common to all, there is need to determine whether they derive from an expert disposition [*technikê diathesis*] or a non-expert [*atechnos*] one. For the virtuous man's function is not to care for his parents and honour them in other respects, but the virtuous man's function is to do so motivated by prudence [*phronêsis*]. And just as caring for health is common to both the doctor and the layman but caring for health in the medical way is peculiar to the expert, so also honouring one's parents is common to both the virtuous [*spoudaios*] and the non-virtuous person, but honouring one's parents motivated by prudence is peculiar to the sage. So, he indeed has an art concerned with life [*technê peri ton bion*], whose peculiar function is to do every deed motivated by an excellent disposition (*M* XI.200–201).

---

[43] It is worth noting the development in the conception of *diathesis* with regard to Aristotle, according to whom *diathesis* is a temporary condition: see Burnyeat 2002. I owe this remark to Thomas Johansen.
[44] As remarks Gourinat 2011: 248 n. 21, this text is not included in SVF.

Thus, according to Sextus' testimony, the *technikê diathesis* coincides with the wholly virtuous disposition of the sage. Only the sage acts invariably in accordance with prudence or in accordance with a *technê* concerned with the whole of life and directed to human happiness (Stobaeus, *Ecl.* II. p. 7d7, 16–17). The rest of us, moral progressors, may occasionally or even frequently do the right thing but without acting expertly, that is, by applying prudence or the art concerned with life.

Clearly, there are structural similarities between this latter and the Stoics' conception of every first-order *technê*. In addition to the fact that both are dispositional states of the commanding faculty,[45] like every first-order art, the art of living is assumed to be rule-governed and to have its own domain and its own end. Moreover, as we shall see in some detail, the art of living is comparable to first-order arts in respect to involving practice as well as theory and of advancing methodically and systematically towards its own goal. However, similarly to the art of the user in Plato's *Republic*, it can be viewed as a second-order or higher-order *technê* jointly on account of its very general scope and its ultimately evaluative function,[46] which is exercised with regard to the whole of life and comprises the ethical assessment and right use of all first-order arts.

V   The Stoic Art of Living

At the outset however, and although we shall go over well-trodden ground, some brief comments need to be made about the Stoics' understanding of the goal of the art of living, namely, happiness. The core idea to which every Stoic subscribes is stated by Zeno: happiness is 'living in agreement' or having 'a good flow of life'. This idea receives elaboration by Zeno himself as well as his successors: 'living in agreement' is 'living in agreement with nature', 'living in accordance with one concordant reason', 'living in accordance with virtue', 'living harmoniously and free of conflict', or, as Chrysippus puts it, 'living in accordance with experience of what happens by nature', for our own natures are related to the nature of the whole.[47] Arguably, the relations between living a fully natural life, living a fully rational life and living a fully virtuous life are relations of identity,[48] although the conception of happiness in terms of a life in

---

[45] Simplicius, *In Aristotelis categorias* 237,25–38,20.
[46] See the discussion of the *Republic* by R. Barney, Chapter 3 in this volume.
[47] Cf. Stobaeus, 2.75,11–76,8, 77,16–17; D.L. VII.87–89.   [48] See Striker 1996b; 1996c.

agreement with nature is the most fundamental.[49] Again, we should note the Platonic roots of these seemingly paradoxical identifications,[50] and contemplate the degree to which the Stoic art of living is indebted to the analogy between virtue and the *technai* explored by Plato's Socrates.

What does the Stoic art of living consist in? What are its substantive contents? To address this question in a useful manner, it will not do to offer a survey of these latter. Rather, I shall talk briefly and selectively about certain crucial aspects of *technê biou*, and also draw attention to certain features that invite comparison with the Epicurean counterpart of that *technê*. First, does the sage's possession of the art of living entail that he is an expert in all first-order arts, that is, the totality of 'artistic' knowledge? Next, assuming that the art of living centrally involves the virtues, in what way does it do so? Then, how do the Stoics spell out the relations between the art of living and the cultivation of *logos*? And, finally, how are the *technai* as well as the *technê biou* related to the artful and providential ways of Nature? Let us take these topics in turn.

In view of the global nature and perfect consistency of the sage's knowledge, many ancient and modern interpreters of Stoicism have inferred that the sage is omniscient: namely, he is the greatest expert in every first-order art according to the criteria internal to that art. Indeed, some texts may appear to lend support to this view. For instance: 'they [sc. the Stoics] say that the wise man does everything [in accordance with] all the virtues. For everyone of his actions is perfect and therefore is lacking no virtue' (Stobaeus, *Ecl.* II 65,12). Also, consider the following passage:

> for in all movements and all relations the virtuous man deserves praise, inside as well as outside the household; he is both a politician and a household manager, on the one hand, setting straight the inside affairs of the household in the capacity of an administrator and, on the other hand, in the capacity of a politician rectifying the affairs outside the household where it is profitable. (Philo, *de fortitudine* II p. 426)

For the most part, however, the evidence indicates that the canonical Stoic position lies closer to common sense.

---

[49] See Inwood 2017.
[50] Plato's Socrates repeatedly suggests that the good life is a life in accordance with our distinctively human nature, namely, the rational element in us (e.g. *Phd.* 65e–67b). Since virtue is the healthy condition of the rational soul but vice a pervasive disease calling for remedy (e.g. *Grg.* 464b–66a, 477a, 523a–27e), a life guided by our nature as humans is a life lived in accordance with reason, and this latter is a virtuous life.

They [sc. the Stoics] claim that, indeed, it is evident that the wise man does well everything he does. For as we say that the flute-player or the lyre-player does everything well, while it is implied, in the one case, 'everything having to do with flute-playing' and, in the other, 'everything having to do with lyre-playing', so the wise man [*ton phronimon*] does everything well in so far as it concerns whatever he does, but not of course also whatever he does not do. In their view, the doctrine that the wise man does everything well follows from the thesis that he does everything in accordance with right reason and, in a way, with virtue, which is an art [*technê*] concerned with the whole of life. Analogically, the fool does whatever he does badly in accordance with all the vices. (SVF III.560)[51]

Hence, it seems that the sage is not omniscient nor is he better than every other expert in every given area of expertise. Rather, the Stoics advance a more intuitive and moderate claim: the sage's superiority in everything he does derives not from his expertise in every *technê*, but from his expertise in the *technê biou*, the art of living. If he does happen to be superior to other first-order experts, for example, doctors, this would be because he is more knowledgeable in the art of medicine, not because he masters the art of living. As for the cognitions that constitute the sage's expertise, they form an entirely coherent system but not an all-comprising one. The sage, then, is cognitively superior to others not because he has *more* knowledge or *all* knowledge, but because whatever knowledge he has is available to him *in the right way*: in a stable, firm and thoroughly integrated manner, so that the sage can always make *right use* of it. Compare Plato's remarks concerning the cognitive advantage of the user over the maker. The former's knowledge is of a special sort: it need not have anything to do with expertise in first-order arts, but it has everything to do with expertise in virtue.

The Stoics conceive of the virtues as corporeal states of the commanding faculty, that is, *epistêmai* or *technai* that extend over the entire range of value. According to Plutarch, Zeno accepted several different virtues, namely, prudence, courage, moderation and justice, contrary to Aristo who held that virtue is a unitary state of the soul equivalent to psychic health (*De virt. mor.* 440E–41A).[52] Also, Plutarch continues, 'like Plato', Zeno maintained that the virtues are inseparable but distinct from each other (*de Stoic. repugn.* 1034C); and he ascribed a sort of primacy to *phronêsis*, since he treated the latter both as one of the four cardinal virtues

---

[51] I follow the translation by Long and Sedley 1987: 1: 379–80, with modifications.
[52] See Schofield 1984.

and as a defining element of each of the other three virtues.[53] Chrysippus follows the founder of the school, in so far as he too determines the virtues as *epistêmai* or *technai*, sciences or arts, sharing the same theorems but each having its own domain of application. Thus, courage is the art or science of what is and is not to be feared. Temperance is the art of things to be chosen and avoided and neither. *Phronêsis* is the art of what we ought or ought not to do or neither, or, alternatively, the art of things good and evil and neither. And justice is the art of distributing to each individual his own deserts (Stobaeus, *Ecl.* II 63, 6). Moreover, like Zeno, Chrysippus counts *phronêsis* among the four virtues, and also assigns to it a predominant position among these latter. For as the science of good and evil and neither *phronêsis* is a master-virtue extending over the realms of the other virtues. Notwithstanding arguments to the contrary, there is no reason to believe that Cleanthes deviates from the orthodox position of the school. For while he contends that *ischus* and *kratos*, strength and might, lie at the core of all the virtues (Plutarch, *de Stoic. repugn.* 1034D–E),[54] this need not mean (as has been taken to mean) that the virtues essentially consist in training and habit at least as much as in knowledge. Rather, Cleanthes' point is, simply, that the sage uses the virtues in a perfectly firm and steadfast manner, unlike the rest of us.[55]

In its capacity as a master-virtue or a master-*technê*, *phronêsis* may be treated as coextensive with the art of living[56] not only as a theoretical system, but also as a practical philosophy leading to happiness.[57] For *phronêsis*, more than any other virtue, guarantees the performance of a special class of *kathêkonta*, namely, right or appropriate actions rooted in

---

[53] Plato's influence on Stoicicm is especially marked in respect of the double role ascribed by both parties to *phronêsis*: on the one hand, it is one of the cardinal virtues, but, on the other, it is treated as a higher sort of virtue capable of turning apparent courage, apparent temperance and apparent justice into their true counterparts (*Phd.* 69a–c), and also capable of ensuring the beneficial or harmful use of the other virtues (*Men.* 87c–89a). Discussion of the relevant Platonic passages is found in Schofield 2013: 14–17.

[54] According to several interpreters, Cleanthes' position derives from Antisthenes' and Xenophon's portraits of Socrates. For Antisthenes claimed that physical and psychic training (*askêsis*) as well as 'Socratic strength' suffice for the achievement of happiness. See the study of Goulet-Cazé 1986.

[55] As Schofield 2013: 21 remarks, only if *enkrateia* has a cognitive dimension can it focus on 'what is evidently called for' in the special sphere of each of the virtues. In fact, I am inclined to believe that 'what is evidently called for' is not just a necessary condition of having *enkrateia* but, rather, the very essence of this latter. Overall, I think Cleanthes' position is inspired not so much by Antisthenes and Xenophon as by Plato's Socrates. A different view is held by Sellars 2003.

[56] The evidence suggests that the same can be said about *sophia*, that is, the wisdom of the sage. Consider the intuition of Sara Magrin that *phronêsis* and *sophia* probably refer to the same thing but with different emphases: while the former picks out primarily the practical aspects of the sage's wisdom, the latter highlights its theoretical aspects.

[57] See, for instance, Kidd 1978; Long and Sedley 1987: 1: chs. 57–61; Bénatouïl 2006.

natural impulses,[58] which, in the ideal case of the sage, are *katorthômata*, perfect actions deriving from a thoroughly rational disposition. As for moral progressors, the increasingly consistent selection of natural preferables (*proêgmena*) and avoidance of dispreferables (*apoproêgmena*) leads to the gradual improvement of their disposition and aids them in their efforts to approximate the moral perfection of the sage. In this way, philosophical theory and ethical practice can be considered aspects of one and the same art. Like the first-order *technai*, this latter, in my view, owes its 'technicity' primarily to the method, principles and rules that govern it. Also, like its first-order counterparts, the master-*technê* identified as *phronêsis* is not confined to the realm of barren theory but is put to use. But while the first-order arts aim at relatively profitable things, *phronêsis* as the art of living aims at the good.

Nowhere is the interplay between theory and practice more evident than in Stoic debates concerning the relation between *decreta* and *praecepta*, doctrines and precepts. To give an example, on the one hand, Seneca suggests that the *technê* of living has to do, first of all, with systematicity and understanding. For, he claims, the *decreta* are the 'causes' or reference points of everything (*Ep.* 94.16, 95.12, 58). They constitute the basis of demonstrations concerning good and evil; determine the content of moral judgements; ground all genuine teaching, learning and understanding and provide the final justification of *katorthômata*, the perfect right actions of the sage (94.10, 33–34, 95.35, 61). In short, only if one fully assimilates the Stoic doctrines, one will be able to judge correctly what to do in *any* given situation (*Ep.* 95.5).[59] On the other hand, Seneca also highlights the importance of precepts, when he traces the cognitive process by which we extract from our experience of right-but-not-perfect actions a conception of virtue and the good (117, 120).[60]

Contrary to Aristo, who contended that 'old wives' precepts' are useless while all benefit derives from doctrines and the Stoic conception of the good (124.2–18), Seneca argues that the *praecepta* too have a significant role to play. They supply specific instructions that Nature does not give (19–22), can help both people much advanced towards wisdom and others who are less advanced (22–23), sharpen one's attention and

---

[58] See Long and Sedley 1987: 1: 365.
[59] Kidd 1978: 252–53 suggests that precepts are like hypothetical imperatives, whereas doctrines are like categorical imperatives: one can opt out of the former, not the latter.
[60] See Inwood 2005b.

memory (21, 24), strengthen one's mental powers to the best of one's ability (30–31)[61] and benefit one's soul as moral exemplars do (41–42).[62] But while we, moral progressors, do need precepts to direct us towards doing the right thing, the wise man does not really need precepts, concrete guidance or training. He both has and exercises the virtues, and his perfect rationality suffices to ensure that he will act rightly in every circumstance.[63] One is tempted to think of Plato's Socrates in this connection as well. He too directs our attention to the seamless continuity between knowledge and action, theory and practice, philosophical examination and the moral quality of one's life (e.g., *Ap.* 28e; *Cri.* 46b–e, 48b–e; *Lach.* 187e–88c; *Grg.* 500c). And while he advocates the importance of *askêsis* (e.g., *Grg.* 507c) often illustrating it in his own conduct, he also suggests that, ideally, virtue alone suffices to supply the motivation and ultimate justification of action.[64]

Finally, it is important to look at certain aspects of Stoic dialectic in connection with the art concerned with life. According to the Stoics, dialectic as 'the science of things true and false and neither' (D.L. VII.42)[65] is a *technê* coextensive with virtue (VII.178). Probably influenced by his Academic mentor Polemo, Zeno thinks of dialectic primarily as argumentative conversation by question and answer and compares it with rhetoric, the art of speaking well, by using the metaphor of a clenched and then open fist: dialectic is brief and condensed, whereas rhetoric is the art of more extended and thinly spread speeches (Sextus, *M* II.7). Without ever ceasing to be an art of argument by question and answer, the Stoic art of dialectic underwent development and acquired a vast and varied scope. It comprises rationality and reasoning, cognitions and truth, naming and speaking, but also the nature of what is, the correct use of one's

---

[61] Seneca echoes Plato on that point too: there are natural differences between people with regard to their mental capacities.
[62] Also, see *Ep.*124. 33, 45–47, as well as Seneca's defense of the use of preludes in the Plato's *Laws* vis-à-vis the criticisms of Posidonius (*Ep.*124.38).
[63] Plato may be evoked in this connection as well. While, in their youth, the Guardians of the *Republic* are educated by means of instructions as well as doctrine, in their adulthood, they are led solely through abstract thinking towards the contemplation of the Good. The lower classes, however, are not exposed to the mathematical sciences and to dialectic but, presumably, follow concrete instructions and precepts to perform their tasks.
[64] See Aristotle's remark that, according to Socrates, for example, knowing justice and being just come together (*EE* 1216b6–9). Evidently, I disagree that Socrates' concern 'is not with argument or definition or rational understanding, but rather with life' (Sellars 2003: 33).
[65] To my mind, Long 1978 makes a compelling case to the effect that Chrysippus was the author of this definition and the Stoic philosopher primarily responsible for the expansion of dialectic in the directions of epistemology and language.

impressions and the study of discourse concerning the good (D.L. VII.83). Since it is a *technê* equivalent to virtue, the Stoics describe it also in terms of a corporeal disposition of the commanding faculty oriented towards the good life (VII.46). And, in the spirit of Plato's Socrates,[66] they suggest that the only true dialectician, as well as the only true orator, is the philosopher (Alexander, *On Aristotle's Topics*, 1.8–14) or, ideally, the Stoic sage.

This idea lies at the basis of Chrysippus' definition of dialectic as the science of what is true and false and neither, as well as Diogenes of Babylon's self-advertising claim that he can *teach* the art of speaking well and of distinguishing between the true and the false (Cicero, *De Or.* II.157–58). By styling himself as a teacher of a *technê*, 'which he called by the Greek term "dialectic"' (Cicero, *De Or.* II.157–58), Diogenes implicitly takes a position with regard to the teachability of virtue[67] and assumes something that Chrysippus probably also assumes,[68] that is, that dialectic is both the ability to argue in the question-and-answer form and a part of logic devoted to the apprehension of reality and the application of criteria of truth. The Stoics' attested interest in definitions (e.g., D.L. VII.60–62) and the relation that they draw between definitions and concepts (St Augustine, *De civ. dei* VIII.48) also belong to the *technê* under discussion and have a recognisably Socratic flavour (cf. Galen, *Contra Lyc.* 3.7).

Comparably to Plato, the Stoics view dialectic as the ideal method of philosophical enquiry and the only route to reality and truth. Hence, many members of the school, and especially Chrysippus, place it at the heart of the philosophical enterprise and of the sage's wisdom (*sophia*). Moreover, according to Aetius, the Stoics believe that philosophy, the loving pursuit of wisdom, is 'an exercise (*askêsis*) of *technê* in utility' (*technê epitêdeia*),[69] while virtue is the most accomplished *technê* of that sort (Aetius I, *Preface* 2).[70] Logic, 'which is concerned with *logos*, reasoning, as well as discourse, and which they also call dialectic' (Aetius I, *Preface* 2), corresponds to one of the three generic virtues related, respectively, to the three parts of philosophy – the other two parts being ethics, which occupies itself with human life, and physics, which investigates the world and its contents.

But although the sage's *sophia* jointly consists of these three interconnected forms of expertise, Chrysippus marks out dialectic by observing

---

[66] See the classic study by Long 1978. [67] Recall that, according to the Stoics, dialectic is a virtue.
[68] See Long 1978: 112–13.
[69] I follow the translation of this phrase by Long and Sedley 1987: 1: ch. 26A.
[70] On the Stoic provenance of this definition, see Brouwer 2014: 8–18.

that it concerns itself with the arguments of the other two parts of philosophy as well as its own (D.L. I.18). Not only is dialectic the expertise in 'things true and false and neither' as well as reasoning and language (D.L. 7.42), but it also offers support to the Stoics' account of a providentially created *cosmos* and their ethics of virtue. Another Stoic definition of *sophia*, wisdom, as '*technê* in utility', which is also cognition [*katalêpsis*] of things both human and divine (ps.-Galen, *De hist.phil.* 602.19–3.2 Diels), places greater emphasis on the progress towards attaining *epistêmê* of these matters than on the permanent character of *epistêmê* itself.[71] The same holds, I think, for the claim that philosophy is *askêsis* in the 'art in utility', which pertains to the best life (ps.-Galen, *De hist.phil.* 602.19–3.2 Diels). This claim too concentrates more on the moral progress of the trainee and less on the end of that progress. Whatever we may think about *askêsis*, the point to retain is that the aforementioned '*technê* in utility' is the only intrinsically useful art: it is practised by Stoic philosophers to the best of their ability, and aims to *epistêmê*, virtue and happiness.[72] We may conclude, therefore, that 'the *technê* in utility' actually is the art of living, assuming that this latter is taken in a sufficiently broad sense to include moral progressors as well as the sages themselves. The Platonic origins of the above set of views have been discussed in the secondary literature and require no further comment at present.[73]

To the extent that the '*technê* in utility' depends on cognitions, it presupposes that one should endeavour to assent only to true impressions and not to unclear or false ones. In fact, philosophical practice crucially involves the correct use of rational impressions (*phantasiai*) or thoughts (*noêseis*), whose propositional contents are the objects of assent. While the sage has complete command over this latter, Stoic progressors are supposed to administer their assent as well as they can, since this is fundamental to

---

[71] This definition also can be traced back to the Aetius passage, but contains new material as well. See the comments by Mansfeld and Runia 1997 on that passage.
[72] See Long and Sedley 1987: 2: 163, cited also by Brouwer 2014: 43 n. 134.
[73] Even so, the following remark seems particularly pertinent to our discussion. In Plato's *Apology*, which allegedly motivated Zeno to move to Athens and begin his studies in philosophy (Themistius, *Oratio* 23.295a), Socrates describes his search not only in terms of a requirement to achieve moral expertise, but also in terms of tireless and open-ended philosophical practice. He declares that the latter is supremely beneficial to all concerned. And he suggests that the dialectical pursuit of moral understanding constitutes the only wisdom available to human beings, while the *technê* or *epistêmê* of value is perhaps possessed only by the gods. On Socrates' view, therefore, the practice of philosophy closely parallels the '*technê* in utility' of the Stoic sage: it involves pieces of cognition (for instance, Socrates claims to know that no harm can come to a good person), but not full causal knowledge, which would be comparable to the scientific knowledge of the sage. Further discussion of these suggestions is offered by Tsouna 2017.

the analysis as well as the moral evaluation of action (Epictetus, *Diss.* I.1.7–12, I.6.12–22). The difference between the sage and the rest of mankind in that regard is conveyed by the following analogy: as an art critic 'sees' a painting differently from laymen because of his particular expertise, so the wise man perceives impulses and actions differently from other people because of his perfect virtue and expertise about the whole of life (D.L. VII.51). Since he never supposes or opines or errs (Sextus, *M* VII.151–53; Plutarch, *de Stoic. repugn.* 1056E–F), and since he accomplishes whatever he undertakes scientifically and well, he is the supreme expert in the fields in which he is engaged. He is the only dialectician and the only orator, supremely beautiful and supremely wealthy, self-sufficient and free, a powerful king and a lucky hero, a man of unshakeable tenor and scientific knowledge, a divine spirit or even a god (Plutarch, *Synopsis* 4.1–5). Moreover, like the Platonic Socrates, he has beauty, wealth and freedom, even though he may be ugly, poor and a slave.[74] There is no need to dwell more on such paradoxes to reiterate this point: the profit deriving from the *technê* of living is not mundane profit. While philosophical practice involves the correct use of external goods, including the achievements of first-order *technai*, its ultimate goal basically has to do with the cultivation of reason and the best possible approximation of expertise in value. Recall that, in the Stoic view, living in accordance with nature is living in accordance with *logos*. And to live in that manner, one must make a sustained effort to understand both human reason and the rational nature of the world.

VI Craft in Stoic Cosmology

In this latter respect, too, the Stoics position themselves with regard to the tradition of Platonic creationism and the corresponding conception of an omniscient and benevolent Maker, responsible for the creation of a world in which everything moves towards its providential end within the constraints of matter. A compelling case has been made to the effect that Plato uses the 'seductive explanatory power of the craft analogy to insist on a genetic, rather than a static, account of the world's divine causation'.[75] He draws on general assumptions about the *technai* in order to invite us to

---

[74] Likewise, Socrates claims to be the only dialectician, even though he has no true knowledge of dialectic; the only orator, even though he avows knowing nothing about rhetoric; an expert in love without really having a beloved; and so on.

[75] Sedley 2007: 106–7, and, on the basic features of divine craftsmanship: 107–13.

consider what sort of world the divine craftsman or, more impersonally, divine craftsmanship[76] would create,[77] and through what sort of activity this latter would be brought about. For present purposes, the features of Plato's account that I wish to single out include the perfect rationality of the Demiurge, which is supposed to parallel the rationality inherent in every human *technê*; his planned and controlled activity, comparable to that of experts in human arts; the invariable orientation of that activity towards the best possible product and the parallels between the divine and the human ways of life, which derive from the suggested similarities between the engagement of the Demiurge in creationist activity and men's engagement in the *technai*.

While the Stoics account for the genesis and function of the world in comparable terms, they reject the idea (rightly or wrongly attributed without qualification to the *Timaeus*) that the operations of the divinity that brought the world into being are like those of a craftsman (*cheirotechnês*) whose intellect remains distinct and separate from the material on which he acts. Rather, they claim, Zeus is a Demiurge (*dêmiourgos*) thoroughly pervading and wholly present in the totality of matter. Depending on the context, Zeno and his followers refer to Zeus as the soul (*psuchê*) of the world, the mind (*nous*) of the world, tenor (*hexis*), reason (*logos*), nature (*phusis*) and a certain sort of fire (*pur*) (Aetius I.7,23 DDG p. 303,11; Themistius, *in de An.* II p. 64,25 Spengler). While these terms have ultimately the same referent, they semantically pick out different aspects of the demiurgic power suffusing matter, sometimes focusing on its active agency as the force holding together every existing thing, other times stressing the thoroughly rational and teleological character of that force as it manifests itself in the workings of fire.

Unlike Plato's cosmological first principle, which is incorporeal, the Stoics' fire is a corporeal substance (Aristocles apud Eusebius *praep. evang.* XV p. 816d) that plays a twofold role in their system. It is an element of Nature as well as identical with Nature, an ingredient of the world as well as the intelligent power responsible for cosmogony, a destructive substance as well as the essence of all living things. These dualities are captured by a distinction attested by the sources between two kinds of fire: *atechnon* and *technikon*, fire that does not have *technê* and fire that does have that capacity. As Cleanthes puts it, the fire that we encounter in ordinary life differs from the fire constituting the life of living creatures (Cicero, *ND* 40–41). The former consumes and destroys everything that feeds it, the

---

[76] See the suggestion defended by Johansen 2004: 83–86. [77] See Broadie 2012: especially 31–38.

latter causes things to grow and preserve themselves, and constitutes the nature or soul of animals and plants (Stobaeus, *Ecl.* I.25, 3 p. 213, 15). The stars too are made of craftsmanlike fire and, consequently, their fiery essence (*ousia*: Stobaeus, *Ecl.* I.25, 3 p. 213, 15) is intelligent and wise. So far as living beings are concerned, the *technê*-like sort of fire is responsible for the regular, methodical manner in which plants and animals go through their respective natural cycles, and also for the orderly movements of the stars and the intelligibility of the phenomena related to them.

The supreme rationality and wisdom of craftsmanlike fire finds its fullest manifestation in the nexus of causes necessarily determining everything that has happened, is happening or will happen. The necessary interconnection and consequentiality of these causes is equivalent to providence and fate, as well as scientific knowledge (*epistêmê*), truth, and Nature itself (e.g., Aristocles apud Eusebius *praep. evang.* XV p. 816d). The belief that Nature is *pur technikon*, craftsmanlike fire, 'proceeding through a road to generation' (D.L.7. 156) underlies Chrysippus' doctrine of mixture (Galen, *methodi med.* I.2 Vol. X 15K)[78] and lends support to the Stoic conception of Nature as a sort of tenor accomplishing its goals in the same manner as the arts do, that is, methodically, by following a certain road (Olympiodorus, *In Platonis Gorgiam* 12.1, p. 70 Westerink). Cicero summarises the Stoic position as follows:

> Zeno gives this definition of nature: 'Nature', he says, 'is a craftsmanlike fire [cf. *ignem artificiosum*], proceeding methodically to the work of generation'.[79] He holds that the special function of an art is to create and generate, and that what in the procedures of our arts is done by the hand is accomplished with much greater craftsmanship by Nature, i.e. as I said, by the craftsmanlike fire which is the teacher of the other arts. Also, according to this theory, while the nature of each thing[80] is craftsmanlike in the sense of having a sort of path marked out for it to follow, the nature of the world itself, which encloses and contains all things in its embrace, is called by Zeno not merely craftsmanlike [*artificiosa*] but actually a craftsman [*artifex*] whose foresight plans out the work to serve its use and purpose in every detail .... Such being the nature of the world-mind [*mens mundi*], it can, therefore, correctly be designated as prudence [*prudentia*] or providence [*providentia*], for in Greek it is called *pronoia*. This providence is

---

[78] According to Galen (Broadie 2012: especially 31–38), Chrysippus accepts from Hippocrates and Aristotle the basic dualities of hot and cold, dry and wet, and he claims that everything is ultimately a mixture of these elements, which interact with each other by acting or suffering change. Also, he accepts other relevant Hippocratic views as well. The same holds for the Peripatetics, although these latter slightly differ from the Stoics in respect of the nature and ingredients of mixture.
[79] See DL. VII.156.   [80] Rachman renders *omnis natura* by 'each department of nature'.

chiefly oriented towards and concerned with three objects: to secure for the world the structure best fitted for it to survive; then, to make sure that it lacks nothing; and, chiefly, to adorn it with beauty and embellishment of every kind. (*ND* II 57–58)

In sum, as the external manifestation of the *logos* pervading matter, the craftsmanlike fire operates providentially at the cosmic level to ensure the preservation, completeness and beauty of the cosmos. Therefore, in addition to being unique, the world is optimally administered and it is the best world possible (D.L. VII.143). Moreover, the world retains these qualities through successive cycles of conflagration and eternal recurrence, in which the artful fire plays a protagonistic role. For it is the ultimate element into which everything is reduced and from which everything is recreated exactly as it was (Eusebius, *praep.evang.* XV 18,3; II.188,7, I.111.20; II.183.19). It is eternal and incorruptible (Plutarch, *de comm.not.* 1066A). And it is divine – in fact, certain sources identify it with the supreme deity or Zeus (Porphyrius, *de anima*, apud Eusebius, *praep. evang.* XV p. 818c). The ultimate goal of the Stoic *technê* of living is to help us understand as best we can the artful workings of divinity and align ourselves with the rationality permeating the world and all its parts.[81]

---

[81] As mentioned, this chapter and the next (Chapter 8) are companion pieces: the introduction to both the Stoics and the Epicureans is at the beginning of the present chapter, whereas the conclusions concerning both schools are drawn at the end of the chapter on the Epicureans. Both studies have greatly benefitted by the comments and criticisms of many colleagues, whom I shall have the pleasure to thank at the end of the chapter on the Epicureans.

CHAPTER 8

The Epicureans on Technê and the Technai

Voula Tsouna

As is well known, the Epicureans defend a mechanistic account of the universe based on the atomic theory, and they explicitly reject the providentialist creationism of Plato and the Stoics together with the sort of teleology that this latter implies. In this way, their system stands at the antipodes of Stoicism, and the radical differences between the two doctrines are especially evident in the respective approaches of the two schools to Nature, the relation between Nature and *technê* and the manner in which human beings engage with natural things and processes to develop the *technai* and reliably provide for their own needs.

A cautionary note concerns the evidence available to us. In the first place, very little survives from what Epicurus and his early associates said about *technê* and the *technai*. Moreover, it seems that the Founders left several issues underdetermined and open to debate. So, while I shall try to piece together their views, there should be no expectation that these latter will amount to a fully fledged theory about *technê* and the *technai*. In the second place, although the surviving works of Lucretius and Philodemus give substantial information about our subject, Lucretius is mainly concerned with the genealogy of the arts rather than their nature and structure, whereas Philodemus' systematic treatment of this latter topic is often difficult to reconstruct or evaluate. On the one hand, we are now in a better position to do so because of much recent work on Philodemus' aesthetic writings, that is, *On Rhetoric*,[1] *On Poems*[2] and *On Music*,[3]

---

[1] The edition by Francesca Longo Auricchio 1977 remains a standard point of reference for anyone working on that treatise. I rely on Longo Auricchio's text, and also on the translations of *Rhetoric* I and II in Italian by Longo Auricchio 1977 and in English by Chandler 2006. As Clive Chandler indicates, his translation is based on Longo Auricchio's text, as well as on conjectures proposed by David Blank that Chandler had access to. A new edition of the first book of the *Rhetoric* has been published by Nicolardi 2018. The entire surviving text of the *Rhetoric* is in preparation by David Blank.
[2] I use the following editions and translations of *On Poems*: Book I by Janko 2003; Books III and IV by Janko 2010; Book V by Mangoni 1993, translated by Armstrong 1995.
[3] I use the edition and translation of *On Music* Book IV by Delattre 2007.

and also on his treatise *On Property Management*.[4] On the other hand, especially in the case of the *Rhetoric*, the poor physical condition of certain parts of the papyri on which it has been written, as well as the complex dialectical structure of the treatise, make it hard or sometimes impossible to distinguish with any degree of certainty Philodemus' own views from those of his rivals. Hence, the claims that I make about Philodemus are tentative and susceptible to revision in the light of future papyrological research.

I Epicurean Determinations of *Technê*

Epicurus' surviving writings contain no definition or outline of his conception of *technê*. However, he probably would see no reason to object to a sort of definition[5] attributed to the Epicureans in general: 'they define *technê* as follows: *technê* is a method [*methodos*] achieving what it profitable for life' (*Scholia ad Dionysius Thrax* 108.27). As in the case of the Stoics so in the case of the Epicureans 'method', both point to a body of knowledge or a set of true beliefs that concern a certain subject matter, constitute a particular field of expertise and are governed by principles and rules extending through that entire field (*to diêkon*: Philodemus, *De poem.* 5 XXVII.25–36). Moreover, this conception of *technê* as a method[6] implies, like its Stoic counterpart, that the technical process advances systematically, step by step, towards the achievement of a final goal. If so, the Epicureans too determine art not in an accumulative manner, by compiling a list of necessary and sufficient characteristics, but in a systematic way, by emphasising the coherence, directionality and methodical nature of every art.

---

[4] I use my own translation of the text (Tsouna 2012), which is based on Jensen 1906 with some new conjectures by David Sedley, Daniel Delattre and myself. For the columns relaying Metrodorus' views, I also consult Tepedino Guerra 2007 and the French translation of *On Property Management* by Delattre and Tsouna 2012.

[5] The Epicureans disapprove of definitions in a technical or philosophical sense of the term. Later sources attribute to Epicurus the theses that words (*onomata*) are clearer than definitions (*horoi*) (Anonymous, *in Theaet.* 22.42–23.8) and that definitions are redundant or even harmful, since they destroy the clarity that words have in ordinary language (Erotian, *gloss. Hippocr. praef.* p. 34, 10 Klein). On the other hand, Epicurus insists that some sort of outline of the subject of investigation is necessary in order to conduct clear and coherent enquiries. Generally, Epicurean definitions can be viewed as summary descriptions of the corresponding preconceptions (Asmis 1984: 42), or as demarcations of what is empirically known to be a commonly shared conception of the topic of discussion (Tsouna 2007: 66).

[6] It is not clear from the surviving evidence whether the relation between *technê* and method is biconditional.

Comparably to the Stoic authorities, the Founders of the Garden believe that art crucially depends on experience, is optimally or only[7] practised by experts and enables these latter to accomplish their function in a regular and predictable manner. However, while Zeno and Chrysippus account for the empiricist basis of an art in terms of the *katalêpseis*, cognitions, that constitute it, the Epicureans stress the role of observation (*paratêrêsis*) in identifying the common principles running through all or most particular instances belonging to the domain of each art. A further similarity between the two schools has to do with the fact that the Epicureans too conceive of *technê* also in terms of a *hexis* or *diathesis*. Hence, they too determine the nature of an art in two different and complementary ways, the one epistemological and methodological, the other psychological and behavioural. According to the former, an art is a method applied on the basis of a set of beliefs concerning a specific subject matter and systematically pursuing the relevant goals, while, according to the latter, an art is a capacity or faculty developed through the observation of commonalities and disposing the experts to apply that capacity in order to achieve their goal. Perhaps there is reason to stress that the *hexis* that the Epicureans identify with *technê* is not a Stoic tenor.[8] Rather, it has a quasi-Aristotelian flavour: it is the habitual capacity of experts in a *technê* to act in a certain way.

Due to the peculiarities of Philodemus' evidence, it is harder to assess how the positions of the two rival schools can be compared in respect to the importance of the theoretical elements composing a *technê* vis-à-vis its practical aspects. If the relevant excerpts of Philodemus' *Rhetoric* mean what they have been taken to mean, and if they accurately reflect Epicurus' own view, Epicurus may have suggested that, while some *technai* involve both theory and training, others consist in *epistêmê* alone.[9] In any case, Epicurus as well as his followers treat *technê* and *epistêmê* as synonyms in certain contexts, while in other contexts they take *technê* to be a species of *epistêmê* (cf. *Rhet.* I, PHerc. 1427 fr. 4.3–15 /Longo 7). Yet in other circumstances, Philodemus refers to a sharper distinction drawn between *technai* and *epistêmai* on the grounds that the former are absolutely incapable of having the same power as the latter (*Rhet.* II, PHerc. 1674 XVIII.1–4 /Longo 79). Nonetheless, it is not clear whether this distinction

---

[7] See οὐδείς in Blank 2003, 71, adopted by Chandler (cf. Chandler 2006: 190 n. 70).
[8] See Chapter 7 in this volume.
[9] Philodemus, *Rhet.* II, PHerc. 1672 XIII.2–3 /Longo 183; cf. also XII.1–10 /Longo 179; *Rhet.* I, PHerc. 1427 fr. 4.1–15 /Longo 7.

belongs to Philodemus' rivals or is also endorsed by Philodemus and other Epicureans. In general, Philodemus' methodological approach to art and the arts accords with his contention that not all the *technai* can be made to conform to a single and uniform notion of expertise (cf. *Rhet.* I, PHerc. 1427, fr.1.2–21 /Longo 3).

We shall return to this contention later but, for the moment, it is important to mention another set of contrasts also to be revisited at a later stage of our discussion. Namely, Epicurus and his followers appear to oppose *technê* to mere experience, unreflective practice, habitual skill or talent.[10] For instance, as we shall see in more detail, Philodemus' defense of the position that sophistic[11] rhetoric is a *technê* while political rhetoric and forensic rhetoric are not *technai* comprises the suggestion that, according to the authorities of the school, the former has 'science and method', whereas the latter depend on ordinary experience of civic affairs, familiarity with the relevant audiences and perhaps talent. Unlike Plato's Socrates, who sometimes suggests that even the most successful politicians are both artless and harmful in so far as they have no expert knowledge of the good (e.g., *Grg.* 513d–17c), the Epicureans concede that the skill to speak persuasively in a political gathering or a courthouse can be useful in certain ways. However, they claim that such a skill does not amount to a *technê*, for a reason that Plato's Socrates too would endorse: it does not involve the sort of knowledge that could be systematically applied, explained and taught to others.

Although the authorities of the Epicurean school address to some extent the methodological and epistemological issue of technicity, nonetheless, they appear chiefly interested in the ethical question whether or to what extent certain *technai* are profitable for the Epicurean sage and those who wish to emulate him.[12] Diogenes Laertius' *Life of Epicurus* contains important evidence about this topic, which is complemented by other sources as well.

According to Diogenes Laertius, the sage abstains either partly or wholly from the practice of several arts, ranging from politics and property management to rhetoric, poetry and music. Even though the sage will do his duty as a citizen, he will not actively engage in politics, let alone endeavour to become a tyrant (D.L. X.119). Nor will he be an expert money-maker (X.120), although, as Metrodorus contends, he should try

---

[10] Compare the position of the Stoics as well as Plato's: see the discussion of the Stoics in Chapter 7.
[11] This branch of rhetoric is also called epideictic or panegyric.
[12] See Longo Aurrichio 1985: 42; 1988: 150.

to avoid penury and to preserve a proper measure of wealth (Philodemus, *Oec.* XII.43–XIV.23). He will be fond of living in the country (D.L. X.120), but probably won't cultivate the land with his own hands (*Oec.* XXIII.7). He will earn an income from his wisdom alone (D.L. X.120), but will not conduct himself as a professional teacher or sophist. He will found a school and will occasionally give readings in public, without doing these things in the manner in which the sophists do: he will not try to attract crowds and will not volunteer to read in public unless he is requested to do so (X.120). While sophistic rhetoric probably qualifies as a *technê*,[13] the sage won't be an expert in it: he won't compose fine speeches as an expert does (X.118), nor will he compose panegyrics (X.120). Of course, he will take a case to court if he needs to do so (X.120). But he won't become skilled in forensic rhetoric, which is a *kakotechnia*, (Ammianus Marcellinus, XXX.4.3, *Deperditorum librorum reliquiae* 20.3.2; Sextus, *M* II.12), that is, a bad form of rhetorical art, presumably as opposed to sophistic rhetoric, which is a proper form of rhetorical *technê*.[14] Nor will he compose poems, although he will take pleasure in poetry and will be the only person that can talk correctly about poetry as well as music (D.L. X.120). The general idea is this: regarding at least some of the *technai*, the sage and his adherents will not become experts in them, but they may practise these *technai* up to a certain point. As indicated in Section V, later members of the school clarify and elaborate this position further.

II *Technê* and Human Development

In line with tradition, the Epicureans take the *technai* to be profitable for life. Assuming that the contents of the monumental inscription by Diogenes of Oinoanda are based on canonical writings, the authoritative position of the Founders is that, initially, the *technai* arose from need and circumstance (*chreiai kai periptôseis*: Diogenes, fr.12 II.9–10; cf. Lucretius, *DRN* V.1029), and, then, were gradually developed with the aid of paradigms found in Nature[15] and through the inventiveness of the human mind. The fullest defense of that thesis is offered by Lucretius (*DRN* V),

---

[13] As we shall see, this claim is under debate: Philodemus contends that Epicurus and the other authorities of the Garden did consider sophistic rhetoric an art, while other Epicureans deny this. On balance, however, Philodemus' interpretation of the canonical writings seems fairly convincing.
[14] Compare Chandler 2006:12 and n. 72 and Ferrario 1981 (also mentioned by Chandler 2006).
[15] Monte Johnson remarked that the Epicurean position that art imitates nature lies closer to Aristotle than to Plato. This suggestion is worth exploring in the light of Aristotle's *Protrepticus*, and

who gives a detailed account of the transition from the primitive condition of humans to *homo technicus*. More specifically, Lucretius locates the development of the arts, as well as of religion and language, in our world – one of an infinite number of worlds composed of atoms and void. And he constructs a complex and ambiguous story[16] of how different *technai* gradually came into being as the primitive men moved in successive steps away from animality and towards civilisation.[17]

During the primitive phase (Lucretius, *DRN* V.925–1010), men were hardier than they are now and physically better equipped to deal with natural challenges (925–30). They lived like wild beasts (*more ferarum*: 930–31). They did not know how to cultivate the land (933–36), but fed on what Nature provided (936–44). They hunted much in the way in which wild animals hunt, overpowering their victims through physical strength and natural weapons, such as stones (966–69). They had no clothing (954–57) and made no dwellings, but wandered around in the wild (948–50), lived in the woods and in caves (955) and slept on the ground without fearing the dark (970–76). Because they had become used to the alternation of day and night, they never felt wonder (*mirarier*: 979) nor did they ever think that the sun might disappear and the world might be covered by everlasting night (977–81). However, they did live in fear of the wild beasts much more than we do (982–87). And they were far more vulnerable than we are to bodily affections and maladies. They were decimated by hunger, poisoned plants and wounds (988–1010), for they did not know how to cook or to cure themselves. Sex was merely a matter of animal instinct (962–65) and, generally, every man lived for himself. There was no concern for the common good, no laws and customs and no system of governance (958–61).

---

especially the following claim made by the character Aristotle: 'just as in the other craftsmanlike arts the best of their tools were discovered from nature ... similarly the statesman must have certain guidelines taken from nature itself and the truth, by reference to which he judges what is just, what is good, and what is advantageous' (Iamblichus, *Protrepticus*, ch. X, 54.24–55.4; cf. also X.55.7–56.2). I am grateful to Monte Johnson for making the forthcoming edition of the *Protrepticus* by D. S. Hutchinson and himself available to me, and also for extensive discussion concerning the topic of Aristotle's influence on Epicurus. On this latter, see also Bignone 1936, and, in particular, his defense of the claim that Epicurus was influenced by Aristotle's exoteric works, including the *Protrepticus*.

[16] On the ambiguity of Lucretius' account see Tsouna 2020, who also suggests that Lucretius' story is presented neither as history nor as myth, but as a plausible account of the successive steps of human development.

[17] On the demarcation of the different phases of human development, I follow Gigandet 2003. I am also indebted to Morel 2016, and Isnardi-Parente 1969.

In this original phase of mankind, then, the arts are altogether absent, principally because the first men can neither produce fire nor keep it going for their use. Whatever benefits are available to them are provided by Nature. But, unlike modern utopias of primitivism, Lucretius' picture has bad as well as good or neutral aspects. On the one hand, the first men are terribly vulnerable to natural dangers, but, on the other, they are not threatened by the dangers caused by the development of human civilisation. In fact, Lucretius suggests that the evils besetting primitive people are lesser than or inferior to those threatening the modern man. For unlike the latter's fears and anxieties, the fears of primitive men had real causes. Also, although primitive humans did not have fire and the *technai* whereas subsequent generations do, it is not at all clear that the former were less well off than the latter. Primitive men died from natural causes, not the greed motivating 'the wicked art of navigation', which was 'hidden and obscure' in the dawn of mankind (1006). They perished from hunger, not gluttony (1008). They were destroyed by eating or drinking things that they did not know to be poisonous, not by being deliberately poisoned by someone else (1009–10), etc. We should bear these contrasts in mind as we move to the next stage of Lucretius' cultural anthropology.

In this next phase (*DRN* V.1011–1241), much of the hardiness and endurance of the first men weakens as men acquire the use of fire, learn how to make things and form small societies. Fire was not a gift from Prometheus or some other god[18] but from Nature.[19] Lucretius tells us relatively little about this momentous event (cf. 1091–1104) but, none-

---

[18] Lucretius does not explicitly refer to Prometheus, but can of course assume that his audience is aware of the relevant myth. Compare Protagoras' myth in Plato's *Protagoras* (cf. 320d–22d) and see Edward Hussey, Chapter 1 in this volume. In general, Protagoras appears to have a fairly optimistic idea of technological progress. On the other hand, according to my own account, the Epicureans worry about technical progress going well beyond covering natural needs. It is worth noting that, according to Protagoras' myth, social order and the bonds of friendship develop *well after* Prometheus gave to men fire and wisdom in the practical arts as means of survival. As Protagoras explains, wisdom enabling men to live together in society, that is, political wisdom, was not accessible to Prometheus because it was in the keeping of Zeus (321d). And it became available to humans only when Zeus ordered that justice and shame be distributed evenly among all members of the human race (322c–d). According to Lucretius' account, however, friendship and the social skills develop *at the same time as* the first *technai*. I thank Thomas Johansen and an anonymous reader of Cambridge University Press for their remarks on this topic.

[19] On the reinterpretation of the myth of Prometheus, see Morel 2016. As Morel argues, the capacity to develop the *technai* and the actualisation of that capacity are the distinguishing marks of humanity, since they imply the emancipation of man with regard to both the gods and the constraints of our animal nature.

theless, he says enough to suggest that, on any plausible explanation,[20] men came to acquire and maintain fire by discovering and imitating Nature. The use of fire was absolutely pivotal to the emergence of primitive technical practices, elementary political and social structures and new ways of life (cf. 1105–1240). Human beings now live in huts, wear animal skins, coexist in family-like groups and, prompted by a kind of friendship (*amicitia*), reach mutually protective agreements neither to do nor to suffer harm (1019–20). Here, then, lie the origins of the arts of building, clothing, legislation and perhaps politics. Lucretius' story indicates that, just like the uses of fire, these latter arts too aim to reproduce things or processes observed in Nature. Because human beings have the natural capacity to make artefacts as well as the natural ability to reason (they are both *technikoi* and *logikoi*), they can imitate the examples given by Nature and also use their mind to explore further possibilities. Moreover, as Lucretius' account intimates, there is no cut-off point at which Nature ends and the *technai* begin, nor is there an objective boundary beyond which a practical activity turns into a *technê*. On the contrary, there is continuity between primitive techniques or practices and fully fledged *technai*. The development of each art is viewed as an open-ended continuum, not a gradual progress towards some determinate form.[21]

Strikingly similar observations apply to Lucretius' account of language development.[22] Language is neither the gift of Hermes (cf. Diogenes, fr. 12.III.1–8) or some other god nor the artificial creation of an anonymous name-giver, but originates in human physique and gradually becomes both richer and clearer under the influence of convention and of the new discoveries of human reason (cf. Epicurus, *ad Herod.* 75–76). Initially, as the primitive men meet the challenges of their environment naturally and spontaneously without using anything artificial, so also they react vocally to those challenges by producing sounds expressive of their feelings and impressions. Later on, however, men regularly replicate the vocal sounds expressing feelings to label the things prompting such feelings, in a manner comparable to the manner in which they regularly imitate the ways of Nature to produce certain artefacts for the purpose of satisfying natural needs. Subsequently, new terms are continually added to the language and

---

[20] Lucretius proposes two explanations of how fire came to the possession of mankind. Both of them involve a natural event as well as man's powers of observation and inventiveness, and each of these explanations implicitly excludes the benevolent intervention of a divinity.
[21] On this point, see the incisive remarks by Gigandet 2003.
[22] On the stages of linguistic development, see the analysis by Long and Sedley 1987: 100–101.

their meanings are determined by consensus. This latter process loosely corresponds to what happens in the last phase of Lucretius' genealogy of the arts: the discovery of metals and the dramatic increase of technical activities due to the increasingly more sophisticated use of metals achieved through the ingeniousness of the human mind.

A further parallel between language and the arts can be drawn as well. According to standard Epicurean doctrine, while the 'words' or 'names' of a language or dialect can be employed in metaphorical or catachrestic ways, each 'word' or 'name' has a proper use or 'natural' use determined by a corresponding preconception (*prolêpsis*), that is, a naturally formed fundamental concept whose propositional content is always true.[23] Likewise, although artful practices can be applied in different ways and for different purposes at every stage of their development, each of them has a proper or 'natural' use determined by the relevant preconception. We shall revisit this suggestion, but for the moment it is worth noting that, during the phase of human civilisation currently under discussion, the construction and use of artefacts by quasi-primitive men mostly does not overstep the boundaries set by nature. Their dwellings protect them from the wild beasts, their clothing from the cold, their laws from harming each other, and they use language 'to signify by voice and gesture with stammering tongue that it was right for all to pity the weak' (*DRN* V.1022–23). Overall, it seems that, during this period, the practice of the *technai* remains fairly close to natural paradigms and aims to satisfy, first of all, natural and necessary needs. However, the situation changes in a spectacular manner in the subsequent stage of Lucretius' genealogy.

This latter stage (*DRN* V.1241–378) is marked by the discovery and use of metals: gold, silver, copper, iron and lead. Lucretius proposes multiple explanations to account for the hypothesis that metals oozed up to the surface of the earth, filling up and taking the shape of the hollows in which they gathered. According to his narrative, people did eventually observe the capacity of metals to melt and take the form of all sorts of objects, and they also found out by trial and error which metal was most suitable for certain functions and which was not. Again, the origins of this new *technê*, metallurgy, had to do with the discovery of natural materials and the imitation of what Nature does with them, while further experimentation by trial and error led humans to acquire greater empirical knowledge of the metals, their basic properties and their optimal uses. Initially, the natural

---

[23] The primary use is not the only proper use, but nonetheless it is the only use based on the corresponding preconception and, therefore, the only use that can never be misleading.

properties of metals determined their value. Bronze was worth more than gold, because it was harder and could be made sharper. Iron acquired greater value than bronze for a similar reason, etc. A number of peaceful arts related to metallurgy was developed as well: bronze and iron tools were used in agriculture (1361–78), looms were constructed for weaving and cloth production (1351–53) and so on. Vegetables, fruits and grains used to be collected in a happenstance manner, whereas, in this third phase of human history, they came to be reliably produced through the cultivation of the land. As for animal skins and plaited garments, they were replaced by woven clothes. While it is questionable whether certain activities undertaken in the previous phase of human history qualify as *technai*, there is no doubt that metallurgy and other related endeavours are arts. They are based on the discovery of natural resources, the observation of their properties, the imitation of their natural behaviour by technical means, and further improvements effected through the mental faculties of man. Technical knowledge gets gathered through experimentation by trial and error, rules are discovered and men begin to pursue methodically and reliably the goals of the various arts.

The life of men during this latter period, however, has far darker aspects than in earlier periods of the human race. For metallurgy implies the development of metal weapons, and these weapons are used not only for purposes of self-preservation and self-defense (*DRN* V.1283–84), but also for wanton aggression and destruction. Lucretius' reference to the use of bronze weapons used to subdue weaker people evokes the great conflicts of the bronze age, which of course presuppose the development of the military art (cf. V.1287–92). The art of war becomes more elaborate during the iron age, when struggles become 'doubtful and equal' and violence escalates (V.1293–96). As other arts, this too is susceptible to further innovations and refinements. One of these latter is the use of horses and elephants for purposes of warfare, which proved successful over time and which can reasonably be considered an integral part of the art of war. On the other hand, Lucretius depicts a horrific scene in which wild animals such as bulls, boars and lions, are used by men in the battlefield and throw everything into havoc (V.1297–1340). The source of this scene may be Epicurus' treatise *On Nature*,[24] and Epicurus may have relied on some literary paradigm unknown to us. In any case, Lucretius' nightmarish representation raises serious doubts as to whether this sort of practice could

---

[24] I owe this suggestion to David Sedley. On Lucretius' use of Epicurus' work *On Nature*, see Sedley 1998b.

ever belong to the art of war. For, first, a *technê* presupposes that its materials are brought under rational control but, as the aforementioned scene illustrates, no rational control can be exercised over bulls, boars and lions unleashed into the field of battle. Second, innovations are introduced into a *technê* in order to make it all the more useful, but it seems that nothing profitable can derive from the technique of employing wild beasts in the battlefield. Lucretius suggests that the use of the technique under discussion is possible in a world different from ours: 'you might rather maintain that this happened somewhere in the universe, in the different worlds made in different ways, than in any single and particular earth that you please' (V.1344–46). As for the purpose of depicting such a bizarre scene, the point seems to be this: experiments like that one are bound to backfire on men because they go against nature. People get carried off with the idea of innovation, are blinded by their anthropocentric arrogance and overstep the boundaries within which the arts can flourish to the benefit of mankind. Arguably, this implicit lesson holds true of advanced forms of *technai* producing, for example, strong fortifications, well-built roads, great ships, large quantities of agricultural goods, treaties and legislation, but also of the arts of reading and writing, history and literature, poetry, painting and sculpture (V.1440–57). Philodemus has more to say on this subject, as we shall see.

Lucretius makes another observation too: 'rolling time changes the seasons of things' (*DRN* V.1276). For example, the relative values of metals change because of the passage of time and because people's perceptions about the usefulness of different metals change with time. The same applies to the *technai* as well as their products or effects (cf. 1379–1457). For instance, the woodland people get from Nature the idea of music by listening to the singing birds or the whistle of the wind through the hollow reeds. Then, they gradually learn[25] to play the pipe and find pleasure in that activity (V.1379–1411). On the other hand, Lucretius' contemporary readers are bound to recall that, in their own era, music is a sophisticated discipline involving theory as well as performance and constitutes a topic of debate. While Lucretius does not make any explicit reference to this latter fact, he does invite his audience to compare and contrast the manner in which the woodland people attend to music with the manner in which his contemporaries do so. For he makes the significant point that the

---

[25] In this case too, then, there is sequential systematicity: people learn music step by step, steadily moving towards a certain direction (*DRN* V.1452–3). There is method, even if it has not yet been fully articulated.

former drew *as much* pleasure from playing their primitive instruments as the latter.

Why, then, did the art of music develop over time? And, more generally, why did the *technai* develop, and why do they continue to develop, beyond some fairly elementary point? Lucretius' answer is that, in fact, human beings cannot help desiring to make progress in the arts. Their natural tendency is to seek novelty and delight in it. They are content with the goods they have *until* some superior form of these goods gets discovered (*DRN* V.1412–35). Socrates' 'city of pigs' (cf. *Rep.* 369b–73a) may come to mind: arguably, it cannot be viewed as an ideal, because it does not take into account the complexity of human desire.[26] Likewise, according to Lucretius, the *technai* of earlier societies cannot constitute definitive paradigms, because such paradigms are not able to accommodate man's longing for novelty and progress. Perhaps the parallel between Plato and Lucretius can go further. Socrates' 'city of pigs' is replaced by another city in which the numerous desires of people for all sorts of pleasures, on the one hand, are related to corruption but, on the other, generate the need for the institution of the guardian-soldiers: men and women who, in Socrates' thought experiment, become the representatives of the noblest achievement of humanity. In a somewhat comparable manner, Lucretius' woodland people yield their place to ever more cultivated generations of humans, who use increasingly more elaborate forms of *technai*. On the one hand, these men and women often practise sophisticated forms of the arts in order to satisfy unnatural desires deriving from empty beliefs and a corrupt disposition. On the other, increasing progress in the *technai* is inextricably bound to the complex rationality and psychology of fully developed human beings, and it matches their desire for novelty in ways in which primitive arts cannot. Hence, if sophisticated arts are used correctly, they can substantially promote pleasure or remove trouble and pain.

In general, Lucretius' account repeatedly highlights a very important point, in respect of which the Epicurean position resembles the positions of the Stoics and of Plato: the value of first-order *technai* and of their products is relative to their use. They are beneficial if they are employed correctly, but neutral or harmful if used incorrectly. The next issue to discuss, then, is how the Epicureans determine what constitutes right use.

---

[26] On the nature and philosophical purpose of the 'city of pigs', see the subtle analysis by Narcy 2015 and the sustained argument developed by Diaco 2016.

III *Technê* and the Epicurean Art of Living

Comparably to the Stoics and Plato, Epicurus and his adherents treat their philosophical doctrine as a higher-order *technê* whose sphere is the whole of life and whose values ought to guide everything that one does, including one's engagement in the *technai*. Even though we cannot be sure that the school's authorities actually described their doctrine as the 'art of living', the surviving writings of the Founders and their later followers strongly suggest that all known members of the school thought of their doctrine in that manner. What follows is not intended to be a summary of this latter. Rather, I shall highlight briefly and selectively certain aspects of the Epicurean art of living that are especially relevant to the school's conception of *technê*.

Similarly to the Stoic doctrine, the Epicurean doctrine was traditionally divided into three parts. The physical part consists of the atomic theory and its implications for the Epicurean conception of Nature, including of course human nature. The part called *Canonics*, which constitutes the introduction to the system and is contained in Epicurus' *Canon* (D.L. X.29–30), roughly corresponds to the Stoic 'logical part' of philosophy. It includes the empiricist epistemology and scientific methodology introduced by Epicurus, but does not include dialectic (X.31). The ethical part is coextensive with Epicurean hedonism, whose core is the vastly controversial contention that pleasure or the absence of pain is the ultimate goal of human life. Although one might feel tempted to equate the art of living with 'the ethical part', Epicurus makes clear that Physics and Canonics are also integral parts of this latter. For they too bear crucially on the rational pursuit of the supreme good.

To begin with Canonics, the Founder and his adherents underscore the epistemological as well as ethical importance of the thesis that all sense-impressions are true and irrefutable (*KD* XXIII), of the role of sense-impressions (*aisthêseis*), preconceptions (*prolêpseis*) and feelings (*pathê*) as criteria of truth (D.L. X.31), and of the correct method of drawing inferences on the basis of trustworthy evidence (Epicurus, *ad Herod.* 37–38). Relatedly, they defend their empiricism vis-à-vis the epistemological and ethical disadvantages, on the one hand, of scepticism and, on the other, of arbitrary judgements leading one to confuse truths with falsehoods. Specifically concerning the *technai*, Canonics guarantees the epistemological integrity of *paratêresis*, observation, the reliability of the evidence relevant to the method and goal of an art, the utility of further experimentations by trial and error and, ultimately, an art's technicity as opposed to lay practice.

Moreover, the Epicureans must assume that expertise in the *technai* entails that the experts follow the basic rules of Epicurean scientific methodology. Namely, beliefs about facts potentially falling within our direct experience are verified if they are 'attested' by evident things, or falsified if they are 'unattested' by any instances that might have confirmed them. Also, theories about non-evident things are verified if 'uncontested' by what is evident, or falsified if 'contested' by what is evident (Sextus, *M* VII.211–16).[27] In the arts as in other domains of knowledge, these procedures involve both inductive and deductive reasoning, although, as Zeno and Philodemus maintain, the former has priority over the latter. Inferences on the basis of direct or analogical similarities lay the necessary empirical grounds for deduction (Philodemus *De sign.*, PHerc. 1012 XI.32–XII.31). Overall, Epicurus' Canonics outlines a robust form of epistemological and methodological empiricism that has philosophical value in its own right. At the same time, however, Canonics is intended to serve a paramount ethical purpose: protect us from the pitfalls of error and the anxiety of doubt, restore confidence in the natural ability of human beings to attain truth and hence promote our well-being. For this reason, above all, Canonics has a legitimate claim to be considered an essential aspect of the Epicurean *technê* concerned with the whole of human life.

Turning to Physics, Epicurus and his followers waste no opportunity to state the crucial importance of *phusiologia*, the study of nature, for a serene and happy life (*ad Herod.* 37; *ad Pyth.* 84). All known Epicureans defend the view that only if we understand thoroughly the atomic theory and its implications, shall we be able to rid ourselves of the pain caused by harmful falsehoods and groundless fears and attain happiness. The extant remains of Epicurus' monumental work *On Nature* contain explanations of the atomic structure of the world and its contents, including, importantly, the nature and functions of human beings. Moreover, Epicurus composed works on specific aspects of his natural philosophy (e.g., On Atoms and Void, On the Angle in the Atom, On Images, On Imagination, On Vision), as well as two Letters summarising, respectively, the fundamental positions of atomism and the explanations of the *meteôra*, astronomical and meteorological phenomena. This latter epitome, the *Letter to Pythocles*, indicates that Epicurus views the physical part of philosophy both as an integral part of philosophy or the art of living and as a specific *technê* oriented towards its own proper end. He contrasts the multiple

---

[27] See, e.g., the analysis by Long and Sedley 1987: 1: 94–96.

explanations that he offers regarding the turnings of the sun and the moon, which derive from atomism and are compatible with the facts, with the 'servile artifices' (*andrapodôdeis techniteiai*: *ad Pyth.* 93) of the astronomers, which are pseudo-explanations contradicted by the empirical evidence. While the former set of explanations belongs to a genuine *technê*, that is, Epicurean *phusiologia*, and therefore are greatly profitable, the latter are the products of arbitrary views and must be harmful. Epicurus calls them 'servile', presumably because the arbitrary explanations of the astronomers fetter people through fear and superstition and close off their minds to the liberating truths delivered by Epicurus.

In particular, Epicurean *phusiologia* frees the mind by advancing four cardinal tenets. The first pertains to the nature of the gods: the gods are atomic constructs whose eternal and blessed existence can be contemplated by the human mind and whose perfect serenity precludes their interference in the affairs of humans. The second explains the nature and implications of death: death is the dissolution of the compound composed of body atoms and soul atoms, and it implies the destruction of the self and the complete loss of all sensation. The third and the fourth tenets presuppose the correct understanding of human nature and, in particular, of human feelings and desires: the good, that is, pleasure, has natural limits beyond which it cannot be increased. And something similar holds also for the bad, that is, pain: it has natural limits within which it can be tolerated, and when it transgresses these limits it destroys us utterly. We shall return to these positions promptly, for they are central to the ethical part of philosophy, but it is worth stressing here that all of them are anchored in different ways on Epicurus' natural philosophy.

Without going into details, I wish to make two observations especially relevant to the connection between atomism and the Epicurean conception of *technê*. The one has to do with the *technê*-like nature of Epicurus' physical system. As Torquatus' exposition suggests (Cicero, *De fin.*, I),[28] Epicurus deploys his natural philosophy in a methodical and systematic manner comparable to the structure of a first-order *technê*. Moreover, the Epicurean pedagogic techniques resemble those frequently used in first-order arts. They include regular surveys of the cardinal principles (*kuriôtata*), systematic repetition and memorisation and improvement through trial and error, correction and admonishment. My other remark concerns an explicit connection drawn by Lucretius between the atomic structure of the world and the products of the *technai*. Namely, all things

---

[28] See Sedley 1998a.

are material compounds composed of atoms and void. They abide by the laws of nature and 'the strong statutes of time' (*DRN* V. 55–58; see also 923–24). The law-like regularity of natural processes can exhaustively explain how everything in the world works. In fact, the world and all its contents, animate or inanimate, are perishable. And this includes the arts as well, which are initially introduced by Lucretius in that connection in order to stress, precisely, the mortality of our world and all its parts. Upon reflection, as Lucretius suggests, one comes to realise that a world is but a small patch of order in a chaotic universe in which all possible combinations are bound to obtain in the infinity of time. Nothing is permanent and everything is subject to the contingencies of the movements of atoms in void. Thus all natural things will perish, just as all arts and artefacts shall. Mountains and rocks must eventually fall into pieces, and the same must hold for turrets, the gods' temples and their statues, and all the monuments constructed through the craftsmanship of men (V.306–17).

Lucretius also makes another point connecting the Epicurean accounts of nature and of the development of the *technai*. Our world is not only mortal, but also young and still developing. It is not god's perfected creation, nor are any of its contents designed to suit the needs of man. Rather, the world is in continuous progress, and so are the *technai*. Time brings men before every existing thing and reason brings it to light (*DRN* V.1454–55). 'They saw one thing after another grow clear in their minds, until they attained the highest pinnacle of the arts' (*artibus ad summum donec venere cacumen*: V.1457). As indicated, this peak is not absolute, but relative to a given time. Moreover, different arts have been developing at different paces, with the result that some of them have greatly advanced, while others are in earlier stages of growth (V.331–37).

> Today [*nunc*] many improvements have been made in ships, yesterday musicians invented their musical tunes. Again, this nature and rationale of the world [*rerum ratio*] has been discovered but lately, and I myself am now found to be the very first to be to describe it in our mother tongue. (V.333–37)

In sum, the world as well as the *technai* and philosophy are relatively new. These latter represent achievements of the humans inhabiting our world and no other. And they will eventually disappear, when our world will. But while the arts and crafts will vanish altogether, Epicurus' system shall hold true even if nobody is left to practise it.

The ethical part of philosophy is interconnected with the other two parts, but also extends over them in so far as it concerns itself with their theses and arguments as well as the ones falling within its own proprietary domain. Comparably to the other two parts, Epicurean ethics is artful in the requisite sense: it consists of a set of systematically interrelated beliefs bearing on a certain subject matter and oriented towards a certain end. More specifically, it is about the things to chose or to avoid and, generally, human life (D.L. X.30).[29] As for its proper goal, it is the ultimate end of everything we do (D.L. X.30): pleasure or the absence of pain, which, as the Epicureans determine it, is equivalent to *eudaemonia*, happiness. To acquire an idea of the highly methodical and indeed 'technical' nature of Epicurean ethics (cf. *DRN* V.10) we should briefly survey some of its key points.

Generally speaking, the hedonistic eudaemonism introduced by Epicurus is a fairly optimistic ethical outlook that, on the one hand, relies on a quasi-normative conception of nature and, on the other, implies great confidence in the capacities of the human mind. Thus, the Epicureans appeal to the fact that all newborn creatures while still uncorrupted seek pleasure but avoid pain to support their normative contention that we ought to seek pleasure as the supreme good but avoid pain as the greatest evil (Cicero, *De fin.* I.29–30). On the account that I favour,[30] this normative inference is drawn on the strength of the premise describing how baby animals actually behave. The right way to behave is the way living beings do naturally behave, and the right goal to seek is the goal that newborn animals are prompted by nature to seek. In the words of the Founder, pleasure is a good primary and akin to us, from which all choices are derived; it is 'the beginning and the end of the blessed life' (*ad Men.* 129). And since all goods refer to it but it does not refer to anything else (Cicero, *De fin.* I.21), it is reasonable to view pleasure as the final objective of a higher-order sort of *technê*: a *technê* whose scope comprises the whole of life and whose axiological system is used to assess the value of everything, including the first-order *technai*.

This idea gains plausibility in the light of two peculiar features, which distinguish Epicurean hedonism from every other sort of ancient hedonism and also render it immune to the charge commonly levelled against

---

[29] We must beware of turning natural philosophy and the Canon into mere means to an end external to them. In my view, the Founder entertains only counterfactually the possibility that one might reach happiness in some different manner. In so far as we are rational beings, truth and a thorough understanding of the nature of things are steps towards as well as essential constituents of our well-being.

[30] Sedley 1998; Tsouna 2017. Different interpretations of the Cradle Argument are proposed, notably, by Brunschwig 1986; Annas 1993: 240–44; Cooper 1999; and Woolf 2004.

Epicurus, namely, that he offers a theoretical alibi to those who wish to live a profligate life. The first of these features has to do with the predominant role of the mind in moral choice, its capacity to set limits to bodily desire and its power to overcome the effects of physical suffering.[31] All known members of the Epicurean schools reject a day-to-day search for pleasure in favour of its rational pursuit through the application of the so-called hedonic calculus.[32] Whether or not we are fully conscious of what we are doing, we do choose certain pleasures but avoid others on the basis of a relative calculation of their hedonic advantages or disadvantages in the long run.[33] Moreover, we ought to reason and act in that way if we aspire to the good life.

Contrary to common prejudice, the Epicureans make clear that the calculus should not be viewed as an effective means to ever greater pleasures. Rather, it consists in the methodical assessment of the long-term implications of one's actions in the light of Epicurean values. It is the mind and not the flesh, reason and not instinct, that determines how an Epicurean will pursue pleasure. Indeed, while Epicurus and some of his adherents stress the fundamental character of bodily pleasure and the basic contentment deriving from the satisfaction of bodily needs (*VS* 33; *De Epic.*, PHerc. 1232 XVII.15, XVIII.10–17; Zeno, fr.8 Angeli and Colaizzo),[34] they also argue that mental pleasures are far more intense and more influential than bodily pleasures in respect to the overall quality of one's life. For the former comprise present as well as past and future pleasures, whereas the latter are necessarily confined within the limits of the present (D.L. X.137; Cicero, *De fin.* I.55). An artful aspect of Epicurean ethics, admirably illustrated by the Founder on his deathbed (D.L. X.22), consists in the recollection of past pleasures and their systematic use in order to offset even the most acute physical suffering.

The second distinguishing feature of Epicurean hedonism bearing on the conception of the art of living is Epicurus' controversial claim that the *telos*, moral end, is pleasure or the absence of pain. Related to that claim is the equally controversial distinction between kinetic pleasure, which involves an agreeable stirring of the senses or the mind typically caused

---

[31] In this sense, the Epicureans are rationalists of a kind.
[32] This expression is commonly used in the secondary literature but, in fact, it can be misleading: see Mitsis 1988: ch.1.
[33] Epicurus, *ad Men.* 129–30, *KD* 8, *SV* 73; Cicero, *De fin.* I.32; Philodemus, *De elect.*, PHerc. 1251 XI.7–20; Diogenes, fr. 34 II.4–V.1, III.13–IV.1.
[34] Epicurean iconography points to this sort of contentment by using as a symbol the pig. See Warren 2002: 129–49.

by some desirable object, and katastematic pleasure, which may but need not result from the fulfillment of desire and is characterised as a stable condition of painlessness (*aponia*) or tranquillity (*ataraxia*). The evidence about this topic is not decisive but, nonetheless, there is good reason to surmise that the distinction between kinetic and katastematic pleasure was first introduced by Epicurus and Metrodorus (cf. D.L. X.136; *KD* 3, 10, 18–21; *SV* 33, 51, 59, 81),[35] and also is presupposed by later members of the school.[36] Leaving aside the vexed issue how kinetic pleasure and katastematic pleasure are related to each other it seems clear that, according to the canonical sources, katastematic pleasure is a condition of health (cf. *ad Men.* 128). It constitutes the limit of pleasure beyond which this latter cannot be increased (*KD* 3, 18). And, from an ethical point of view, it is designated as the highest good (cf. *ad Men.* 122, 135; *KD* 33). If we have it 'we feel joy, as the gods do, as long as we live' (fr. 112.38–40).

Hence, in so far as the ethical part of philosophy qualifies as a higher-order art, its ultimate aim is the attainment of a godlike life: a dynamic condition of painlessness and serenity enriched by kinetic pleasures and governed by reason. Again, only the mind can secure and preserve that condition, since only the mind can grasp the limit of pleasure by reflecting on the facts of nature and the human constitution (*KD* 3, 20) and by removing our deepest anxieties and fears. As for the man who discovered all this through the power of his intellect and bequeathed it to us, 'a god he was' (*deus ille fuit*: *DRN* V. 8), 'who by means of his art (*per artem*: V.10) brought life out of so many tempests and the depths of darkness and settled it in such tranquillity and clear light' (V.10–12). Indeed, from the point of view of posterity, the most valuable aspect of Epicurus' *technê* lies in its purging and therapeutic function. While the products of other, greatly prized arts and discoveries are not necessary for our survival or happiness, 'the good life would be impossible without a purged mind; all the more reason why he [sc. Epicurus] seems to us a god, from whom even now spreading abroad through great nations come sweet consolations of life to soothe our minds' (V.18–21). This 'purging' of the mind presupposes the capacity to distinguish between natural and non-natural desires (D.L. X.127–28, *KD* 29, Cicero, *De fin.* II.9, 26) and to seek the pleasures deriving from the satisfaction of the former but not the latter.

---

[35] Information about the different views advanced in the secondary literature is found in Tsouna 2017.
[36] For instance, it is presupposed by Lucretius' account of the passions and their methods of therapy, Philodemus' analyses of vices and emotions and Diogenes' attacks against Cyrenaic hedonism.

Philodemus adds that it is useful to pay attention also to the different factors contributing to the arousal of desires and the different ways in which desires and pleasures are felt (Philodemus, *De elect.* VI.7–21). Importantly, desires as well as emotions and character traits consist of beliefs whose truth or falsehood has, respectively, a positive or negative affective impact on us. True beliefs can provide a most effective shield against pain or disturbance, whereas empty convictions shatter our tranquillity or intensify the manner in which bodily pain is felt. Expertise in Epicurean ethics as well as in *phusiologia* and Canonics are necessary in order to expel the former sort of beliefs and replace it with the latter. In this way, too, each of the three branches of Epicurean philosophy has a legitimate claim to technicity, since the truths that each branch consists of are systematically evoked with a view to a certain end.

We may now return to the four articles of the so-called Fourfold Remedy (*tetrapharmakos*: cf. Philodemus, *Ad contubernales* IV.9–14), whose basis lies in the Epicurean philosophy of nature but whose purpose is clearly ethical. Even if the expression 'Fourfold Remedy' was not used by Epicurus, there is no doubt that his 'art' (cf. *DRN* V.10) aims to remove the beliefs and fears corresponding to each of the items of the drug: the gods are not to be feared, death is nothing to us, the good is easy to get, and the bad is easy to avoid. Only if we assimilate the truths of Epicurean atomism shall we be able to stop dreading the gods' wrath and the sting of death. And only if we truly understand Epicurus' doctrine concerning the limit of pleasure and the limited power of pain can we put an end to greed and ambition as well as fear. On the positive side, katastematic pleasure is pursued through the exercise of the virtues, that is, dispositions that, like emotions and character traits, involve axiological beliefs and can be explained by reference to these beliefs. Epicurus contends that one lives pleasantly if and only if one lives virtuously (*KD* 5), and he also suggests that the virtues form a sort of psychological unity and grow together in one's soul. Moreover, like Plato and the Stoics, Epicurus treats *phronêsis* as both one of the cardinal virtues and the source of the other virtues – a virtue more precious than philosophy itself (*ad Men.* 132). Torquatus equates *sapientia* with the *ars vivendi*, but he also says that *sapientia* would not be desired if it produced no good effect; if it is desirable, this is because it is the artificer (*artifex*) of pleasure (Cicero, *De fin.* I.41).[37] Generally, the evidence indicates that the Epicureans value

---

[37] So, according to Torquatus, the art of living gets its value from the goal that it is oriented towards, but has no value in itself. It is doubtful, however, that this interpretation of the canonical position would be acceptable to the Founder himself.

wisdom and the other virtues, ultimately, for instrumental reasons, that is, because they constitute the only reliable means to pleasure.

To summarise this stretch of argument, each of the three parts of the Epicurean system qualifies as a *technê* and all three of them taken together constitute the art by which Epicurus settled human life 'in such tranquillity and clear light' (*DRN* V.10–12). Like first-order *technai*, this art is principle-governed, methodical and directed towards a conceptually distinct end. Moreover, Epicurus and his known followers make deliberate efforts to structure their doctrine in ways that make the latter fairly easily transmissible, and they explore ways in which it can be taught at different levels of difficulty and to different audiences. These comprise the composition of extensive philosophical treatises as well as compendia, the study and interpretation of the school's authoritative writings and the development of various learning techniques. Such endeavours find parallels in first-order *technai*, for example, mathematics and medicine, whose experts also are concerned with the training of students, the composition of handbooks and the clarification and elaboration of the theoretical elements of their arts.

As we move towards the end of the Hellenistic era, the debates concerning *technê* and the *technai* become subtler, richer and more theoretical. Consequently, the methodological issue concerning the criteria of arthood receives fuller treatment than ever before, and the same holds for the ethical question whether or to what degree the practice of an art is useful for the philosopher. These two issues are addressed independently of one another. A case study is the ongoing debate about the nature and usefulness of rhetoric, to which Philodemus is known to be a prominent contributor.

IV Rhetoric As a *Technê* in Philodemus

First, something should be said about the background of Philodemus' *Rhetoric*. The art of rhetoric was an integral aspect of the traditional education and, ever since Plato, it was set up as philosophy's principal rival. Hermarchus' conversion from rhetoric to philosophy (D.L. X.24; cf. also Diogenes fr. 127 Smith) was received as a case in which philosophy won. Moreover, Epicurus' assertion that the sage will not deliver fine speeches (D.L. X.118) has been taken by many to indicate that Epicurus rejected rhetoric altogether. In fact, however, it seems that the Epicurean authorities left their views on rhetoric under-determined and open to different readings. In his treatise *On Rhetoric* (*Rhet.*) Philodemus undertakes to rectify the situation on the basis of his own interpretation of the Founder's position. Taking into consideration the investigations concerning the *technai* conducted in Athens by Zeno and his colleague Bromius (*Rhet.* II, PHerc. 1674 XXXIV.11–31 /Longo 115), Philodemus devotes a substantial part of the *Rhetoric* to refute rival arguments to the effect that rhetoric is or, alternatively, is not a *technê*. Judging from the surviving part of the text, these arguments entertain various criteria for technicity and suggest either that rhetoric does fulfill them or, alternatively, that it does not. On the other hand, they do not directly address the ethical issue whether or to what degree rhetoric is beneficial for those who endorse Epicurus' doctrine and wish to live in accordance with it. In rough outline, the extant remains of the first two books of the *Rhetoric* are structured as follows: initially, Philodemus offers a critical overview of the aforementioned arguments, presenting and refuting each of them in turn. Next, he elucidates the meaning of *technê* in order to remove certain misconceptions entertained by Epicureans as well as other authors. Subsequently, he defends the position that sophistic rhetoric is a *technê*, as opposed to forensic rhetoric and political rhetoric which are not, both by appealing to the writings of the Founders and by arguing the case afresh. At present, I cannot discuss this remarkable text with a high degree of confidence and with sufficient attendance to textual matters.[38] I only intend to draw attention to certain claims and assumptions that Philodemus makes, generally, about the nature of *technê* and, specifically, about rhetoric.

At the outset, I should mention one way in which my own approach differs from that of other interpreters. Contrary to what is commonly assumed, I think that not all of Philodemus' replies to his rivals have a mere dialectical function. While some of them are indeed ad hoc, others appear to derive from Philodemus' own conception of *technê* or, at least, are compatible with it.[39] Therefore, I view them not only as dialectical moves, but also as preliminary considerations pointing forward to Philodemus' own criteria of arthood.

To begin, we may consider Philodemus' criticism of the method followed by certain unknown rivals in order to judge whether or not rhetoric is an art. These latter determine prescriptively what constitutes an

---

[38] Not only is the text fragmentary and its restitution conjectural, but also the argumentation is very dense and complex and it is sometimes difficult to distinguish the view that is being criticised from Philodemus' response.

[39] Compare Chandler 2006: 67, who maintains that Philodemus' refutations are strictly ad hoc without any intellectual commitment on his part.

epistêmê[40] and then go on to show that rhetoric does or does not fit that prescriptive conception. Philodemus objects, however, that this sort of definition is too rigid and too narrow to comprise the variations between different arts (*Rhet.* I, PHerc. 1427 fr. 1.2–21 /Longo 3). As he will argue in the systematic part of the treatise, the right method is to attend to the primary use of '*technê*' in ordinary language, compare it to various secondary or katachrestic uses, and thus reach an empirically based understanding of the sort of thing that *technê* denotes. A crucial advantage of this approach is that it can accommodate different conceptions of *technê*, formed from different perspectives and according to different criteria.

> (Some say that art is) that which exhibits established theorems (*h]estêkota theô[rêma]ta*), for instance grammar, others that which consists in wisdom alone, others that which has an account (*logos*) 'in virtue of which it accomplishes what it accomplishes', as Plato claims, yet others that which has been introduced for the sake of some advantage of life' (*Rhet.* I, PHerc. 1427 fr.3.2–11 /Longo 7).[41]

An art, then, can be defined from the point of view of method, or cognition, or explanation, or outcome, or some other perspective as well. Furthermore, Philodemus suggests that a rigid notion of art like the one advanced by his rivals cannot capture the fact that certain arts or sciences (cf. *epistêmôn*) owe their technicity to their own structure without any help from training, while others require also training or talent or both (PHerc. 1427 fr.4.3–15 /Longo 7). In addition to their adversative dimension, we shall see that the above observations correspond to an aspect of Philodemus' own method too.

Another case in point in this: to the argument that, while a genuine art has an exclusive claim to its professed goal, rhetoric is not the only practice that can claim to attain persuasion, Philodemus replies that this need not always be the case; for what occurs by means of an art can also be achieved incidentally by some other *technê* (*Rhet.* I, PHerc. 1427 II.7–11 11a–16 Blank /cf. Longo 11).[42] Rhetoric persuades through its proper means, that is, through speeches, but there are also other ways of achieving persuasion (III.25–IV.1 Blank /cf. Longo 13, 15). Again, the distinction that Philodemus draws for dialectical purposes also underlies his own view of how a goal is attained by artful means. Something similar holds for his

---

[40] This is yet another instance in which *epistêmê* is either a synonym of *technê* or refers to the genus of which *technê* is a species.
[41] I rely on the translations by Longo Auricchio 1977 and Chandler 2006, with modifications.
[42] See also Chandler 2006: 65.

reply to the argument that, since there exist bad as well as good orators, it follows that what they practise is not a genuine *technê*. Philodemus contends that this is not the case. Certain arts, such as medicine, are successful only for the most part and yet their technicity is taken for granted (III.14–21 Blank /cf. Longo 13). Invariable success is neither a necessary nor a sufficient condition for arthood.

Turning to those who claim that rhetoric is an art, the surviving part of the text indicates that these people draw their conclusion on the following grounds:

(1) Pupils pay fees.
(2) Students in rhetorical schools do actually acquire a skill that they did not have beforehand, that is, they become better speakers.
(3) The rhetors themselves do send their sons to the schools.
(4) Like music and grammar, rhetoric can be methodically taught.

Although Philodemus' responses to these arguments are ad hoc, they contain nothing that would prevent him from endorsing them in his own right. Let us take them in turn:

(1) The payment of fees is no criterion for arthood. As Epicurus notes, many people have paid fees in order to be trained in political rhetoric, but subsequently came to realise that they have not learned anything useful for civic life (*Rhet.* II, PHerc. 1674 X.24–XI.34 /Longo 63, 65).
(2) Nor is it true that everyone who has studied in a school comes out a better orator. Some come out worse, while there are laymen that speak better than those trained by the rhetors (XIII.28–XIV.4 / Longo 69, 71). In general, the best orators have acquired their skill by what they have observed in assemblies and courts (*en dêmois kai dikastêri[ois]*: XIV.23–25; cf. XIV.18–XV.5 /Longo 71, 73).
(3) While there are rhetors that do take their sons to the schools, others don't. Or if they do, they make that decision so that their sons may receive a well-rounded education rather than technical training in rhetoric (XVI.2–11 /Longo 75).
(4) Finally, the transmission of knowledge is necessary but not sufficient for technicity. There are kinds of knowledge that are transmissible, but nonetheless do not qualify as *technai* (cf. XVI.18–24 /Longo 75).

These replies are fully compatible with Philodemus' own stance, as is also his reaction to the argument that since there exist technical manuals about rhetoric (cf. *technol[o]g[ias]*: *Rhet.* II, PHerc. 1674 XVII.34 /Longo

77), rhetoric must be an art. Philodemus retorts that astrologers and soothsayers also compose technical manuals, but this does not mean that their skills qualify as *technai* (XVIII.5–12 /Longo 79). A last case worth considering is the accusation that Philodemus himself and his companions fall prey to *adialêpsia*, namely, they are incapable of distinguishing the sorts of things that are accomplished by artful means from those that are achieved in an artless manner (XVIII.29–35 /Longo 81). In fact, the criticism continues, just as when one sees a statue one recognises spontaneously and without reflection (*chôris logou*: XIX.18 /Longo 83) that it is a fine work of art, so when one examines the achievements of the politicians one acknowledges without reflection their artful character (XIX.16–21 / Longo 83).

Once again, Philodemus' response is compatible with, or indeed part of, his own stated view. For, on the one hand, he concedes that one can recognise quasi-automatically the technicity of the epideictic orator. The concession is appropriate, since Philodemus considers epideictic rhetoric an art. On the other hand, he denies that political or forensic speeches could be immediately recognised as artful (XIX.22–XXI.1 /Longo 81–87) – naturally so, since Philodemus does not believe that these types of rhetoric are *technai*.

To summarise, in the dialectical part of the *Rhetoric*, Philodemus refutes effectively the arguments of his rivals, and also draws attention to the distinction between three different branches of rhetoric, assesses various proposed criteria for arthood and explores the necessary and sufficient conditions of this latter. Thus, he paves the ground in order to further clarify the terms of the debate, advance what he takes to be the authoritative position of the Founders and defend that position in his own right as well.

Here is not the place to discuss Philodemus' interpretation of the canonical writings in respect of the technicity of rhetoric.[43] Suffice it to say that, in his view, the Founders do acknowledge the status of sophistic rhetoric as an art, but deny arthood to the other two branches. Presumably, the relatively elevated status of sophistic rhetoric vis-à-vis the other two branches is due to the features that it is governed by rules, has a determinate sphere consisting in stylistic and argumentative aspects of discourse, is teachable, and is useful in so far as it brings pleasure. On the contrary, Philodemus argues that, according to the school's authorities, political and legal rhetoric lack those features. Because of the contigencies

---

[43] Chandler 2006: 105–46 offers extensive discussion of this topic.

of their material, they have no fixed rules and no clearly delineated domain of application. In addition, they are not transmissible in the way in which an art is transmissible, and it is doubtful that they are beneficial always or even for the most part. In fact, as Metrodorus apparently pointed out, the only way to successfully address the assembly or the court is to acquire the requisite experience of the ways in which society functions. In general, on Philodemus' account, the canonical position of the school is that forensic and political rhetoric are very far removed from the defining characteristic of *technê*, namely, method and universal principles (*me[th]odois kai stoicheiôses[i]n [ka]tholikais*: *Rhet.* II, PHerc. 1672 XI.27–34 /Longo 177). Apparently, Polyaenus too held similar views.[44]

As mentioned, not only does Philodemus appeal to textual authority in order to present his own position as legitimate, but he also argues for it on independent grounds. The first step that he takes is to examine what an art is said to be in ordinary language.[45] Clearly, Philodemus assumes that, if we carefully attend to the ordinary use of '*technê*', we shall be safely led to understand the sort of thing that *technê* is; and thus we shall find ourselves better situated to address the question whether rhetoric, or some particular branch of it, is a *technê*. This assumption, however, calls for a brief explanation.

According to Epicurus, only if we grasp the primary concept (*to prôton ennoêma*) underlying our utterances, and only if we test our opinions, problems and investigations by reference to that primary concept, shall we be able to avoid circular reasoning and empty talk (*ad Herod.* 37–38) as well as error arising from the manifold applications of the words (*De Nat.* XXVIII, PHerc. 1479 fr. 12 col. III.2–12 Sedley). Error is related to one's misuse of 'preconceptions and appearances' and, therefore, we must take care not to be misled by the ambiguities of common speech or other factors (*De Nat.* XXVIII, PHerc. 1479 fr. 12 col. III.2–12 Sedley). Chiefly, we need to make sure that our use of a given word accurately reflects the content of the corresponding preconception (*prolêpsis*), which determines the truth-conditions related to the word's meaning.[46] Now, while philosophical or technical language often deviates from the preconceptual meaning of the terms, ordinary language constitutes a reliable if not unfailing guide to the relevant *prolêpseis*. And since these latter are criteria

---

[44] See Tepedino Guerra 1991: 64–65.
[45] Cf. *kata tên sunêtheian*: *Rhet.* II, PHerc. 1674 XXXVII.1–31 /Longo 121 and, for lines 7–31, Blank 2003.
[46] See Barnes 1988; Tsouna 2016.

The Epicureans on Technê *and the* Technai

and therefore always disclose truths and never falsehoods, if we pay attention to the ordinary, proleptic meaning of a given term, we stand an excellent chance of discovering the nature of the thing that the term refers to (cf. *De nat.* XXVIII, PHerc. 1479 fr. 13 col. IV inf.1–V sup. 12 Sedley).[47] Furthermore, since our preconceptions are outlines rather than detailed sketches of the kind of thing that each of them represents, definitions grounded on the *prolêpseis* are sufficiently broad and flexible to accommodate individual variations and peculiarities occurring within each class of items to be defined.

In the light of this view set forth by Epicurus, Philodemus' strategy of looking, first, at the conception of art inherent in ordinary language is methodologically sound and epistemologically promising. The following passage purports to convey what *technê* commonly denotes.

> Well, then, among the Greeks *technê* is conceived and spoken of as a faculty [*(he)xis*] or disposition [*diath(e)si(s)*] derived from observation of certain common and fundamental elements which extend through [*diêkei*] most particular instances, a faculty which both[48] grasps and produces an effect such as only a few who have not learned the art can accomplish in a similar way, and doing this firmly and securely, or even[49] conjecturally. (*Rhet.* II, PHerc. 1674 XXXVIII.5–19 /Longo 123)[50]

According to Philodemus, this kind of definition marks out the distinguishing characteristics of every *technê*, if it is called *technê* in any sense at all.[51] Regardless of the peculiarities of each art, ordinary language suggests that all the arts are capacities that derive from the observation of commonalities holding through specific instances of a certain kind, and which are directed methodically and systematically (XXXVIII.13–15)[52] towards the apprehension (cf. *katalambanousa*: XXXVIII.9–10 /Longo 123) and successful execution (cf. *[s]untelousa*: XXXVIII.11 /Longo 123) of their respective goals.

Taking these elements into consideration, and also relying on the distinction between firm or exact arts, which are invariably successful in achieving their goal, and conjectural arts, which are not effective on every occasion (*Rhet.* II, PHerc. 1674 XXXVIII.35–XXXIX.24 /Longo 123, 125), Philodemus uses firm arts as a model in order to address afresh,

---

[47] See also Chandler 2006: 89 and nn. 28, 29.
[48] I render Blank's reading τε: Blank 2003. So also Chandler's translation of the passage and his n. 69.
[49] [ἢ τ]ε Barnes 1986; see also Blank 1995: 179 n. 3.
[50] I rely on the translations by Blank and Chandler, with modifications.
[51] XXXVIII.15–29 and especially ll.24–29 /Longo 123; Blank 2003.
[52] See Chandler 2006: 92–93.

and also answer, the question whether rhetoric is an art. The detailed discussion of his strategy and argument transcends the scope of my study. However, we should register that his task becomes possible precisely because he has done enough conceptual work to remove certain ambiguities surrounding the concept of *technê*. In brief, his thesis is the following: sophistic rhetoric does indeed exhibit the distinguishing marks of arthood, whereas political rhetoric and forensic rhetoric do not. The former has the form (*eidos*) that grammar and sculpture do, whereas deliberative and forensic speeches do not have an artistic form but rather an 'observational form' (*paratêrêtikon eidos*).[53] In the end, technicity has everything to do with method, and the reason why sophistic rhetoric deserves to be called an art is that it exhibits just that distinguishing feature (*[idi]ômati ke [char]achthai*: XLIII.20–21 /Longo 133), while the other two branches of rhetoric do not.

V Epicureans on the Usefulness of *Technê*

To complete the discussion of our topic we should explore the ethical question of usefulness: whether or to what degree those who live according to the Epicurean values may profit from engaging in the *technai*. Recall that the Epicureans treat this question independently of the question of technicity: an art need not be useful, nor does every useful knowledge or skill qualify as an art.

Clearly, the Epicureans take for granted that the *technai* are useful in a prudential sense of the term, since they trace the origins of the arts in need and circumstance and determine *technê* as a method achieving *to sumpheron*, the profitable (*Scholia ad Dionysius* Thrax 108.27). Indeed, on the one hand, Epicurus or his followers are known to commend one's ability to read and write, speak clearly and coherently, count or add or subtract, draw a circle, enjoy music and poetry or make astronomical and meteorological predictions on the basis of the observation of phenomena. On the other hand, however, Sextus (who draws on Epicurean sources to compose his attacks against the professors of arts and sciences)[54] attests that Epicurus rejected the study of such subjects (*mathêmata*) on the grounds that they do not contribute to the perfection of wisdom (*M* I.1, 1.4). The subjects in question comprise grammar, rhetoric, geometry, arithmetic,

---

[53] Nonetheless, these two sorts of rhetoric cannot be reduced to mere experience (*empeiria*) or practice (*askêsis*) (cf. PHerc. 1674 XL.24–29 /Longo 127).
[54] See Blank 1995: 178; 1998.

astronomy and music. We know independently of Sextus that the Epicurean sage shall not practise them in an artful manner (e.g., D.L. X.119–20). Moreover, Sextus says that the Epicureans tried to prove dogmatically that music is not necessary for happiness (*M* VI.4).[55]

Their attitude appears similarly complex with regard to other arts as well. Lucretius intimates that navigation is harmful when practised because of greed (*DRN* V.1006), but he does not condemn sailing altogether. He suggests that cooking can cause death from gluttony (V.1008), but also mentions how cooked food improved the life of the early generations of men. The value of medicine is self-evident, but nonetheless in that case too there are two aspects to it. People fearful of death turn to medicine in the vain hope that they may remain alive for ever. But the followers of Epicurus will avail themselves of the services of medicine in a rational manner, to restore or preserve their health in so far as this is possible (Philodemus, *De elect*. XII.4–5, 9–10, XXIII.2–13). Yet another notable example is *oikonomia*, property management – a topic that occupies the Epicurean school throughout its long history.[56] In Epicurus' view, the wise man should try to secure a living through his wisdom but, if necessary, he will occasionally earn his living by paying court to a monarch (D.L. X.120). In a similar spirit, Metrodorus rejects the Cynics' proposal that the philosopher provide for his needs on a day-to-day basis; rather, he contends, the philosopher will try to secure stable sources of natural wealth, so as to live a peaceful and pleasant life (Philodemus, *Oec.*, PHerc. 1424 XII.17–25; cf. also XIV.19). Following suit, Philodemus maintains that the difference between possessing and lacking wealth is small (XVIII.25–31), but, on balance, 'more' wealth is preferable to 'less', because of the serenity and comfort that it brings when it is correctly used. While Philodemus does not specify what 'more' amounts to, he argues that 'more' is never identical with the open-ended goal of traditional *oikonomia*, namely, amassing as many riches as possible by lawful means. In this case too, then, there are two aspects to the *technê* under discussion, one suitable for the philosopher, the other unsuitable. And, again, what Philodemus questions is not whether traditional *oikonomia* qualifies as an art, but only whether the expert practice of that *technê* is useful or appropriate for the followers of Epicurus.

---

[55] In this second instance, the Epicureans are not identified by name, but it seems certain that they are the philosophers that Sextus is referring to.
[56] See Laurenti 1973; Natali 1995; Tsouna 2007: 163–94; Tsouna 2012.

To clarify the relation between the different forms or aspects of each *technê* and thus disambiguate the question pertaining to an art's usefulness the Epicureans use several interconnected pairs of contrasts.[57] Some of them focus on objective factors, others on subjective or psychological ones, others on the structure and content of each form of a *technê*, others on their respective outcomes, others on the requirements that each of the two forms of an art imposes on their practitioners and yet others on the semantic and epistemological implications of referring to a *technê* by its habitual name. Ordinary capabilities, such as reading and writing or basic arithmetical calculations or land-measurements, are opposed, respectively, to the *technai* of grammar, arithmetic and geometry, as these arts have been theorised and taught by their expert practitioners. According to Sextus, the ordinary, 'lower' versions of such arts generally preserve a close connection to Nature, whereas their 'technical' or 'higher' counterparts have lost sight of this latter. The former practices aim to satisfy natural desires and therefore are profitable, while the latter aim to achieve technical perfection, typically involve false beliefs and empty desires, and hence are harmful. A related contrast is drawn in terms of the hedonic calculus: while the pedestrian forms of the arts bring far greater pleasure than pain, the opposite holds for the corresponding 'expert' forms. Their practitioners devote a great deal of effort and trouble to achieve the goals of their *technai*, without giving any consideration to the natural end that all human beings ought to seek.

Another way of opposing 'lower' to 'higher' forms of certain *technai* concerns benefit. While, for example, reading and writing or playing an instrument for pleasure are believed to be profitable in a specific and modest manner, experts in the 'higher' *technai* of Grammar or Music claim that their arts can secure our happiness better than philosophy is able to. Since this topic has been addressed in the secondary literature,[58] a few remarks should suffice. The Grammarians contend that poetry and prose need the aid of Grammar to disclose the meaning of poems and prose writings, and thus make accessible the wisdom that they contain and that is conducive to happiness (*M* I.270). Likewise, the Musicians defend the belief that music produces better results than philosophy in repressing the passions and giving harmony to human life (cf. *M* VI.7). Comparable claims are also made by experts in the 'higher' arts of Rhetoric, Geometry, Arithmetic and Astronomy. The Epicureans counter such pretensions both by opposing the practical usefulness of the 'lower'

---

[57] See Blank 1995: 180.   [58] See Blank 1995; 2009.

forms of these arts to the excessively difficult and theoretical character of their 'higher' counterparts,[59] and by upholding the role of philosophy as the only *technê* securing happiness. Precisely because the sage masters this latter, he can prioritise his activities in the right manner and thus can engage in first-order *technai* or *epistêmai* (cf. *epistêmê*: *M* VI.1) to an appropriate degree, which usually coincides with some 'lower' form of an art. In that light, we can now better understand Epicurus' assertions that the sage will take pleasure in poetry and music but he will not compose poems, or that he will speak well but not like an orator (D.L. X.120). Regardless of the sophistication of their writings, Philodemus as well as Sextus elaborate a line of thought that, as it seems, can be traced back to the Founder of the Epicurean school.

Finally, to delimit the boundaries of the sage's engagement with a *technê* and indicate the line beyond which the sage will refuse to go, Epicurus and his followers draw yet another contrast, also mentioned above, between the primary or proleptic use and the non-proleptic uses of *technê*, and also of words denoting particular *technai*. A clear example is found in Philodemus' treatise *On Property Management* (*Oec.*). Philodemus opposes the proleptic use of 'the good property manager' with the non-proleptic use of that expression and, correspondingly, he compares and contrasts the Epicurean conception of property management (*oikonomia*) with the traditional notion of what property management consists in. While this latter aims at the lawful acquisition and preservation of wealth and property to the greatest extent possible, Epicurean *oikonomia* prescribes that one should have a relaxed psychological attitude towards the acquisition and preservation of material possessions, recognise that these have only instrumental value, and regulate all financial activities with an eye to the natural good. Thus, Philodemus opposes the traditional property manager (*oikonomos*) to the Epicurean *oikonomos* regarding several counts, psychological and moral as well as practical. Notably, the former is willing to subject himself to the gravest troubles and the most troublesome and laborious practices and, therefore, lives a life full of labours and concerns, tension and fear, abrupt changes of fortune and great loneliness. On the other hand, the Epicurean manager is emotionally detached with regard to financial objectives (*Oec.* XIV.23–XV.3), takes no great risks, is generous and

---

[59] Notably, sophistic rhetoric is useful partly because it helps the sages to express themselves with clarity as well as elegance and persuasion. On the importance of *saphêneia*, clarity, for the Epicureans, see Angeli 1985. On the meaning of '*saphêneia*' with regard to Epicurus' writings, see Leone 2000. I am indebted to Francesca Longo-Auricchio for written comments on this topic.

philanthropic, has a sense of decorum, honours the claims of friendship and is free of greed (cf. XVII.2–14, XXV.3–XXVII.12). He has true beliefs, well-ordered desires, and moral virtues, and these features too contribute to the good administration of his estate.

One might object, however, that although the Epicurean property administrator may be a better person than his traditional counterpart, nonetheless he is worse as an *oikonomos*, that is, expert in the 'higher' art of *oikonomia*. Part of Philodemus' answer to that putative objection relies on an appeal to the proleptic use of *oikonomia* and other related terms.

> But we must not [violate] this [sc. the meaning of the expression 'the good moneymaker'] through linguistic expressions, as sophists do, for we would be showing nothing about the acquisition and use (of wealth) pertaining to the wise man. Rather, we must refer to the preconception that we possess about the good money-maker, ask in whom the content of that preconception is substantiated and in what manner that person makes money, and ascribe the predicate 'good moneymaker' [to whomever it may be in whom] those features are attested. (*Oec.* XX.1–16)[60]

The method that Philodemus follows in this case resembles the one applied in the case of the *Rhetoric*. Namely, he draws attention to the proleptic use of the word designating the relevant *technê*, and he relies on the clarity and criterial power of the preconception in order to settle the issue under debate. In the present context, the preconceptual use of *oikonomia* and its cognates delimits the boundaries of that *technê* in accordance with the natural good, and thus distinguishes Epicurean property management from the 'higher' or 'expert' form of that art, which is motivated by greed and has turned away from the aim set by Nature.[61]

Implicitly, the Epicureans acknowledge the plain fact that the acquisition of expertise in a *technê* is usually an all-consuming task. Devoting one's life to the 'higher' form of an art takes a great deal of time and effort and, most importantly, it entails that one will endorse the value-system

---

[60] Translation by Tsouna 2012: 55, with modifications.
[61] One may wonder whether the traditional expert in a 'higher' art and the Epicurean philosopher who engages in its 'lower' counterpart do, in fact, practise the same *technê*. Generally, the Epicurean authors appear to presuppose that the latter engages in the same art as the former, but in a different manner and in accordance with different values. However, I think that this presupposition is more defensible in some cases than in others. For instance, on the one hand, it seems quite natural to take for granted that the Epicurean manager and the traditional manager engage in the same art, but pursue the goal of this latter in different ways and with a different ultimate end in sight. On the other hand, it may be more problematic to argue that the Epicurean philosopher's competence in 'lower' grammar, for example, his literacy or his understanding and enjoyment of poetry, is actually the same art as the *technê* of the Grammarians.

internal to that *technê* and will make it one's own. Ultimately, the choice of becoming an expert or remaining an amateur depends on the sort of person that one wants to be: a servant to one's *technê* who adopts its objectives like those of a master, or a free person who subordinates all other activities to the Epicurean art of living and practises this latter with a view to happiness.

VI Conclusion

To conclude these two studies on the Stoic and the Epicurean conceptions of *technê*, I wish to summarise the salient points of comparison and contrast of these conceptions with each other and with Plato's idea of *technê*, and also suggest some ways in which they can be related to our own intuitions and interests.

On the one hand, the Epicureans' approach to art and the arts is antithetical to the approaches of the Stoics and of Plato on several counts. While these latter assume some sort of external finality determining the development and orientation of the *technai*, the Epicureans completely reject the creationist model and the versions of providentialism related to the latter. Nowhere is this contrast more pronounced than in the conceptions of Nature defended, respectively, by each of the two Hellenistic schools. Depending on the context, the Stoics identify Nature with god or *logos* or craftsmanlike Fire, from which everything is created and by which everything is consumed according to the necessity entailed by the nexus of causes constituting the rational governance of the world. Plato's explanation of demiurgic activity in the *Timaeus* constitutes the closest parallel to that account. On the contrary, although the Epicureans claim that the *technai* originated in Nature and developed by imitating natural paradigms, they strip Nature of every sort of purposeful activity akin to human craftsmanship and oriented towards the good of the whole. Nature is neither rational and providential, as the Stoics and Plato want it, nor artful in the way in which Aristotle believes. Natural things and processes as well as living beings are what they are and function as they function: in a regular and orderly manner and in accordance with what we might call natural law, namely, in accordance with principles deriving from the properties and behaviour of atoms. Thus, the works of Nature are mechanistic and unintentional, and there is no room for teleology of any kind in respect to them. Both these rival approaches are still with us, for example, in certain forms of religious creationism setting itself in opposition to scientific theories of natural evolution or in scientific explanations of the factors precipitating climate change.

On the other hand, several similarities and parallels appear to hold, surprisingly so, between the Stoics and the Epicureans, and also between each or both of them and Plato. First of all, the Stoics and the Epicureans agree, and Plato would not disagree, that the principal feature of *technê* is method: to progress, methodically and systematically, towards the achievement of a certain goal. Moreover, both these Hellenistic schools highlight in different ways the empirical grounds of the *technai*: the Stoics stress the role of cognitions as the basis of the methodical advancement of each *technê* towards its goal, while the Epicureans emphasise the importance of the observation of commonalities exhibited through many particular instances of the same kind. Plato would not be hostile to this latter element of Hellenistic *technê* either: while he too would resist the idea that an art is reducible to experience, he too would acknowledge that experience plays a role in acquiring as well as practising all or most of the arts.[62] Contrary to what is sometimes believed, the sciences composing the educational curriculum of the Guardians do not suggest that Plato tries to do away with experience altogether.

At the same time, however, Plato as well as the authorities of Stoicism and of Epicureanism sharply distinguish the *technai* from unmethodical skills. While the latter two schools view *technê* as a *hexis* of some kind, neither of them reduces that *hexis* to a mere habitual tendency; rather, both of them connect the artful *hexis* to pursue a certain goal with the expert's mastery of a corresponding method, a set of principles and rules and a body of true beliefs grounded on experience. Like Plato, the Stoics and the Epicureans relate these features to an expert's capacity of providing explanations and of transmitting his or her *technê* to others. Such features, I propose, also characterise mutatis mutandis our own notions of expertise in the arts and sciences as well. An important difference is, however, that we have significantly relaxed the rigid assumption (endorsed by all the philosophers under discussion) that every *technê* must be determined by reference to a sharply delineated domain and must have a goal distinct and peculiar to itself. Interdisciplinary work in the arts and sciences presupposes, precisely, that such boundaries are blurred or crossed and that experts coming from different arts or sciences can jointly pursue a common end.

A final word concerns the art of living. Both the Stoics and the Epicureans react in quite similar ways to the suggestions of Plato's

---

[62] Hulme Kozey 2019a argues that, according to Plato, *empeiria* is not the opposite of *technê* but part of it (see, e.g., *Rep.* 466e–67a; *Phdr.* 269d).

Socrates, that is, that moral expertise may be structurally analogous to expertise in first-order *technai*, that only that kind of expertise might enable one to assess objectively the achievements of the *technai* and that, therefore, only expert knowledge of value could ensure the right use of many things, including the results of artful activities. In particular, both schools conceive of the art of living by reference to or by contrast with their respective conceptions of the first-order *technai*. On the one hand, the art of living too is methodical, governed by principles but also anchored on experience, applicable to its own domain, and oriented towards its own final end. On the other, not unlike Plato's Socrates, the Stoics and the Epicureans consider the art of living the only higher-order art. And they intimate that it owes its special status chiefly to its second-order axiological function but also its very general scope and goal: contrary to the other arts, the art of living concerns itself with the whole of life and aims to an overarching goal, that is, happiness.

Sometimes the two schools identify the art of living with some branch of their respective systems, for example, physics or dialectic or ethics, while at other times each school treats the art of living as coextensive with the school's doctrine in its entirety. In ways also reminiscent of Plato's Socrates, the Stoics and the Epicureans indicate that the true expert in the art of living constitutes an ideal never or seldom encountered in reality. Only the Stoic sage masters the expertise concerned with life, and only Epicurus and maybe his closest associates fully possessed the *ars vitae*. What both schools encourage everybody else to do constitutes sound advice and, once again, bears the mark of their common Platonic heritage. That is, only by endeavouring to acquire an ever better understanding of value may we be able to make right use of the goods of life, including, importantly, the benefits deriving from the practice of the *technai*.[63]

---

[63] The task of writing this chapter and Chapter 7 proved more difficult that I expected. My work benefited greatly from the comments and criticisms of several colleagues on earlier drafts. I extend my warmest thanks to Thomas Johansen and the two anonymous readers of the press, as well as to Thomas Bénatouïl, Francesca Longo-Aurrichio, Sara Magrin, Carlo Natali, David Sedley and James Warren for detailed written comments. Also, I had the privilege of discussing specific aspects of my work with Richard Arneson, Gabor Betegh, John Cooper, Dimitri El Murr, Jean-Baptiste Gourinat, Monte Johnson, Paul Kalligas, Pierre-Marie Morel, Maria Protopapas, Samuel Rickless, Donald Rutherford and Cristina Viano, and I am very grateful for their input. I learned much from the PhD dissertations of Sara Diaco and Emily Hulme Kozey, and I thank both of them for their critical remarks. I presented some of the material of these chapters at the Research Centre on Greek Philosophy at the Academy of Athens (April 2018), at the University of California at San Diego (February 2019) and at the École Normale Supérieure in Paris (April 2019); it is my pleasure to thank the organisers of these events as well as the audiences for their valuable input.

CHAPTER 9

The Sceptic's Art
Varieties of Expertise in Sextus Empiricus

Stefan Sienkiewicz

I Introduction

At *M* 2.10 Sextus offers us a definition of *technê*. He informs us that

> Every art is a body of organized items of knowledge with reference to an end useful in life. (*M* 2.10)

Sextus' remark has a Stoic flavour. In fact, in several of the dozen or so texts in which a formulation of this kind occurs, it is attributed to the Stoics or, more particularly, to Zeno.[1] Two features of Sextus' characterisation are in particular worth noting: that the items of knowledge that compose a *technê* are organised (*suggegumnasmenôn*) and that the end (*telos*) of a *technê* is useful (*euchrêston*). It is clear from a text like *M* 2.10 that these two conditions – which we might label the Systematicity Condition and the Utility Condition – were thought by Sextus to be jointly necessary for something's being a *technê*.[2] Indeed, Sextus' strategy throughout *M* 1–6 is to argue that some putative *technê* is in fact no *technê* at all either because it fails the Systematicity Condition or because it fails the Utility Condition. How exactly these two conditions are to be understood is the issue that I take up in this chapter. In particular, I shall be concerned with the following question: does the sceptic's own art satisfy both the Systematicity Condition and the Utility Condition and thereby qualify as a *technê*?

This is not an idle question. For if it turns out that the sceptic's art does qualify as a *technê*, then one might reasonably ask whether, on pain of inconsistency, Sextus ought not to train his guns on the sceptic's art just as

---

[1] See, for example, Olympiodorus *in Platonis Gorgiam* 12, 1; pseudo-Galen, *Scholium in Dionysium Thracem* 31–33; pseudo-Galen, *Definitiones medicae* 8 Vol. XIX, p. 350. See Hülser 1987: 420–26, von Arnim 1903–1905, 1: 73, 2: 93–97.
[2] These two conditions are clearly logically independent of one another. There can be perfectly systematised bodies of truths that serve no useful function whatsoever and there can be very useful bodies of non-systematised truths.

he trains his guns on the liberal arts of grammar, rhetoric, geometry, arithmetic, astrology and music in *M* 1–6.

In what follows, I suggest that Sextus does not in fact fall victim to this sort of inconsistency. Though the sceptic's art might reasonably be thought to satisfy the Utility Condition – or at least reasonably be thought by Sextus to satisfy the Utility Condition – I shall argue that it fails to satisfy the Systematicity Condition. To suppose otherwise rests on two mistakes. Speaking somewhat roughly, the first mistake conflates two things that should be kept apart and the second mistake opposes two things that should be brought together.

The first mistake involves confusing Sextus the author with the sceptic referred to in his pages. Though it is certainly true that Sextus himself organises his material in a systematic fashion and indeed in places reflects on his own systematic methodology, that is not to say that Sextus' hero – the sceptic – undermines his dogmatic opponents in an equivalently systematic manner. The second mistake involves wrongly treating as opposed the two central argumentative methods of the sceptic – namely, the Equipollent Method and the Agrippan Method. Whereas many commentators have emphasised the systematicity of the Agrippan Method and have contrasted this method with the Equipollent Method, on my heterodox interpretation of the sceptic's practice, both these methods turn out to be manifestations of the sceptic's distinctive non-technical expertise, an expertise that is to be distinguished both from those sorts of *technai* that Sextus criticises (such as geometry and arithmetic) and those that he is perfectly happy to countenance (such as navigation and agriculture).

II Utility

The Utility Condition emerges at various points throughout the course of *M* 1–6. Take, for example, Sextus' remarks about rhetoric at *M* 2.26:

> if rhetoric is an art [*technê*] at all, then either it will be of use to its possessor or to the cities, like the other arts. But it is of use neither to its possessor nor to the cities, as we shall establish. Therefore, it is not an art.

That is as clear an illustration as any that utility was viewed by Sextus as a necessary condition for something's being a *technê*. But how is Sextus construing utility here? In the subsequent argument, Sextus spells out the ways in which rhetoric might be thought to be harmful to the rhetorician and to the *polis*, but there is no positive characterisation of how he is construing utility.³ However, turning to the rest of *M* 1–6 it is possible to fill in the picture.

There are two senses – as noted by Jonathan Barnes⁴ – in which Sextus speaks of *technai* being useful. One sense is straightforwardly practical. This is the sense that is in play at the opening of *M* 5 where Sextus speaks positively of Eudoxan astronomy, which is useful in so far as it enables us 'to forecast droughts and rainstorms, plagues and earthquakes' (*M* 5.1).⁵ Sextus places this Eudoxan art on a par with the *technai* of agriculture and navigation. As Barnes puts it, arts such as these 'ameliorate the conditions of everyday life'.⁶

But there is a second sense in which a *technê* might be useful that also emerges from the pages of *M* 1–6. For instance, at *M* 1.294, which occurs during a discussion of grammar, Sextus writes:

> It is one thing for something to be useful to a city, it is another for something to be useful to oneself. The art of the cobbler and the art of the bronze-smith are necessary for the city but it is not necessary that we become bronze-smiths and cobblers in order to be happy [*pros eudaimonian*]. Therefore, the art of grammar is not necessarily useful to us, just because it is useful to the city.

The passage draws a pair of distinctions. There is a distinction between what is useful to the agent and what is useful to others. And, more significantly, there is a distinction between two kinds of utility. This second distinction is not stated explicitly but it does not lie far below the surface of Sextus' text. Sextus observes – and is perfectly correct in observing – that it is illegitimate to infer that some *technê* benefits the practitioner of the *technê* from the fact that the *technê* in question benefits the wider community. The implication is that there are two different sorts of benefit involved here. The art of the cobbler benefits the community in the practical sense in which Eudoxan astronomy and agriculture benefit

---

[3] Sextus claims that rhetoric is harmful (*epiblabês*) (*M* 2.30) to its possessor inasmuch as the rhetorician is compelled to keep company with knaves and cheats (*meta mochthêrôn ... kai sukophantôn*) (*M* 2.27) and is perpetually wearied by the troubles of others (*kopoumenon nuktôr kai meth'hêmeran hupo tôn pragmata echontôn ochleisthai*) (*M* 2.30). It is harmful to the community inasmuch as it undermines the laws that bind the city together (*M* 2.31–42). For further discussion of Sextus' treatment of rhetoric, see Barnes 1986.

[4] See Barnes 2014: 523–25.

[5] As well as devising a system of homocentric spheres to explain the motion of celestial bodies – as described by Simplicius, *in* Cael. 492.31ff – Eudoxus compiled detailed descriptions of the constellations including a calendaric record of their risings and settings. See Corti 2015: 134–35 for further details. Barnes 2014: 529 is sceptical of whether Sextus' overly empiricised description of Eudoxus does justice to Eudoxus' theoretical achievements.

[6] Barnes 2014: 523.

the community. But this need not – and, according to Sextus, presumably in and of itself will not – benefit the cobbler in the sense of amounting to a life of *eudaimonia* for the cobbler. He will have to look elsewhere if he wishes to achieve that. One place he might look – if the grammarians are to be believed – is the art of grammar itself. Sextus goes on to describe how the grammarians argue that the art of grammar is useful not only for life (*biôphelês*) but is also useful for the cultivating of wisdom and the achieving of *eudaimonia* – in so far as a grasp of grammar enables one to understand poetry, and in so far as poetry, so the grammarians argue, provides many starting points towards wisdom and the happy life (*pollas ... aphormas pros sophian kai eudaimonia bion*) (*M* 1.270).[7]

From the pages of *M* 1–6, then, there emerge at least two kinds of utility that a *technê* might promote: what we might label *Eudoxan utility*, on the one hand, and what we might label *eudaimonistic utility*, on the other. Turning now to consider the sceptic's own art, it is clear that Sextus thought that scepticism promoted utility in at least the second, *eudaimonistic* sense. As he writes,[8]

> we say, up to now, that the aim [*telos*] of the sceptic is tranquillity [*ataraxia*] in matters of opinion and moderation of feeling in matters forced upon us. (*PH* 1.25)

The *telos* of scepticism, then, is mental tranquillity, just as the *telos* of medicine might be physical health.[9] Furthermore, according to Sextus' discussion at *M* 11.110–61, this mental tranquillity promotes the agent's *eudaimonia* more effectively than the alternatives suggested by the sceptic's dogmatic competitors. Here is not the place to engage with the merit of Sextus' arguments regarding the connection between tranquillity and

---

[7] *Eudaimonistic* utility recurs in Sextus' discussion of music in *M* 6. See, for example, *M* 6. 4, 27, 34, 36.
[8] See also *PH* 1.12 where Sextus claims that the causal principle (*archê*) of scepticism is the hope of becoming tranquil.
[9] In fact, the picture is a little more complicated than this. A few lines later at *PH* 1.30 Sextus observes that certain eminent sceptics – Timon and Aenesidemus, if Diogenes Laertius (9.107) is to be believed – take a further aim of scepticism to be suspension of judgement (*PH* 1.30). And at *PH* 1.232 Sextus claims that Arcesilaus stated that suspension of judgment was the aim. Be that as it may, it is clear from a passage like *PH* 1.25 that Sextus is contrasting the kind of scepticism with which he is concerned and which has tranquillity as its aim with those forms of scepticism – Timonian, Aenesideman or Arcesilaun – that have suspension of judgement as theirs. And in any case, one could argue that, for all that Sextus and Diogenes Laertius say, these other forms of scepticism are not committed to denying that the ultimate goal of scepticism is tranquillity. They are just committed to saying that there is an additional – perhaps intermediate – goal, namely, that of suspension of judgement.

eudaimonia.[10] What is relevant, for present purposes, is that Sextus takes scepticism to be useful in precisely the second of the two senses of 'useful' discussed above.

Scepticism therefore seems to satisfy the Utility Condition of *M* 2.10. But does it satisfy the remainder of the *M* 2.10 definition, which informs us that a *technê* must be an organised body of knowledge? Before addressing the question of as to whether scepticism is systematic in the same or in a different sense to the way in which the various *technai* are systematic, it is important first to clear up a possible confusion regarding the nature of the subject matter of scepticism.

III Subject Matter

When undermining the so-called *technai* in *M* 1–6, Sextus' attacks are often connected with the supposed subject matter of the *technai* in question. Broadly speaking, Sextus offers two kinds of objection to these *technai* – one moderate, one radical. The moderate kind of objection maintains that the *technê* in question lacks a subject matter that is susceptible of a systematic treatment. The radical kind of objection denies that the *technê* in question has a coherent subject matter at all.[11]

Take the discipline of geometry, as an example. The subject matter of geometry is constituted by various geometrical entities such as points, lines, planes and bodies. At least, that is geometry's *supposed* subject matter. In fact, Sextus goes on in *M* 3 to offer a variety of sceptical arguments against there being such things as points, lines, planes and bodies. Geometry, if Sextus' arguments are to be believed, turns out not to have a subject matter after all. Or, to put it more carefully, the existence of such things as points and lines is the kind of thing over which one should suspend judgement – Sextus' arguments against the existence of such entities should be construed as one limb of an equipollent strategy to get his interlocutor to suspend judgement regarding the existence of such entities.

---

[10] On this question see, for example, Striker 1990: 97–110; Annas 1993: 351–63; Nussbaum 1994: 315.
[11] Barnes speaks of Sextus' 'Two Voices' in connection with these two types of strategy. He distinguishes an Epicurean Voice, which he associates with the moderate sort of objection and a Pyrrhonian Voice, which he associates with the radical sort of objection. For different attempts to reconcile these two different voices in *M* 1–6, see Hankinson 1995: 251–56; and Barnes 2014: 530–35.

This radical kind of objection, which attacks the items foundational to the various *technai*, resurfaces at various points in *M* 1–6: there is no subject matter of grammar because there are no syllables (*sullabai*) (*M* 1.121–41), no subject matter of rhetoric because there are no meaningful sentences (*logoi*) (*M* 2.48), no subject matter of arithmetic because there are no numbers (*arithmoi*) (*M* 4.1) and no subject matter for music because there are no notes or rhythms (*oute ta melê . . . oute hoi rhuthmoi*) (*M* 6.38–68).

Here is not the place to assess the various and varied arguments Sextus gives for these sweeping conclusions. But it is worth reflecting on what it is about these foundational items – whether they be numbers or points or lines – that makes it the case that they are open to these sorts of sceptical arguments in the first place. Sextus does not address this question explicitly in *M* 1–6, but when we turn to other parts of Sextus' oeuvre the issue becomes clearer.

Running through all of Sextus' writings is a distinction between what is evident (*prodêlon* or *enargês*) and what is non-evident (*adêlon*). In a much-discussed passage of the *Outlines*, *PH* 1.13, Sextus addresses the question as to whether or not the sceptic can hold beliefs. In elucidating this question, Sextus distinguishes between those beliefs that have as part of their content any unclear items (*pragmata adêla*) and those beliefs that do not – the latter being those sorts of beliefs that a sceptic is able to hold and the former being those sorts of beliefs that a sceptic is barred from holding. Later on in the *Outlines*, during his discussion of signs (*sêmeia*), Sextus elaborates on the distinction between those objects that are evident and those that are by nature non-evident.[12] He writes, at *PH* 2.97–98,

> What comes of itself to our knowledge, they say, is evident [*prodêla*] (for example that it is day) . . . and what does not have a nature such as to fall under our evident grasp is non-evident [*adêla*] by nature (for example imperceptible [*noêtoi*] pores – for these are never evident of themselves but would be deemed to be apprehended, if at all, by means of something else, for example by sweating or something similar).

Sextus' illustrative examples are heterogenous. The first is propositional (the proposition that it is day is evident) while the second is non-

---

[12] In this passage, Sextus also distinguishes two other kinds of non-evident item: there are those things that are non-evident once and for all and those which are non-evident for the moment. I pass over these two senses because they are not relevant when it comes to elucidating the respects in which the items that constitute the subject matter of the disciplines of *M* 1–6 are non-evident. For further discussion of the evident/non-evident distinction and its history, see Burnyeat 1982; Sedley 1982; Ebert 1987; Hankinson 1987; and Allen 2001: 87–146.

propositional (imperceptible pores are items that are by nature non-evident). For the sake of uniformity let us recast the distinction in propositional terms. We might say that,

> for some subject S, some proposition P and some time t, it is evident to S that P at t if and only if it is possible for S to know that P at t without inferring that P; and it is by nature non-evident to S that P at t if and only if it is not possible for S to know that P at t without inferring that P.[13]

I open my curtains and see that it is day. It is possible for me to know that it is day and it is possible for me to know this without inferring it from any other piece of knowledge with which I am furnished – I know that it is day by directly perceiving that it is day. On the other hand, it is not possible for me to know that there are imperceptible pores in my skin without inferring this from some further fact – for example, from the fact that I am doused in sweat.

Equipped with this distinction between evident and non-evident items it is possible to offer an explanation as to what is motivating Sextus' attack on the foundational items of the various disciplines considered in M 1–6. Take the example of arithmetic. One might think that just as it is not possible for me to know that there are imperceptible pores in my skin without making some kind of inference from some further fact; equally, it is not possible for me to know that 977 is prime without inferring this from some further facts about the divisibility or non-divisibility of 977 by numbers greater than 1. It is not possible for me to directly know that 977 is prime in the way in which it is possible for me to directly know that it is day when I draw back the curtains and perceive that it is day. In this sense numbers – the abstract entities – are non-evident by nature and it is in virtue of this fact that the theorems and axioms that constitute the discipline of arithmetic are open to being challenged by the sceptic's arguments.

At this stage, the following question suggests itself. If the subject matter of arithmetic are those propositions that make reference to abstract items like numbers, and if the subject matter of geometry are propositions that make reference to abstract items like points and lines, what is the subject matter of scepticism? In answering this question, it is important not to confuse the *target* of scepticism with the *subject matter* of scepticism.

The target of scepticism is not fixed but changes. More precisely, it changes depending on the dialectical context in which the sceptic finds

---

[13] Lorenzo Corti draws a similar distinction. See Corti 2015: 141.

himself. When a sceptic is confronting a geometer, then his target will be the geometrical theses and geometrical theories put forward by his opponent. If, instead, he faces an arithmetician, then the propositions over which the sceptic and his opponent will lock horns will be arithmetical ones, and so on. But this is not, of course, to say that the *subject matter* of scepticism is a body of geometrical propositions or a body of arithmetical propositions. Geometrical propositions are the subject matter of geometry, and arithmetical propositions the subject matter of arithmetic. What then is the subject matter of scepticism? Is there a body of propositions – systematically organised – that constitutes the science of scepticism as there is a body of geometrical propositions that constitutes the science of geometry or a body of arithmetical propositions that constitutes the science of arithmetic? It is to this question that I now turn and to which I offer a negative answer.

IV Systematicity

As with utility, it is clear that Sextus thought that a *technê* could not be a genuine *technê* unless it displayed a certain degree of systematicity. So at *M* 1.249, the historical part of grammar is said not to be a *technê* because it arises from unsystematic matter (*tês amethodou hulês*) and at *M* 3.21 geometry is said not to be a *technê* because it lacks *sustasis* ('structure'). But before broaching the question as to whether the sceptic is in command of some systematised body of propositions that constitutes his sceptical expertise, it is important to be clear on at least two issues. The first is what we are to understand by the term 'systematic'. The second is to clearly distinguish between questions pertaining to the systematicity of Sextus' method and that of the method of the sceptic found in Sextus' pages. I deal with these issues in reverse order.

The second issue is significant because if our focus is on Sextus the author, then any cursory reading of *M* 1–6 (indeed of his oeuvre in general) suggests a certain degree of systematicity – sober and sensible systematicity – in his approach. Indeed, there are occasions where Sextus explicitly reflects on his own systematic methodology. In the prologue to *M* 1–6, for instance, he claims that in attacking the various *technai* he will not examine each and every thesis of those dogmatists whom he is refuting. That, he observes, would be unsystematic (*amethodon*) if not altogether impossible (*adunaton*). It is better, he suggests, to target the dogmatists' foundational claims, upon which the edifices of their *technai* are constructed. Sextus emphasises the point with a military metaphor:

> By 'equipollence' [*isostheneia*] we mean equality with regard to being convincing [*pistin*] or unconvincing: none of the conflicting accounts takes precedence over any other as being the more convincing.

To give a well-worn example, suppose that our sceptic confronts some dogmatist who maintains that Tom Tower is square because it appears square from nearby.[17] If the sceptic is a skilled practitioner of his art then to the little piece of reasoning

(1) Tom Tower appears square from nearby
therefore (2) Tom Tower is square,
he will oppose the rival argument
(1*) Tom Tower appears round from a distance
therefore (2*) Tom Tower is round.

Sextus does not explain why he takes an opposition of this kind to count as equipollent but it is not too difficult to conjecture why. Both pieces of reasoning advert to the same type of reasons to support their different conclusions – namely, to reasons that make reference to the way Tom Tower appears to some observer. Of course, our dogmatist might quite reasonably respond to the sceptic by arguing that one should privilege appearances from nearby to appearances from a distance, but if he does this he will have abandoned his initial argument and will have supplied the sceptic with another sort of argument against which the sceptic can exercise his art.

Now the pieces of reasoning in the above paragraph are extremely simple, and Sextus is well aware of this. Indeed, he puts forward the tower example as a toy example to give us an instance where the sceptic is opposing a *phainomenon* to a *phainomenon*.[18] Any sceptic worth his salt will have to be able to exercise his ability when he faced with more complicated arguments than the ones adduced above. This is why it is a non-trivial skill – a skill that requires training and practice.

This fact is highlighted by Sextus' celebrated medical analogy that closes the *Outlines*. He writes:

> Just as doctors for bodily afflictions have remedies which differ in potency and apply severe remedies to patients who are severely afflicted and milder

---

[17] See *PH* 1.32. I have gained a great deal from the treatment of this passage by Morison 2011: 269–87. I discuss the passage in greater detail in Sienkiewicz 2019: 34–41.
[18] Sextus also goes on to offer an example of a *phainomenon* being opposed to a *nooumenon* (an object of thinking) and an example of a *nooumenon* being opposed to a *nooumenon* but these need not concern us here.

remedies to those mildly afflicted, so Sceptics propound arguments which differ in strength – they employ weighty arguments, capable of vigorously rebutting the dogmatic affliction of conceit, against those who are distressed by a severe rashness, and they employ milder arguments against those who are afflicted by a conceit which is superficial and easily cured and which can be rebutted by a milder degree of plausibility. (*PH* 3.280–81)

The comparison between sceptic and doctor is suggestive. Sextus himself was a doctor and wrote medical treatises alongside his sceptical works (*M* 7.202; *M* 1.61), but the Hellenistic period knew at least three different kinds of medical sect, namely, the Rationalists, the Empiricists and the Methodists. Whether and to what extent the method of sceptics was similar to or distinct from the methods of the Rationalists, the Empiricists and the Methodists is a question too large and complex to pursue here – it is a question that exercised Sextus himself no less than contemporary commentators.

For present purposes, it is only necessary to stress that in comparing the sceptic to the doctor, Sextus should not be interpreted as comparing him to the Rationalist doctor. For the Rationalists went beyond a reliance on experience of the *phainomena* and claimed that – at least in some cases – correctly exercising the medical art depended on theoretical knowledge, that is to say, knowledge of the underlying causes of disease and health. The reasons why this is not the right way to think about the analogy in the above passage, should be clear. To compare the sceptic to a doctor of this stripe would be to compare the sceptic to an agent with knowledge of just those sorts of matters that – according to Section III – were unclear by nature, and over which the sceptic would suspend judgement.

Rather, Sextus should be understood to be comparing the sceptic to a non-Rationalist doctor, that is to say, a doctor whose practice is grounded in experience and accumulated observation, but not in any theoretical knowledge of underlying causes. Whether Sextus thought that the kind of doctor to which the sceptic ought to be compared was the Empiricist doctor or the Methodist doctor is a puzzle that cannot be entered into here.[19] For want of a better label, I shall refer to the sort of doctor Sextus

---

[19] While the Methodists, in common with the Empiricists, confined themselves to the *phainomena* – and in this respect were both equally opposed to the Rationalists – the Methodists differed from the Empiricists inasmuch as they did not base their medical practice on experience and memory but on a kind of non-inferential grasp of the relevant underlying physiological condition of the patient. Whether this kind of approach was coherent was an issue that exercised commentators since Galen's time (*Sect. ingred.* III 24, 19–22). To complicate matters further, despite his own soubriquet and despite Diogenes Laertius' remarks about the long-lived association between medical Empiricism

has in mind in the above passage as a 'non-Rationalist doctor' though this label should of course be understood as being neutral between thinking of the doctor as a Empiricist doctor and as a Methodist doctor.

The analogy between this kind of doctor and the sceptic is as follows. Just as such a doctor, through training and practice is in a position to correctly prescribe the right strength of potion or poultice to cure his patient's ailments, so the skilled sceptic is able to craft exactly the right sort of arguments to counterbalance the arguments of his dogmatic opponent, bring him to suspend judgement and ultimately achieve tranquillity. Some of the dogmatists' arguments will be more intricate and powerful than others and they will require correspondingly more intricate and powerful arguments from the sceptic. The more experienced the sceptic is in exercising his equipollent ability the more likely he is to meet with success.

VI The Agrippan Method

If the sceptic's Equipollent Method is best understood as a kind of expertise along the lines of the expertise of the non-Rationalist doctor, what of the sceptic's Agrippan Method? At first blush, it seems that this aspect of the sceptic's art is more theoretically loaded, more of a piece with the putative *technai* of arithmetic and geometry that Sextus is keen to target. The Agrippan Method, like the Equipollent Method, has as its aim the promotion of the suspension of judgement and, ultimately, cognitive tranquillity. However, unlike the Equipollent Method, the Agrippan Method codifies not one but four different kinds of argument forms (or 'modes' in Sextus' language) that are meant – both individually and collectively – to bring about suspension of judgement. These are the modes of disagreement, relativity, infinite regression, reciprocity and hypothesis.[20] At *PH* 1.170–77, Sextus combines all five of these modes into a 'sceptical net' (to use Barnes' gladiatorial language)[21] – a combined

---

and Pyrrhonian scepticism (D.L. 9.115–16), Sextus himself aligns the sceptics more closely with the Methodists than with the Empiricists (*PH* 1.236–41). For more details on how to interpret the distinctions between Empiricists and Methodists see, for example, Frede 1990: 225–50 and Hankinson 1995: 225–36, and for an attempt to make sense of Sextus' puzzling remarks about Methodism, see Allen 2010: 232–48.

[20] There is also a fifth Agrippan mode – of relativity – which I pass over here because, on my view, it does not – indeed cannot – form part of a combined Agrippan strategy because it is incompatible with one of the other Agrippan modes, namely, the mode of disagreement. I argue for this position and discuss some of the many complexities the mode of relativity throws up further in Sienkiewicz 2019: 125–53.

[21] See Barnes 1990: 113.

strategy that was supposed to be a perfectly general method for bringing about suspension of judgement regarding any object of investigation.

To fully elaborate on the puzzling and complicated *PH* 1.170–77 passage would require a chapter in its own right. For present purposes, it will suffice to give a brief sketch of the kind of strategy that is being invoked here so that the prima facie differences between the sceptic's Equipollent Method and Agrippan Method can be highlighted. In the *PH* 1.170–77 passage, the modes fit together in something like the following way. For any claim that the dogmatist endorses – call it P – that claim will either be subject to undecided disagreement or not, where there being an undecided disagreement over P amounts to there being, trivially, a disagreement over P (for example, as to whether P or not-P) and, furthermore, to there being no argument that tells in favour of P over not-P (and vice versa). If the disagreement over P is undecided, then suspension of judgement follows according to the mode of disagreement. If, on the other hand, the disagreement is decided (in favour of P, say), then that amounts to there being an argument that tells in favour of P. Furthermore, this putative argument in favour of P either will be an argument that goes on ad infinitum or not. If it is an argument that goes on ad infinitum, then P will be supported by some reason R_1, R_1 by some further reason R_2, R_2 by some further reason R_3 and so on without end, where none of these reasons is identical to P and no two reasons are identical to one another – but this option is ruled out by the mode of infinite regression. If, on the other hand, the argument in favour of P does not go on ad infinitum, then there are two forms it can take. Either the sequence of reasons adduced to support P loops back on itself or it does not. If the sequence of reasons loops back on itself, then we have a reciprocal argument for P. For example, P might be supported by R_1, R_1 by R_2 and R_2 by P – but this is ruled out by the mode of reciprocity.[22] If, however, the sequence of reasons does not loop back on itself then, qua finite sequence, it must stop at some reason R_n that is itself supported by no further reason R_{n+1}. This is what it is for a claim to be adduced as a 'mere hypothesis' – but this is ruled out by the mode of hypothesis.

The Agrippan Method, then, on the face of it seems to display a kind of systematicity that the Equipollent Method does not – a systematicity that

---

[22] There is no requirement that it be P that is both supported and supporting. Here is another reciprocal argument in favour of P: 'P because R_1, R_1 because R_2, R_2 because R_3, R_3 because R_1'. There are countless others.

has often been remarked on by commentators.[23] A cursory reading of a text like *PH* 1.170–77 might suggest that, in his Agrippan incarnation, the sceptic comes closest to being a *technikos* – someone in command of a body of truths about the kinds of ways of organising reasons there can be, and the defectiveness of all those ways of organising reasons.

But this judgement is precipitous. On closer inspection, the Agrippan Method can be seen to have much more in common with the non-technical, experience-based skill constitutive of the sceptic's Equipollent Method. Let us consider, as a test case, just one of the four modes alluded to above – the mode of disagreement.

VII The Art of Disagreement

The mode of disagreement is a lynchpin of the sceptic's Agrippan strategy. For any proposition, P, endorsed by a dogmatic philosopher, the sceptic first brings to bear the mode of disagreement. Then, depending on the response of the dogmatist, suspension of judgement will either follow immediately (if the disagreement in question is undecided) or he will be forced into a trilemma and confronted with either the mode of infinite regression, reciprocity or hypothesis.

Much is buried within that description. First, we might ask: what is it for the sceptic to 'bring to bear the mode of disagreement' against his dogmatic opponent? There are two ways in which the sceptic might be thought to do this, which I shall distinguish by speaking in terms of the sceptic being, on the one hand, a *chronicler* of disagreements and, on the other, a *creator* of them.[24]

As a chronicler of disagreement, all it is for a sceptic to deploy the mode of disagreement against some dogmatic opponent who endorses P is for the sceptic to philanthropically draw the dogmatist's attention to the fact that there is an undecided disagreement over whether P. Put under this description, the sceptic's activity in deploying the mode of disagreement is not expressive of any kind of technical mastery. Indeed, this kind of activity does not even amount to the kind of capacity the sceptic evinces when he deploys the Equipollent Method. For the sceptic to deploy the mode of disagreement in this sense is just for him to be able to point to some relevant disagreement over P. He becomes a reporter of the various

---

[23] See, for example, Barnes 1990: 113–44; Hankinson 1995: 191–92; Thorsrud 2009: 147–50; Woodruff 2010: 223–26.
[24] I discuss this distinction between chronicler and creator further in Sienkiewicz 2019: 47–51.

and varied undecided disputes that rage between the dogmatists.[25] To be sure, for this to be a dialectically effective strategy against the dogmatist, the sceptic will have to be well versed in the relevant controversies – both in philosophical contexts (in logic, in physics and in ethics) and in the context of the liberal arts. But this is a matter of learning, not expertise.

Of course, were this the only respect in which the sceptic deployed the mode of disagreement, then the power of the mode would be considerably reduced. For if the sceptic were a mere chronicler of disagreement, then the efficacy of the mode would depend on the sceptic, when confronted by some dogmatist who maintains P, being aware of some relevant undecided dispute over P and drawing the dogmatist's attention to this dispute. But in those situations in which the sceptic was unaware of there being any relevant undecided disagreement over P, the mode of disagreement would be toothless.

However, the sceptic is not only a chronicler of disagreement, he is also a creator of them. This is the second of the two respects in which the sceptic might be said to deploy the mode of disagreement. And it is when the sceptic creates disagreement that he exercises that very capacity that he does when he employs his Equipollent Method. For example, suppose some dogmatist offers an argument for some claim he maintains, and that the sceptic opposes to that argument an equipollent argument with a conclusion incompatible with the conclusion of the dogmatist's original argument. In doing so, the sceptic has thereby created an undecided disagreement between himself and the dogmatist – in so far as the sceptic's argument and the dogmatist's argument – by virtue of their equipollence – are as convincing as one another.

So neither qua chronicler nor qua creator of disagreement does the sceptic's deployment of the mode of disagreement amount to the sceptic having a full-blown technical grasp of a body of truths constitutive of some science of Agrippan scepticism. In his first guise, the sceptic turns out merely to be a well-informed chronicler of the varied undecided disputes that obtain between dogmatists. In his second guise, he turns out merely to be exercising his non-technical sceptical ability – namely, opposing to each and every argument he encounters an argument of equal force with a conclusion incompatible with the conclusion of the original argument.

---

[25] Sextus emphasises the role of sceptic as chronicler at the beginning of the *Outlines*. At *PH* 1.4 he writes, 'we report things descriptively' (*historikôs apaggellomen*) as opposed to 'affirming that things certainly are just as we say they are' (*diabebaioumetha hôs houtôs pantôs kathaper legomen*).

Of course, the above is only an account of how the sceptic might be thought to deploy one of the Agrippan modes. Space does not allow for a similar treatment of the other Agrippan modes – though my contention is that it is possible to interpret each of the other of the Agrippan modes in terms of the sceptic's non-technical equipollent ability. However, there is also a sense in which, given my present purposes, it is not necessary to embark upon that task here. Suppose, for example, that our dogmatist maintains that P and that our good sceptic exercises his skill and crafts an equipollent argument that Q. Now, if the dogmatist is to continue to endorse P, he will have to provide some reason for privileging P over Q but – as the modes of infinite regression, reciprocity and hypothesis show – this is not possible. The sceptic must be skilled in his equipollent art to get the dogmatist into the position of offering reasons for his belief that P. But once this is done, the trilemma emerges as a natural consequence of the fact that there are only three ways in which reasons can be organised and that all three of these ways of organising reasons are defective (or at least judged to be defective by the sceptic's dogmatic opponents). The sceptic does not have to have some technical grasp of the possible forms chains of reasons can take for the dogmatist to find himself in this trilemma. That the sceptic successfully exercises his equipollent art such that his dogmatic opponent is forced into a position to offer reasons for his beliefs is, dialectically speaking, all the sceptic need do.

VIII Varieties of Expertise

Let us now take stock. From the preceding remarks it is possible to distinguish between at least two levels of expertise alluded to in the pages of Sextus. At the higher level – let us call it Level 2 – would be found the sorts of disciplines Sextus argues against in *M* 1–6. These are *technai* that purport to delineate and correctly describe a part of reality (or *phusis* to use Sextus' language). For example, geometry is that systematically organised body of truths concerned with the properties of various geometrical entities like points, lines and planes, arithmetic is that systematic body of truths concerned with the properties of mathematical entities like numbers, and so on.

At the lower level – which we might call Level 1 – are those types of expertise that do not – and which do not purport to – illuminate any part of *phusis*. For example, at *M* 5.2 Sextus describes the art of Eudoxan astronomy as well as the arts of agriculture (*geôrgia*) and navigation (*kubernêtikê*) in terms of the observation of appearances (*têrêsis epi phainomenois*). Alongside these we might also include the Empiricist – or at least the non-Rationalist – version of the medical art as discussed in Section V. These sorts of arts, unlike geometry and arithmetic, do not purport to penetrate behind the surface of the *phainomena* and discourse on the nature of things. Rather they are based on observation (*têrêsis*) and grounded in the *phainomena*.

It is also possible to make more fine-grained distinctions between the Level 1 arts. Some, for example, will exhibit a greater degree of systematicity than others. At one end of the Level 1 spectrum would be the sciences of agriculture, navigation and the sort of medicine practised by the non-Rationalist doctors. Unlike the Level 2 arts, these arts are grounded in the *phainomena* but, for all that, they might reasonably be thought to contain universal generalisations and exhibit a systematic structure. At the other end of the Level 1 spectrum would reside those non-technical expertises that are to be best understood in terms of possessing some sort of ability, the possessing of which does not require the agent to have grasped any systematically organised body of propositions whether containing universal generalisations or not.

For instance, consider Sextus' remarks about the two senses in which one might speak of the discipline of grammar. At *M* 1.49 he writes:

> Since there are two arts of grammar [*grammatikê*], one professing to teach the alphabet and its combinations and being a general type of expertise of writing and of reading, the other being a more profound ability in comparison to that, consisting not in mere acquaintance with letters but also in the investigation of their origin and their nature ... it is not our purpose now to argue against the former.

The distinction being drawn here is between the ability to read and write, which Sextus labels 'grammatistic' (*grammatistikê*) (*M* 1.52), and the science of grammar (*grammatikê*), which involves a grasp of a body of truths concerned with the origin and nature of letters. Unlike the science of grammar – which would count as a Level 2 *technê* alongside geometry and arithmetic – grammatistic is a particular kind of ability, namely, the ability to read and write. Possessing this ability does not require the agent to have grasped a systematically organised body of propositions. Successfully exercising the grammatistic ability is a matter of experience, habituation and the following of custom and convention (*sunêtheia*) (*M* 1.186). As Sextus goes on to observe

> we possess no natural criterion regarding what is good Greek and what is not good Greek ... unless it be the customary practice of each person, which is neither technical nor natural. (*M* 1.187–88)

Alongside grammatistic one might also include the arts of sculpture and painting, which Sextus mentions at *M* 1.182 as examples of 'true arts' (*hai men toi onti eisi technai*) in contrast to the pseudo-*technê* of Chaldean astrology (*Chaldaikê*).

But if Level 1 types of expertise should be thought of as existing on a spectrum that ranges from the more systematised (agriculture, navigation, medicine as practised by the non-Rationalist doctor) to the less systematised (sculpting, painting, grammatistic), it is still, of course, an open question as to where precisely the sceptic's expertise is to be located on that spectrum. In this chapter, I have offered some reasons for thinking that scepticism should not be considered to be a Level 2 type of expertise. Furthermore, by taking the sceptic's use of the Agrippan mode of disagreement as a test case, I have suggested that the sceptic's art be located on the less systematised end of the Level 1 spectrum alongside those types of ability like grammatistic, sculpting and painting.[26]

During his discussion of grammatistic at *M* 1.235, Sextus writes that, even absent the technical knowledge of the grammarians, those who rely merely on practice and custom are equally able to speak impeccable Greek. 'Deftly responding on each occasion with just the right word, we shall be held to speak faultless Greek.' Such a remark could quite easily serve as a general motto for the sceptic's philosophical practice. In skilfully exercising his sceptical ability, which is grounded not in any grasp of a systematic body of truths, but which is a matter of practice, sensitivity and experience, the sceptic will seem to argue faultlessly too.[27]

---

[26] Though to fully defend this claim would require a more detailed examination of the ways in which the other four Agrippan modes function, which is an enterprise that must be left to another occasion.

[27] My thanks to the anonymous readers for their most helpful remarks about this chapter.

CHAPTER 10

Plotinus on the Arts
Eyjólfur Kjalar Emilsson

I Introduction

The first thing to note in connection with the topic announced in the title here is the fact that Plotinus does not have a whole lot to say about the arts, at least not as compared with his illustrious predecessors, Plato, Aristotle and the Stoics: there is no extended discussion such as we have in Plato and Aristotle of the nature of art as such and of what distinguishes it from other human capacities and endeavors. Admittedly, there are some remarks. In connection with his discussion of Aristotle's *Categories*, for instance, he suggests that the arts can generally be said to belong to two categories: 'in so far as they dispose the soul, they are qualities, but in so far as they do or make, they are doings and makings, and in this way they are other-directed and relative' (I.6.12, 28–30). We also see a grouping of the arts into productive arts (house-building is the example), arts that help nature keep in the right state such as medicine and agriculture, and arts such as rhetoric and music that are directed at the human soul and aim at influencing it for better or worse (IV.4.31, 17–23; cf. V.9.11).

In the *Timaeus*, Plato famously describes the cosmos as a work of a divine artisan and his assistants, and we see throughout that dialogue references to this craftsmanship. In other dialogues, Plato is liable to use analogies or metaphors from the arts, for example, the art of weaving or the art of grammar, to make ontological and epistemological points. Aristotle too is full of illustrations of his metaphysical doctrines drawn from the arts – I have in particular mind his much-discussed pieces of bronze or marble that are turned into statues by art, and bricks and timber that art turns into houses. We see very little of this in Plotinus in spite of the fact that he draws heavily on both Plato's and Aristotle's writings on themes where one might think that such an appeal to the arts could be relevant. In so far as he draws on the arts to make general philosophical points, the art of dancing is the most conspicuous and striking. I shall have something to say about that later on. Nor is Plotinus inclined to regard ethical knowledge as analogous to the mastery of arts as Socrates did or as a kind of art, the art of living, as the Stoics did.[1] At least he does not make such a point explicitly. There are two areas, however, where it seems especially appropriate to discuss Plotinus' thought in relation to the arts.

The first set of issues we shall address has to with the relation between the arts and the intelligible sphere. In the early treatise 'On Intellect, the Forms, and Being' (V.9.[5]), Plotinus discusses a traditional school question among Platonists, that is, whether the arts are there in the intelligible realm and concludes that in part they are. This claim is reaffirmed in the later treatise 'On the intelligible beauty' (V.8. [31]).[2] It raises a number of questions. We must first of all address how Plotinus understands the question. Is it whether there are Forms of the arts? Or whether there are Forms of sensible art objects? Or whether artists must have access to the intelligible realm? Secondly, what is exactly the principle of division for which arts or which parts of an art belong to the intelligible realm? Thirdly, because at least some of the arts do have a place in the intelligible realm, even such arts as painting and sculpture, the question arises whether Plotinus' view here deviates from that of Plato in the tenth book of the *Republic*, assigning a higher status for what Plato calls the imitative arts. His position in this regard together with certain statements of his about the relationship between sensible and intelligible beauty has often been praised as highly original and has secured him a significant place in the history of aesthetic theory.[3] His views here left deep marks on philosophers and artists of the Italian Renaissance, not least Michelangelo.[4] As I see it, the main question here is to what extent this is justified: did Plotinus have a distinct philosophy of beauty and the fine arts? I shall not address this last question in full generality here but I'll attempt to do some groundwork concerning it.

The second topic is rather different. For Plotinus, the *Timaeus* was one of the most important Platonic dialogues. He does, however, not take its wording at face value and is very much concerned about eliciting its true philosophical message as he sees it. In other words, Plotinus seeks to demythologise the *Timaeus*.[5] This means among other things that, as

---

[1] See Chapter 7 in this volume.
[2] The number in square brackets refers to the place of a treatise on Porphyry's chronological list of Plotinus' treatises.
[3] See, e.g., Bosanquet 1904: 11–119 and Beardsley 1966: 78–89.
[4] See Panofsky 1939, chapters IV and V.
[5] On the art of world-making in Plato's *Timaeus*, see Johansen's contribution in Chapter 5.

opposed to Plutarch and Atticus, he doesn't think that the story of a temporal beginning of the cosmos is to be taken literally and the figure of the divine craftsman, the Demiurge, very much disappears. That is to say, what the Demiurge does in the *Timaeus* is there in Plotinus in some form and he keeps citing the *Timaeus*. But the Demiurge as a character is pretty much gone as is much of the language of craftsmanship associated with him and his sons.[6] Lots of questions arise in this connection, but I shall focus on issues that have a direct bearing on our topic. If we take the *Timaeus* at face value, the divine craftsman and his helpers reason in a craftsmanlike manner about how to get optimal results, given a perfect intelligible model and sensible materials that put serious constraints on the full realisation of the ideal. In Plotinus, the tasks of the divine craftsman are divided between the Intellect and the hypostasis Soul. He, however, consistently insists that neither Intellect nor Soul reasons. In general, they do not make plans or seek to obtain particular results. Nevertheless, what they produce is so intelligently done that it is as if it had been carefully planned and reasoned through with an optimal result in mind (V.8.6). This raises the question about the nature of the thought that goes into making the world according to Plotinus. As we shall see, considerations of the nature of *technê* are lurking in the background of this topic.

I shall now discuss these two topics in turn.

II The Status of the Arts in the Plotinian Hierarchy

Plotinus famously claims that action (*praxis*) is posterior to contemplation (*theôria*). In the treatise 'On nature, contemplation and the One' (III.8.), he argues that action is a kind of by-product of contemplation, a sort of substitute for those unable to think properly.[7] Since the working of the arts must in general fall under action, one would presume that they have the same, relatively low, place in Plotinus' hierarchical order of things. This seems to be confirmed by a passage in 'On the problems of soul I', where in comparing the productive activity of the World-Soul with that of art he writes:

---

[6] See, however, II.3.18, 13–16; II.4.7; IV.8.1, 44 and various mentions of *dêmiourgos* and *dêmiourgein* in the so-called *Großschrift*, which consists of *Enneads* III.8., V.8., V.5. and II.9 and was originally written as one long treatise, culminating in II.9, 'Against the Gnostics'. Especially the last-mentioned treatise refers multiple times to the Demiurge, presumably because the adversaries Plotinus is addressing do so.

[7] For the placement of action in the Plotinian scheme and its Platonic sources, see Emilsson 2012.

> For whatever comes into contact with soul is made according to the substance of the nature of soul; and it makes not with an external goal nor waiting upon planning or search. For art is posterior to soul, and imitates it, making dim and weak imitations, toys not worth much, bringing in many devices to help it in producing an image of nature. (IV.3.10, 13–19)[8]

The passage suggests that art is something posterior to natural production. Artistic production is here contrasted with that of the World-Soul, which does not employ reasoning, planning or searching to create and maintain the cosmos. I take it that it is suggested here that art, as opposed to the world-making thought of the World-Soul, has a goal given from the outside and that reaching this goal involves planning and searching.

There are, however, strong reasons to believe that this account does not fully capture Plotinus' views on the nature of art. Slightly later in 'On the problems of soul I', he remarks that 'in the arts reasoning occurs when the artisans are in perplexity, but when there is no difficulty, the art dominates and does its work' (IV.3.18, 5–7). This suggests a rather different picture from that expressed in the previous passage: art, at least when it functions as it should, does not involve reasoning. Thus, according to this account, when 'the art dominates and does its work' the craftsman becomes rather similar to the World-Soul in the previous passage. Other treatises indeed suggest that Plotinus granted at least some of the arts a higher status than the passage cited above suggests. We shall now consider the evidence of these other treatises.

The ancient Platonists both before and after Plotinus discussed the question of what things there are Platonic Forms. While the membership of such impeccable Forms as that of Justice, the Triangle or Man would not be questioned, there were a number of doubtful members of the realm of Forms. In the second century AD, Alcinoos reports that the majority of Platonists hold

> that there are no Forms of artificial objects such as the shield or the lyre, nor of unnatural things such as fever or cholera, nor of individuals such as Socrates, nor of worthless things such as dirt and straw, nor of relations such as bigger or greater. (*Didaskalikos* 9, 24–30)

In Plotinus' early treatise, 'On Intellect, the Forms and Being' (*Ennead* V.9), we find a general discussion of membership in the intelligible world,

---

[8] The translations of passages from the *Enneads* quoted here are those of Armstrong in the Loeb Classical Library, often with modifications.

where Plotinus addresses the question of such doubtful members as Alcinoos mentions. In chapter 11, he turns to the arts: are they there in the intelligible world? It is noteworthy that Plotinus changes the traditional question: he does not ask whether there are Forms of artificial objects such as the shield or the lyre but rather whether there are Forms of the arts. He does not think that the arts of farming and medicine have anything to do with the intelligible realm, but otherwise his answer is surprisingly positive. All arts in so far as they employ mathematics are there in the intelligible realm. This claim may seem to entail that it is really the mathematics that essentially belongs there. The arts that employ mathematics include all music, he says, because it is concerned with melody and rhythm (10–12); also arts that produce sensible objects are there in so far as they make use of proportions and intellectual thoughts. The same holds for the arts of rhetoric, generalship, administration and kingship; these too have a share in the intelligible: 'if any of them communicate beauty in the field of action', he says, 'they have a share of knowledge from the knowledge there' (22–24). The status of what he calls the imitative arts – painting, sculpture, dancing and mime are his examples of these – is less clear. I shall address this shortly.

Two remarks about Plotinus' take on this question in general. First, we should note that in this whole discussion of membership in the intelligible realm, he does not simply ask the question whether there is a specific Platonic Idea of this or that. His conception of the intelligible realm is wider than that. If a given feature of a thing is, for instance, due to the *logos* of the thing rather than to its matter or some external influence, that feature has an intelligible cause. To take an example: curly hair may be congenital to a person and due to the intelligible *logos* (formative principle) of the person. Somebody else's curly hair may be artificial or have another cause. In the former case, the curly hair has an intelligible cause, the *logos,* which is a member of the intelligible realm. That does not necessarily mean, however, that there is a specific Platonic Idea of curly hair or of a curly haired human being. Thus, Plotinus widens the scope of the school question about of which things there are Platonic Forms. The *logos* of something is typically an item of the order of soul rather than Intellect and not exactly identifiable with a classical Platonic Idea. Secondly, when Plotinus gives a positive answer to the question whether a given art has a place in the intelligible realm, he doesn't mean that there is a specific Idea or even a specific intelligible *logos* of the art in question. As Bréhier 1931 noted long ago in his 'Notice' to *Ennead* V. 9, Plotinus transforms the school question into the question whether a given sort of artist or artisan makes use of the intelligible realm in performing his or her art. So when he concludes that, for example, carpentry has at least partially a place in the intelligible realm, this is because he thinks this art makes some use of mathematical proportions; the knowledge of these belongs to that realm and the practitioner who applies this knowledge has some kind of access to that higher realm.

With all this in mind, let us have a closer look at what Plotinus says about the imitative arts. He says:

> As for the imitative arts, painting and sculpture, dancing and mime, which are in some way composed of elements from this world and use a model perceived by sense and imitate their forms and movements and transpose the proportions they see, it would not be reasonable to trace them back to the intelligible world except through the *logos* of a human being. (V.9.11, 1–6)

To begin with, this sounds as if the imitative arts have no place in the intelligible world: they merely imitate sensible models. Thus, Plotinus' view of these arts would be in conformity with Plato's account in book 10 of the *Republic*, according to which the products of the imitative arts are 'shadows of shadows'. Nevertheless, the qualification at the end, 'except by means of the *logos* of the human being', or however we translate the Greek phrase,[9] should give us reason to pause. Evidently, there is some qualification of the previous statement being made here, the question is just exactly what it means. There is no agreement among the translators. Armstrong, for instance, translates the phrase as 'except as included in the formative principle of man' and MacKenna as 'except indirectly, through the Reason-principle of humanity'. Schniewind, on the other hand, has 'were it not in virtue of human reason'.[10] I shall not go into the details about grammatical and semantic possibilities here but let it be said that for Plotinus, as for other Greek philosophers, *logos* is a highly ambiguous word. A very common meaning, which I have already invoked, owes a lot to Stoicism: *logos* is then an internal intelligible principle that causes and directs the sensible features of things. This is what often is translated by 'formative principle' and it is evidently this sense that Armstrong had in mind. But *logos* can, of course, also be other things, for instance, reason, the human capacity of thinking. This is the sense reflected in Schniewind's translation. I fail to get a good meaning out of Armstrong's translation or in general from any translations in terms of

---

[9] *ei mē tôi anthrôpou logôi*.
[10] 'si ce n'est en vertue de la raison humaine', see Schniewind 2007, ad loc.

'formative principle'. Schniewind's proposal makes reasonably good sense in the context, for Plotinus continues:

> But any artistic skill which starts from the proportions of [individual] living beings and goes on from there to consider the proportions of living beings in general would be a part of the power which also there [i.e., in the intelligible realm] considers and contemplates the proportions of all things. (V.9.11, 7–10)

The idea is then that the imitative arts do indeed employ human reason. This, however, does not quite amount to their using the intelligible realm, unless they move on from imitating particular sensible proportions to considering proportions generally. There is no strong affirmation here that imitative artists necessarily ascend to the intelligible level in their work but it is hinted that they may, at least so far as proportions are concerned.

Let us now have a look at another passage from a later treatise where Plotinus also discusses the question whether the imitative arts use the intelligible realm. This is the treatise 'On the intelligible beauty', which Porphyry puts as number 31 of his chronological list of Plotinus' treatises (*Life of Plotinus* 5). It is one of the four treatises comprising the so-called *Großschrift* – originally a single treatise but split by Porphyry into four and put into different *Enneads*.[11] In the first chapter of this treatise, Plotinus notes that the beauty of sensible things is due to their form rather than to their matter. A stone, for instance, that has been made beautiful by art has not changed its matter but it has been given form by the art. That form was in the thought of the artist prior to being in the stone. Plotinus writes:

> Now the material did not have this form, but it was in the man who had it in his mind even before it came into the stone; but it was in the craftsman, not in so far he had hands and eyes, but because he had a share in art. So this beauty was in the art and it was far better there; for the beauty in the art did not come into the stone, but that beauty stays in the art and another comes from it into the stone which is derived from it and less than it. (V.8.1, 15–22)

He continues, arguing in a familiar way, that the beauty in the artist's soul is stronger and superior to the one in the product because the latter is spread out in a spatial magnitude, and the loss of unity always involves a loss of strength. For Plotinus, dispersion in space as contrasted with the togetherness characteristic of soul and the higher realms is always a loss of

---

[11] The *Großschrift* consists of *Enneads* III.8., V.8., V.5 and II.9. The last treatise is entitled 'Against the Gnostics'. Presumably, the whole *Großschrift* was written with the primary aim of setting certain Gnostics straight about the status and value of the sensible region.

strength, presumably primarily the loss of strength for self-maintenance and begetting.

We can glimpse behind these claims several principles of Plotinian metaphysics. One of them is actually quite explicit here: (1) 'More unified' implies 'stronger and better' and vice versa. Spatial dispersion comes with a very low degree of unity; hence, the beauty in spatially extended things has a low degree of unity. (2) Causes are more unified, hence stronger and better, than their effects. The cause of the sensible beauty of a statue, say, is more unified, hence stronger and better, than the beauty of the extended statue. (3) We have here a version of the Platonic-Aristotelian principle of prior actuality: what is to become F, becomes so through the agency of something that is actually F.[12] At least the Platonic version of this principle insists that the cause is somehow more fully F than the effect, which has a status as a mere image or imitation of an F. (4) We see here Plotinus' particular version of this kind of causation, which in the literature has been called the theory of double activity.[13] Double activity is seen at work throughout the Plotinian hierarchy. The first principle, the One, has self-contained, internal activity and at the same an external activity as a kind of by-product of the internal activity. It is this by-product that is often called emanation. A new hypostasis is established when the external activity turns back toward its source. Thus, the emanation from the One, converts toward the One and the hypostasis Intellect is established. Soul comes to be from Intellect through a similar process. This idea of an external activity or by-product is also at work in the sensible world. For instance, Plotinus describes human action in general in terms of external activity of the soul and the sensible features of the physical world as the external act of the *logoi* contained in nature, which is the lowest phase of the World-Soul.[14]

---

[12] On this principle, see Makin 1991, and especially with respect to Plato, Sedley 1998.

[13] For the principle of double activity and its relationship with emanation, see Emilsson 2007, chapter 1. This principle is also at work in later Platonists such as Proclus: see Opsomer on Proclus (Chapter 11).

[14] A few remarks about the sources of the double activity theory. The exact sources are somewhat disputed, but here is what I think: The internal and external activities along with the emanation metaphors are Plotinus' interpretation of Platonic causes. He sees this as suggested by passages such as the *Republic* on the Idea of the Good, *Phdr.* 245 C, which distinguishes between the internal, innate, motion of the soul and the motion the soul imparts on other things, and Diotima's speech in the *Symposium*, where Diotima makes the point that Beauty itself is unaffected by causing other things to be beautiful (cf. Gerson 1993: 23–24). This last point is of great importance in the metaphysical application of the two acts: the internal activity loses nothing by having the external activity. So, even if the vocabulary of activity is Aristotelian and even if aspects of the doctrine clearly make use of Aristotelian views (e.g., concerning the last-mentioned claim that agents do not suffer from acting), Plotinus sees the double act doctrine primarily as an account of the causality of

Aspects of this double activity are clearly at work here and particularly evident in the following phrase in the passage just quoted: 'The beauty in the art did not come into the stone, but that beauty stays in the art and another comes from it into the stone which is derived from it and less than it.' What Plotinus describes here is something characteristic of double activity: the internal act itself isn't transferred to the effect. It loses nothing of itself in its external causation but nevertheless produces the external act as a weaker image of itself.

Thus, Plotinus sees double activity going on in the relationship between the arts and their products. In this case, he focuses on one property in particular, namely, beauty. Let us see how he continues:

> But if anyone despises the arts because they produce their work by imitating nature, we must tell him, first, that natural things are imitations too. Then he must know that the arts do not simply imitate what they see, but they run back up to the forming principles [*logoi*] from which nature derives; then also that they do a great deal by themselves, and, since they possess beauty, they make up what is defective in things. For Phidias too did not make his Zeus from any model perceived by the senses, but understood what Zeus would look like if he wanted to make himself visible. (V.8.1, 32–40)

Let us first note that it is clear from the context, where beauty is the theme, that even if Plotinus speaks about the arts generally, he has primarily in mind arts that aim at making beautiful objects. The imitative arts such as sculpture and painting would be prime examples of these. Secondly, it is noteworthy that Plotinus uses the word 'nature' (*phusis*) in a somewhat unusual way here: here it seems to refer to the sensible object or the sensible features of things. Most often in contexts such as this one 'nature' refers to an internal intelligible principle that produces the sensible features. As such, normally, nature is the same as the *logos*. But, as noted, here he is using the word in a non-typical way. In any case, we see here that the artists may ascend to the *logoi* of the sensible things they express in their art, presumably *logoi* of the sort the transcendent World-Soul thinks in terms of. Put somewhat boldly, perhaps, but I hope understandably, we might say that the claim is that the imitative artist can grasp the intelligible nature of things, the very intelligible content from which the World-Soul

---

Platonic principles. As to the idea of conversion, that the external act should turn towards its source and become informed by it, is without doubt derived from Platonic and Aristotelian notions of imitation and love such as we find in *Metaphysics* XII.7. These claims are argued for at greater length in Emilsson 2007, chapter 1, where references to other literature on the double act theory can also be found.

makes the sensible features of things. Moreover, he says that the arts can even improve on what nature has produced. What does he have in mind by that? He might have been thinking of arts such as agriculture and medicine, which he says help nature to stay intact. In this context, however, he more probably means that the World-Soul, well-organised and clever though she is, leaves some things much less beautiful than they could be. Stones, for instance: there is ample evidence that Plotinus thinks little of stones and that they would be benefitted by some artistic treatment.

Many scholars have noted that this account of the imitative arts differs widely from that of Plato in the tenth book of the *Republic* according to which the imitative arts have no recourse beyond the sensible level. There was in antiquity a rival theory to Plato's about the nature of the imitative arts. We see it expressed for instance by Philostratus in *De vita Apollonii* VI.19, where he has Apollonius say that the artist does not simply imitate what he sees but uses the imagination, *phantasia*, to supply what he does not know about. This is of course especially relevant in the case of representations of the gods, whom few have seen. The artist, using his or her memory and power of imagination, forms a mental image that is not a copy of anything they have directly experienced and seeks to convey this image in the work of art. Plotinus is, however, most commonly understood as taking a further step in holding that some artists can have access to the Forms themselves and make perceptible representations of them. For this reason, Plotinus has been granted a place as an important innovator in the field of aesthetics.[15]

Recently, however, in a well-argued short monograph, Oiva Kuisma (2003) has questioned the innovative nature of Plotinus' thought in this regard, a view that has become some kind of orthodoxy. Kuisma holds that Plotinus does not depart far from Plato at all. He objects to the whole idea of giving the Platonic Forms a perceptual representation, mostly on the ground that there cannot be any similarity between timeless, purely intelligible Forms and perceptible things. Despite his making a well-informed and well-argued case, I am not convinced by Kuisma's revisionary view and stick to the orthodoxy, slightly revised. I shall not argue against Kuisma's account in detail here but let the following be noted:

---

[15] See Kuisma 2003: 52–53 with a large number of references. A clear and well-argued statement of the orthodox view is given by Rich 1960.

(1) Though Kuisma may be right that there is no evidence that, according to Plotinus, imitative artists may ascend to the level of Forms, to Intellect itself, he clearly indicates the artist may be an agent parallel to the World-Soul with access to the same kind of rational principles as she: 'but [the arts] run back up to the forming principles [*logoi*] from which nature derives', he says in the passage from V.8.1 quoted above at greater length. Kuisma 2003: 92–93 takes the *logoi*, the forming principles in question, to be discursive definitions that are, as it were, man-made and do not reflect the pre-ordained structure of the intelligible realm. It seems to me, on the contrary, that the passage clearly suggests that these *logoi* belong to this structure. They would not necessarily be of the order of Forms in Intellect. There are *logoi* at the level of soul according to Plotinus (cf. III.8.1–5). These are themselves imitations of the Forms but they belong to the intelligible order. Artists can have access to such *logoi* and are thus in a way at a level parallel to the World-Soul. This is indeed a radically different picture from that suggested by book ten of the *Republic*.

(2) Kuisma is certainly right that the idea of an imitation of intelligible entities in a perceptible form is philosophically perplexing. Nevertheless, whatever we might wish to say about it, Plato, Plotinus and the whole hoard of ancient (and modern) Platonists insist that such an imitation is possible: however we explain this, the sensible world is an imitation or representation of an intelligible realm. It is in principle no more questionable that a human mind could accomplish such an imitation than the soul that fashions the world. So whatever inherent problems there may be in the notion of perceptible imitations of intelligible things, these are problems that Plotinus and any Platonist are saddled with in any case.

III The Art of World-Making

Let us turn to the topic of cosmological art. I mentioned at the outset Plotinus' tendency to demythologise Plato's *Timaeus*. But despite demythologising – dehumanising we might even say – the divine craftsman, Plotinus describes the creative cosmological activity of souls as artistic, *technikos*, and he compares it with human arts. The main question I wish to address is what he has in mind by this claim.[16]

---

[16] For recent accounts of world-making in Plotinus, differing in some respects from what is said here, see Noble and Powers 2015 and Caluori 2015, especially chapter 2, 51–68.

In order to come to better grips with Plotinus' position on the kind of thought that goes into making the world, a little excursion back to Plato's *Timaeus* and its ancient interpretations may be helpful. Plato's views on the generation of the sensible world are often presented as if there are just two sorts of things: the Forms and physical objects that participate in, or imitate, the Forms. If we only had, for example, the *Republic* and the *Phaedo* we might easily be led to adopt this simple picture. Human souls are of course prominent in both these dialogues but there is no hint that they or any other souls are involved in making the world. The *Timaeus*, which was of central importance to the ancient Platonists, has a much more complicated account. We have there the realm of Forms, which is called the Living Being. We have in addition the character of the divine Craftsman or Demiurge, the maker of the world. The Craftsman fashions the world on the model of the Forms with the help of his children, whom he gave the final task of 'weaving mortal bodies' (*Tim.* 42d). Before he had made the World-Soul and other souls and set the world in uniform circular motion, thereby creating time as 'a moving image of eternity'.

Plato relates all this in a semi-mythical language, which he presumably didn't mean to be taken literally in every respect. So Plato's ancient followers had the formidable task of interpreting the *Timaeus* so that it made good philosophical sense. Some of Plotinus' Platonist predecessors noted that the divine Craftsman seems to be engaged in two rather different kinds of activity. On the one hand, he is engaged in pure intellection of the Forms. On the other hand, the Craftsman must think about what he is about to make and how. This observation gave rise to theories such as that of Numenius, which split the Craftsman's thought into two: pure intellection and providential thought about the world (Numenius fr. 11; cf. *Timaeus* 30c).[17] Plotinus follows this trend and takes it further.[18]

Among other things, this means that the divine craftsman appears as less human in Plotinus than he does in Plato's *Timaeus*. Actually, as already noted, there is not a whole lot about the divine Craftsman as such in the *Enneads*. The Craftsman's tasks have been split into two: on the one hand, he is the Intellect that thinks the Forms and the One in so far as the One lets itself be thought; on the other hand, the task of the Craftsman is given to the hypostasis Soul, which, through contemplating Intellect, makes

---

[17] For Numenius' interpretation of the generation of the world, see Frede 1987.
[18] For an overview of the developments in the interpretation of the *Timaeus*, see Michalewski 2014 and Caluori 2015: 25–36.

some sort of scheme of the sensible world and makes it through the agency of the World-Soul. This is not a process with a temporal beginning; the thinking that goes into making the world is itself timeless and the creation or making is everlasting. Plotinus describes this thought from which the world is made as providential, that is, the world to be made is as good as a sensible being can possibly be.

How does this providential thought differ from pure intellection at the level of Intellect according to Plotinus? The following is reasonably clear:

(1) The Soul's thought is less unified than Intellect's grasp of the Forms. Though there is little explicit about this, a crucial way in which the Soul's thought is less unified is presumably that it is propositional, whereas Intellect's thought is non-propositional.[19]
(2) Soul's thought is derived from that of the Intellect by means of the soul's vision of Intellect in its conversion.
(3) Soul's thought has a practical aspect in that it involves thinking about how to make the sensible world according the maxim that it is to be as good as a sensible image can be.
(4) Nevertheless, the thought the Soul is engaged in is not a temporal process that involves deliberation.

Plotinus often emphasises that there is no searching (*zêtêsis*), or deliberation (*bouleusis*), or reasoning (*logismos*) involved in the Soul's thought when it makes the world.[20] On the other hand, the world is made in such a way that it is possible to see afterwards good reasons for each thing in it being such as it is. In other words, the sensible world is rationally arranged and as if it had been well reasoned through but there is no reasoning behind its making.

Plato, in the *Timaeus* 30b–c, actually attributes 'reasoning' (*logisamenos, logismos*) to the divine Craftsman's providential thought. Plotinus seems to wish to explain away this reference to reasoning as our afterwards reconstruction of what happened; it does not accurately describe the Demiurge's thought (see V.8.6). He also insists in one passage that reasoning does not have to imply a temporal searching process, which is what 'reasoning' usually means for him. Thus, after denying that undescended souls are engaged in reasoning, he qualifies his statement by noting that the term 'reasoning' can also be applied to the undescended souls:

---

[19] See Caluori 2015: 44–51.   [20] See, e.g., IV.4.11; V.8.6; VI.7.1.

> But one must understand reasoning in this sort of sense; because if one understands reasoning to be a state of mind which exists in them always proceeding from Intellect, and which is a static activity and kind of reflection of Intellect, they [the souls] would employ reasoning in that other world too. (IV.3.18, 10–13)

For the embodied human soul, discursive reasoning is a searching temporal process. But this is not how undescended souls think (see IV.4.15). This admission on Plotinus' part, that there is room for reasoning that is a 'static activity', presumably reflects his wish not to speak against Plato but rather to sway the latter's meaning towards his understanding.

Plotinus expressly compares the thought of the divine world-maker with artistic production: in comparing embodied and undescended souls, he notes that 'just as in the arts reasoning occurs when the artisans are in perplexity, but when there is no difficulty, the art dominates and does its work' (IV.4.18, 5–7). (Even if the undescended souls here are not necessarily occupied with world-making, the comparison can certainly be transferred to the World-Soul.) 'Reasoning' here is clearly meant as a temporal, searching reasoning. Good craftsmen do not normally need to go through such a process. Their mastery of their art ensures effortlessness. We might be tempted to describe this situation by saying that artists who do not have to stop to think about what they are doing act mechanically and unthinkingly. As Plotinus sees it, this is not the case at all: on the contrary, they are thinking excellently, much better than those who have to reason their way through! A source of this view is no doubt Aristotle's saying in *Physics* II 198b18 that art does not deliberate. That claim is of prime importance for Plotinus' understanding of how art works. The upshot of this is that in so far as the making of the world is comparable with artistic production, it is artistic production at its best, an idealisation, we might say, of the sort that does not involve deliberative reasoning.

How plausible is such a model for the case of the world-maker? We may suppose it is most natural to compare the world-maker with architects or builders. The world-maker is indeed constructing something. According to a common conception of the task of the architect, it consists very much in taking into account several, sometimes opposite requirements for the building that is to be constructed and seeking to do justice to them all in a harmonious way. The architect does not know beforehand how to achieve this in detail: the building has to look graceful from a distance; it has to function well as a museum; it has to accommodate access for handicapped people; it has to allow visitors to enjoy the splendid view from the inside and so forth. In this kind of situation, the architect would try to put a certain feature in place in a certain way just to realise that this would conflict with certain other requirements. Then a process of deliberation starts, moving different pieces around, until everything falls into place to the architect's satisfaction. Clearly, this kind of account is rather different from what Plotinus envisages Soul to be doing when she makes and administers the world. He is clearly assuming an idealised model of the arts according to which the artist has no need to pause and deliberate.[21]

Plotinus, however, does not compare the world-maker with an architect or manufacturer of any kind. He draws on other kinds of art when he uses arts to illustrate how the World-Soul works. We get a sense of how he conceives of this from a passage in the treatise 'On providence', where he explicitly says that the working of nature is artistic, *technikos*:

> All life, even worthless life, is activity; activity not in the way fire acts; but its activity, even if there is no perception there, is a movement which is not random. For with living things when there is no perception present and any one of them has any share in life, it is immediately enreasoned [*lelogôtai*], that is informed, since the activity which is proper to life is able to form it and moves it in such a way that its movement is a forming. So the activity of life is an artistic [*technikê*] activity, like the way in which one who is dancing is moved; for the dancer himself is like the life which is artistic in this way and his art moves him, and moves in such a way that the actual life is somehow of this [artistic] kind. (III.2.16, 17–27)

The life and the activity of life spoken of here is any sort of life at the sensible level: the life of an oyster or that of the whole sensible cosmos, which is actually what Plotinus is interested in in the context: both are artistic. The reason given for this is that life is not random but movement and formation according a rational pattern. In the natural world, there are intelligible *logoi*, which are like computer programs that direct the movements and formations at the sensible level. These *logoi* parallel the position of the art in artistic production: in 'On the kinds of being III', VI.3.16, 13–14, it is explicitly said that the arts are *logoi* having the soul (of the artist) as their matter.

---

[21] Arna Mathiesen, my wife, who is a practicing architect, informs me that while architects do go about their work along the lines just suggested, employing a trial-error-improvement procedure, with experience they do so much less and that much falls right into place right away without a whole lot of deliberation. Now, what she describes as 'with experience' could presumably just as well be described as 'with full mastery of the art', mastery that novices do not have, even if they have finished school and can call themselves architects.

In drawing the analogy between the cosmological art and dance, Plotinus speaks about the arts generally but he seems to have a preference for mentioning dance when it comes to giving examples.[22] There is a natural explanation of this preference. Performance arts can, more obviously than other arts, be said to enact immediately and without deliberation a pattern that the artist sees in his or her mind in a different medium. The artists, so to speak, look upwards and inwards and translate what they see into some movement. In 'On the problems of soul II' (IV.4.33 and following chapters) he goes on about pantomimic dance, which he introduces to shed light on the movements of the cosmos and the relations between its parts. In such a dance, a single dancer may enact a whole myth. The art would in this case be the dancer's appropriation of the myth that is to be enacted and his or her disposition to move according to that appropriation. The art in act is the dance itself: 'The dancer's intention (*proairesis*) looks elsewhere, but his limbs are affected in accordance with the dance and serve the dance, and help make it perfect and complete' (IV.4.33, 17–19). The dancer's grasp of the myth itself would in this case correspond to the intellectual vision Soul has of Intellect in making and administering the world.

IV World-Making without Deliberation

An important aspect of dance, as Plotinus sees it, that renders it suitable to illustrate cosmological causation is the absence of deliberation and, what for Plotinus amounts to the same thing, the absence of goal-directedness in the sense of lack of a direct aim for a particular result.[23] Let us consider the latter first. In 'On the intelligible beauty' he writes:

> You can explain the reason why the earth is in the middle, and round, and why the ecliptic slants as it does; but it is not because you can do this that things are so there; they were not planned [*bebouleutai*] like this because it was necessary for them to be like this, but because things there [in the intelligible realm] are disposed as they are, the things here are beautifully

---

[22] See, in particular, 'On the problems of Soul II', *Ennead* IV.4.33–34 but also IV.4.8, 43–50 and VI.9.8, 45–49.

[23] Sarah Broadie (1987) argues, convincingly, that in so far as art serves as a model in explaining the work of nature in Aristotle, the notion of art in question is an abstract, idealised one. It is art in this idealised sense that does not deliberate or concern itself with particular results. Plotinus may of course have been influenced by Aristotle on this point. The lack of concern with the outcome is also a feature of the Stoic conception of wisdom, the art of life, which the arts of acting and dancing are in fact said to resemble more closely than navigation and medicine in that the former have an internal end (Cicero, *De fin.* 24–25)

disposed: as if the conclusion was there before the syllogism which showed the cause, and did not follow from the premises; [the world-order] is not the result of following out a train of logical consequences [*ex akolouthias*] and purposive thought [*ex epinoias*]: it precedes consequential and purposive thinking. (V.8.7, 37–43)

A lot could be said about this passage, but I shall confine myself to a few observations that are relevant to our topic. Even if the particular results are not aimed at, there is a teleology at work in Plotinus. Stated generally: an agent aims at and imitates a principle above itself, not a particular result ensued from doing this. The *telos* of any lower level is to become like the higher one, its source. In the case of Soul's world-making, the principle – Intellect and ultimately the Good (the One) itself – is good and is aimed at as something good. It follows that in so far as the imitation is successful, it will resemble the principle, hence, be good in so far as an image can be. Thus, if the result is recognised as meaningful and intelligent, this is because its paradigm is and it is assumed that an imitation must reflect this.

How are we supposed to be able to discover afterwards why everything is arranged the way it is? Plotinus does not tell us exactly, but the analogy of the Egyptian hieroglyphics he gives slightly before the passage quoted above (chapter 6), may suggest an answer along the following lines. The principle is not only good, it is intelligent too – its goodness and its intelligence are in Plotinus' view inseparable features – but its intelligence is not the deliberative reasoning sort of thought. Nor is the thought that goes into making the world of that kind: it absorbs its model and translates what it sees in the manner of a skilled portrait painter, or even better, a dancer enacting a myth. However, since the latter kind of thought (and its product, the world) is a good image of a supremely good and intelligent model, it is possible to discover, step by step, the reasons why everything is such as it is.

The performance arts exhibit very well the feature of the cosmological art that was brought up a little while ago: these arts do not deliberate. It is a poor dancer who stops to think: 'Should I put my foot here or perhaps rather over there?' Also, I take it that these performance arts are not goal-directed in the sense that they seek particular sensible results. Well-trained dancers, at least, do not aim at particular positions: they move into particular positions as an expression of the intelligible pattern they have internalised. Presumably, a skilled dancer could afterwards explain, for example, to students or to an audience, every move he or she makes. It does not follow that the dancer ever went through this reasoning. Soul works in a similar manner in its making. It does not do this in order to achieve this or that other thing. We might say that in performance arts such as dance, Plotinus sees a real example of what he wishes to maintain about world-making with regard to the aspects of the arts that Broadie (1987) takes to be unrealistic idealisations on Aristotle's part.

CHAPTER 11

Productive Knowledge in Proclus

Jan Opsomer

I Introduction

Human productive knowledge is not Proclus' most cherished topic.[1] It is no surprise, then, that there is no extensive treatment of it in the extant works. Artisanal production cannot claim to be a science, and hence is of lesser interest to the Platonic philosopher. Nonetheless, the production of things gets Proclus' full attention. As one would expect of a Neoplatonist, it is the *divine* production that counts. And divine production is intimately connected to divine thought. Moreover, whatever gods think they know, and vice versa.

Hence, we have to start our inquiry with divine production and from thence move on to human production and the knowledge that it requires. This strategy is justified not just by the general fact that Platonists tend to understand the earthly through analogy with the divine, that is, what is familiar to us from what is better known in itself, but also by the more specific idea that human production imitates divine production. This does not just mean, as one might think, that we humans try to reproduce things we see in nature, but more interestingly, that our modus operandi imitates certain features of divine production.

One of the key passages for the Platonist is found at the beginning of the tenth book of the *Republic*, concerning the making of the 'third couch' (596b5–98c4), a passage often quoted in connection with the question whether there are Forms of artefacts.[2] Ancient Platonists were not deterred by the fact that the text contains several markers indicating that not everything should be taken at face-value.[3] In this passage Socrates distinguishes three couches:

---

[1] Proclus is cited after the standard editions. In the case of the *Parmenides Commentary*, I opt for Steel 2007–2008.
[2] d'Hoine 2006a; 2006b.   [3] As I argue in Opsomer 2006.

(1) the couch that is, which is the idea or pattern of couch created by a divine Demiurge;
(2) the couch made by a carpenter;
(3) the couch reproduced by a mimetic artist after the image of the second couch.

The idea that god creates the paradigm of the couch is not only unparalleled in Plato, it also creates problems for interpreters wanting to deny that there are eternal Forms of artefacts. More importantly for our purposes, if the human carpenter is to use the first couch for his model, it is not clear how, according to Plato, he would access it. But maybe we are supposed to assume that we can use divinely produced material couches as our models.[4] Socrates calls the divine creator a plantsman (*phutourgon*), the human carpenter a Demiurge – artisan – and maker (*dêmiourgon kai poiêtên*), the painter or poet an imitator (*mimêtês*, 597d4–e8).

Making things is the domain of the crafts, yet not all crafts are productive. When Aristotle in the *Nicomachean Ethics* (VI.3–4, especially 1140a10–20) states that *technai* are concerned with contingent realities, which distinguishes them from *epistêmê*, he is thinking of crafts that are productive. More important for Platonists is a passage in the *Philebus* (55d1–56c9) in which Plato divides the cognitive disciplines (*mathêmata*) first into those concerned with education and nurture, on the one hand, and productive disciplines (*to dêmiourgikon*), on the other, and then distinguishes within the latter group – now called manual arts (*cheirotechnikai*) – those that are closer to knowledge and others that are less closely related. The former are pure and 'leading', the latter are less pure, lack precision and are 'stochastic' in nature (they proceed by guesswork, that is) and are called *technai* once they have been improved through repetition.[5]

In later philosophy, the stochastic crafts formed a more or less established category, which included the productive *technai*.[6] Platonists often

---

[4] Proclus uses the fact that Plato only mentions three couches and calls the representation produced by the mimetic artist 'third from the truth' as proof for his view that there is no transcendent Form of the couch. For if there would be such a divine Form, then the couch produced by the mimetic artist would be fourth, since we also need a model in the mind of the craftsman and the material product of the craft. Cf. *in Parm.* 827.25–28.2; *in Tim.* II, 1.344.5–14; d'Hoine 2006b: 299.

[5] Cf. Damascius, *in Phil.* 225.9–17 Van Riel. A Platonic passage that does not seem to have been discussed very much by later Platonists is *Plt.* 258d8–e7, where it is established that the most basic division of knowledge (*epistêmê*) is that between practical (*praktikê*) and theoretical (*gnôstikê*), with 'manufacture in general' (*sumpasa cheirourgia*) and, more specifically, carpentry belonging to practical knowledge. Simplicius, for instance, uses the contrast *praktikê/gnôstikê* to distinguish physics from crafts (*in Phys.* 308.20–21), but attributes this basic distinction to the Peripatetics (*in Phys.* 1.5–14).

[6] Sextus Empiricus, *AM* 1.72; Alexander Aphrodisias, *Quaestiones* 2.16; Chrysippus, SVF III 64 (p. 16.22).

emphasised the insecurity of their results.[7] They also explained the stochastic nature of these crafts in terms of the external goal at which the craftsman takes aim without being certain of hitting it.[8] Stochastic *technai* need deliberation.[9] Aristotle's statement 'craft does not deliberate'[10] was accordingly often interpreted as pertaining exclusively to the non-stochastic *technai*.[11] Among the latter are the pedagogic, anagogic crafts, which are directed at Forms and can be called sciences.[12] Production requires deliberation, at least when it is in the hands of humans. Divine production is indeed non-deliberative.[13] In this contribution, I deal only with the productive crafts and focus on human productive crafts. The latter fall short of being sciences in the strict sense,[14] yet may be called sciences in a broader sense – already Plato calls them thus.[15]

Whereas Proclus is wont to use human craft as a foil for explaining divine production, I propose to do the opposite and start from his much more extensive treatment of divine production in order better to understand what he has to say about the productive activities of humans.

II Divine Production

In the prologue of his *Commentary on the Timaeus* Proclus criticises Aristotle for his causal theory among other things.[16] To Aristotle's four causes, Proclus and the Platonists of his day add the paradigmatic and the instrumental cause, but they also demote three of them to the status of

---

[7] E.g., Porphyry, ap. Iamblichus, *Responsio* [= *Myst.*] III.15, 1010.3–5 Saffrey-Segonds; Themistius, *in An. post.* 53.18–19.
[8] Philoponus, *in An. post.* 380.35–81.2; 385.15; *in Phys.* 310.3. Themistius, *in Phys.* 61.27–28.
[9] Proclus, *in Alc.* 202.1–3.13   [10] Aristotle, *Ph.* II.8 199b28.
[11] Simplicius, *in Phys.* 385.18–19. The standard example of a non-deliberative skill is the art of writing (Simpl. *in Phys.* 385.17–18; Philop. *in Phys.* 321.6–10). Philoponus, *in Phys.* 321.4–6, also mentions house-building as an example, which is the example already given by Aristotle, *EN* 3.3, 1112a34. For his interesting explanation why even a productive craft does not deliberate, see below, n. 26.
[12] Proclus, *in Parm.* III, 828.15–29.2.   [13] *in Tim.* II, 1.395.10–96.26.
[14] They are images of sciences and their products are images of images: *in Parm.* IV, 947.18–21. Cf. d'Hoine 2006b: 293.
[15] Proclus, *in Remp.* 2.73.18–20; *in Eucl.* 30.8–31.1: occasionally Plato calls *technai* sciences, but never does he call knacks or routines (*empeiriai*) sciences. See Plato *Grg.* 464b2–66a3. In *Republic* VII, Socrates contradistinguishes dialectic from the crafts concerned with human *doxai* and desires with what grows or is put together and the care of those things, but also with geometry (533a10–b5). The latter crafts, he then says, are habitually called *epistêmai*, although they do not really deserve that name, since they are situated between *doxa* and *epistêmê*. In the preceding conversation, he had called them *dianoia*, but, as he now says, one should not bother too much with names (*Rep.* VII, 533d3–9; cf. V, 511d3–e1).
[16] *in Tim.* I, 1.6.21–7.16.

auxiliary causes (the material, instrumental and formal cause, the latter being understood as the form immanent to bodies).[17] The efficient cause (*to poiêtikon aition*) is understood not just as a cause of motion, but as a productive, that is, a creative cause. It bestows being. Accordingly, the productive cause of the world, the Demiurge, gives being to the world at each and every moment of its existence.[18]

The principle of divine production[19] is explained in propositions 26 and 27 of the *Elements of Theology* (*ET*): every productive cause (*pan to paraktikon aition*) produces by its inner activity by which it constitutes itself. This activity, then, is self-directed and not directed at an external product. Yet the product acquires being as a result of the activity of its cause and is constituted as something different from the cause.[20] This activity, at the level of divine causes, is eternal, unchanging and necessary, and these characteristics are transferred to the products. Production is the result of the perfection and abundance of power of the cause. The Neoplatonic realm of the divine is broad. If we look at the specific level of Intellect, which is the ontological level at which the Demiurge is located, its mode of production is defined in proposition 174: 'Every intellect by thinking gives rise to what comes after it: its productive activity consists in thinking, and its thinking consists in producing.' Since thinking is the very being of intellect, this proposition amounts to the claim that an intellect, like any divine cause, produces by its being. Its creative activity is identical with its thinking.[21] At this level, there is no real distinction, but merely a conceptual distinction, between thinking and production. The farther one descends down the ontological scale, however, the activities of thinking and producing will get ever more dissociated.

Every divine cause except the very highest derives its being from a superior cause. This superior cause bestows its being upon the lower cause, which constitutes itself through the activity that can also be described as the reception of what it receives from the higher cause. The lower cause as it were interiorises that which it receives, which is why the higher cause is also the paradigmatic cause for both the lower cause and the products of

---

[17] *in Tim.* II, 1.263.19–30.   [18] *in Tim.* II, 1.267.20–24. See also Sorabji 2004b: 138–40, 6(c).
[19] Their acceptance of divine production and hence divine productive understanding, distinguishes Proclus, and the Platonists more generally, in a crucial aspect from Aristotle. See U. Coope's contribution to this volume (Chapter 7).
[20] This is the theory of the double activity, or the double effect, which is already present in Plotinus. See E. Emilsson's contribution to this volume (Chapter 10).
[21] *ET* 174: proof, p. 152.14–15: 'If, then, it produces by its very being and its being is thought, it produces by thinking.'

the latter. This structure prefigures what happens when the divine craftsman, or the human craftsman, contemplates a model in order to produce something external to him (the use of masculine forms is justified as demiurges are considered to be male gods, who work in team with female life-giving principles).

The work from which the preceding claims were quoted, the *Elements of Theology*, deals with the highest levels of reality, a divine hierarchy of productive causes, where both causes and effects are gods. Production here is eternal and unchanging. It is an ontological causation whereby beings are constituted. I will not go into details nor into the many problems that are connected with this theory. Instead I turn to demiurgy, which is more interesting for our purposes, as it is already closer to human production.

III Demiurgy

It would be a mistake to think that demiurgy is simply the same as ontological derivation. Demiurgy at the divine levels is only a small part of divine production and its lower levels are no longer strictly divine. Proclus restricts the term 'demiurgy' to the production of things that become, *in so far as* they are such. The term 'becoming' (*genesis*) was held to be polysemic: the meaning required here is that of whatever is subject to change of whatever kind.[22] Proclus accepts a multitude of demiurgic causes: subordinated to the demiurges are other demiurgic gods[23] and daemons. The textual basis for his account of demiurgy is, as one would expect, the *Timaeus*. Yet also other dialogues, like the *Sophist*, the *Gorgias*, the *Philebus*, and the *Republic* provide a wealth of demiurgic information. On closer inspection, there are surprisingly many places in Plato's dialogues where demiurgic gods are mentioned.[24]

Plato presents the Demiurge as engaged in discursive thinking and deliberation.[25] Having certain aims, and accordingly being faced with certain problems, the Demiurge thinks about how to achieve his goals given certain material conditions. The Demiurge moreover produces step by step: he conceives the plan to make a world, reflects on what is to be

---

[22] Cf. *in Tim.* II, 1.260.19–26; Opsomer 2017: 144–48. Note that Proclus does not say that demiurgy is the creation *of the physical world*. The expression 'becoming qua becoming' is more precise. Physical things have aspects and constituents that are not subject to becoming, for instance, the prime matter and the principle of dimensionality that are constitutive of hylomorphic entities.
[23] For the lesser demiurgic forces in Plato's *Timaeus*, see Johansen's chapter in this volume (Chapter 4).
[24] Cf. Neschke-Hentschke 2000.   [25] He uses the term *logismos* in *Tim.* 33a6 and 34a8.

done, looks at his model, creates things in sequence. Yet, as readers of the *Timaeus* know, there are problems with the sequence, for instance, with the sequence of body and soul. This provides an important clue for interpreters like Proclus who are opposed to an all too literal reading of the creation story. As the heir to a long tradition in which certain interpretive and philosophical choices were made, Proclus could not accept the idea of a divine craftsman engaged in true deliberation and discursive thinking.[26] He firmly believes that the Demiurge is an intellect, and since the Peripatetic analysis of *nous* had been incorporated in the Platonic framework, this meant that the Demiurge is engaged in an unchanging, non-deliberative way of thinking. Discursive reasoning (reasoning from one thing to the next, *kata metabasin*) is expressly denied,[27] as it could only be seen as a deficiency in the divine. Intellects are held to be outside of time and so are their cognitive and productive activities. As we have seen, thinking constitutes the being of intellects. The same activity, looked at from the perspective of its external effects, is called production. The generation of the world is therefore considered to be the mere result of the Demiurge being what he is, an intellect thinking itself and its contents, which are in turn images from the intelligible paradigm. Timaeus' narrative is accordingly interpreted as a didactic instrument, used in order to explain structural features of the universe and everything in it. The function of the deliberative episodes, so Proclus thinks, is to make us understand how different components and aspects are fitted together. Proclus takes the Demiurge of the *Timaeus* to be the divine cause that creates the world as a unitary whole and all of its unchanging constituents, like the body of the world, the soul of the world, but also particular beings, such as the stars and planets and even the immortal human souls. The creation of other, particular, changing and sometimes also perishable parts is entrusted to lower demiurgic forces, yet the universal Demiurge also somehow oversees their work.[28] Neoplatonism connects an ontologically

---

[26] See also Philoponus, *in Phys.* 321.16–18: 'And what should I say about the crafts, when even the divine kind of demiurgy does not deliberate, but brings forth all things by its very being, whenever it wants, without needing deliberation. For deliberation, as I have explained, comes about only through lack of insight.' The context is provided by Aristotle's famous remark in *Ph.* II.8 199b28 that craft itself does not deliberate. Philop. *in Phys.* 321.1–5 explains that craft indeed does not deliberate, but the craftsman does, namely, if his grasp of the craft is deficient. This is in accordance with the interpretation presented by Sedley 2007: 177–81. For Plotinus' view on the non-deliberative nature of demiurgy, see E. Emilsson's chapter in this volume (Chapter 10).

[27] *Theol. Plat.* 5.17, 62.17–63.5; *in Tim.* II, 1.399.20–24.

[28] Proclus, *in Tim.* V, 3.228.26–28: 'He creates [mortal beings], but through the young gods. For, before the latter create he has already created by his sole thinking'; *in Tim.* V, 3.230.16–18: 'As for

high rank with simplicity. Divine causes cannot therefore be directly responsible for complex effects, except in a 'hidden way' and as anticipating the action of lower causes. And since the world is highly complex, a multiplicity of divine causes is required, assisted by causes of a lower status that are able to handle a greater expressed complexity and actively intervene in the course of events unfurling in time.

The Demiurge marks the transition between a realm in which production is completely timeless and the realm where everything is subject to change. He is himself firmly situated in the eternal, his products are themselves everlasting, but not completely unchanging, whereas the lowest forms of demiurgy produce things that are born and wither away, such as individual plants. At the divine levels of demiurgy, wholes are created before the parts. This is understandable given the universal nature of demiurgy and the intimate connection, at this level, between conceiving of an idea and realising it. The Demiurge contemplates the paradigm that is appropriate to himself, the so-called intelligible living being, and this automatically results in the existence of a world that is itself a divine living being, but one that is material and sense-perceptible. Our world exists as an image and is physical because, as Plato says, such an image can only exist in a receptacle.[29] This receptacle is in fact explained by the Platonists as itself multi-layered, comprising dimensionality, metric and topical space and resistance, *antitupia*, which can be understood as the feature of material bodies that resists co-location.[30] These combined features form the receptacle of the world logically preceding the creation of the world. They were produced by causes superior to the Demiurge. These non-demiurgic effects form the basic conditions for implementation of the first demiurgic act: the living being created by the universal Demiurge has to appear in the receptacle and thereby becomes physical and subject to division, which is in turn a necessary condition for motion.

The universal Demiurge 'wants to' create the world as a divine, living and thinking being. Anything that participates in intellect, needs to be alive, that is, needs to have a soul, as Plato explains (*Tim.* 30b1–6), and a universal soul needs a body to which it is connected. In this manner, the blueprint for the world contains the idea that the world consists of a body

---

what is left, the demiurge certainly brings it into existence, but he immediately hands over its production to the young gods and proclaims them as responsible for the entire mortal nature.'

[29] Of course, some higher, intelligible realities, too, are images. At some point in the descent images become physical rather than merely spiritual. Hence Plato's claim about the need of images to be in a receptacle is better understood as marking a transition between one type of image and another.
[30] Cf. Opsomer 2017: 156–59.

and a soul. The idea that there needs to be a body in turn precedes the idea of the main parts of that body: the four elements, earth, heavens, sun and stars. The living being that is the world is an encompassing living being that contains other living beings. In the paradigm contemplated by the universal Demiurge there are already the blueprints for the four main kinds of living beings mentioned in the *Timaeus*: celestial, aerial, aquatic, and terrestrial.[31] The division of these into *infimae species* takes place also at the level of universal demiurgy, yet not with the highest Demiurge himself, but rather in the divine ancillaries. In all these cases, the rule is that the whole precedes the part.

What makes the prior creation of wholes possible is the non-temporal character of universal demiurgy. The priority is to be understood as essential. This kind of whole, which is more precisely a whole-before-the-parts, does not depend for its being upon the parts, but the parts depend for their essence on the whole, as their essence is defined as being a part of the wholes of which they are parts. Proclus detects evidence for this characteristic of universal creation in the narrative of the *Timaeus*. Plato's narrator talks about the creation of the world prior to mentioning the manufacturing of its parts (31b4). Moreover, he first relates the creation of body, before that of soul, but then adds that soul is body's senior (*Tim.* 34b10–35a1), which is taken to be a sign of the artificiality of the sequence of narration.[32]

At the lower levels of demiurgy, that of the inner-worldly gods, the order of production is reversed.[33] Lower demiurges create in time and implement parts before wholes. Their way of producing things is therefore much closer to that of human craftsmen. They too conceive the whole prior to the parts: wholes are what they intend to make. Yet in the implementation of their ideas, they are forced to produce the parts first and then combine the parts into the desired wholes. These activities are stretched out in time and need to take place in a certain order. Without pre-existing blueprints, that is, paradigmatic causes, these processes would be chaotic and ugly. Beauty and order therefore require Forms. In ordinary processes of generation, Nature (an incorporeal and to some extent divine principle governing bodies) is at work.

---

[31] Cf. *Theol. Plat.* III.19.
[32] Proclus often pays attention to the technical aspects of the narration. Cf. *in Tim.* III, 2.2.9–23; 2.113.19–15.5, and especially V, 3.322.2–17; *Theol. Plat.* III.10, 41.8–12.
[33] *in Tim.* V, 3.321.32–22.17, 322.1–16.

Not all forms that provide the paradigms for things produced exist at the highest intelligible levels. Some exist, for instance, as thoughts in the souls of demiurgic daemons,[34] who conceive of them as ideas by contemplating beings superior to them. In Nature the role of the paradigmatic causes is taken by formal principles called *logoi* that consist in the formulae or blueprints for things generated by nature.[35] The fact that parts are combined into wholes that are unities is supposed to be explained by paradigmatic causes of the wholes, which are superior to the paradigmatic causes of the parts and anticipate, that is, pre-programme, the parts.

As an example, we can think of the creation of the elements. As wholes, the elements are created by the Demiurge. The *Timaeus* indeed gives a separate account of the elements as wholes in immediate connection with the creation of the body of the world. Single atomic elemental corpuscles, however, are created from the combination of elementary triangles, which had to be shaped beforehand. The corpuscles are subsequently combined into larger bodies, for instance, the parts of animal bodies, which are then combined into animal bodies. When the human body is thus shaped, it is ready to receive a soul. This, Proclus thinks, can happen only at the moment of birth, when the embryo is fully formed.[36] The development of a particular human being thus happens bottom-up. A human body is not a random combination of parts, however, but a well-ordered structure after a pre-existing model.

IV Human Production

Once they have been successfully manufactured, human beings proceed to make things of their own. Their arts imitate natural processes of generation (*in Crat.* 54, 23.28–29; *in Parm.* III 828.7–8).[37] Whereas Nature penetrates into the very core of natural things and fashions them from within, human craftsmen are external to their products.[38]

---

[34] Daemons are intermediate between gods and humans, yet in their case too, demiurgic thoughts are identical with the activity of producing. Cf. Procl. *in Tim.* II, 1.332.16–19; V, 3.205.2–3: 'these rational principles (*logoi*) are thoughts and these thoughts are acts of production'.

[35] E.g., *in Parm.* III, 793.10–11, 22–23. *Logos*, in this context, is translated variously as 'reason principle', 'rational principle', 'formal' or 'formative' principle. See also E. Emilsson in this volume (Chapter 10). For Plotinus' use of this term, see also the useful discussion in Gerson 2012.

[36] *in Tim.* V, 3.322.17–31. This is when the soul *properly speaking*, that is, the *rational* soul, enters the living being. Prior to that, non-rational powers were already present. For Neoplatonic embryology, see Wilberding 2017, in particular p. 141 for Proclus' view.

[37] See also *in Tim.* III, 198.11–16, and, with a pejorative twist, Plotinus, 4.3 [27] 10.17–19.

[38] *in Parm.* III, 794.4–6.

Human *technai* are mentioned a few times by Proclus, mostly in the context of discussions of Forms of artefacts.[39] In the *Commentary on the Cratylus* (53–56, 21.6–25.7), he discusses the example of the weaver's shuttle (*kerkis*), and in the *Commentary on the Parmenides* (III, 827.19–29.14) the examples are couch and table (*klinê*, *trapeza*), mentioned in the tenth book of the *Republic*. It is not a coincidence that when Proclus discusses human crafts he happens to be looking for their paradigmatic causes. This issue is so predominant that the definition of art is restricted to it: 'As for art, what else is it than the artefact, minus the matter, in the soul of the artisan?'[40]

If the craftsman has the form of the artefact in the mind, it is tempting to say that he must cognise it or even *know* it. Proclus denies that we can speak of *epistêmê* in this case. His reason for saying so is that artefacts lack the stability required for objects of knowledge. Contrary to products of Nature, such as plants and animals, products of human crafts are unsubstantial. They are subject to all kinds of change depending upon what is useful for us and upon circumstances.[41] Neither their parts nor the relative dispositions of the parts are defined with respect to an essence (*in Crat.* 53, 21.10–12). Proclus invariably links the notion of artefacts with that of usefulness (*chreia*): humans design artefacts in order to fulfil some need, because they find them useful, that is, useful for themselves.[42]

Natural objects receive an essence from divine causes operative in nature. Because of their relation with these causes, they are all in some sense alive.[43] Artefacts, on the contrary, fully depend on humans and their whims.[44] They have no essence communicated to them; their functionality remains external to them and is a function of human intentions. When circumstances change, we stop making certain artefacts or design them differently. Accordingly, Proclus unhesitatingly rejects 'Platonic Forms' of

---

[39] See d'Hoine 2006a; 2006b.
[40] *in Crat.* 53, 23.12–14: ἡ γὰρ τέχνη τί ἄλλο ἐστὶν ἢ τὸ τεχνητὸν ἔξω τῆς ὕλης ἐν τῇ τοῦ τεχνίτου ψυχῇ;
[41] See also U. Coope in this volume (Chapter 5).
[42] E.g., at *in Parm.* III, 829.2–3; *in Crat.* 53, 21.10–13. This idea enjoys Plato's authority: *Phlb.* 58c6; *Prt.* 320d8–21b6. For the link between arts and the good in Stoicism, and the profitable in Epicuraneism, see V. Tsouna in this volume, (Chapters 7 and 8). And for the sceptics, see S. Sienkiewicz (Chapter 9).
[43] *in Parm.* III, 828.10–12.
[44] It is more accurate to say that artefacts depend on rational souls. Daemons, for instance, also manufacture artefacts. For our present purposes, we can neglect this complication but we will come back to the artisanship of daemons when we take a closer look at the different levels of craftsmanship and the corresponding levels of paradigms.

artefacts.[45] This does not mean, however, that there is no formal principle at all for them. According to late Neoplatonic ontology, Plato's Forms are located in Intellect and the Intelligible. Some are higher than others, depending on their degree of generality and unity, but they all are situated in the upper ontological realms (the 'standard' Platonic Forms are actually at the Intelligible-Intellective level). On these levels, nothing corresponds to artefacts.[46] Still, the artisans have some model in their mind when they set out to make something.[47] This content is a *logos* or rational formula, which in itself is nothing special for the soul, since also Platonic Forms, when they are communicated to souls, are received by them in the form of *logoi*.[48] It is peculiar of the *logoi* of artefacts, however, that they are not copies of higher forms. Accordingly, they only exist in *dianoia* and *doxa*, not in human intellect.[49] They are doxastic objects and feature in discursive reasoning (*in Crat.* 53, 23.25).[50]

When an artisan sets out to make a certain object, she looks at what kind of thing it is and what purpose it has, and then produces its likeness in the external material (*in Crat.* 53, 23.10–12). What it takes to express a likeness in matter will be discussed shortly, but first we need to take a closer look at the *logos* (or 'formative principle') that is the model providing the formula for the artefact. These formulae are in the minds of artisans and accessible through introspection. They have their being in the soul, more precisely, in the dianoetic soul. Since these *logoi* are human creations, they are not everlasting. They can only survive the death of an individual in case they are passed on. One implication is that these *logoi* are not found in every human soul.[51] Another is that they have not existed always:

---

[45] Proclus would have nodded approvingly at the arguments put forward by Broadie 2007: 237–38.
[46] *in Parm.* III, 828.13–14; 829.4; *in Crat.* 53, 23.23–25.
[47] The idea of a *logos* or *eidos* in the soul of the craftsman is discussed by Aristotle: *Metaph.* VII.7 1032a32–b1: 'From art proceed the things of which the form is in the soul.', cf. VII.9 1034a22.
[48] Cf. Brisson 1999: 101.   [49] Cf. Syr. *in Met.* 26.35–38.
[50] Cf. also *in Parm.* III, 827.22–24 (where Proclus suggests that Socrates when talking about forms of artefacts may just mean *logoi* in *dianoia*), and Calc. § 343: p. 335.24–36.3 Waszink: 'And he calls this form [of the statue] "knowable by the senses", because the form imprinted upon a work is seen by the eyes of the spectators, but also "knowable by belief" because the mind of the artisan transfers the form, not from a fixed model, but drawing it from their own mind to the best of their abilities' (*sensibus autem noscendam dicit hanc speciem, quia impressa forma operi spectantium oculis videtur, opinione vero noscendam, quia mens opificis non de certo exemplari transfert hanc speciem, sed ex propria mente haustam pro viribus*). For Proclus *doxa* and *dianoia* are separate faculties. They are both faculties belonging to the rational soul and accordingly grasp wholes before parts. Cf. *in Tim.* II, 1.249.12–22; 251.5–7; III, 2.299.6–7. Ultimately, however, the doxastic and the dianoetic *logoi* are the same *logoi*, that is, they stem from the same causes and belong to the same series: 2.241.29–42.2. Cf. Helmig 2012: 223–61, 254–60, 305.
[51] When C. Helmig argues that every human soul contains exactly the same *logoi*, he does not take into account the special case of *logoi* of artefacts. Cf. Helmig 2012: 252–53, 277. Helmig can be

artefacts were invented sometime, which means that once upon a time some creative individual reflecting upon what was needed in a particular situation or type of situation newly created their *logos*.[52] The blueprints for artefacts are then psychic *logoi*, invented and transmitted:

> For [human artisans] do not look to the [intelligibles] when they create, but to the forms [*eidê*] at their own level and to the rational principles [*logous*] which they possess of artefacts. These rational principles they either discovered or received from others. For the first manufacturer of the couch or the shuttle considered what the shuttle should be like by looking to, and being guided by, its function [*chreia*], and constructed in themselves its rational formula [*logon*]. But those who learned it from that person first acquired knowledge of the form and then produce the image of the shuttle in accordance with it. (*in Crat.* 53, 22.30–23.7)

Proclus undeniably has an intellectualist conception of the process of invention and discovery. There is as it were an armchair stage in which the artisan perceives a certain need and then reflects on how to make a tool that could be useful in this way. Proclus does not mention trial and error, a back and forth between reflecting and manipulating of matter, or the discovery in nature of a structure that could be adapted so as to fulfil a new purpose or to be better suited for something for which it was already used. The expression 'he composed a formula', that is, a *logos* (*logon sunestêsato*), indicates that the inventor indeed creates a novel *logos*. He does not make it out of nothing, however, but Proclus does not tell us out of which elements the inventor puts it together. One may assume, however, since the *logoi* are propositional, they will be assembled from the elements of a proposition. Those will in turn reflect intelligible structures and are images of Forms (for instance the Form of Being).[53]

Proclus explicitly states that our souls have the capacity to produce and evaluate the *logoi* of the products of crafts. This power resides in the opinative faculty (*in Parm.* III, 829.4–7). Why humans are able to be genuinely creative is not further explained nor is there much more detail about the creative process. It clearly involves the awareness of what is useful and of deficiencies in the existing situation or room for improvement. Then we search for solutions while making plausible guesses[54] by imagining the effect of the solutions to be attempted, and possibly also

---

excused, since the master himself obviously disregards human-made *logoi* of artefacts when claiming that all particular souls contain the same *logoi*: cf. *in Tim.* V, 3.255.30–56.21.
[52] Proclus shares the emphasis on human inventiveness with the Epicureans. See Tsouna, Chapter 8.
[53] Cf. *in Crat.* 16 p. 6.12–16; 36, p. 12.14.
[54] Simplicius mentions the role of informed guessing in our use of instruments: *in Ench.* 4.367–70.

testing and retesting solutions or partial solutions.[55] A necessary condition for this ability certainly consists in the fact that human souls are self-movers: they have the capability to cause motion without being determined by anything external and are therefore a source of spontaneity in the material world. Divine intellects, on the contrary, are unmoved, invariably thinking the same thoughts and producing the same effects, as long as the further condition of the suitability of the recipients is met. If the recipients develop a different suitability, that is, if the material conditions are different, even in the case of divine production a different result may come about – but this will be a rather rare occurrence that is limited to the transitional zone between the hypercosmic and the cosmic realms (for only the so-called hypercosmic gods are in direct contact with the realms in which contingency obtains), and moreover it does not involve the origin of something truly new (the effect will be of the same type, i.e., correspond to the invariable nature of intellect,[56] but due to the material conditions certain features may appear in different degrees of intensity or not appear at all).[57] The self-motion of the soul, on the contrary, is a source of genuine initiative and is connected with the ability to inspect and evaluate input from the senses and from intellect, to ponder reasons, entertain propositions and connect them in novel ways.

While the power of creativity is safely rooted in the rational soul, opinative (doxastic) and discursive reason need to cooperate closely with the faculty of imagination, which constitutes the summit of the irrational faculties. Proclus asks his reader to think of the person who invented the ship. This requires an extraordinary creativity. Their 'modelling power' (*dunamis anaplastikê*) distinguishes inventors from mere artisans who are only capable of producing accurate copies.[58] The true inventor recognises a practical need[59] and then 'models' or 'shapes' (*aneplase*) in her own mind (*en heautôi*) a paradigm[60] of the ship and does so with the aid of her imagination (*phantastikôs, in Tim.* II, 1.320.5–10). While the *logoi*

---

[55] For a contemporary account of these mental processes and abilities involved in creativity, as well as attempts to define (different types of) creativity, see (Kozbelt et al. 2010), especially pp. 30–40, with further bibliography. U. Coope argues that for Aristotle, too, productive understanding requires the ability to deal with (genuinely) new cases. See her contribution to this volume (Chapter 5), and also that of R. Bolton (Chapter 6) .
[56] Cf. *ET* 18.   [57] Cf. *ET* 103.
[58] This distinction echoes Aristotle's when he says that art either completes what nature cannot finish or imitates it: *Ph.* II.8 199a15–16. See also Procl. *in Tim.* II, 1.263.6.
[59] Cf. *in Tim.* II, 1.320.8: ἔργων ἀναγκαίων πρὸς τὰς χρείας.
[60] The antecedent construction of a concept that is to serve as a paradigm is also mentioned at *in Tim.* II, 1.266.16–18; see also Asclepius, *in Met.* 189.10–15.

comprising the model of the artefact are propositional, imagination *pictures* not only what the artefact will look like, but also how it will function in the environment and for the purpose for which it is designed. Proclus does not say whether the inventor first pictures the artefact as a solution for a practical problem and only afterwards constructs the corresponding *logos* or whether it is the other way around. Possibly they are being developed together over time. Whatever the temporal relation, reason, being the higher faculty, should always take the lead. While the ability to picture a ship may be a useful and even necessary part of the creative process, rational calculation and the connecting of the *logoi* with a view to the functional aspects of the artefact will definitively be of greater importance.

The concept of creative imagination (*phantasia*) predates Proclus by far.[61] Philostratus (*Vit. Ap.* 6.19) calls imagination a Demiurge far subtler than mimicry, thus drawing the same opposition as Proclus at *in Tim.* II, 1.320.5–10.[62] Imagination, Philostratus explains, makes what it has not seen. It is not, however, divorced from reality and for Philostratus still involves an element of imitation, as it conceives its ideal with reference to the real (*hupothêsetai gar pros tên anaphoran tou ontos*). By the time of Philostratus it was already a commonplace to cite Phidias as an artist who used his imagination to express the invisible, namely, Zeus, in his art.[63] Plotinus uses the same example in a rare passage in which he praises the crafts: Phidias imagines what Zeus *would* look like if he had wanted to make himself visible.[64] Subsequently, he expressed his vision in his famous sculpture. More generally, arts do not merely imitate what they see, but make up for what is deficient or lacking (*Enn.* V.8 [31] 1.32–40).[65] Plotinus' example of Phidias speculating about what Zeus would look like if he were visible, again assumes that there is some objective standard of the sense-perceptible image, albeit not one that has itself the perceptible qualities that need to be portrayed. Plotinus seems to think that Zeus has certain features that should find a specific expression if they are to be expressed in a visible way at all. The creative imagination in some of the cases Proclus describes goes beyond this. One could think that the person who first invented a ship took her idea from seeing pieces of wood floating on the water with animals on top of them, in which case we would have

---

[61] Cf. Watson 1994: 4767–69.
[62] For Philostratus, see also Emilsson's contribution to this volume (Chapter 10).
[63] Cf. Cic. *Or.* 7–10. [64] See also Emilsson's discussion of this example in Chapter 10.
[65] Watson 1994: 4770, 4789; see also ps.-Longinus, *De subl.* 35; Calcidius, *Commentary on Plato's Timaeus* § 343: p. 335.19–36.3 Waszink.

what could be described as a discovery,[66] rather than the origin of something radically new. Yet other examples, like the shuttle mentioned already by Plato but without the idea of its invention, or a more complex instrument for weaving of which the shuttle is a part, do not seem to have ready-made examples in nature or natural objects close to them. Proclus does not explain what cognitive processes lead to the invention of new artefacts, but he probably thinks these may vary. It is very well possible that one and the same artefact was invented independently at different times, in different places, and in different ways. One person could think of making a boat in the way described above, whereas another could come to the same result by pondering on the specific qualities of water and wood. Also the question whether resembling artefacts are in fact one and the same type is open. Since artefacts do not have a stable definition and essence, and their purposes and outlook may allow for some variation, one could argue that they can only be considered to belong to the same type in so far as rational beings consider them to be such and assign the same purpose to them.

Once a new *logos* has been invented, we may learn it from others, and whoever has learned or invented them can thereupon recollect them when needed. The different possibilities that Proclus envisages contain some startling examples. He claims that it is possible to have learnt them in another life and then recollect them, which is surprising as Platonic 'recollection' is usually believed to have transcendent ideas or at least *their* images in the soul as its objects (before recollecting the Forms themselves, we become aware of their *logoi*-images).[67] Proclus may think that since standard Platonic recollection is not of the Forms directly, but of the *logoi* that are their images,[68] it would be possible to recollect *any* logoi, irrespective of whether they have a direct transcendent origin. The ways in which we came to possess the *logoi* in a previous life are again multiple: by learning it from others, by discovering it ourselves, either through reflection or by another instance of recollecting.

Any well-ordered production process needs to have a goal (*skopos*) and a standard to measure the product by (*metron tou poiêmatos*). The concept that is the craftsman's paradigm serves this double purpose. To use a paradigm in this manner is a hallmark of rationality. Reason is indeed necessary to find the right measure and to steer and adjust the process of

---

[66] The need for discoveries was already stressed in *On Ancient Medicine*: see E. Hussey's Chapter 1 in this volume.
[67] Helmig 2012: 306–7.   [68] E.g., *in Tim.* II 1.248.11–13; 1.251.4–9; cf. Helmig 2012: 249–51.

production accordingly. Without his paradigm craftsmen would not know when they have reached the endpoint, the point of completion (*telos*). They could not tell whether something needs to be removed or added. Lack of rationality would therefore inevitably lead to excess or deficiency (*in Tim.* II, 1. 1.320.10–22).[69]

The possession of the corresponding *logos* is of course not sufficient for the ability to produce the artefact. It is not even the only necessary cognitive condition. The *logos* tells one 'of what kind an artefact it is and what it is for'.[70] The expression 'of what kind' presumably refers to the standard shape of the artefact, its parts, and the disposition of its parts. Proclus has told us, however, that all this is not strictly defined in the case of artefacs. We can nonetheless assume that the *logos* provides a sufficient grasp of what kind of thing it is, the kind of grasp that would allow us to recognise the artefact when we see it, for instance, and also, to use it more or less appropriately. However, we need to know more than that if we want to produce it. For we would have to possess knowledge – which however falls short of *epistêmê* – of the conditions for the implementation of the form in matter, and we would in many cases also need knowledge of specific circumstances for the intended use of the artefact, which may require us to make adaptations to the design.[71]

Proclus is aware of at least some of the additional cognitive resources needed. He mentions the varying circumstances and in his account of demiurgy has shown himself to be very much aware of the difficulties of implementation. Proclus neatly separates the two stages of conceiving a concept of an artefact and thinking about its realisation. In the conceptual stage, a further similarity with divine production shows up: we too conceive of the whole prior to the parts. It is only in the implementation that the order is typically reversed: we prepare the matter, shape the parts and combine them into a whole. Contrary to intelligible production, material production requires a step-by-step methodical reasoning. Divine demiurges, too, have to take into account the aptitude (*epitêdeiotês*)[72] of the material structures.[73] This is what it means to make necessity obey

---

[69] This is why, Proclus adds, Plato introduced the paradigmatic cause together with the productive cause (i.e., the efficient cause, ποιητικὴ αἰτία), whereas Aristotle by spurning the former unwittingly abolished the latter (*in Tim.* II, 1. 1.320.23–26).
[70] *in Crat.* 53, 23.11–12: ὅτι ἐστὶν τοιαδὶ καὶ τοῦδε ἕνεκα γίνεται.
[71] Aristotle gives a partly overlapping account at *Metaph.* VII.7 1032b15–31.
[72] Cf. *ET* 79, p. 74.23–24. According to Proclus' explanation of the 'theologians', the mirror fashioned by Hephaestus for Apollo symbolises that aptitude or receptivity: *in Tim.* III, 2.80.19–24.
[73] E.g., *in Tim.* V, 3.321.7–22.31.

reason. But in their case no special effort and no intermediate steps are required. Good results are obtained because higher causes already created a material receptivity.[74] Nature provides not only the form but also the most appropriate matter.[75] Human craftsmen, on the contrary, must use the material they find[76] and have to prepare it themselves. To that aim they need tools. Whereas gods completely dominate matter, humans do not have that kind of power but use instruments in order to make matter apt to their purposes. These tools, too, need to be made. Artisans will produce their tools from matter that is suitable for the function they need to perform.[77] With these instruments they then set to work on other matter in order to produce the desired end-product. Human artisans drill, carve and chisel, not however in order to realise the form in matter, but to remove what is unsuitable and thus to prepare matter for the reception of form. Once the obstacles are removed, the form is installed in a timeless manner: it is instantaneously transferred from the craft into matter, the craft being nothing other than the artefact as it exists in the soul of the artisan.[78]

V Divine Patronage

The preceding discussion of the *logoi* of artefacts has left out one important complication: gods also appear to play a role in the invention of (certain types of) artefacts. Quoting the example for *Republic* X, Proclus talks about god who eternally produces the Couch-itself (*in Remp.* II. 86.14–16). In Greek religion, some gods were traditionally associated with crafts and were considered as their patrons. They communicate their powers to us.[79] For instance, Athena and Circe are connected with

---

[74] Cf. *ET* 72, p. 68.20–22 Dodds: 'And the principles which bring into existence things that serve as substrate for others are causes of more products, since they bring into existence even the aptitudes preceding the presence of the Forms in question (ὑφιστάντα καὶ τὰς ἐπιτηδειότητας πρὸς τῆς τῶν εἰδῶν παρουσίας).'

[75] *in Crat.* 54, 23.28–30.

[76] d'Hoine 2006a: 330. See also Aristotle, *EN* I.10 1101a3–6, giving the example of the shoemaker who has to make the finest shoe out of the leather provided to him.

[77] *in Crat.* 54, 23.26–28 (commenting on *Crat.* 389b8–d3): 'That all forms of tools have to have their own receptive matter proper to them and adapted to the task for which we need the tool. For also the paradigm of art, nature, not only attends to the form of the tools, but also to the kind of matter that is most appropriate.'

[78] *in Tim.* II, 1.395.13–22.

[79] In *in Parm.* III, 827.24–25, this is just a tentative suggestion. It is confirmed, however, at *in Parm.* III, 829.7–9.

weaving, Hephaestus with bronze-working.[80] Yet divine crafts are much more abstract and general. We should not think that Athena's way of weaving involves the same operations on material objects as in the case of humans. As we have seen, gods completely dominate matter and therefore do not need chisels and hammers. *Specific* crafts only come about at the level of daemons, who are the true patrons of human crafts and are probably the first to use tools. They also guide us in the discovery of new types of instruments and assist us in our developing *logoi* that become even more specific when we tailor them to our own needs.[81]

Should we assume then, that gods produce transcendent Forms of artefacts? Such a claim, which has strong textual support from *Republic* X, would sit uneasily with Proclus' view that rational souls invent new rational formulae for artefacts. In fact, Proclus emphatically denies that there are transcendent, eternal Forms of artefacts and claims that Plato actually means the *logos* in the mind of the craftsman, of which god is the cause in so far as he provides us with our technical abilities.[82]

Our *technai* imitate the demiurgic art and our *logoi* are analogous to the intellective Forms, since both are paradigms. And just like the Demiurge and his ancillaries provide stability to the world and preserve it, for instance, by replacing things that perish, using the paradigm to create a new but specifically identical individual, so human craftsmen can replace a broken tool by a new one or also repair a broken tool by resorting to the *logoi* in their souls.[83] However, as Proclus admits, crafts in the divine realm are merely analogous to our crafts, and they receive their name only because certain powers of theirs are also operative in our crafts.[84] The power of separating, for instance, has a real function in the realm of the Forms, and is connected with the power of the shuttle. Hence, there is an analogue of the shuttle in the divine realm,[85] which is part of the reason why we also speak of a divine craft of weaving. However, the fact that divine production is merely analogous to human production also implies

---

[80] *in Crat.* 53, 21.19–22.15. For the theological interpretation, see d'Hoine 2006a: 331–34; Syrianus, *in Met.* 26.24–26; Philoponus, *in Nicomachi introductionem arithmeticam* I, 34, with d'Hoine 2006a: 340 nn. 94–95.

[81] d'Hoine 2006a: 331–42.

[82] *in Parm.* III, 827.20–24; *in Tim.* II, 1.344.5–14; d'Hoine 2006b: 297. For this issue in Plotinus, see Emilsson in this volume (Chapter 10).

[83] *in Crat.* 53, 23.14–21. Compare Syrianus, *in Met.* 26.35–38: 'The same indeed obtains also in relation to arts: for they survive, even if their concern is destructible things, since they are controlled by universal reason-principles. And even if these are projected by souls which find themselves in coming-to-be, arts of this sort also must remain.' (trans. D. O'Meara-J. Dillon).

[84] *in Crat.* 53, 21.13–22.25. See also *in Parm.* III, 829.7–14.   [85] *in Crat.* 53, 22.25–26.

that there are important differences. Divine productive *technê* is homonymous with human productive *technê*. The homonymy is, however, not arbitrary, because the two cases are linked through analogy. Whereas separating and weaving apply even to the upper levels of the transcendent realm, other divine crafts are associated rather with demiurgy. Welding, harmonising and gluing are activities that are characteristic of demiurgy, both that of the principal Demiurge and that of his assistants.[86]

The similarities between human and divine productive crafts are undeniable: in both cases, a productive cause makes use of a paradigm, which specifies the form and the function of the product; divine and human artisans have to take into account conditions of material realisation and where necessary have to prepare the matter or have it prepared for them; in the conception of the product wholes precede parts. Moreover, at least if we restrict divine production to demiurgy, both divine and human production first realise the parts in matter and then combine them into wholes.

The main disanalogy, however, turns out to be the following. Whereas we can attribute generative power to the gods and notice an analogy between the function of Forms and *logoi* in productive thinking, it is hard to see how genuine discursive creativity could stem from the Neoplatonic gods. Genuine creativity, in the modern sense of the term, implies innovation, and that is something divine intellects are incapable of. This is understandable, since according to the Platonists, the need for innovation is born from deficiency. This is where the activity of rational souls of daemons and humans is required and creativity comes into play.

VI Conclusion

Crafts, and especially those of the stochastic type to which the productive crafts belong, are not the highest of our activities. Humans involved in technical activity are 'playing':[87] 'all those [crafts] typical of a soul that is at

---

[86] *in Tim.* V, 321.1–25. Also medicine, divination, archery and music have divine analogues, at many different levels even: see *in Crat.* 174, 96.12–100.7, commenting on *Crat.* 405a3. For the welding, riveting and weaving done by the lesser gods in Plato's *Timaeus*, see Johansen's Chapter 4 in this volume.

[87] Just as the lesser gods and daemons are playing when engaged in the lower forms of demiurgy consisting in the regeneration of perishable things. Hephaestus, patron of the crafts, is one of them. Cf. *in Parm.* III, 829.10–11; *in Remp.* 1.92.9–17 (a lower, daemonic Hephaestus as patron of bronze-working); 1.127.1–11; *TP* V.24, p. 87.22–89.8; *in Tim.* 1.142.23 (*ergotechnitês*, the name given to Hephaestus by the Theologians); *in Tim.* 1.147.7 (Porphyry calls Hephaestus the *technikos nous*). See also Plotinus, 3.6 [26] 7.24; 4.3. [27] 10.18.

play, occupied with mortal things and catering to human needs' (*in Parm.* III, 829.2–3). Yet human craft enjoys a high patronage. Several gods, as we have seen, are linked to specific crafts. Of course, they are not really craftsmen (*technitai*), but are merely called technicians either by analogy – because their activity bears structural similarities to those of specific human crafts – or symbolically. When they are concerned with the mortal world and perishable things, gods too are said to play.[88]

Even if human crafts, other than the anagogic crafts, do not involve true *epistêmê* and are not sciences, they do require advanced rational capacities. Our souls form *logoi* of artefacts by employing dianoetic thinking combined with creative imagination and use further dianoetic thinking to put them to work. This activity is considered as an image, spread out through time, of what in the divine realm is unified. After all, every craftsman is a demiurge.

---

[88] *TP* V.24, p. 88.2.

Bibliography

Alesse, F. 2000. *La Stoa e la Tradizione Socratica*. Rome: Bibliopolis.
Algra, K., Barnes, J., Mansfeld, J., and Schofield, M. (eds.) 1999. *The Cambridge History of Hellenistic Philosophy*. Cambridge: Cambridge University Press.
Allen, J. 2001. *Inference from Signs*. Oxford: Oxford University Press.
  2010. 'Pyrrhonism and Medicine', in *The Cambridge Companion to Ancient Scepticism*, ed. R. Bett. Cambridge: Cambridge University Press: 232–48.
  2015. 'Practical and Theoretical Knowledge in Aristotle', in *Bridging the Gap between Aristotle's Science and Ethics*, eds. D. Henry and K. M. Nielsen. Cambridge: Cambridge University Press: 49–70.
Angeli, A. 1985. 'L'esattezza scientifica in Epicuro e Filodemo', *Cronache Ercolanesi* 15: 63–84.
Angier, T. 2010. *Technê in Aristotle's Ethics: Crafting the Moral Life*. London: Continuum.
Annas, J. 1981. *An Introduction to Plato's Republic*. Oxford: Oxford University Press.
  1993. *The Morality of Happiness*. Oxford: Oxford University Press.
  2011. *Intelligent Virtue*. Oxford: Oxford University Press.
Annas, J., and Betegh, G. (eds.) 2016. *Cicero's De Finibus: Philosophical Approaches*. Cambridge: Cambridge University Press.
Arnim, H. von (ed.) 1903–1905. *Stoicorum veterum fragmenta*, 4 vols. Leipzig: B. G. Teubner Verlag.
Asmis, E. 1984. *Epicurus' Scientific Method*. Ithaca: Cornell University Press.
  1996. 'Lucretius on the Growth of Ideas', in *Epicureismo greco e romano: Atti del congresso internazionale*, vol. 2, eds. G. Giannantoni and M. Gigante. Naples: Bibliopolis: 763–72.
Balansard, A. 2001. *Technê dans les Dialogue de Platon*. St. Augustin: Academia Verlag.
Barnes, J. 1986. 'Is Rhetoric an Art?', *DARG Newsletter* (University of Calgary) 2: 2–22.
  1988a. 'Epicurean Signs', *Oxford Studies in Ancient Philosophy*, suppl. vol. 1988: 91–134.
  1988b. 'Scepticism and the Arts', in *Method, Medicine and Metaphysics*, ed. R. J. Hankinson. Edmonton: Academic Print and Publishing; reprinted in

Barnes, J. 2014. *Proof, Knowledge and Scepticism*. Oxford: Oxford University Press: 512–35.
   1990. *The Toils of Scepticism*. Cambridge: Cambridge University Press.
   2003. *Porphyry Introduction*. Oxford: Clarendon Press.
Barnes, J., Brunschwig, J., Burnyeat, M. F., and Schofield, M. (eds.) 1982. *Science and Speculation*. Cambridge: Cambridge University Press.
Barney, R. 2006. 'Socrates' Refutation of Thrasymachus', in *The Blackwell Guide to Plato's Republic*, ed. G. Santas. Oxford: Blackwell: 44–62.
   2008a. 'Aristotle's Argument for a Human Function', *Oxford Studies in Ancient Philosophy* 34: 293–322.
   2008b. 'The Carpenter and the Good', in *Pursuing the Good: Ethics and Metaphysics in Plato's Republic*, eds. D. Cairns, F.-G. Herrmann and T. Penner. Edinburgh: University of Edinburgh Press: 293–319.
Beardsley, M. C. 1966. *Aesthetics from Classical Greece to the Present: A Short History*. New York: Macmillan.
Beere, J. 2009. *Doing and Being: An Interpretation of Metaphysics Theta*. Oxford: Oxford University Press.
Bénatouïl, T. 2006. *Faire usage: La pratique du Stoïcisme, Histoire des doctrines de l'Antiquité Classique*. Paris : Vrin.
   2009. '*Theôria* et vie contemplative du stoïcisme au platonisme: Chrysippe, Panétius, Antiochus, Alcinoos', in *The Origins of the Platonic System: Platonisms of the Early Empire and Their Philosophical Contexts*, eds. M. Bonazzi and J. Opsomer. Louvain: Éditions Peeters; Société des Études Classiques: 3–31.
Bénatouïl, T., and Bonazzi, M. (eds.). 2012. *Theoria, Praxis, and the Contemplative Life after Plato and Aristotle*. Leiden: Brill.
Bengson, J., and Moffett, M. (eds.) 2011. *Knowing How: Essays on Knowledge, Mind, and Action*. Oxford: Oxford Universtiy Press.
Betegh, G. 2003. 'Cosmological Ethics in the *Timaeus* and Early Stoicism', *Oxford Studies in Ancient Philosophy* 24: 273–302.
Bett, R. 2010. *The Cambridge Companion to Ancient Scepticism*. Cambridge: Cambridge University Press.
Bignone, E. 1936. *L'Aristotele perduto et la formazione filosofica di Epicuro*. Firenze: La Nuova Italia.
Blank, D. 1995. 'Philodemus on the Technicity of Rhetoric', in *Philodemus and Poetry: Poetic Theory and Practice in Lucretius, Philodemus and Horace*, ed. D. Obbink. Oxford: Oxford Univesity Press: 178–88.
   1998. *Sextus Empiricus: Against the Grammarians (Adversus Mathematicos I)*. Clarendon Later Ancient Philosophers. Oxford: Oxford University Press.
   2003. 'Atomistic Rhetoric in Philodemus', *Cronache Ercolanesi* 33: 69–88.
Bolton, R. 2012. 'The Aristotelian Elenchus', in *The Development of Dialectic from Plato to Aristotle*, ed. J. Fink. Cambridge: Cambridge University Press: 270–95.
   2013. 'Dialectic, Peirastic and Scientific Method in Aristotle's Sophistical Refutations', *Logical Analysis and History of Philosophy* 15: 267–85.

2017. 'The Search for Principles in Aristotle: *Posterior Analytics* II and *Generation of Animals* I', in *Aristotle's Generation of Animals*, eds. A. Falcon and D. Lefebvre. Cambridge: Cambridge University Press: 227–48.

2018. 'Two Conceptions of Practical Skill (Technê) in Aristotle', in *Aristotle – Contemporary Perspectives on His Thought*, ed. D. Sfendoni-Mentzou. Berlin: De Gruyter: 279–96.

(Forthcoming). 'Phronesis: Aristotle on Moral Wisdom and Its Origins in Philia', in *Wisdom, Love and Friendship in Ancient Philosophy*, eds. E. Keeling and G. Sermamoglou-Soulmaidi. Berlin: De Gruyter.

Bonazzi, M., and Helmig, C. (eds.) 2007. *Platonic Stoicism – Stoic Platonism: The Dialogue between Platonism and Stoicism in Antiquity*. Leuven: Leuven University Press.

Bosanquet, B. 1904. *A History of Aesthetics*. London: Macmillan.

Bréhier, É. 1931. *Plotin: Ennéades*, vol. V. Paris: Les Belles Lettres.

Brandom, R. B. 2011. *Perspectives on Pragmatism: Classical, Recent and Contemporary*. Cambridge, MA: Harvard University Press.

Brennan, T. 1996. 'Reasonable Impressions in Stoicism', *Phronesis* 41: 318–34.

Brickhouse, T. C., and Smith, N. D. 1994. *Plato's Socrates*. Oxford: Oxford University Press.

Brisson, L. 1999. 'Logos et logoi chez Plotin: Leur nature et leur rôle', *Les Cahiers Philosophiques de Strasbourg* 8: 87–108.

Broadie, S. 1987. 'Nature, Craft and Phronesis in Aristotle', *Philosophical Topics* 15: 35–50.

1991. *Ethics with Aristotle*. Oxford: Oxford University Press.

2007. 'Why No Platonistic Ideas of Artefacts?' in *Maieusis: Essays in Ancient Philosophy in Honour of Myles Burnyeat*, ed. D. Scott. Oxford: Oxford University Press: 232–53.

2014. *Nature and Divinity in Plato's Timaeus*. Cambridge: Cambridge University Press.

Broadie, S., and Rowe, C. 2002. *Aristotle: Nicomachean Ethics. Translation, Introduction and Commentary*. Oxford: Oxford University Press.

Brown, E. 2000. 'Justice and Compulsion for Plato's Philosopher-Rulers', *Ancient Philosophy* 20: 1–17.

2009. 'Socrates in the Stoa', in *A Companion to Socrates*, eds. S. Ahbel-Rappe and R. Kamtekar. Oxford: Blackwell.

Brown, L. 1993. 'Understanding the *Theaetetus*', *Oxford Studies in Ancient Philosophy* 11: 199–224.

2010. 'Division and Definition in Plato's *Sophist*', in *Definition in Greek Philosophy*, ed. D. Charles. Oxford: Oxford University Press: 151–71.

Brouwer, R. 2014. *The Stoic Sage*. Cambridge: Cambridge University Press.

Brunschwig, J. 1986. 'The Cradle Argument in Epicureanism and Stoicism', in *The Norms of Nature*, eds. M. Schofield and G. Striker. Cambridge: Cambridge University Press: 113–44.

Burnyeat, M. F. 1982. 'The Origins of Non-Deductive Inference', in *Science and Speculation*, eds. J. Barnes, J. Brunschwig, M. F. Burnyeat and M. Schofield. Cambridge: Cambridge University Press: 193–238.
  1990. *The Theaetetus of Plato*. Indianapolis: Hackett.
  2002. 'Aristotle on Learning to Be Good', *Journal of the History of Philosophy* 40: 141–62.
Calabi, F., and Castaldi, S. (eds.) 2012. *Immagini delle origini: La nascita della civiltà e della cultura nel pensiero antico*. Sankt Augustin: Academia Verlag.
Callard, A. (unpublished). 'Reasoning about Particulars in *Prior Analytics* B21'.
Caluori, D. 2015. *Plotinus on Soul*, Cambridge: Cambridge University Press.
Cambiano, G. 1991. *Platone e le Tecniche*, Bari: Laterza.
Chadwick, J., and Mann, W. A. 1978. *Hippocratic Writings*, 2nd ed. London: Penguin.
Chandler, C. 2006. *Philodemus on Rhetoric Books 1 and 2: Translations and Exegetical Essays, Studies in Classics*. London: Routledge.
Charles, D. 2000. *Aristotle on Meaning and Essence*. Oxford: Oxford University Press.
Cole, T. 1990. *Democritus and the Sources of Greek Anthropology*. American Philological Association Monograph Series 25. Atlanta: Scholars Press.
Cooper, J. M. 1982. 'Aristotle on Natural Teleology', in *Language and Logos*, eds. M. Schofield and M. C. Nussbaum. Cambridge: Cambridge University Press 197–222.
Cooper, J. M. (ed.) 1997. *Plato: Complete Works*, Indianapolis: Hackett.
  1999. 'Pleasure and Desire in Epicurus', in *Reason and Emotion: Essays on Ancient Moral Psychology, and Ethical Theory*, ed. J. M. Cooper. Princeton: Princeton University Press: 495–514.
  2012. *Pursuits of Wisdom*, Princeton: Princeton University Press.
Corti, L. 2015. 'Scepticism, Number and Appearances: The ἀριθμητικὴ τέχνη and Sextus' targets in M I–VI', *Philosophie Antique* 15: 123–47.
Crager, A. 2013. 'The Infinite in Aristotle's Logical Epistemology', in *Master of Logic Thesis Series*, ed. R. Fernádez. Amsterdam: Institute for Logic, Language and Computation Scientific Publications: 1–80.
Craik, E. 1998. *Hippocrates: Places in Man*. Oxford: Clarendon Press.
Cuomo, S. 2007. *Technology and Culture in Greek and Roman Antiquity*. Cambridge: Cambridge University Press.
Delattre, D. 2007. *Philodème de Gadara: Sur la Musique: Livre IV*, 2 vols. Paris: Les Belles Lettres.
d'Hoine, P. 2006a. 'The Status of the Arts: Proclus' Theory of Artefacts', *Elenchos* 27: 305–44.
  2006b. 'Proclus and Syrianus on Ideas of Artefacts: A Test Case for Neoplatonic Hermeneutics' in *Proklos: Methode, Seelenlehre, Metaphysik*, eds. M. Perkams and R. M. Piccione. Philosophia Antiqua 98. Leiden: Brill: 279–302.

Diaco, S. 2016. 'Plato and Lucretius on the Origins and Development of Human Society', PhD diss., Faculty of Classics, Cambridge University.
Diels, H., and Kranz, W. 1952. *Die Fragmente der Vorsokratiker*, 8th ed. Diels: Weidmann.
Dillon, J. 2003. 'Philip of Opus and the Theology of Plato's *Laws*' in *Plato's Laws: From Theory into Practice*, eds. S. Scolnicov and L. Brisson. Proceedings of the VI Symposium Platonicum. Sankt Augustin: Academia Verlag: 304–11.
Dillon, J., and Gergel, T. (eds.) 2003. *The Greek Sophists*, trans. J. Dillon and T. Gergel. London: Penguin.
Dodds, E. R. 1973. 'The Sophistic Movement and the Failure of Greek Liberalism', in *The Ancient Concept of Progress and Other Essays on Greek Literature and Belief*, ed. E. R. Dodds. Oxford: Oxford University Press: 92–105.
Druart, T.-A. 1999. 'The *Timaeus* Revisited', in *Plato and Platonism*, ed. J. M. van Ophuijsen. Washington, DC: Catholic University of America Press: 163–78.
Düring, I. 1957. *Aristotle in the Ancient Biographical Tradition*. Göteborg: Acta Universitatis Gothoburgensis.
Ebert, T. 1987. 'The Origin of the Stoic Theory of Signs in Sextus Empiricus', *Oxford Studies in Ancient Philosophy*: 82–126.
Emilsson, E. K. 2007. *Plotinus on Intellect*, Oxford: Oxford University Press.
    2012. 'Plotinus and Plato on Soul and Action', in *Plato and the divided self*, eds. R. Barney, T. Brennan and C. Brittain. Cambridge: Cambridge University Press: 350–67.
Farrar, C. 1988. *The Origins of Democratic Thinking*. Cambridge: Cambridge University Press.
Ferejohn, M. 1984. 'Socratic Thought-Experiments and the Unity of the Virtue Paradox', *Phronesis* 29: 105–22.
Ferrario, M. 1981. 'La concezione della retorica da Epicuro a Filodemo', in *Proceedings of the XVI International Congress of Papyrology*. Chicago: Scholars Press: 145–52.
Frede, M. 1985. *Galen: Three Treatises on the Nature of Science*. Indianapolis: Hackett.
    1987. 'Numenius', in *Aufstieg und Niedergang der römischen Welt 36.2*, ed. W. Haase. Berlin: Walter de Gruyter Verlag: 1034–75.
    1990. 'An Empiricist View of Knowledge: Memorism', in *Companions to Ancient Thought 1: Epistemology*, ed. S. Everson. Cambridge: Cambridge University Press: 225–50.
    1992. 'Introduction', in *Plato Protagoras*, trans. S. Lombardo and K. Bell. Indianapolis: Hackett: vii–xxxiii.
Gerson, L. P. 2012. 'Plotinus on Logos', *Neoplatonism and the Philosophy of Nature*, eds. C. Horn and J. Wilberding. Oxford: Oxford University Press: 17–29.
Giannantoni, G., and Gigante, M. (eds.) 1996. *Epicureismo greco e romano*, 2 vols. Atti del congresso internazionale. Naples: Bibliopolis.

Gigandet, A. 2003. 'Les Épicuriens et le problème du paradigme artificialiste', in *Ars et ratio: Sciences, art et métiers dans la philosophie héllenistique*, eds. C. Lévy, B. Besnier and A. Gigandet. Collection Latomus 273. Brussels: Édition Latomus: 221–30.
Gomperz, T. 1900–1912. *Greek Thinkers: A History of Ancient Philosophy*, 4 vols, trans. L. Magnus and G. G. Berry. London: Murray.
Gottlieb, P. 2009. *The Virtue of Aristotle's Ethics*. Cambridge: Cambridge University Press.
Goulet-Cazé, M.-O. 1986. *L'ascèse cynique: un commentaire de Diogène Laërce VI, 70–71*. Paris: Vrin.
Gourinat, J.-B. 2001. 'Le Socrate d'Epictète', *Philosophie antique* 1: 137–66.
  2008. 'Le Platon de Panétius: à propos d'un témoignage inédit de Galien', *Philosophie antique* 8: 139–51.
  2011. 'Les définitions de l'*epistêmê* et de la *technê* dans l'ancient stoïcisme', in *L'Homme et la Science, Actes du XVIe Congrès international et quinquennal de l'Association Guillaume Budé*, eds. J. Jouanna, M. Fartzoff and B. Bakhouche. Paris: Les Belles Lettres: 242–56.
Grote, G. 1875. *Plato and the Other Companions of Socrates*, 3rd ed. London. John Murray.
Gulley, N. 1968. *The Philosophy of Socrates*. London: Macmillan.
Hankinson, R. J. 1987. 'Causes and Empiricism: A Problem in the Interpretation of Later Greek Medical Method', *Phronesis* 32: 329–48.
  1995. *The Sceptics*. London: Routledge.
  2013. 'Lucretius, Epicurus, and the Logic of Multiple Explanations', in *Lucretius: Poetry, Philosophy, Science*, eds. D. Lehoux, A. D. Morrison and A. Sharrock. Oxford: Oxford University Press: 69–97.
Hard, R. (trans.) 2014. *Epictetus: Discourses, Fragments, Handbook*. Oxford: Oxford University Press.
Harte, V., McCabe, M. M., Sharples, B., and Sheppard, A. (eds.) 2010. *Aristotle and the Stoics Reading Plato*. BICS Supplementary, vol. 107. London: Institute of Classical Studies.
Harte, V. (Forthcoming). 'The Fourfold Classification and Socrates' Craft Analogy in the Philebus', in *Cambridge Companion to Plato*, rev. ed., eds. R. Kraut and D. Ebrey. Cambridge: Cambridge University Press.
Hasper, P.-S., and Yurdin, J. 2014. 'Between Perception and Scientific Knowledge: Aristotle's Account of Experience', *Oxford Studies in Ancient Philosophy* 47: 119–50.
Heinimann, F. 1961. 'Eine Vorplatonische Theorie der τέχνη'. *Museum Helveticum* 18: 105–30.
Helmig, C. 2012. *Forms and Concepts: Concept Formation in the Platonic Tradition*. Commentaria in Aristotelem Graeca et Byzantina, 5. Berlin: de Gruyter.
Henry, D. 2015. 'Holding for the Most Part: The Demonstrability of Moral Facts', in *Bridging the Gap between Aristotle's Science and Ethics*, eds. D. Henry and K. M. Nielsen. Cambridge: Cambridge University Press: 169–89.

Henry, D., and Nielsen, K. M. (eds.) 2015. *Bridging the Gap between Aristotle's Science and Ethics*. Cambridge: Cambridge University Press.

Hicks, R. D. 1925. *Diogenes Laertius: Lives of Eminent Philosophers*. London: Heinemann.

Hulme Kozey, E. L. 2019a. 'Philosophia and Philotechnia: The Technê Theme in the Platonic Dialogues', PhD diss., Princeton University.

 2019b. 'The Good-Directedness of Τέχνη and the Status of Rhetoric in the Platonic Dialogues', *Apeiron* 52: 223–44.

Hülser, K. (ed.) 1987. *Die fragmente zur Dialektik der Stoiker*, vol. 2. Stuttgart-Bad Cannstatt: Frommann-Holzboog.

Hussey, E. 1990. 'The Beginnings of Epistemology: From Homer to Philolaus', in *Epistemology*, ed. S. Everson. Companions to Ancient Thought 1. Cambridge: Cambridge University Press: 11–38.

 1996. 'Rescuing Protagoras', in *Essays for David Wiggins: Identity, Truth and Value*, eds. S. Lovibond and S. G. Williams. Oxford: Blackwell: 185–200.

Hutchinson, D. S. 1988. 'Doctrines of the Mean and the Debate concerning Skills in Fourth-Century Medicine, Rhetoric, and Ethics', *Apeiron* 21: 17–52.

Inwood, B. 2004. 'Review of Sellars 2003', *Notre Dame Philosophical Reviews*. https://ndpr.nd.edu/news/the-art-of-living-the-stoics-on-the-nature-and-function-of-philosophy/.

 2005a. *Reading Seneca: Stoic Philosophy at Rome*. Oxford: Oxford University Press.

 2005b. 'Getting to Goodness', in *Reading Seneca: Stoic Philosophy at Rome*, ed. B. Inwood. Oxford: Oxford University Press: 271–301.

 2017. 'Stoic Ethics', in *The Cambridge History of Moral Philosophy*, eds. S. Golob and J. Timmerman. Cambridge: Cambridge University Press: 75–87.

Irwin, T. 1977. *Plato's Moral Theory: The Early and Middle Dialogues*. Oxford: Oxford University Press.

 1995. *Plato's Ethics*. Oxford: Oxford University Press.

 2000. 'Ethics As an Inexact Science: Aristotle's Ambitions for Moral Theory', in *Moral Particularism*, eds. B. Hooker and M. O. Little. Oxford: Oxford University Press: 100–29.

Isnardi Parente, M. 1966. *Techne: Momenti del Pensiero Greco da Platone ad Epicuro*. Firenze: Nuova Italia.

Janko, R. 2000. *Philodemus on Poems Book One*. Oxford: Oxford University Press.

Johansen, T. K. 2004. *Plato's Natural Philosophy: A Study of the Timaeus-Critias*. Cambridge: Cambridge University Press.

 2012. *The Powers of Aristotle's Soul*. Oxford: Oxford University Press.

 2014. 'Why the Cosmos Needs a Craftsman: Plato, *Timaeus* 27d5–29b1', *Phronesis* 59: 297–320.

 2017. 'Aristotle on the *Logos* of the Craftsman', *Phronesis* 62: 97–135.

 2020. 'From Craft to Nature: The Emergence of Natural Teleology', in *The Cambridge Companion to Ancient Science*, ed. L. Taub. Cambridge: Cambridge University Press: 102–20.

Jouanna, J. 1990. *Hippocrate II 1: De l'Ancienne Médicine (Budé series)*. Paris: Les Belles Lettres.
Kahn, C. 1996. *Plato and the Socratic Dialogue: The Philosophical Use of a Literary Form*. Cambridge: Cambridge University Press.
Kalligas, P. 2016. 'Platonic Astronomy and the Development of Ancient Sphairopoiia', *Rhizomata* 4: 176–200.
Kamtekar, R. 2006. 'The Politics of Plato's Socrates', in *A Companion to Socrates* eds. S. Ahbel-Rappe and R. Kamtekar. Oxford: Blackwell: 214–27.
Kato, M. 1986. *Techne und Philosophie bei Platon*. Frankfurt am Main: P. Lang.
Kidd, I. G. 1978. 'Moral Actions and Rules in Stoic Ethics', in *The Stoics*, ed. J. Rist. Berkeley: University of California Press: 247–58.
Korsgaard, C. 1996. *The Sources of Normativity*. Cambridge: Cambridge University Press.
  2009. *Self-Constitution: Agency, Identity, and Integrity*. Oxford: Oxford University Press.
Kozbelt, A., Beghetto, R. A., and Runco, M. A. 2010. 'Theories of Creativity', in *The Cambridge Handbook of Creativity*, eds. J. C. Kaufman and R.J. Sternberg, Cambridge University Press: Cambridge: 20–47.
Kraut, R. 1989. *Aristotle on the Human Good*. Princeton: Princeton University Press.
  1991. 'Return to the Cave: *Republic* 519–521' *Proceedings of the Boston Area Colloquium in Ancient Philosophy* 7: 43–62.
  1992. 'The Defense of Justice in Plato's *Republic*', in *Cambridge Companion to Plato*, ed. R. Kraut. Cambridge: Cambridge University Press: 311–37.
Kube, J. 1969. *TEXNH und ARETH: Sophistisches und Platonisches Tugendwissen*. Berlin: De Gruyter.
Kuisma, O. 2003. *Art or Experience: A Study on Plotinus' Aesthetics*. Helsinki: Societas scientiarum fennica.
Laks, A., and Most, G. W. 2016. *Early Greek Philosophy*, 9 vols. Loeb Series. Cambridge, MA.: Harvard University Press.
Laurenti, R. 1973. *Filodemo e il pensiero economico degli Epicurei*. Milan: Cisalpino —Goliardica.
Lee, D. (rev. T. K. Johansen) 2008. *Plato: Timaeus and Critias*. London: Penguin.
Lehoux, D., Morrison, A. D., and Sharrock, A. (eds.) 2013. *Lucretius: Poetry, Philosophy, Science*. Oxford: Oxford University Press.
Lennox, J. 2021. *Aristotle on Inquiry. Erotetic Frameworks and Domain Specific Norms*. Cambridge University Press.
Leone, G. 2000. 'Epicuro fondatore del Giardino e l'opera sua conservata nei papiri', *Cronache Ercolanesi* 30: 21–33.
Löbl, R. 1997. TEXNH *–TECHNE, Untersuchungen zur Bedeutung dieses Worts in der Zeit von Homer bis Aristoteles, Band I: Von Homer bis zu den Sophisten*. Würzburg: Königshausen und Neumann.
Long, A. A. 1978. 'Dialectic and the Stoic Sage', in *The Stoics*, ed. J. Rist. Berkeley: University of California Press: 101–24.
  1988. 'Socrates in Hellenistic Philosophy', *Classical Quarterly* 38: 150–71.

2002. *Epictetus: A Stoic and Socratic Guide to Life*. Oxford: Clarendon Press.
Long, A. A., and Sedley, D. N. 1987. *The Hellenistic Philosophers*, 2 vols. Cambridge: Cambridge University Press.
Long, A. G. (ed.) 2013. *Plato and the Stoics*. Cambridge: Cambridge University Press.
Longo-Aurrichio, F. 1977. Φιλοδήμου Περὶ Ῥητορικῆς *libros primum et secundum*. Naples: Bibliopolis.
  1985. 'Testimonianze della Retorica di Filodemo sulla concezione dell'oratoria nei primi maestri epicurei', *Cronache Ercolanesi* 15: 31–61.
  1988. *Ermarco: Frammenti*. Naples: Bibliopolis.
Lovibond, S., and Williams, S. G. (eds.) 1996. *Essays for David Wiggins: Identity, Truth and Value*. Oxford: Blackwell.
Maier, J. 2018. 'Ability, Modality, and Genericity', *Philosophical Studies* 175: 411–28.
Makin, S. 2006. *Aristotle Metaphysics Book Theta*. Oxford: Clarendon Press.
Mansfeld, J. 1978. 'Zeno of Citium', *Mnemosyne* 31: 134–78.
  1983a. 'Techne: A New Fragment of Chrysippus', *Greek, Roman, and Byzantine Studies* 24: 57–65.
  1983b. 'Zeno's Definition of Geometry in a Fragment of I. Calvenus Taurus', *Phronesis* 28: 59–74.
  1986. 'Diogenes Laertius on Stoic Philosophy', *Elenchos* 7: 295–382.
Mansfeld, J., and Runia, D. T. 1997. *Aëtiana I*. Leiden: Brill.
  2009. *Aëtiana II*. Leiden: Brill.
Marrou, H. I. 1948. *Histoire de l'Éducation dans l'Antiquité*. Paris: Éditions du Seuil.
Maucolin, B. 2009. *Untersuchungen zur hippokratischen Schrift 'Über die alte Heilkunst'*. Berlin: Walter de Gruyter.
Menn, S. 1995. 'Physics As a Virtue', in *Proceedings of the Boston Area Colloquium in Ancient Philosophy 11*, eds. J. Cleary and W. Wians. Washington, DC: University Press of America: 1–45.
Michalewski, A. 2014. *La puissance de l'intelligible: La théorie plotinienne des Formes au miroir de l'héritage médioplatonicien*. Leuven: Leuven University Press.
Mitsis, P. 1988. *Epicurus' Ethical Theory: The Pleasures of Invulnerability*. Ithaca: Cornell University Press.
Moraux, P. 1951. *Les Listes Anciennes des Ouvrages d'Aristote*. Louvain: Éditions Universitaires.
Morel, P.-M. 2016. 'Travail et émancipation dans l'épicurisme antique: Prométhée revisité', *Revue Internationale de Philosophie* 278: 451–67.
Morison, B. 2011. 'The Logical Structure of the Sceptic's Opposition', in *Essays in Memory of Michael Frede*, eds. J. Allen, E. Emilsson and W. Mann. Oxford Studies in Ancient Philosophy 40. Oxford: Oxford University Press: 265–95.
  2014. 'Sextus Empiricus', in *The Stanford Encyclopedia of Philosophy*, ed. E. N. Zalta. http://plato.stanford.edu/archives/spr2014/entries/sextus-empiricus/.

2019. 'The Sceptic's Argumentation', in *Dialectic after Plato and Aristotle*, eds. T. Bénatouïl and K. Ierodiakonou. Cambridge: Cambridge University Press: 283–319.
Moss, J., 2014. 'Right Reason in Plato and Aristotle: On the Meaning of *logos*', *Phronesis* 59: 181–230.
Narcy, M. 2015. 'Cité naturelle et cité juste dans la *République* de Platon', *Bulletin de la Société Française de Philosophie*, séance du 22 novembre 2014: 1–40.
Natali, C. 1995. '*Oikonomia* in Hellenistic Political Thought', in *Justice and Generosity: Studies in Hellenistic Social and Political Philosophy*, eds. A. Laks and M. Schofield. Cambridge: Cambridge University Press: 95–128.
  2008. 'Aristotle's Conception of *Dunamis* and *Technê*', in *Reading Ancient Texts Volume II: Aristotle and the Neoplatonists, Essays in Honour of Denis O'Brien*, eds. S. Stern-Gillet and K. Corrigan. Leiden: Brill: 1–21.
Nawar, T. 2013. 'Knowledge and True Belief at *Theaetetus* 201a–c', *British Journal for the History of Philosophy* 21: 1052–70.
  2017. 'Platonic Know-How and Successful Action', *European Journal of Philosophy* 25: 944–62.
  2018. 'Thrasymachus' Unerring Skill and the Arguments of *Republic* I', *Phronesis* 63: 359–91.
  (unpublished). 'Aristotle on Skill and Rational Ability'.
Nehamas, A. 1987. 'Socratic Intellectualism', *Proceedings of the Boston Area Colloquium in Ancient Philosophy* 2: 275–316.
  1998. *The Art of Living: Socratic Reflections from Plato to Foucault*. Berkeley: University of California Press.
Neschke-Hentschke, A. 2000. 'Der platonische *Timaios* als Manifest der platonischen Demiurgie', in *Le Timée de Platon: Contributions à l'histoire de sa réception: Platos Timaios, Beiträge zu seiner Rezeptionsgeschichte*, ed. A. Neschke-Hentschke. Bibliothèque philosophique de Louvain, 53, Éditions de l'Institut Supérieur de Philosophie. Leuven: Peeters: ix–xxvii.
Nicolardi, F. 2018. *Filodemo: Il primo libro della Retorica*. La Scuola di Epicuro, vol. 19. Naples: Bibliopolis.
Noble, C. I., and Powers, N. M. 2015. 'Creation and Divine Providence in Plotinus', in *Causation and Creation in Late Antiquity*, eds. A. Marmodoro and B. D. Prince. Cambridge: Cambridge University Press: 51–70.
Nussbaum, M. 1986. *The Fragility of Goodness: Luck and Ethics in Greek Tragedy and Philosophy*. Cambridge: Cambridge University Press.
Opsomer, J. 2005. 'Demiurges in Early Imperial Platonism', in *Gott und die Götter bei Plutarch: Götterbilder – Gottesbilder – Weltbilder*, ed. R. Hirsch-Luipold. Berlin: De Gruyter: 51–99.
  2006. 'Drittes Bett, Artefakt-Ideen und die Problematik, die Ideenlehre zu veranschaulichen', in *Metaphysik als Wissenschaft: Festschrift für Klaus Düsing zum 65. Geburtstag*, ed. D. Fonfara. Freiburg: Alber: 73–88.
  2017. 'The Natural World', in *All from One: A Guide to Proclus*, eds. P. d'Hoine and M. Martijn. Oxford: Oxford University Press: 139–66.

Panofsky, E. 1939. *Studies in Iconology: Humanistic Themes in the Art of the Renaissance*. Oxford: Oxford University Press.
Primavesi, O. 2012. 'Aristotle, *Metaphysics A*', in *Aristotle's Metaphysics Alpha*, ed. C. Steel. Oxford: Oxford University Press: 385–516.
Reeve C. D. C. 1989. *Socrates in the Apology: An Essay on Plato's Apology of Socrates*. Indianapolis: Hackett.
  (trans.) 2004. *Plato: Republic*. Indianapolis: Hackett.
Rich, A. N. M. 1960. 'Plotinus and the Theory of Artistic Imitation', *Mnemosyne*, 4th series 13: 233–39.
Rist, J. (ed.) 1978. *The Stoics*. Berkeley: University of California Press.
Robin, L. 1928. *De rerum natura: Commentaire exégétique et critique*, 3 vols. Paris: Les Belles Lettres.
Roochnik, D. 1996. *Of Art and Wisdom: Plato's Understanding of Techne*, University Park: Pennsylvania State University Press.
Rosetti, L. 1973. '"Socratica" in Fedone di Elide', *Studi Urbinati* 47: 364–81.
Ross, W. D. 1924. *Aristotle's Metaphysics, a Revised Text with Introduction and Commentary*. Oxford: Clarendon Press.
Rowe C. J., and Schofield, M. (eds.) 2000. *The Cambridge History of Greek and Roman Political Thought*. Cambridge: Cambridge University Press.
Ryle, G. 1949. *The Concept of Mind*. London: Hutchinson.
Schaerer, R. 1930. ΕΠΙΣΤΗΜΗ *et* ΤΕΧΝΗ: *Etude sur les notions de connaissance et d'art d'Homère à Platon*. Mâcon: Protat Frères.
Schiefsky, Mark J. 2005. *Hippocrates on Ancient Medicine*. Studies in Ancient Medicine 28. Leiden: Brill.
Schiller, F. C. S. 1908. *Plato or Protagoras?* Oxford: Oxford University Press.
Schniewind, A. 2007 *Plotin, Traité 5: I, 9: Introduction, traduction, commentaire et notes*. Paris: Les éditions du Cerf.
Schofield, M. 1984. 'Ariston of Chios and the Unity of Virtue', *Ancient Philosophy* 4: 83–95.
  2013. 'Cardinal Virtues: A Contested Socratic Inheritance', in *Plato and the Stoics*, ed. A. G. Long. Cambridge: Cambridge University Press: 11–28.
Sedley, D. N. 1982. 'On Signs', in *Science and Speculation*, eds. J. Barnes, J. Brunschwig, M. F. Burnyeat and M. Schofield. Cambridge: Cambridge University Press: 239–72.
  1998. 'Platonic Causes', *Phronesis* 43: 114–32.
  1998a. 'The Inferential Foundation for Epicurean Ethics', in *Ethics*, ed. S. Everson. Companions to Ancient Thought 4. Cambridge: Cambridge Unnversity Press: 129–50.
  1998b. *Lucretius and the Transformation of Greek Wisdom*. Cambridge: Cambridge University Press.
  1999. 'The Stoic-Platonist Debate on *kathêkonta*', in *Topics in Stoic Philosophy*, ed. K. Ierodiakonou. Oxford: Oxford University Press: 128–52.
  2007. *Creationism and Its Critics in Antiquity*. Sather Classical Lectures, 66. Berkeley: University of California Press.

2010. 'Teleology, Aristotelian and Platonic', in *Being, Nature, and Life in Aristotle*, eds. J. Lennox and R. Bolton. Cambridge: Cambridge University Press: 5–29.

Sellars, J. 2003. *The Art of Living: The Stoics on the Nature and Function of Philosophy*. London: Bloomsbury.

Sienkiewicz, S. 2019. *Five Modes of Scepticism*. Oxford: Oxford University Press.

Smith, M. F. 1992. *Diogenes of Oinoanda: The Epicurean Inscription*. Naples: Bibliopolis.

2003. *Supplement to Diogenes of Oinoanda: The Epicurean Inscription*. Naples: Bibliopolis.

Smith, R. 1997. *Aristotle,* Topics*: Books I and VIII*. Oxford: Oxford University Press.

2009. 'Aristotle's Theory of Demonstration', in *A Companion to Aristotle*, ed. G. Anagnostopoulos. Malden: Wiley-Blackwell.

Solmsen, F. 1929. *Die Entwicklung der Aristotelischen Logik und Rhetorik*. Berlin: Weidmann.

Sorabji, R. 2004a. *Aristotle on Memory*, 2nd ed. London: Duckworth (1st ed. 1972).

2004b. *The Philosophy of the Commentators, 200–600 AD: A Sourcebook: Volume 2, Physics*. London: Duckworth.

2010. 'The Ancient Commentators on Concept Formation', in *Interpreting Aristotle's* Posterior Analytics *in Antiquity and Beyond*, eds. F. de Haas and M. Leunissen. Leiden: Brill: 3–26.

Sparshott, F. E. 1978. 'Zeno on Art: Anatomy of a Definition', in *The Stoics*, ed. J. Rist. Berkeley: University of California Press: 273–90.

Stanley, J. 2011. *Know How*. Oxford: Oxford University Press.

Stanley, J., and Williamson, T. 2017. 'Skill', *Noûs* 51: 713–26.

Steel, C. 2007–2008. *Procli In Platonis Parmenidem Commentaria I-V*, 2 vols. Oxford Classical Texts. Oxford: Oxford University Press.

Striker, G. 1990. '*Ataraxia*: Happiness As Tranquillity', *The Monist* 73: 97–110; reprinted in Striker, G. 1996a. *Essays on Hellenistic Epistemology and Ethics*. Cambridge: Cambridge University Press: 183–95.

1991. 'Following Nature: A Study in Stoic Ethics', *Oxford Studies in Ancient Philosophy* 9: 1–73.

1996a. *Essays on Hellenistic Epistemology and Ethics*. Cambridge: Cambridge University Press.

1996b. 'Antipater, or the Art of Living', in Striker, G. *Essays on Hellenistic Epistemology and Ethics*. Cambridge: Cambridge University Press: 298–315.

1996c. 'Plato's Socrates and the Stoics', in Striker, G. *Essays on Hellenistic Epistemology and Ethics*. Cambridge: Cambridge University Press: 316–24.

Taylor, C. C. W. 1991. *Plato* Protagoras, rev. ed. Oxford: Oxford University Press.

Tepedino Guerra, A. 1991. *Polieno*. Frammenti, La Scuola di Epicuro 11. Naples: Bibliopolis.

Thorsrud, H. 2009. *Ancient Scepticism*. Stocksfield: Acumen.

Tieleman, T. 2003. *Chrysippus' On Affections: Reconstruction and Interpretation.* Leiden: Brill.

   2007a. 'Onomastic Reference in Seneca: The Case of Plato and the Platonists', in *Platonic Stoicism – Stoic Platonism: The Dialogue between Platonism and Stoicism in Antiquity*, eds. M. Bonazzi and C. Helmig. Leuven: Leuven University Press: 133–48.

   2007b. 'Panaetius' Place in the History of Stoicism, with Special Reference to His Moral Psychology', in *Pyrrhonists, Patricians, and Platonizers: Hellenistic Philosophy in the Period 155–86 BC*, eds. A. M. Ioppolo and D. Sedley. Naples: Bibliopolis: 103–42.

Tsouna, V. 2007. *The Ethics of Philodemus.* Oxford: Oxford Universtiy Press.

   2012. *Philodemus on Property Management.* Williston: Society of Biblical Literature.

   2016. 'Epicurean Preconceptions', *Phronesis* 61: 160–221.

   2017. 'Epicureanism and Hedonism', in *The Cambridge History of Moral Philosophy*, eds. S. Golob and J. Timmerman. Cambridge: Cambridge University Press: 57–74.

   (Forthcoming). 'Lucrèce: Les origines et le développement des arts', *Aitia*.

van Riel, G. 2013. *Plato's Gods.* Farnham: Ashgate.

Vander Waerdt, P. A. 1988. 'Hermarchus and the Epicurean Genealogy of Morals', *Transactions of the American Philological Association* 118: 87–106.

Vander Waerdt, P. A. (ed.) 1994a. *The Socratic Movement.* Ithaca: Cornell University Press.

   1994b. 'Zeno's Republic and the Origins of Natural Law', in Vander Waerdt, P. A. *The Socratic Movement.* Ithaca: Cornell University Press: 272–308.

Vlastos, G. 1983. 'The Socratic Elenchus', *Oxford Studies in Ancient Philosophy* 1: 27–58.

   1985. 'Socrates' Disavowal of Knowledge', *Philosophical Quarterly* 35: 1–31.

   1991. *Socrates: Ironist and Moral Philosopher.* Cambridge: Cambridge University Press.

Warren, J. 2002. *Epicurus and Democritean Ethics: An Archaeology of Ataraxia.* Cambridge: Cambridge University Press.

Watson, G. 1994. 'The Concept of "Phantasia" from the Late Hellenistic Period to Early Neoplatonism', *Aufstieg und Niedergang der römischen Welt, II* 36 (7): 4765–810.

White, N. 2002. *Individual and Conflict in Greek Ethics.* Oxford: Oxford University Press.

Wiggins, D. 1996. 'Reply to Edward Hussey', in *Essays for David Wiggins: Identity, Truth and Value*, eds. S. Lovibond and S. G. Williams. Oxford: Blackwell: 274–76.

Wilberding, J. 2017. *Forms, Souls, and Embryos: Neoplatonists on Human Reproduction, Issues in Ancient Philosophy.* New York: Routledge.

Witt, C. 2015. 'In Defense of the Craft Analogy: Artifacts and Natural Teleology', in *Aristotle's Physics: A Critical Guide*, ed. M. Leunissen. Cambridge: Cambridge University Press: 107–20.

Woodruff, P. 1990. 'Plato's Early Theory of Knowledge', in *Companions to Ancient Thought, 1: Epistemology*, ed. S. Everson. Cambridge: Cambridge University Press: 60–84.
  2010. '*The Pyrrhonian Modes*', in *The Cambridge Companion to Ancient Scepticism*, ed. R. Bett. Cambridge: Cambridge University Press: 208–31.
Woods, M. 1986. 'Intuition and Perception in Aristotle's *Ethics*', *Oxford Studies in Ancient Philosophy* 4: 145–66.
Woolf, R. 2004. 'What Kind of Hedonist Was Epicurus?', *Phronesis* 49: 303–22.
Wright, G. H. 1976. 'Replies', in *Essays on Explanation and Understanding*, eds. J. Manninen and R. Tuomela. Dordrecht: Reidel: 371–413.
Zedda, S. 2000. 'How to Build a World Soul: A Practical Guide', in *Reason and Necessity: Essays on Plato's Timaeus*, ed. M. R. Wright. London: Duckworth: 23–41.

General Index

account (*logos*), 6–8, 30, 32, 48, 53, 59–60, 63–64, 66, 73–74, 85, 135, 162, 168, 174, 180, 213, 223
Aeschylus
  Prometheus Bound, 3
Anaxagoras, 89, 92, 111
Annas, J., 43, 63, 70, 75, 207, 230
Aristotle
  lost work on *technê*, 131
  Metaphysics I., 7–8, 47, 111, 126
  Nicomachean Ethics, 6, 8, 50, 59, 81, 119, 264
art. *See technê*
art of living, 12, 52, 62, 65–66, 68, 167, 186, 203–4, 208, 210, 246
  and natural philosophy, 60

Balansard, A., 2, 64, 66
Beere, J., 52, 56, 59, 127

Chrysippus, 170–72, 175, 179, 182, 184–85, 189, 193
Cleanthes, 170–72, 182, 188
craft. *See technê*

dêmiourgia. *See* craft
Demiurge (divine craftsman)
  as cause of the cosmos, 42
  in Plotinus, 74
  in Proclus, 82
  Stoic reception of, 188
democracy, 38
dialectic, 7, 50, 53, 60, 136–37, 185, 203, 225
Diodorus Siculus, 34

Empiricism, 237, 243
Epictetus, 62, 65, 78, 82–83, 85, 187
Epicureans
  on method in *technê*, 57, 224
Epicurus, 55, 168, 225
Eudoxus, 228–29, 242
Evenus, 63, 67

experience (*emperia*), 121, 224
  and knowledge, 47

Farrar, C., 26
forms, 2, 7, 12, 14, 35, 52, 93–95, 103, 109, 135, 153, 185, 201–2, 220, 223, 229, 238, 242, 250, 254, 267, 271, 279, 281
  of artefacts, 85, 249, 264
Frede, M., 16, 24, 159, 238, 256

Galen, 159, 170–71, 177, 185–86, 189, 226, 237
Gorgias of Leontini, 4

happiness (*eudaimonia*), 12, 40, 52, 64, 66, 68, 70, 72, 84–85, 167, 186, 204, 207, 209, 219–20, 223, 225
  and the end of scepticism, 67
hedonism
  Epicurean, 62
Hippocratic writers, 3–5
  On Ancient Medicine, 16, 33
  On the Art, 4–5, 45–46
Homer, 3

imitation (*mimêsis*), 6, 42, 199–200, 252–53, 255, 261, 276
intellectualism, 9, 63–65, 70, 85
Irwin, T., 17, 63, 66
Isocrates, 36, 40, 65

kairos (appropriate time), 4
knowledge that/how, 174
Korsgaard, C., 78
Kuisma, O., 254–55

lesser gods
  creation of human beings, 42
Lucretius, 57, 191, 205–6, 209, 219

297

Makin, S., 34, 127, 252
mathematics, 1–2, 4, 35–36, 119, 159, 211, 249
medicine, 1–3, 5, 9, 19–21, 23, 25, 29, 32–37, 40–42, 45–46, 49, 60, 62, 66–68, 72, 81, 115–17, 148, 160, 167, 174–75, 181, 211, 214, 219, 229, 249, 254, 260, 281
   analogous to political *technê*, 18, 33–35
memory, 59
Methodism, 237
Moss, J., 53–54, 112

Numenius, 256

Pausanias, 3
Pericles, 23–24, 38, 67
Philodemus, 55, 63
Philostratus, 254, 276
Plato
   Apology, 5–6, 63, 67, 186
   Charmides, 46, 66–67, 70, 81–82, 168, 176
   Euthydemus, 45–46, 49, 67, 70, 81–82, 168
   Euthyphro, 66
   Gorgias, 4, 7, 67
   Hippias Minor, 11, 41, 46, 49, 56, 79
   influence on Stoics, 51
   Ion, 6, 67
   Laches, 66–67
   Laws, 89, 107, 184
   Meno, 7, 66, 69–70
   Philebus, 10, 65, 264, 267
   philosophical rulers (guardians), 40
   Protagoras, 5, 15, 17–19, 67
   Republic, 5–7, 11, 14, 35, 39–41, 43, 47, 49–50, 93–94, 100, 141, 168, 179, 184, 246, 250, 252, 254–56, 263, 265, 267, 272, 279–80
   Statesman, 6, 49, 65, 168
   Theaetetus, 2, 7, 15–16, 24, 26–27, 32–34, 67
   Timaeus, 42, 74, 86, 223, 276
Plotinus
   on imitation (*mimêsis*), 73
   on reasoning in craft, 258
poetry, 26, 36, 194, 201, 218, 220, 222, 229
practical wisdom (*phronêsis*), 52, 62
productive knowledge. See *technê*
property management (*oikonomia*), 66
Protagoras of Abdera
   perception and empiricism, 27–31
   political thinking, 11, 37
   relationship to character in Plato's *Protagoras*, 11

rationalism, 237–38, 243–44
rhetoric, 2, 4, 37, 48, 60, 63, 67, 116, 132, 155, 159–60, 184, 187, 194–95, 211, 221, 227–28, 231, 245, 249
Roochnik, D., 49, 63–64, 66, 166–67
Ryle, Gilbert, 9

sage, the Stoic, 12, 52, 167–68, 173, 176, 194–95, 211, 219, 221, 225
scepticism
   Agrippan method, 71
   method of equipollence, 69
   mode of disagreement, 71
   on levels of craft, 72
   subject matter of, 67
Seneca, 183
Socrates. See Plato
Sophists. See *Plato*, *Gorgias*, *Protagoras*
Sophocles
   Antigone, 3, 68, 79
Stoics
   on cosmic fire, 54
   on knowledge (*epistêmê*), 52
systematicity
   as a condition of *technê*, 226, 233

technê, 4, 11
   as architectonic, 6, 37, 41, 100
   and beauty, 72, 176, 187, 190, 260
   and biological creation, 42
   as a capacity (*dunamis*), 40
   and causal knowledge, 8–9, 51, 54, 71, 81, 89, 93–94, 106–8, 110, 118, 134, 136, 147, 219, 249, 261, 275, 280–81
   and combining and dividing, 99
   and cosmology, 10, 12–13, 42, 72, 186, 190, 259
   and creativity, 110, 275, 281
   and deliberation, 10, 13, 24, 31, 59, 62, 67–68, 70, 72, 77, 81, 84, 119–20, 126, 135, 145
   and desire, 55, 60
   directed at the good in Aristotle, 34
   directed at the good in Plato, 28, 40
   directed at the good in Stoicism, 173
   and ethics, 12
   and exceptional circumstances, 45
   and experience (*empeiria*). See experience
   and explanations, 42
   as fine arts, 1, 246
   first and higher-order, 51, 211
   and human development, 57
   and imagination, 10, 14, 85, 254, 275–76, See Proclus
   and innovation, 129, 201, 281

as necessitating outcome in Aristotle, 34
as necessitating outcome in Plato, 29
non-scientific forms of, 49
not of the accidental, 43
and performance arts, 13, 75, 182, 201, 261
and politics, 4–5, 11, 37, 41, 63, 77, 111, 197–98
and practical identity, 78, 83
and practical need, 195, 272, 274–75
practical value of, 50
as productive knowledge, 8
and progress of civilization, 34
proper object of, 66, 71, 110, 156, 167, 171, 176, 224
and proper use, 22
stochastic, 10, 264–65
as a system of cognitions, 51, 174
as tenor (*hexis*), 172, 193
and theoretical science, 42
and tools, 87
and training (*askêsis*), 184–86, 218
as a two-way capacity, 11, 50–51, 53
as two-way capacity in Aristotle, 30
of the universal, 48, 115
as two-way capacity in Plato, 25
usefulness of, 65

vs. luck (tuchê), 4, 68
and virtue (*aretê*), 35, 49
technodicy, 42, 100
teleology, 13, 191, 223, 261
theoretical science (*epistêmê*), 109
and gods, 46
principles, 111
relationship to *technê*, 42, 49
Thrasymachus
in Plato's *Republic*, 29, 38, 80

utility
as a condition of *technê*, 226–27, 230

wisdom (*sophia*), 46, 53, 134
World-Soul
in Plotinus, 13, 73, 247–48

Xenophanes, 5, 27–37
influence on Protagoras, 29–31
Xenophon, 6, 47, 182

Zeno (Stoic philosopher), 51, 212
Zhuangzi, 63

Index Locorum

Aetius

Opinions of the Philosophers (Placita)

I.7,23 188

Alcinoos

Didaskalikos

9, 24–30 248

Alexander of Aphrodisias

On mixture (De mixtione)

223 171
225 171

On Aristotle's Topics

1.8–14 185

Questions

2.16 45

Ammianus Marcellinus

History (Res Gestae)

XXX.4.3, 195

Anonymous in Theaetetum

XV.26–30 178
22.42–23.8 192

Anonymous Londiniensis (Anon. Lond.)

18.8–29 42

Aristotle

Eudemian Ethics (EE)

1112b13 119
1216b2–25 161
1216b4–10 64
1216b6–9 184
1216b11–19 111
1216b16–19 60
1216b19–20 60
1217b34ff 156
1227b27 119
1227b28ff 112
1246a26–35 60

Generation of Animals (GA)

734b37–35a4 52
739b12–23 52
743a25 124
744b15–16 123
770b9–11 124
778a5–9 153

History of Animals (HA)

491a6–19 132
491a10–13 164
604b25–26 164
614a12–30 164
631b8 164
633a9 164

Metaphysics (Metaph.)

980a27–81b13 134
980b25–26 140
981a1 145
981a1–3 154
981a1–20 4
981a5–30 152
981a7–9 140
981a7–12 54
981a10 139
981a12–17 55
981a15–16 54
981a16 54
981a18–20 140
981a20–24 58
981a28–29 135
981a28–30 54
981a29–b1 6
981a30 110
981a30–b6 134
981a32 2
981b5 139
981b5–6 164
981b13 135
981b22 2
991a20–92b9 141
991a21–30 7
995a15–20 153
998b2–4 36
1003a33–b10 165
1004b22 156
1018a25–35 51
1019a15–16 50
1019a15–18 50
1021b16–17 128
1025a1–13 57
1025a30–34 112
1026a18–19 159
1026a21 57
1026b2ff 116
1026b4–10 109
1026b27–27a28 59
1027a20–21 114
1028a10–15 156
1032a3–6 169
1032a12–33a22 146
1032a32–b1 273
1032b3–5 53
1032b5–6 52
1032b6–26 145
1032b9–22 169
1032b15–31 278
1032b21–28 52
1032b26–29 42
1034a21–32 51
1034a22 273
1034b14–19 51
1036a31–32 169
1044a25–32 169
1046a10–11 50
1046b1 50
1046b2 53
1046b2–24 135
1046b3 109
1046b3–4 50
1046b4–9 51
1046b5 53
1046b6 44
1046b6–14 60
1046b7–8 52
1046b8–9 53
1046b12–14 53
1046b12–15 53
1046b16–17 52
1046b20–22 53
1046b22–23 53
1046b36–47a2 58
1047a24–26 169
1047b31–35 50
1047b35–48a2 56
1047b35–48a8 51
1048a10–15 55
1048a13 53
1048a13–15 59
1048a15–21 56
1048a16–21 57
1048a2–3 53
1048a3 53
1048a5–7 51
1048a32–33 169
1049a5–12 169
1050b6–22 127
1050b33–34 51
1051a4–17 51
1055a3–b29 51
1063b36–64a1 109
1064a1ff 110
1064a10ff 109
1069b29–34 169
1070a29–30 52
1070b33 52
1173a23–28 42
1074b25–26 128
1074b28–29 128
1177b26–34 128
1178b18–22 127

Index Locorum

Movement of Animals (MA)

700b4–11 147
701a7–32 146

Nicomachean Ethics (EN)

1094a1–2 59
1094a27–28 37
1094b12–27 143
1094b16 144
1094b19–22 143
1094b19–23 146
1095b2–13 139
1095b2–3 131
1095b4–13 143
1097a5–13 59
1097a10–15 141
1101a3–6 123
1102a19–25 144
1102a26–32 139
1026a18–19 159
1103a14–25 148
1103b28–04a11 143
1104a3–10 146
1104a5–10 150
1104a7–10 121
1105a26–b2 62
1106a9 144
1106b5–28 143
1107a28–b8 138
1107a33–b8 138
1109b20–23 143
1112a34 265
1112b9–16 143
1112b11–20c 147
1112b34–13a2 119
1126b4 143
1129a13–14 53
1137a13–18 143
1137b12–32 143
1139a3–17 135
1139a6–15 50
1139a6–17 161
1139b19–21 115
1140a1–23 1
1140a2–3 139
1140a3–5 53
1140a3–24 162
1140a6f 159
1140a10–13 162
1140a10–20 264
1140a14–15 159
1140a20–21 50
1140a25–28 60
1140b1–7 62
1140b21–25 62
1141b14–21 138
1141b20 138
1143b5 143
1143b6–14 143
1044b12–15 163
1145b2–7 144
1146b6–8 144
1146b35–47a9 142
1147a24–31 144
1147a24–b5 147
1155b2–15 144
1155b8–9 144
1155b27–31 48
1165a35 138
1179b20 144
1179b24–31 143
1180b8–10 59
1180b8–10 149
1180b13–23 149
1180b30–81a12 148
1181b3–12 142
1181b15–23 132
1181b17 132
1181b2–5 132

On Generation and Corruption (GC)

320b17–21 51
323b18–24a10 51
324a10–24 52
324a15–19 42
324b7–9 51

On Interpretation (Int.)

17a37–b16 152
23a23–24 127

On Memory (Mem.)

450a11–25 145
452a13 157
452a14 157
453a4–14 160

On Sense and Sense Objects (Sens.)

436a19–22 154

On the Heavens (DC)

302b10ff 111

On the Soul (DA)

402b16–403a2 132
403b20ff 165
408a1–3 42
413a8–20 163
416b15–17 92
417a18–20 51
417a26–28 57
434a7–10 145
434a8 145
434a9 145
434a16–21 147
451b10–16 145
453a4–14 145

On Youth and Old Age (Juv.)

480b22–28 154

Parts of Animals (PA)

648b2–10 53
658a23–24 123

Physics (Ph.)

184a16–b14 132
184a19–21 163
184a21–26 163
184a23–b14 153
184b2 163
184b3–4 164
187b10–11 111
193a9–17 169
193a23–28 169
195a11 51
198b18 258
199a15–16 275
199a33–b7 169
199a33–35 58
199b15–18 57
199b26–27 13
199b27 265
199b28 268
199b31–32 92
200a7–13 169
200b5–7 169
202a5–9 51
202a9–12 51
204a34–b3 42
210a20 42
244a14–b2 51
246b3–6 42
251b1–8 57

255a34–b1 51
255b4 51
260b1–5 51

Politics (Pol.)

1282a3–6 131

Posterior Analytics (Post An)

73b26–74a32 151
73b32–74a3 151
74a32–b4 151
75a12–13 115
78a22–26 135
78a26–38 136
78b18–27 146
78b34–79a16 161
78b35ff 111
79a2–4 136
87b21–23 115
87b28–34 140
87b29–30 153
87b39–88a4 135
87b39–88a17 141
88a2–4 162
89a20 152
89b23–31 135
90a6–7 112
93a16–21 135
93a16–24 162
93a23 162
94b12–21 113
97b25–28 115
99b28–100a 141
99b36–100a2 140
100a3–6 162
100a3–9 154
100a6 152
100a6–9 152
100a8–9 164
100a9 135
100a16–b1 134
100a17 153
100a17–b1 152

Prior Analytics (Pr An)

25a1–13 148
46a17–27 132
46a22 135
48a36–37 112
67a12–16 115

Rhetoric (Rhet.)

1354a1–11 155
1355a21 60
1355b12–14 58
1355b17–21 60
1356a32–33 159
1356b30–33 149
1356b30–35 116
1356b30–57a7 142

Sophistical Refutations (SE)

172a11–20 155
172a21–b4 156
172a34–36 155
172a39–b1 131
183a37–b14 157
184a25–b8 132

Topics (Top.)

101a28–30 157
101b5–10 157
101b8–10 58
105a13–16 136
105b30–31 157
121b29–22a2 157
123b20–32 157
126a30–b3 60
129a28–31 157
139b21 146
141a23–b2 158
141b6–14 137
141b12–14 143
141b15–19 131
142a12–16 158
142a13–16 157
145a16 109
155b34–56a10 137
157a10–11 109
160b14–23 157
163a29–b16 157
163b23–33 157
163b24–33 157
163b33–64a3 137
164a7–8 137

Aquinas, Thomas

On Physics II

Lec.14, 268 129

Summa Contra Gentiles

I.69 129

Asclepius

On Aristotle's Metaphysics, Books A–Z (in Met.)

189.10–15 275

Augustine (St.)

The City of God (De civ. Dei)

VIII.48 185

Calcidius

Commentary on Plato's Timaeus

343: 335.19–36.3 276
343: 335.24–36.3 273

Chrysippus

SVF II 64 264

Cicero

Academica

I.42 178

On Ends (De Fin.)

I.21 207
I.29–30 207
I.32 208
I.41 210
I.55 208
II.9, 26 209
III.24 65
24–25 260

On Invention (De Inv.)

II.6. 132

On Duties (De Off.)

I.107–17 78

On the Orator (De Or.)

7–10 276
II.157–58 185

On Divination (de div.)

I.34 175

On the Nature of the Gods (ND)

40–41 188
II 57–58 190

Posterior Academics (Acad.post.)

I.41 177

Cleanthes

SVF I.490 172

Damascius

On Plato's Philebus (in Phil.)

225.9–17 264

Diodorus Siculus

1.7–8 34
1.8.1 34

Diogenes of Oinoanda

fr.12 II.9–10 195
fr. 12 III.1–8 198
fr. 34 II.4–V.1 208
fr. 34 III.13–IV.1 208
fr. 127 211

Diogenes Laertius (D.L.)

Lives of the Eminent Philosophers (VF)

I.18 186
V.21 131
V.24 131
V.25 154
V.27 132
VII.42 184
VII.46 185
VII.47 177
VII.51 187
VII.60–62 185
VII.83 185
VII.87–89 179
VII.143 190
VII.156 171
VII.178 184
IX.50 38
IX.51 32
IX.55 34
IX.107 229
IX.115–16 238
X.22 208
X.24 211
X.29–30 203
X.30 207
X.31 203
X.118 195
X.119 194
X.119–20 219
X.120 194
X.127–28 209
X.136 209
X.137 208

Epictetus

Discourses (Disc.)

I.1.1–6 82
I.1.7–12 187
I.2.25–27 65
I.6.12–22 187
I.20.1–6 82
I.20.13 62
II.5 65
II.10.1–12 78
II.10.13–16 79
II.13.15 85
III.23 85
III.23.4 83
IV.1.165 65
IV.5.22 85
IV.8 85
IV.12.14 85

Epicurus

Principal Doctrines (KD)

23 203
29 209
33 209

Index Locorum

Letter to Menoeceus (ad. Men.)

122 209
128 209
129 207
132 210
135 209

Letter to Herodotus (ad Herod.)

37 204
37–38 203
75–76 198

Letter to Pythocles (ad Pyth.)

84 204
93 205

On Nature (De Nat.)

XXVIII 216

Erotian

Glossary of Hippocratic Words (gloss. Hippocr.)

praef. p. 34, 10 (Klein) 192

Eusebius

Preparation for the Gospel (praep. Evang.)

I.111.20 190
II.183.19 190
II.188.7 190
XV, 18.3 190
XV, 816d 188
XV, 818c 190

Galen

Against Lycus (Contra Lyc.)

3.7 185

On the motion of the muscles (de musculorum motu) I

7, 8 171

Medical Definitions (defin. Medicae)

II.7 177

Method of Healing (methodi med.)

I.2 189

On Sects for Beginners (Sect. ingred.)

III 24, 19–22 237

Hippocrates

Ancient Medicine (VM)

1.2 25
2–3 34
2.1 37
2.3 35
3 34
3.4 23
3.5 19
4.1 19
4.2 37
5 34
7.1 19
7.2 34
7.3 20
9.3 20
9.4 25
9.4–5 33
14–18 35
20 4
22–24 35

Art. (On the Art)

4 4
6 45
7 45
7–8 46
8 4
9 4
11 4
13 45
14 5

Nature of Man (Nat. Hom.)

2 42
4 42

Index Locorum

Places in Man (Loc. Hom.)

9 42
46 45

Regimen (Vict.)

3 42

Homer

Iliad

1.571 3
18.143 3

Iamblichus

On the Egyptian Mysteries (Myst.)

III.15, 1010.3–5 265

Protrepticus

X.54.24–55.4 196
X.55.7–56.2 196

Isocrates

Antidosis

33 40
35 40
117 40
230 40

Lucretius

On the Nature of things (DRN)

Book V

10 207
10–12 211
55–58 206
306–17 206
331–37 206
333–37 206
923–24 206
925–1010 196
1011–1241 197
925–30 196
930–31 196
933–36 196
936–44 196
948–50 196
954–57 196
955 196
958–61 196
962–65 196
966–69 196
970–76 196
977–81 196
979 196
982–87 196
988–1010 196
1006 197
1008 197
1009–10 197
1019–20 198
1022–23 199
1029 195
1091–1104 197
1105–1240 198
1241–378 199
1276 201
1283–84 200
1287–92 200
1293–96 200
1297–1340 200
1344–46 201
1351–53 200
1361–78 200
1379–1411 201
1379–1457 201
1412–35 202
1440–57 201
1452–53 201
1454–55 206
1457 206

Marcus Aurelius

Meditations (Med.)

V.1.3 85
VII.61 65

Numenius

Fragment 11 256

Olympiodorus

On Plato's Gorgias (in Plat. Gorg.)

12.1 226
12.1, 70 189
53 170
54 170

308   *Index Locorum*

Pausanias

Description of Greece

ii 4.5 3

Philo

On Courage (Fort.)

426 180

Allegorical Interpretation (Leg. Alleg.)

II & 22 172

Philodemus

To Friends of the School (Ad contubernales)

IV.9–14 210

On Choices and Avoidances (De elect.)

VI.7–21 210
XI.7–20 208
XII.4–5 219
XII.9–10 219
XXIII.2–13 219

On Poems (De poem.)

5 XXVII.25–36 192

On Property Management (Oec.)

XII.43–XIV.23 195
XIV.23–XV.3 221
XVII.2–14 222
XX.1–16 222
XXIII.7 195
XXV.3–XXVII.12 222

On Rhetoric (Rhet.)

I 213
II 212

Philoponus

On Posterior Analytics (in An. post.)

380.35–81.2 265
385.15 265

On Nicomachus' Introduction in Arithmetics

I, 34 280

On Physics (in Phys.)

310.3 265
321.1–5 268
321.4–6 265
321.6–10 265
321.16–18 268

Philostratus

Life of Apollonius (Vit. Ap.)

VI.19 254

Plato

Apology (Ap.)

19d–20c 66
19d–21c 63
19e–20c 67
22c9–d2 48
22d 63
23d 5
28e 184

Charmides (Chrm.)

164a9–b9 48
165c–66b 176
165c–66c 176
165c8 42
165c10–e2 48
166b1–3 42
167b 176
168b2–3 42
170e5–71a9 42
171c 174
171d1–2 48
171d1–72a5 46
171d–74d 82
171d–75a 176
171d–75d 82
173a–74e 66
173a–77e 70
174a 174
174a10ff 49
174c2–3 42

Cratylus (Crat.)

389b8–d3 279
405a3 281

Crito (Cri.)

46b–e 184
48b–e 184

Euthydemus (Euthyd.)

278d 66
278e–82d 66
279d8–e6 46
279e–81b 66
280a6–b3 46
281a6–b4 46
282e 66
288b3–93a6 48
289b 6
289c–92e 82
291b–93a 70
291b7 49
292c 66

Euthyphro (Euthphr.)

13a1ff 48
13a4–c20 47

Gorgias (Grg.)

447c2 72
447d–48a 4
448e 174
449a 174
449d2–4 42
449d2ff 42
450d 2
450e 175
451a–c 176
451c1–5 42
452a 174
452e 4
453b–54a 67
459c–60e 67
459c6ff 49
460a–c 64
464b–66a 66
464b2–66a3 265
464b4 42
464c 174
464e2–65a2 48
465a 63
465a2–5 53
465a2–7 48
477a 180
500a1 49
500a7–b5 48
500b3–5 48
500c 184
500e–501a 66
500e4–501b1 48
501a–b 63
501a1–3 53
501a3–4 48
501b 86
501e1–3 48
502e2–7 47
504a 89
504d5–e4 47
507c 184
509e1–10a4 72
511c7–12b2 47
511e–12b 82
512b1–2 48
512c 3
513d–17c 194
513d1–5 49
513e–14b 66
513e2–3 47
514d3–16d3 47
517d6–18e1 49
519c 77
520e 77
521a2ff 49
521d 66
523a–27e 180

Hippias Minor (Hp. Mi.)

366b7–c4 46
366e3–67a5 41
373c7 41
373d5–7 41
374a1–3 41
375a7–b2 41
375b–c 11
375b4–7 41
376a 72
376b 79

Ion

537e–41b 67

Laches (Lach.)

185a 174

185c–e 176
186a–87a 66
187e–88c 184
195c–d 82
195c7–d2 47

Laws (Leg.)

903c 89
903d–4c 107

Meno (Men.)

70a 69
72c 7
86d–89d 66
87c–89a 182
89d–96d 66
98a 7
99e–100a 70

Phaedo

65e–67b 180
69a–c 182
98b 89
100a 70

Phaedrus (Phdr.)

245c 252
268a8–b7 42
268a–9c 80
269d 224
270b4–9 42

Philebus (Phlb.)

55d1–56c9 264
55e–57d 10
55e1ff 42
55e1–56c6 48
58c6 272

Protagoras (Prt.)

311a1–2 38
311b–12b 172
312a7–b4 18
312b7–14b4 22
312d5–e2 40
314e3–15a3 38
316c5–d3 21
316c5–17c5 17
316c7–d2 24
316d–17a 67
316d3–9 34
316d3–17b5 17
316d8–e5 34
317b3–c1 37
317b4–5 21
317d–e 67
318a–19a 67
318a6–9 21
318d7–e5 17
318e 4
318e1–3 35
318e5–19a2 16
318e5–19a3 31
319a 17
319a3–7 17
319a4 67
319b–c 174
319b–20b 66
319b3–d7 24
319c8–d1 24
319d7–20b3 24
320c8–22d5 16
320c8–23a4 34
320c8–28d2 24
320d–22d 197
320d–28d 67
320d8–21b6 272
321d 197
322b1–c3 19
322b3–d5 23
322c–d 197
322d4–5 23
323c2–d5 23
324a3–c5 16
327c4–e1 23
328a8–c2 25
328c–d 69
328e1–3 25
331a9–32b6 18
331d1–33c9 41
331d5 40
338a8–b1 41
338e6–39a3 26
346d1–3 40
351b–57e 16
352c2–3 33
353a7–8 38
356c–57e 66
356e8–57c1 42

Republic (Rep.)

332d10 72

332e4 72
333a1–3 40
333e–34a 80
333e3–4 40
333e6–7 40
334a5 40
338c2–3 43
338e1–39a4 43
339b9–11 43
339c1 45
339c7–8 43
339c10–12 43
339d5–9 43
339d5–10 43
339e4 43
340c–41a 73
340c7 44
340d–41a 71
340d2–e5 44
340d8–e1 45
340e2–3 43
341b3–43a4 47
341c–42e 73
341c–47d 71
341c10–d4 44
342e 96
343b–44c 73
345d 86
345d–47e 77
346a1–47a5 49
346a2 73
346b1 73
346d5 73
347a 86
349b–50c 71
349b1–50c11 42
351b–52b 71
352b–54a 71
353a11 73
353c1 73
353c10 73
353c7 73
354a 77
366e 72
367a–b 72
367e 72
369b–73a 202
406c–7a 85
436b6–37c10 40
438c6–e9 42
443c–44a 141
444d3–5 42
466e–67a 224
477d1ff 42
491d4–5 40

493a6–c8 48
493c 175
508a9 93
508b13 93
510c 7
511d3–e1 265
516c–e 141
520a–d 141
520e1 79
523e1–24a3 42
533a10–b5 265
533d3–9 265
596b 7
596b5–98c4 263
597d4–e8 264
601b–e 81
601c–2b 176
601d 175
601e 176
601e–602b 6

Sophist (Soph.)

219a10–b2 47
222c5–7 48
243d8–e6 42
253a8–b3 42
265a–68d 73

Statesman (Plt.)

258c–60c 6
258d8–e7 264
259c 2
260a 100
260a4–7 45
260a9–b1 42
261b7–8 48
273b 95
275d8–e1 49
283b–5c 71
283c3–84a3 42
285a3–4 42
304b 2
305c–d 100
305d 4
293a6–e5 47
296c4–97b3 48

Symposium (Symp.)

186d5–e3 42
201e10–b5 40
207d–208b 92

Theaetetus (Tht.)

146d–e 2
146d1 1
151e4–52c7 27
162d5–e4 29
163a6–65e4 27
166a2–66c2 27
166a2–68c2 26
166d1–67b4 28
166d3–67a4 33
167b2 28
167b4–d3 17
167b5–c2 34
169d2–72b7 27
169d3–72b7 30
177c6–79c1 30
186a9ff 42

Timaeus (Tim.)

27d–28a 92
28a–b 101
28a–29a 74
28a6–b2 98
28b1–2 96
28c3–4 91
28c6–29a2 96
29a 86
29a3 96
29a6 98
29b–c 92
29d–30b 74
29e1–3 96
29e2–3 91
30a–b 86
30a6–7 98
30b 94
30b–c 257
30b1–6 269
30c 94
30c–d 100
31b4 270
31c 102
32c 99
33a–b 93
33a6 267
33b5 103
34a8 267
34b10–35a1 270
35a8 99
37a1–2 92
37a4 99
37c6–d1 95
37c7 92
37d 92
41a–d 87
41a8–b5 93
41b7 91
41b7–8 101
41c2–3 91
41c4–5 99
41d 92
41d1 92
42d 256
42d–e 106
42d6 92
42e–43a 102
43a–e 104
43c–e 105
44e2 103
46d–e 108
47b–d 108
47e–48a 74
48a 88
50b 93
50d1–2 93
50d3 106
51c–e 88
61c3ff 42
68d 99
69c 103
69d–72d 103
71d–72b 175
73c–d 104
75c–d 90
76d–e 106
81e6–82b7 42
88b–89d 108
91a–b 104
91d–92c 105
91e–92a 105

Plotinus

First Ennead

I.6.12, 28–30 245

Second Ennead

II.3.18, 13–16 247
II.4.7 247
II.9 247

Third Ennead

III.2.3 90
III.2.16, 17–27 259

III.2.17 107
III.6.7, 24 281
III.8. 247
III.8.1–5 255

Fourth Ennead

IV.3.10, 13–19 248
IV.3.10, 17–19 271
IV.3.10, 18 281
IV.3.18, 5–7 248
IV.3.18, 10–13 258
IV.4.8, 43–50 260
IV.4.11 257
IV.4.15 258
IV.4.18, 5–7 258
IV.4.31, 17–23 245
IV.4.33 260
IV.4.33, 17–19 260
IV.4.33–34 260
IV.8.1, 44 247

Fifth Ennead

V.5 247
V.8 246
V.8.1 255
V.8.1, 15–22 251
V.8.1, 32–40 253
V.8.6 257
V.8.7, 37–43 261
V.9 246
V.9.11 245
V.9.11, 1–6 250
V.9.11, 7–10 251
V.9.11, 10–12 249
V.9.11, 22–24 249

Sixth Ennead

VI.3.16, 13–14 259
VI.7.1 257
VI.9.8, 45–49 260

Plutarch

Against the Stoics on Common Conceptions (de comm. not.)

1066A 190
1085C 171

On Stoic Self-Contradictions (de Stoic. repugn.)

1034C 181
1034D–E 182
1053F–54B 171
1056E–F 187

On Moral virtue (De virt. mor.)

440E–41A 181

Life of Pericles

36.5 38

Platonic Questions

2 91

Synopsis

4.1–5 187

Proclus

Elements of Theology (ET)

18 275
26 266
27 266
72, 68.20–22 279
79, 74.23–24 278
103 275
174 266
174, 152.14–15 266

On Euclid (in Eucl.)

30.8–31.1 265

On Plato's Alcibiades I (in Alc.)

202.1–3.13 265

On Plato's Cratylus (in Crat.)

16, 6.12–16 274
36, 12.14 274
53, 21.10–12 272
53, 21.10–13 272
53, 21.13–22.25 280
53, 21.19–22.15 280
53, 22.25–26 280

53, 22.30–23.7 274
53, 23.10–12 273
53, 23.11–12 278
53, 23.12–14 272
53, 23.14–21 280
53, 23.23–25 273
53, 23.25 273
53–56, 21.6–25.7 272
54, 23.26–28 279
54, 23.28–29 271
54, 23.28–30 279
174, 96.12–100.7 281

On Plato's Parmenides (in Parm.)

III, 793.10–11 271
III, 793.22–23 271
III, 794.4–6 271
III, 827.19–29.14 272
III, 827.20–24, 280
III, 827.22–24 273
III, 827.24–25 279
III, 827.25–28.2 264
III, 828.7–8 271
III, 828.10–12 272
III, 828.13–14 273
III, 828.15–29.2 265
III, 829.2–3 272
III, 829.4 273
III, 829.4–7 274
III, 829.7–9 279
III, 829.7–14 280
III, 829.10–11 281
IV, 947.18–21 265

On Plato's Republic (in Remp.)

1.92.9–17 281
1.127.1–11 281
2.73.18–20 265
II. 86.14–16 279

On Plato's Timaeus (in Tim.)

I, 1.6.21–7.16 265
I, 1.142.23. 281
I, 1.147.7 281
II, 1.248.11–13 277
II, 1.249.12–22 273
II, 1.251.4–9 277
II, 1.251.5–7 273
II, 1.260.19–26 266
II, 1.263.6 275
II, 1.263.19–30 266
II, 1.266.16–18 275
II, 1.267.20–24 266
II, 1.320.8 275
II, 1.320.5–10 275
II, 1.320.10–22 278
II, 1.320.23–26 278
II, 1.332.16–19 271
II, 1.344.5–14 264
II, 1.395.10–96.26 265
II, 1.395.13–22 279
II, 1.399.20–24 268
II, 2.241.29–42.2 273
III, 2.2.9–23 270
III, 2.80.19–24 278
III, 2.113.19–15.5 270
III, 2.299.6–7 273
III, 198.11–16 271
V, 3.205.2–3 271
V, 3.228.26–28 268
V, 3.230.16–18 268
V, 3.255.30–56.21 274
V, 321.1–25 281
V, 3.321.7–22.31 278
V, 3.321.32–22.17 270
V, 3.322.1–16 270
V, 3.322.2–17 270
V, 3.322.17–31 271

Platonic Theology (Theol. Plat.)

III.10, 41.8–12 270
III.19 270
5.17, 62.17–63.5 268
V.24, 87.22–89.8 281
V.24, 88.2 282

Protagoras

DK 80 A14 (=LM R 21) 27
DK 80 B1 (=LM D 10) 29
LM D 11–32 18
LM D 26–30 32

ps.-Galen

Medical Definitions (Def. med.)

8 170

History of Philosophy (De hist. phil.)

602.19–3.2 186

ps.-Longinus

On the Sublime (De subl.)

35 276

Quintillian

Institutes of Oratory (Instit.orat.)

II.17.41 172

Scholiast on Dionysius Thrax

31–33 226
108.27 192

Seneca

Letters (Ep.)

94.10, 33–34 183
94.16 183
95.12, 58 183
95.35, 61 183
95.5 183
124.2–18 183
124.19–22 183
124.22–23 183
124.21 184
124.24 184
124.30–31 184
124.33 184
124.38 184
124.45–47 184
124.41–42 184

Sextus Empiricus

Against the Mathematicians (M.)

1–6 226
1, 1.4 218
1.39–40 234
1.49 243
1.52 243
1.61 237
1.72 264
1.121–41 231
1.182 244
1.186 243
1.187–88 243
1.221 234
1.235 244
1.249 233
1.270 220
1.294 228
2.7 184
2.10 226
2.26 227
2.27 228
2.30 228
2.31–42 228
2.48 231
3.21 233
4.1 231
5.1 228
5.2 242
5.49 234
6.1 221
6.4 219
6.7 220
6.27 229
6.34 229
6.36 229
6.38–68 231
7.151 177
7.151–53 187
7.202 237
7.211–16 204
8.141 234
9.1–3 234
11.110–61 229
11.200–201 178

Outlines of Pyrrhonism (PH)

1.4 241
1.8 235
1.10 235
1.12 229
1.13 231
1.25 229
1.30 229
1.32 237
1.170–77 238
1.232 229
1.236–41 238
2.97–98 231
3.280–81 237

Simplicius

On Epictetus' Handbook (Ench.)

4.367–70 274

On Aristotle's Categories (In Cat.)

237,25–38,20 179

On Aristotle's On the Heavens (in Cael.)

492.31ff 228

On Aristotle's Physics (in Phys.)

1.5–14 264
308.20–21 264
385.17–18 265
385.18–19 265

Sophocles

Philoctetes

83–85 79
1049–52 79

Stobaeus

Eclogues (Ecl.)

I.25,3 189
II.62,15 176
63,6 182
65,12 180
66,14 (=SVF III.560) 181
73,1 172
74,16 177
75,11–76,8 179
77,16–17 179
80,22 173

Syrianus

On Aristotle's Metaphysics (in Met.)

26.24–26 280
26.35–38 273

Themistius

Paraphrase of Aristotle's On the Soul (in de An.)

64,25 188

Paraphras of Aristotle's Posterior Analytics (in An. post.)

53.18–19 265

Orations (Or.)

23.295a 186

Thucydides

History of the Peloponnesian War

I.139 67

Xenophanes

DK B7a 36
DK B18 (=LM D 53) 28
DK B34 (=LM D 49) 29
DK B35 (=LM D 50) 29

Xenophon

Economicus

I 6

Memorabilia

I.2.32 47

Lightning Source UK Ltd.
Milton Keynes UK
UKHW022107260121
377741UK00004B/30